Global Criminology

Crime and Victimization in a Globalized Era

Global Criminology

Crime and Victimization in a Globalized Era

Edited by
K. Jaishankar and Natti Ronel

CRC Press
Taylor & Francis Group
Boca Raton London New York

CRC Press is an imprint of the
Taylor & Francis Group, an **informa** business

Cover Image: Designed by Ueilon Teixeira, based on his winning entry of an open competition at http://www.worth1000.com. Published with permission.

Design work on Cover Image: A. Ravisankar, Sun Graphics, Tirunelveli, Tamil Nadu, India.

CRC Press
Taylor & Francis Group
6000 Broken Sound Parkway NW, Suite 300
Boca Raton, FL 33487-2742

© 2013 by Taylor & Francis Group, LLC
CRC Press is an imprint of Taylor & Francis Group, an Informa business

No claim to original U.S. Government works

Printed on acid-free paper
Version Date: 20130204

International Standard Book Number-13: 978-1-4398-9249-7 (Hardback)

Library of Congress Cataloging-in-Publication Data

Global criminology : crime and victimization in a globalized era / editors, K. Jaishankar, Natti Ronel.
    pages cm
    Includes bibliographical references and index.
    ISBN 978-1-4398-9249-7 (hbk. : alk. paper)
    1. Transnational crime. 2. Criminology--Cross-cultural studies. 3. Criminal justice, Administration of--Cross-cultural studies. I. Jaishankar, K. II. Ron'el, Nati.

HV6252.G5556 2013
364--dc23   2012050907

**Visit the Taylor & Francis Web site at
http://www.taylorandfrancis.com**

**and the CRC Press Web site at
http://www.crcpress.com**

To my "Second Brain" and incredibly supportive friend and wife, Debarati, and our sweet little heart, our daughter Mriganayani.

K. Jaishankar

To my closest friend and beloved wife, Gila, and our hopeful next generation, our children Dror and Tohar.

Natti Ronel

Contents

Section I

TERRORISM

Section II

CYBER CRIMES AND VICTIMIZATION

Section III

MARGINALITY AND SOCIAL EXCLUSION

Foreword

The editors point out in their introduction that when criminality becomes global, also the response to it must become global. We need a global criminology.

The earliest pioneers in criminology and victimology emerged in Western Europe and North America: Cesare Lombroso, Enrico Ferri, Raffaele Garofalo, Hermann Mannheim, Leon Radzinowicz, Hans von Hentig, and many others. Ever since that time, the two sides of the North Atlantic have been the bedrock and point of reference for these disciplines. This has been both a strength and a weakness. Strength, in that the two regions have provided a welcoming academic and governmental background for the study of crime and victimization, allowing for the development, testing, and application of new theories and research methods. Weakness, in that the research interests in capitalistic, urbanized, and postindustrialist societies are likely to follow specific paths. Because of the dominance of Western research, its conclusions may all too readily be assumed to apply to societies around the world, East and West, North and South, industrialized and industrializing.

It is true that Western criminology and victimology have spawned comparative studies, which have tried to offset this imbalance. Even so, Western researchers cannot totally shake their research interests and cultural blinkers. Comparative studies in these fields have tended to assume that Western research should remain the touchstone. If a topic or a research approach is suitable for Western Europe and North America, it is assumed to be more or less equally so for Latin America, Africa, and Asia. The fundamental interest seems to be to find out how different or similar the situation is elsewhere—but using Western yardsticks in the process.

We should go beyond this. In order for criminology and victimology to become truly global, we should follow the mantra of the environmentalists: "Think global, act local." We should seek to understand and respect the interests and concerns of the different regions and integrate these into our research.

For this reason, the initiative of the South Asian Society of Criminology and Victimology (SASCV) to start a series of peer-reviewed international conferences is more than welcome. The themes of the first such conference, held in Jaipur, India, in January 2011, were wisely selected to allow for discussion of traditional mainstay criminological and victimological themes, as well as of cutting-edge concerns. The themes were also selected to allow equally for participation of researchers from inside and outside the region, which led to spirited discussion and the cross-fertilization of ideas. The 19 contributions included in the present volume are but a sample of the papers delivered in Jaipur, but even these reflect the diversity.

The chapters of this book have been grouped into four sections. The first section looks at terrorism, an issue that is torn out of today's headlines and operates at the intersection of international law, international politics, crime, and victimization. The second section looks at cybercrimes from a variety of angles, including law, the motivation of offenders, and the impact on victims. The titles of the third and fourth sections—marginality and social exclusion, and theoretical and practical models of criminal victimization—may have a comfortably familiar ring in the ears of Western criminologists and victimologists, but the reader will find that the authors often take the discussion away from classic Western discourse, into new and intellectually refreshing (albeit often substantively troubling) areas.

The volume is an admirable example of how global criminology and global victimology can be enriched by studies that start from the local or national level, often outside of the dominant Western mainstream. "Eve-teasing," witch hunts, nonstate armed groups, begging, trokosi, levirate—these are not the traditional topics of Western research, but they are deserving of attention.

This book, *Global Criminology: Crime and Victimization in a Globalized Era*, goes a long way to connecting the dots between phenomena such as these and wider globalized concerns. I find that this edited volume will be a very welcome contribution to the fields of criminology and victimology, nationally, regionally, and globally. I thank the editors for allowing me to be a (small) part of this process.

Matti Joutsen, PhD
Director
European Institute for Crime Prevention and Control
affiliated with the United Nations (HEUNI)
Helsinki, Finland

Acknowledgments

We sincerely thank the reviewers of this book: Adam Bossler, Ety Elisha, Glenn Dawes, Inna Levy, Janice Joseph, Kam C. Wong, Keren Cohen-Louck, Keren Gueta, Kushal Vibhute, Mark David Chong, Michael Bacchman, Michael Pittaro, Moshe Bensimon, Muzammil Quraishi, Orly Benjamin, Orly Turgeman-Goldschmidt, Sarah Ben David, Simha Landau, Sophie D Walsh, Stanley Yeldell, Stephen Z Levine, Thomas Holt, Tina Patel, Uri Yanay, and Yuning Wu. Without these people, the quality of the book would not have been ensured.

Ueilon Teixeira, a 16-year-old child prodigy from Brazil, was kind enough to provide his image for the cover page of this book without any fees, which aptly fitted with the theme of the book. We thank him from the bottom of our hearts. A. Ravisankar, the official designer of the first International Conference of the South Asian Society of Criminology and Victimology (SASCV 2011), had several sleepless nights and we sincerely thank him for his dedication, patience, and passion. Ravisankar also designed the text for the cover page of this book. Our heartfelt thanks are due to Periyar and Sivakumar, the editorial assistants, for their dedicated and sincere support in bringing out this publication.

We met Matti Joutsen, the Director of the European Institute for Crime Prevention and Control, affiliated with the United Nations (HEUNI), at the 14th International Symposium of the World Society of Victimology (WSV) held during May 20–24, 2012, at The Hague, the Netherlands. We requested him to write a foreword to this book and he was kind enough to write an excellent one. We are very grateful to him for accepting our request.

We earnestly thank all the keynote speakers, plenary speakers, and panel chairs of SASCV 2011. We thank all the sponsors, advertisers, and knowledge partners who provided a great support to the conference, which greatly helped us in this intellectual pursuit. Our respective employing establishments, the Manonmaniam Sundaranar University, India, and the Bar-Ilan University, Israel, provided a working environment conducive to critical refraction. Without their support, it would not have been possible to conduct such a large event and also bring out this publication on time.

Editors' Introduction: Crime and Victimization in a Globalized Era

K. JAISHANKAR
NATTI RONEL

The phone call was from an unidentified number. A young man on the other end of the line explained politely that he worked for the security department of the bank in Israel where she held her account. He went on to explain that they suspected that a criminal group had somehow obtained her credit card details and would produce a forged card to be used later on. "Did you withdraw money from the ATM at that location?" he asked, and described a location not far from her house with the exact amount that she had recently withdrawn. "Well, yes. But what can I do now?" "Don't worry, your card is already cancelled. You will get a new one very soon." A few hours later, there was another call from the security department, with a very strange question: "Are you in Israel right now?" "Of course I am." "Well, just now there was an attempt to withdraw money using a card with your details in Brussels! We just wanted to be sure that it was not you. Since you are in Israel at this very moment, you can't be in Brussels!" "But what I should do in order to prevent any loss?" "Don't you worry about it—that is what we are here for! It is already taken care of. Have a good day."

Crime and criminality are as old as humanity and are widespread almost everywhere humans go. Although crime is almost always occurring, its definitions and manifestations might greatly vary through societies and cultures. Respectively, the postmodern, hi-tech, global world meets typical manifestations of crime in addition to the known localized ones. Some manifestations are new since they are the results of present-day means, as the example above represents. Some, however, are old phenomena with new, globalized manifestations. The above-described true story, which recently occurred, exemplifies what it is to live in a hi-tech global village in regard to criminology: The details of a credit card were electronically stolen from an ATM and, almost immediately, they were transferred to a faraway location, in another country even, to be criminally used. One characteristic of the global village is that it is an easy task to obtain money from a bank account almost anywhere in the "village." But it is almost as easy a task to abuse this convenience for easy money. However, this story exemplifies not only the globalization of opportunity and crime, but also of the response. A global type of crime requires a global response. In this case, there was such a response, as sophisticated and hi-tech as the crime itself was, with international cooperation, and luckily the offenders failed.

To successfully meet the new challenge of globalized crime, there is a need for a cooperation, resources, and knowledge at every level, including the research-based and scholarly level. Sharing scientific criminological knowledge is a must in the global effort to study, explore, and reduce global crime. In a global era where criminality becomes global, there is a need for global criminology as well.

First International Conference of the South Asian Society of Criminology and Victimology (SASCV 2011)

The South Asian Society of Criminology and Victimology (SASCV) is an international association founded in 2009 to nurture criminology and victimology in South Asian countries. Academics, researchers, and practitioners worldwide have joined hands to establish SASCV and share best practices in the context of South Asia. SASCV hosted its first international conference during January 15–17, 2011, at Hotel Jaipur Greens, Jaipur, Rajasthan. The website of the conference was www.sascv.org/conf2011 and online submission of abstracts as well as registration was facilitated on the site.

The theme of the conference was "Crime and Victimization in the Globalized Era." The major subthemes were terrorism and extremism, cybercrimes, laws and security, crimes of culture and culture of crimes, marginality, social exclusion and victimization, criminal victimization in South Asia, and victimization of South Asians in other countries. The organizing committee of SASCV 2011 was as follows: general chair, K. Jaishankar; vice chair, S. Samuel Asir Raj; program chair, Natti Ronel; administrator, Debarati Halder; event management chair, R. Jayachandran; treasurer, R. Sivakumar; and associate, E. Enanalap Periyar. An international advisory committee comprising members of the SASCV international advisory board was formed to assist the organizing committee.

The first international congress showcased the academic thoughts of professors, practitioners of criminal justice system, professionals in related fields, and students of national as well as international origin from various backgrounds, such as criminology, victimology, law, human rights, digital technology, and socio-health sectors. The conference was inaugurated by Dr. Mahindra Surana, IAS (Retd.), the editorial advisor of *Dainik Bhaskar* (a leading newspaper in India) and Professor Roy King, Institute of Criminology, University of Cambridge, UK, was the opening keynote speaker; he spoke on terrorist gangs and prison torture. The panel of other keynote speakers included: Professor David Wall, Department of Sociology and Criminology, Durham University, who spoke about cybercrime; Professor Mark Groenhujsen, president of the World Society of Victimology, who presented the UN draft bill on victim's rights; and Dr. Gail Mason, director of Sydney Institute of Criminology, who deliberated on the victimization of Indian students in Australia. The conference concluded with the valedictory address by Natti Ronel, Bar-Ilan University, Israel, and a keynote presentation by Professor Emilio C. Viano, Department of Justice Law and Society, American University, Washington DC. More than 300 participants were present at the conference, including 120 paper presenters. The conference was a great success.

A rigorous peer-review process is not the forte of social science conferences held in the South Asian region. SASCV 2011 is unique in this context. Overall, 291 papers were meticulously peer reviewed by the program committee chaired by Natti Ronel, Bar-Ilan University, Israel. The rate of acceptance was 53.26% and the rate of rejection was 46.74%. After the conference, an expert committee was constituted to select quality papers based on the extended abstracts and presentation of the authors at the conference, and revised papers were invited from the selected authors. Papers were rated as A and B. Papers that were rated as A were selected to be published in this book as chapters, and papers that were rated as B were published in a special conference volume of the *International Journal of Criminal Justice Sciences* (the official journal of the SASCV, an open access journal available at www.ijcjs.co.nr). After rigorous peer review, out of 120 papers presented at the SASCV 2011 conference, 19 papers were rated as A and 7 papers were rated as B and were selected for publication.

The peer-reviewed papers, which were presented at SASCV 2011, provide an initial enterprise of defining global criminology and its fields of interest. Most of the various themes of these papers represent the challenges that globalized criminality offers to global criminology:

1. Terrorism: Terrorism is an old, known manifestation of violence. Traditionally, it was mostly narrowly targeted toward certain locations and people and represented a domestic violent and brutal struggle that involved and victimized innocent passersby. However, toward the end of the last millennium, terrorism was transformed into one of the most noticeable threats of our days. Sometime before September 11, it went out of its more localized nature into a globalized one wherein it blindly victimized places, people, and countries. However, the September 11 event took this process further and terrorist groups became more violent, more daring, more universal. Is it a crime issue or a national (global) defense issue? Should

terrorists be treated as war criminals, soldiers, or civil criminals? What are the power relations between international efforts to prevent terrorism and local efforts? Can we define a global law or a global antiterrorism act? Global criminology will have to deal with such issues in an attempt to provide directions for solutions.

2. Cybercrime, cyber security: The cyber, virtual world is newly created. It provides us with resources and opportunities that were but a dream until recently. Naturally, such opportunities created new manifestations of crime that associate old and known criminal motivations with new means to accomplish them. Cyberspace provides anonymity, immediate availability, global access, and the possibility for inventions, and cyber offenders easily abuse these open routes. As cyberspace develops, cybercrime also develops. To achieve better cyber security, there is a need for a new knowledge to be acquired, a task for global criminology.

3. Social exclusion and inclusion: Globalization is manifested, among others, in the fast transition of people between places, societies, social classes, and cultures. Here and there, are but close neighborhoods in the global village and one can easily move in between. Known social constructions are destroyed for new ones. But many are left aside or behind. Being part of the margin, people are excluded from important resources: material, social, or human. They may be victimized, or react in a criminal rebellion, as criminology has known for decades. However, how can we provide inclusion for the marginalized ones in the global era?

4. Victims: Victimology is not so much a new topic as a mature one. However, the process of globalization, as the previous heading shows, creates new victimization. Old and new, victimization calls for better understanding and better responding. During periods of big processes and changes in global creativities, victimology calls for humanity for the weak, in a global perspective that meets the local. Globalization can become an opportunity for better struggle against victimization, for better sharing of knowledge, and global victimology is part of global criminology.

Criminology, similar to other fields of study, attempted to provide universal explanations for the behaviors under its scope. More often than not, universal explanations were replaced by new ones that claim the same power of universalism. The era of globalization recognized pluralism in any field, thus it is possible to hold together less universal explanations or even contradicting ones, each will explain its share and together they portray a larger picture. We therefore anticipate that the emerging global criminology will be the house of diverging attitudes, explanations, and perspectives. In the global village of criminology, there is room for any solid contribution. This edited collection is a move in this direction.

Contents of This Edited Volume

This book is divided into four sections: I, Terrorism; II, Cybercrimes and Victimization; III, Marginality and Social Exclusion; and IV, Theoretical and Practical Models of Criminal Victimization. All the chapters are diverse in nature from contributors across the world and are a blend of theoretical and empirical perspectives.

Chapter 1 explores work at the intersection of international law, international politics, crime, and victimization. India and Pakistan are countries well known for their continuing conflict in the South Asian region. Pakistan encourages terrorism in its home ground and terrorists freely attack India at its borders; the 2008 Mumbai attack proved that they can attack beyond borders. The role of nonstate actors (NSAs) in such terrorist attacks is the prime focus of Chapter 1. The author considers questions of state responsibility and accountability for terrorist acts, using as his frame of reference the horrific attacks in Mumbai in 2008. The objective of this chapter is to explain what the key characteristics of NSAs are; to what extent are terrorist groups in Pakistan nonstate; how accountable is the Pakistani state for the acts of the terrorist groups operating from its territory; and the degree to which international law establishes state accountability toward the acts of NSAs? This chapter presents a brief account of the Pakistan-based terrorist groups, investigates their linkage with the state organs, and draws insights from the Pakistani case for NSAs' activities and state accountability in the international system.

In Chapter 2, the author examines maritime piracy from the perspective of the Southern African Development Community, which is responsible for 3000 km of coastline close to the current nexus of piracy, the coast of Somalia. Following a review of the causes, extent, and modus operandi of maritime piracy, the author lays out a set of detailed recommendations for responding to the growing threat.

Since that fateful day in September 2001, terrorism has been thrust into the limelight of public consciousness like never before. On the international stage, a reinterpretation of preexisting principles such as the "precautionary principle" in novel ways to kick start major "preemptive wars" on transnational terror outfits has come in for heated debate. Such aggressive reform may, however, trigger a dangerous trend if the law of nations were to embrace such a knee-jerk reaction as "customary practice." In India, a people plagued by gory acts of terror since long before the notorious felling of the twin towers, are yet to come to terms with the threat posed by various NSAs and transnational armed groups. Through the enactment of various domestic instruments, such as the TADA, POTA, and UAPA, there have been attempts at curtailing the effects of terrorism. Yet, the author of Chapter 3 believes that uprooting this global crime requires a concerted effort at the global level. The author proposes a three-pronged criticism of the preemptive wars that were launched under the so-called Bush Doctrine's interpretation of the precautionary principle.

In Chapter 4, the author provides an overview of the financing of terrorism in Southern Africa, taking as his point of departure the many international instruments on the subject. The chapter is of particular interest due to the extent of the informal economic and financial sector in Africa. The author concludes his chapter by tailoring the international recommendations to the specific circumstances of this subregion.

Chapter 5 is a legal analysis of the use of electronic evidence in South African law, which reflects the difficulties of applying law in a rapidly changing world. The chapter focuses on critical questions such as: How in particular do we apply the procedural concept of discovery, developed in a time of paper documents, to electronic data? The author's comments on the South African approach will have wide resonance.

Chapter 6 shows how one mainstay of criminology, interviews with self-identified offenders and experts, can be used in the study of cybercrime. Very little is known about those who commit computer crimes. Cybercrime offenders constitute a hidden and hard-to-access population. This is despite the increase in offending rates that have corresponded with the wider availability of computers to the general public from the 1980s and the introduction of the World Wide Web in 1991. These technological advances have increased the reach of offenders as well as the vulnerability of potential victims. Chapter 6 contributes to the literature relating to online victimization, providing insight through the lens of offenders, police officers, and the judiciary. The result, which is firmly grounded in rational choice and neutralization theory, is an interesting exploration of the motives of offenders.

Cybercrime and victimization in cyberspace is a subject of great concern in India. In Chapter 7, the authors take the perspective of victims of cybercrime, examining awareness among Internet users in India of the potential for cyber victimization. Their study includes a component on the experience of the respondents with actual victimization, on their awareness of their rights, and on reporting behaviour. Particular attention is given to the experiences of female Internet users.

Cyberspace creates a unique environment for *hactwers* and terrorists to be able to interact, work together, and learn from each other. The risk of recruiting hackers to work with terrorist organizations is growing remarkably fast. The Islamic world has populated cyberspace and opened up websites propagating Islamic rhetoric and ideology. Some of these websites are established to defend Islam and teach Muslim youth hacking techniques. Unfortunately, the growing Muslim presence in cyberspace has been accompanied by contradictory fatwas, a prevailing fatwa that has affected cyberspace negatively and incited the Arabic Muslim hackers (AMHs) to commit cyber vandalism, and an unpopular fatwa that condemned cyber vandalism against Israeli websites. In Chapter 8, the author through his study locates as many as 154 AMH forums, though many of these are temporary, and they may close down or relocate their operation. The author's study of Arabic Muslim hackers and their relationship with Islamic jihadists is based on extensive research and is very informative. The author also provides an assessment of the impact of fatwas on the activity of these hackers.

Chapter 9 continues the victimological assessment of cybercrime, with a study of sexual harassment over cell phones. In this chapter, the author has tried to answer three questions: (a) Who is using cell phone unethically? (b) Who are the victims of sexual harassment via cell phones? (c) What are the adverse impacts of cell phone sexual harassment on a victim's social life? Through a questionnaire survey in Dhaka City, Bangladesh, this study has tried to explore the various patterns of sexual harassment via cell phones. The contribution is an example of the value of "thinking globally, acting globally." Although the phenomenon itself is global, "Eve-teasing" (as it is known in this subregion) definitely has its own context and its own implications in Bangladesh.

The principal objective of Chapter 10 is to report on the problems of implementing a state-funded, county-implemented, short-term intervention program for mentally ill offenders reentering the community from a large jail. This study focused on program implementation for the treatment of 1278 subjects diagnosed as mentally ill, who were randomly assigned to two groups at jail booking. This contribution deals with a major social, criminal policy, and economic problem in the United States: the jailing of mentally ill offenders. In reporting on an intervention study conducted in California, they also enrich the literature by giving a dispassionate analysis of how shortcomings in the study methodology may have influenced the results.

In Chapter 11, the author has made an attempt to analyze the impact of the imprisonment of women. The author emphasizes that women play various roles, such as mothers, partners, and members of families. The author tried to approach this issue from a global feminist perspective. She emphasizes that women's and girls' interactions with prison systems raise fundamental questions of social exclusion, marginalization, and justice. The author feels that there is a need to link together research on women, girls, and criminal justice with critical perspectives on punishment and the expansion of the prison-industrial complex, to develop radical, critical, and global feminist perspectives, which challenge the power of the prison. This feminist analysis of women in prison is an excellent example of how an analysis can work simultaneously on the local, national, and international levels. The author brings together a wealth of research on key issues from both industrialized and industrializing countries. The reader will come away with a better appreciation of the many difficulties faced by mothers, babies, and children in prison—and of the appalling practice of 'trokosi' in Ghana, Togo, and Benin.

Beggary in India has been in existence since time immemorial for various reasons. Though India lacks a uniform law in this regard, some of the states have laws criminalizing beggary. Though these laws aim to rehabilitate beggars, such rehabilitation comes with criminalization, disregarding the wishes and wants of such beggars. It is this approach that has come under serious criticism from civil society and the general public. The Indian approach, similar to the West's approach toward vagrants, is outdated and goes against not just the constitutional and human rights jurisprudence, but is also contrary to the basic principles of criminalization and criminal liability. In Chapter 12, the author critically analyzes the Indian legal approach to begging and concludes that criminalization of beggary is unjustified and unwarranted as it punishes a person for being poor instead of ensuring alternative means of livelihood, thereby indicating a failure of the "welfare" state. The author considers the present laws to be vague and selectively enforced and further questions the laws on the grounds of morality and of basic criteria for criminalization.

In Chapter 13, the author presents the results of a qualitative study of public statements by Australian parliamentarians in response to the claim that Indian nationals studying in Australia are the victims of racially motivated crime and violence. It examines a sample comprised of press releases, parliamentary Hansard, and media interviews compiled over a 12-month period between June 1, 2009 and May 31, 2010. This chapter goes beyond traditional victimization surveys, to look at the response of decision-makers to claims of victimization. In this case, the focus is on how Australian politicians sidestep the issue of racism when commenting on stories of Indian students being subjected to hate crime in Australia. The author argues that Australian federal parliamentarians have resisted acknowledging that some of the incidents reported by Indian students in Australia are motivated or aggravated by racism.

Considerably fewer studies have been conducted on the psychological effects of internal forced displacement compared to international forced displacement. The aim of the study presented in Chapter 14 was to examine the association between parent–child relations and gender differences and between the pathogenic and saluthogenic effects of internal forced displacement. This contribution looks at how the forced displacement of Israeli settlers from the Gaza Strip affected the adolescents involved psychologically, in the short term and in the long term.

Chapter 15 expands our knowledge of criminal victimization, again taking it in fascinating directions away from classic Western discourse. The author focuses on forced marriages, domestic violence, and allied issues in a few select countries in Africa. This chapter represents a qualitative assessment of the realities of these traditional practices across several African countries. It is a known fact that some African nations still follow some traditional practices in this modern era, which leads to various forms of victimization of women. The author correctly places these within the human rights context, and offers recommendations for addressing the issue.

Chapter 16 aims to explore the multifaceted identity of the female victim, as she courses through the criminal justice process. It is the intention of the author to draw attention to the dilemma that many women face when they seek help for the victimization that they experience. The author offers a fascinating analysis of the applicability of Nils Christie's concept of "ideal victims" to the victims of rape and human trafficking. Although the background is the law in England and English legal cases, the author's theoretical approach has wide applicability.

Despite numerous studies, the answer to why women are the primary targets of witch hunts is much debated. In Chapter 17, the author takes a new approach to the study of the relationship between the instigators of witch hunts and the women victims, by looking at contemporary cases of witch hunts among tea plantation workers in Jalpaiguri, West Bengal, India. The author takes a witch-hunting incident in India and places it squarely within a theoretically well-grounded setting. The author notes the importance of moral entrepreneurs and scapegoats and argues for the adoption of a new concept, "dual deviance," to explain the course of the witch hunt and its aftermath. The chapter also highlights the role of rumor and conspiracy in witchcraft accusations that are used to target the women victims.

Criminology and victimology have traditionally looked at negative phenomenon. In Chapter 18, the author, who is the proponent of the "criminal spin" theory, introduces the new concept, positive criminology. The author suggests understanding criminal conduct as a process that he calls "criminal spin" and advocates an approach called positive criminology, involving, for example, reintegrative shaming, restorative justice, rehabilitation, recovery, and the 12-step programme. The author feels that while strong negative means are necessary to break a criminal spin, especially during an acute phase, positive criminology has the promise of targeting other phenomenological characteristics of the spin, thus reducing its chronic manifestation.

The closing contribution (Chapter 19) is an Indian study comparing a sample of spouses of alcohol dependents with a matched sample of spouses of non-alcohol dependents, examining the incidence of domestic violence. The findings of the study indicate that spouses of alcohol dependents are vulnerable to victimization and require psychological intervention to prevent serious psychopathology from developing.

We close the book with a conclusion in which we try to analyze the merits of global criminology and global victimology.

Editors

K. Jaishankar, PhD, is a senior assistant professor in the Department of Criminology and Criminal Justice, Manonmaniam Sundaranar University, Tirunelveli, India. He was a Commonwealth Fellow (2009–2010) at the Centre for Criminal Justice Studies, School of Law, University of Leeds, UK, and has completed a research project on victims of cybercrimes. He is the founding editor-in-chief of the *International Journal of Cyber Criminology* (www.cybercrimejournal.com) and editor-in-chief of the *International Journal of Criminal Justice Sciences* (www.ijcjs.co.nr). He is the founder president of the South Asian Society of Criminology and Victimology (SASCV) (www.sascv.org) and executive director of the Centre for Cyber Victim Counselling (CCVC) (www.cybervictims.org). Jai was a discussant in the "Opening discussion: Focusing on victims of crime—Comparing crime patterns and improving practice. Researchers' advice to policy" of the Stockholm Criminology Symposium held during June 11–13, 2012, in Stockholm, Sweden, and responded to the questions of Beatrice Ask, the Swedish minister for justice, and Paula Teixeria da Cruz, the Portuguese minister for justice. Jai was a keynote speaker at the 14th World Society of Victimology Symposium held during May 20–24, 2012, in The Hague, the Netherlands. He was the general chair of the First International Conference of the South Asian Society of Criminology and Victimology (SASCV), held during January 15–17, 2011, at the Hotel Jaipur Greens in Jaipur, Rajasthan, India. Among the books he has written/(co) edited are: *Cyber Crime and the Victimization of Women: Laws, Rights and Regulations* (IGI Global, July 2011), *Cyber Criminology: Exploring Internet Crimes and Criminal Behavior* (CRC Press, Taylor & Francis Group, February, 2011), *International Perspectives on Crime and Justice* (Cambridge Scholars Publishing, UK, 2009), *Cyber Bullying: Profile and Policy Guidelines* (DOCCJ, Manonmaniam Sundaranar University, India, 2009), *Crime Victims and Justice: An Introduction to Restorative Principles* (Serial Publications, New Delhi, 2008), and *Trends and Issues of Victimology* (Cambridge Scholars Publishing, UK, 2008). His areas of academic competence are victimology, cyber criminology, crime mapping, GIS, communal violence, policing, and crime prevention.

Natti Ronel, PhD, is an associate professor in the Department of Criminology, Bar-Ilan University, Ramat Gan, Israel. He previously served as the researcher-in-chief of the interdisciplinary Center for Children and

Youth Studies in Tel Aviv University, Israel. He is also a licensed clinical criminologist who has a private practice with the criminal population, youth, and adults who exhibit addiction, violence, and/or victimization. Natti leads continuous training courses for criminal justice and victim assistance professionals and he is a recurring faculty member of the annual postgraduate course of Victimology, Victim Assistance, and Criminal Justice in the Inter University Centre, Dubrovnik, Croatia, where he lectures on therapy for recovering victims. His various writings reflect both his clinical and academic experiences in criminology. He has a special focus on the spiritual aspect of criminology and victimology—its values and impact on individuals and communities: spiritual-based intervention and recovery, moral transformation, and forgiveness and spiritual intelligence. Natti is the proponent of a new criminological theory "the criminal spin," and the conceptualization of a new perspective in criminology and victimology: "positive criminology" and "positive victimology," respectively. Natti is a member of the World Society of Victimology, the Israeli Society of Criminology (board member), and the Israeli Council for Criminology. He is head of the research group for the development and study of positive criminology at Bar-Ilan University, Israel. He has written and edited several books, including coediting *Trends and Issues of Victimology* (Cambridge Scholars Publishing, UK, 2008). He was the program chair of the First International Conference of South Asian Society of Criminology and Victimology (SASCV) held during January 15–17, 2011, in Jaipur, India, and is a member of the advisory board of SASCV.

Contributors

Vinesh Basdeo   Served in the South African Police Service for 16 years, where he worked in various departments, including crime prevention, the detective service, and the VIP Protection Unit. He held the position of assistant director, also known as superintendent or lieutenant colonel. He obtained his master's in law at the University of South Africa. He is currently a senior lecturer in the School of Law at the University of South Africa, and serves on various college and school committees. He teaches undergraduate students and supervises master's students. He has attended various international conferences where he delivered papers on various legal and policing issues, and has published extensively in scientific journals. Mr. Basdeo also serves on the University Student Disciplinary Committee. He has recently submitted his doctoral dissertation, which focused on search and seizure. Vinesh has published extensively on criminal procedure, search and seizure, military policing, and a whole range of criminal justice issues. He was recently invited by the South African parliament to present a paper on the location of South Africa's anticorruption agency.

Gisela M. Bichler   Presently a professor and co-director of the Center for Criminal Justice Research at the California State University, San Bernardino, CA, USA. Professor Bichler joined the faculty at CSUSB in September 2000 after completing her PhD at Rutgers—State University of New Jersey. Professor Bichler is founder and co-director of the Center for Criminal Justice Research. In addition, as the crime analysis division coordinator she is responsible for the new Crime Analysis Certificate Program. Professor Bichler has been extensively involved with the Western Society of Criminology in various capacities, including president and coeditor of their online, peer reviewed professional journal, the *Western Criminology Review*. Professor Bichler has received a number of awards and honors: the J.D. Lohman Award for outstanding service to the Western Society of Criminology; the Provost's Dissertation Award 2000 for the top doctoral dissertation; the Graduate Excellence Award for teaching and scholarship; the Richard J. Hughes Award for graduating from the masters of arts with the highest standing (Rutgers University, 1996); and the Rutgers Excellence Fellowship Award (1995–1999). Her professional specialties are: ecology of crime, applications of geographical information system technology to crime issues, applications of social network analysis techniques to crime issues, environmental criminology and crime analysis, situational crime prevention and problem-oriented policing, crime prevention through environmental design (CPTED), methods and statistics for social scientific research, and maritime corporate crime.

Fawzia Cassim   Associate professor in the Department of Criminal and Procedural Law at the University of South Africa. Her qualifications are BA (law) (University of Durban Westville, now University of Natal); LLB (University of Natal–Durban); and LLM LLD (University of South Africa). She is also an admitted attorney and conveyancer of the High Court of South Africa. Her academic and research interests are in the following fields/disciplines: human rights law, constitutional procedural law, civil procedure, gender law, cyber law/information technology law and Islamic law. She has published a number of articles in academic journals and presented papers at international conferences in the above-mentioned disciplines.

Soma Chaudhuri   Assistant professor at Michigan State University, East Lansing, MI, where she holds a joint position in the Department of Sociology and the School of Criminal Justice. Her research focuses on violence (collective violence and domestic violence), social movements, gender, and witch hunts. Dr. Chaudhuri has published articles in journals such as the *American Journal of Sociology; Mobilization, Violence against Women;* and *Comparative Studies of South Asia, Africa and the Middle East.* Some of her current projects include a book manuscript on contemporary witchcraft accusations in the tea plantations of Jalpaiguri, India (under contract with Lexington Books); and the negotiation of strategies to combat domestic violence in Gujarat, India. Dr. Chaudhuri holds a PhD in sociology from Vanderbilt University, Nashville, TN, master's degrees in sociology from Vanderbilt University (2005) and Jawaharlal Nehru University, New Delhi (2000), and a BA in sociology from Presidency College, Calcutta (1998).

Helen Codd   Reader in law and criminal justice at the Lancashire Law School, University of Central Lancashire, Preston, United Kingdom. She studied law at the University of Wales, Aberystwyth (1987–1990), and then gained an MPhil in criminology at the University of Cambridge, Institute of Criminology (1991). Helen has extensive experience of teaching criminal justice, criminal law, and related subjects at undergraduate and postgraduate levels and has also taught law in a local prison. She has published widely on issues in relation to women, prisons, children, and families and is the author of *In the Shadow of Prison: Families, Imprisonment and Criminal Justice* (Willan Publishing, United Kingdom, 2008) and *Controversial Issues in Prisons* (with David Scott, McGraw Hill, United Kingdom, 2010). Her current research relates to prisoners' families, prisoners' reproductive rights, and feminist perspectives on sentencing. Helen has delivered invited keynote addresses at conferences around the world, most recently in the United States and India, and was an invited participant in the UNHRC Day of General Discussion on Prisoners' Children in September 2011. She has extensive experience of voluntary work with NGOs and is currently chair of THOMAS, a social exclusion and substance abuse charity based in the North of England.

E. Enanalap Periyar Presently an Indian Council for Social Sciences Research (ICSSR) Fellow in the Department of Criminology and Criminal Justice, Manonmaniam Sundaranar University, Tirunelveli, India. He was formerly a lecturer in police science and criminology at APA College of Arts and Science, Nanguneri, Tirunelveli District, India. He is an executive council member of the South Asian Society of Criminology and Victimology (SASCV). His thesis focuses on homicide and victim–offender relationships.

Debarati Halder Advocate and legal scholar. She is the managing director of the Centre for Cyber Victim Counselling (CCVC) (www.cybervictims. org). She received her LLB from the University of Calcutta and her master's degree in international and constitutional law from the University of Madras. She is currently completing her PhD in the National Law School of India University (NLSIU), Bangalore, India. She has published many articles in peer-reviewed journals and chapters in peer-reviewed books. Her work has appeared in scholarly journals, including the *Journal of Law and Religion, Victims and Offenders*; *Murdoch University E-Journal of Law*; *ERCES Online Quarterly Review*; *TMC Academic Journal (Singapore)*; *Temida and Indian Journal of Criminology & Criminalistics*; and edited volumes, *Crimes of the Internet, Trends and Issues of Victimology, Cyber Criminology*. Debarati's research interests include constitutional law, international law, victim rights, cybercrimes and laws. She has presented her research works at many international conferences including the recent Stockholm Criminology Symposium held during June 11–13, 2012.

Alice Hutchings Presently a senior research analyst, in the Global, Economic & Electronic Crime Program of the Australian Institute of Criminology. Alice has extensive experience working across all tiers of government, as well as the academic and private sectors. Alice has undertaken cybercrime-related research since 2007 when she examined risk factors for phishing victimization. Alice is a PhD candidate based at the Centre of Excellence in Policing and Security in Griffith University. Her PhD, titled "Theory and Crime: Does it Compute?", was commenced in 2008. This research consists of testing existing sociological theories of crime to determine whether they explain computer crimes that compromise data and financial security. She has published widely and has presented at various international conferences. She holds a bachelor of arts in criminology and criminal justice (hons.) from Griffith University.

K. Jeevitha Clinical psychology doctoral student (PsyD) at Wright State University School of Professional Psychology, Dayton, OH. She obtained her master's degree in psychology from Bangalore University, an MPhil in mental health and social psychology from the National Institute of Mental Health and Neurosciences (NIMHANS), India. She has also worked as a senior research fellow at St. Johns Research Institute and was a faculty member in the Department of Psychology at Christ University, Bangalore. Her clinical and research interests are in the area of child psychopathology and psychotherapy, pediatric psychology, and domestic violence. She has presented in national and international conferences and has been a volunteer for several Head Start programs for children and families. She is a member of various professional organizations, including the American Psychological Association (APA), the Association for Play Therapy, and Division 53 of APA.

Don A. Josi Serves as professor and program director in the Department of Criminal Justice, South University, based in Savannah, GA. Prior to joining South University, Josi served as a tenured professor of criminal justice at Armstrong Atlantic State University in Savannah, GA. Earlier, he served as an associate professor, chair and on the faculty at California State University, California Polytechnic University, and Chapman University. Josi began his career in criminal justice as a police officer and a detective in the Rialto, CA police department. He later became director of security at a prominent California hospital and has served as a research consultant and juvenile probation control supervisor. He earned a PhD in criminology, law, and society from the University of California—Irvine, a master's degree in criminal justice, and a bachelor's degree in sociology from California State University in San Bernardino, CA.

Avital Laufer Currently the deputy mayor of Netanya, Israel, and in charge of education. Avital is also a senior lecturer at Netanya Academic College. Her studies deal with the well-being of youth in times of terror and political adversities. Her postdoctoral study won the Inbar Fund Award for outstanding research in the field of terrorism (2007). Her dissertation, which examined violence among Israeli youth, won the President and Dean's Award for Excellence (2000). She has published numerous articles in scientific journals and books.

Alaeldin Mansour Maghaireh Lecturer in law at the Centre for Transnational Crime Prevention (CTCP). He is an expert in Islamic criminal law and cybercrime with considerable experience in the First Instance Court in Jordan. His doctoral research, completed in 2009 at Wollongong University, was on "Cybercrime Investigation: A Comparative Analysis of Search for and Seizure of Digital Evidence." He holds a bachelor of laws from Beirut Arab University (1996) and a master of cyber law from Wisdom University, Lebanon (2000). He also holds a graduate certificate in transnational crime prevention from Wollongong University. His primary research interests are: cyber criminology, cyber terrorism, digital evidence, and shariah law. He has published extensively on cybercrime, Shariah law, and related legal issues.

Gail Mason   Associate professor and co-director of the Sydney Institute of Criminology. Her research centers on crime, social justice, and exclusion, particularly: racist and homophobic violence; hate crime law and punishment; and the legal construction of hatred. She is coordinator of the Australian Hate Crime Network and chief investigator on the ARC-funded Hate Crime Law and Justice Project, which is undertaking an international comparison of hate crime laws. She is also involved in research exploring resilience and gendered violence among former-refugee communities in Australia. She is journal director of *Current Issues in Criminal Justice*, associate editor of the *Australian and New Zealand Journal of Criminology*, and series editor for the Sydney Institute of Criminology Monograph Series. Gail is currently the NSW representative on the Australian and New Zealand Society of Criminology Management Committee and sits on the Corrective Services NSW Ethics Committee. She is the author of *The Spectacle of Violence: Homophobia, Gender and Knowledge* (Routledge, 2002) and has published in numerous international scholarly journals and edited books. In 2008, Gail was awarded the Allen Bartholomew Award for the best article published in the *Australian and New Zealand Journal of Criminology*. In 2009, she delivered the distinguished JV Barry Memorial Lecture in Criminology at the University of Melbourne.

Ashutosh Misra   Research fellow at the Australian Research Council Centre of Excellence in Policing and Security at Griffith University. He is a postgraduate gold medalist in history and holds a PhD in international studies from the Jawaharlal Nehru University, New Delhi. He possesses over 18 years of research and professional experience and has published three books *Pakistan's Stability Paradox* (London: Routledge, 2012); *India–Pakistan: Coming to Terms* (New York: Palgrave Macmillan, 2010) and *Pakistan: Engagement of the Extremes* (New Delhi: IDSA and Shipra, 2008). *India–Pakistan: Coming to Terms* was launched by the Honorable Indian Vice President Hamid Ansari in New Delhi in September 2010. He has also extensively published in books, international journals, newspapers, and institutional blogs. He has worked for the United Nations in Jordan and prior to migrating to Australia in 2007, he was a research fellow (2002–2007) at the Institute for Defence Studies and Analyses (IDSA), a premier security think-tank of the Indian Ministry of Defence in New Delhi. Since 2007 at the Griffith University he has initiated and invigorated India/South Asia focused research and facilitated institutional and academic exchanges between the Queensland government and Australian universities with Indian counterparts. Periodically, he also provides policy consultancy to the Department of Foreign Affairs and Trade on India and South Asia and is a visiting faculty with the Department of Defence and National Security College. Dr. Misra regularly features on the Australian television and radio networks commenting on Indian/South Asian affairs.

Moses Montesh Matriculated in Mamelodi-Pretoria in 1990. In 1993, he joined the South African Police. After completing the Basic Police Training, he remained at the Hammanskraal College where he became a physical training instructor. In 1994, he received a scholarship to study for a BA (Pol) at the SAPS Academy in Graaff-Reinet, which he completed in 1996. From 1997 to 1999, Professor Montesh managed to complete a Diploma in Public Management, and an Honours in Police Science. In 2000, he then enrolled for a Masters in Public Administration at the University of Pretoria, which he completed in a record time (one year and six months). In 2007, Prof Montesh completed DLIT et PHIL in Police Science. Professor Montesh's thesis titled "A critical analysis of crime investigative institutions within the South African criminal justice system: A comparative study" provoked debates on whether the SCORPIONS (the Directorate of Special Operations) should be closed or not. In 2005, his draft thesis formed part of an individual submission at the Khampepe Commission of Inquiry, which determined the future of the Scorpions. From October 2001 until January 2004, Professor Montesh was a POPCRU full-time shop steward. After serving 11 years in the South African Police Service, Professor Montesh joined the University of South Africa in February 2004 and, currently, he is an associate professor. Professor Montesh has published papers on public administration as well as criminal justice. He has presented papers locally and abroad (France, Hong Kong, Canada, Malta, Australia, Morocco, Singapore, and India). He has been involved in the training of the Government of Southern Sudan Civil Service. He is currently responsible for undergraduate and postgraduate students in policing.

Colleen Moore Principal lecturer in criminology and deputy head of the Department of Humanities and Social Sciences at Anglia Ruskin University, Cambridge. Colleen's work is concerned with the concept of justice and how it is understood in the criminal justice arena compared to society as a whole. Her main research interests are in understanding everyday "violent" behavior and its intended and unintended impact—upon victims and the community. Colleen is particularly interested in how justice is perceived, sought, and achieved through the criminal justice process. Colleen's past research has involved evaluating the effectiveness of community service (before it was called community payback), young people and their treatment in the youth justice system, parole and the discretionary lifer process, the age of criminal responsibility in Europe, and a comparative examination of legislation in the United Kingdom and the Ukraine relating to trafficking for sexual exploitation. Currently, her work focuses on the treatment of "undesirable" female victims in the criminal justice system and alternatives to justice for victims of domestic (sexual) violence and sexual exploitation. She participated in an international collaboration examining youth justice around the world, through the European Society of Criminology. More recently, she initiated and cofacilitated a project in a young offender's institution that brought undergraduates and young offenders together to edit and produce short films.

A. Nagarathna Presently an assistant professor of law at National Law School of India University, Bangalore has completed her PhD in medical negligence law, LLM (2001) (commercial law), and BAL, LLB (1999). She secured first rank in both the BAL exam (Bangalore University, 1997) as well as the LLB exam (Bangalore University, 1999) and received five gold medals in LLB (Bangalore University, 1999). She taught for over 5 years from 2001 to 2006 at KLE Society's Law College, Bangalore and she joined NLSIU, Bangalore in November 2006 as assistant professor of law. She has published several articles and contributed several chapters to various international and national journals and books. Her research work titled *Patient's Rights under Consumer Law* was published by Karnataka Institute of Law and Parliamentary Affairs in 2009. Her two books, *Failure of Justice—Social Perspective* and *Indian Law Relating to Terrorism* are under publication by Karnataka Institute of Law and Parliamentary Affairs. She has presented various research papers at international and national seminars, conferences, and workshops and has attended national seminars as resource person. Her areas of specialization include criminal law, cyber laws, and commercial law. Her areas of interest include jurisprudence, intellectual property rights, medical law and ethics, legal educational and professional ethics, and women and law.

Ummey Qulsum Nipun Independent researcher in the field of criminology and victimology, holding a master's in development studies (MDS), North South University, Bangladesh and a bachelor degree in urban and regional planning, BUET, Bangladesh. Her main research interests relate to the issues of social security, development of women and adolescents, child development, etc. She is the author of several publications on adolescents, drug trafficking by youth, sexual harassment, child rights and policy formulation, published by UNICEF, ARNEC, and SASCV. Nipun has been working as a "Bangladesh Regional Coordinator" of the South Asian Society of Criminology and Victimology (www.sascv.org). She was a co-chair of a session in the International Conference on Exploring the Linkages between Drug Usage and Criminal Victimization, March 8–10, 2012, organized by the Department of Criminology and Criminal Justice (DOCCJ), Manonmaniam Sundaranar University (MSU), Tamil Nadu, in collaboration with the National Institute of Social Defence (NISD), Ministry of Social Justice & Empowerment, Government of India, New Delhi. She has been working with Save the Children in Bangladesh since 2007.

Dale K. Sechrest   Emeritus professor in criminal justice at the California State University, San Bernardino, CA. Dale Sechrest has practiced, taught, and published in the field of corrections for over 40 years. His work has focused on the evaluation of corrections programs, including juvenile diversion, correctional privatization, substance abuse programs, treatment of mentally ill offenders, victim-offender reconciliation programs, and correctional standards. His publications include articles on correctional standards, privatization in corrections, drug programs, diversion, restorative justice, and community corrections. He is author of *The Role of the Helping Professions in Treating the Victims and Perpetrators of Violent Crime* (2002); *The Changing Career of the Correctional Officer* (1998); *Three Strikes and You're Out: Vengeance as Public Policy* (1996); and *Jail Management and Liability Issues* (1989). Professor Sechrest teaches undergraduate and graduate corrections courses, research methods, and statistics. His professional specialties are: community corrections: juvenile prevention/intervention, drug treatment programs, mentally ill offenders in corrections, privatization of correctional services, correctional standards and program audit procedures, restorative justice, and white-collar crime (telemarketing fraud).

Mally Shechory-Bitton   Senior lecturer in the Department of Criminology in Ari'el University Centre, and a parttime lecturer in Bar-Ilan University, Israel. Her postdoctoral study focused on restorative justice (conducted at the University of Tübingen in Germany). She served 5 years as coordinator, Division of Criminology at the Multidisciplinary Department of Social Sciences in Ari'el University Centre and was the chair of the Israeli Society of Criminology. She also served several years as a senior police officer in the Israeli police force. Her academic work includes both practical and theoretical experience in the fields of victimology, violence and aggression. She has published extensively in scientific journals. She was a member of the Programme Committee of the First International Conference of SASCV held during January 15–17, 2011 at Jaipur, India.

David Shichor   Emeritus professor in the Criminal Justice Department of California State University, San Bernardino, CA, where he has taught since 1975. He has written, coauthored, and coedited several books and he has published numerous articles and book chapters on various topics, including juvenile delinquency, victimization, white-collar crime, corrections, and privatization in criminal justice. He has published four books in the areas of punishment policies, victimization, juvenile delinquency, and private prisons. Professor Schichor completed a typology of juvenile institutions and a study of prison discipline in Israel, both of which were published in that country. He is currently working on several projects on privatization, restorative justice, fraud victimization, and the mental health of jail inmates. Professor Shichor earned his PhD at the University of Southern California (Sociology, 1970), received his MA at California State College, Los Angeles (Sociology, 1966), and his BA at Hebrew University in Jerusalem in 1962. He has held numerous research and consulting positions in the United States and Israel.

Harjass Singh   A BA/BSc (Hons.) LLB student at the National University of Juridical Sciences, Kolkata, India. Having presented his research papers on contemporary legal issues at various reputed international conferences, including a Conference on Protecting People in Conflicts and Crisis Situations conducted by the Refugee Studies Centre, Oxford University, Harjass has recently been invited to present his research on sports and jurisprudence at the Third Annual Sport and Society Conference at Cambridge University. His research work has also been published in numerous reputed journals and books. Discussions with peers and world leaders at the Global Young Leaders Conference in the United States in 2008 were vital in facilitating Harjass's leaning toward research on international legal developments. Although a majority of his writing is devoted to the influence of international law in scenarios pertaining to war, genocide, and crimes against humanity, he retains a keen interest in a number of legal fields. An accomplished debater and public speaker, Harjass's interests range from sports to the UN, international politics, constitutional law, international law, jurisprudence, and environmental and agricultural laws.

R. Sivakumar   Bureau of Police Research and Development (BPR&D) research fellow in the Department of Criminology and Criminal Justice, Manonmaniam Sundaranar University, Tirunelveli, India. He is the treasurer of the South Asian Society of Criminology and Victimology (SASCV). His thesis focuses on cyberbullying among college students in India.

L. N. Suman   Additional professor at the National Institute of Mental Health and Neuro Sciences (NIMHANS), Bangalore, India. She obtained a master's degree in psychology from Bangalore University, an MPhil in medical and social psychology, and a PhD in clinical psychology, both from NIMHANS. She has 25 years experience as a consultant clinical psychologist. At NIMHANS, she is a consultant for an Adult Psychiatry Unit, the Center for Addiction Medicine, and the Center for Psychological Care. She has published papers in national and international peer-reviewed journals and chapters in books and manuals. She is a member of the editorial board of the *Indian Journal of Clinical Psychology* and the *International Journal of Biosciences and Technology*. Her research interests are in the areas of psychosocial issues related to substance use, the mental health of women, positive psychology, and forensic psychology. She has recently initiated an ICSSR-funded research project on cognitive and social factors related to smoking among adolescents.

Victoria M. Time   University professor and associate professor of criminal justice in the Department of Sociology and Criminal Justice, Old Dominion University, Norfolk, VI. Her education comprises degrees in law and criminology, and thus she uses this background to teach law, justice, and criminology courses to both undergraduate and graduate students. Her research revolves around comparative and international law, criminal law, culture and rights, and criminological theory. She has authored a book, and published numerous articles in journals such as *Journal of Criminal Justice*; *International Journal of Comparative and Applied Criminal Justice*; *Women and Criminal Justice*; and *Social Justice*, among others, and she has also published several book chapters. Additionally, she has traveled extensively within the United States and abroad to present papers at conferences and symposiums on a variety of social and justice issues.

Scientific Committee of Reviewers

Inna Levy
Department of Criminology
Ariel University Center of Samaria
Ariel, Israel

Tina Patel
School of English, Sociology, Politics and
    Contemporary History
University of Salford
Manchester, United Kingdom

Michael Pittaro
Crimen et Justitia Consulting
Nazareth, Pennsylvania, USA

Muzammil Quraishi
School of English, Sociology, Politics and
    Contemporary History
University of Salford
Manchester, United Kingdom

Orly Turgeman-Goldschmidt
Interdisciplinary Department of
    Social Sciences
Bar-Ilan University
Ramat Gan, Israel

Kushal Vibhute
University of Brunei Darussalam
Negara, Brunei Darussalam

Sophie D. Walsh
Department of Criminology
Bar-Ilan University
Ramat Gan, Israel

Kam C. Wong
Department of Criminal Justice
Xavier University
Cincinnati, Ohio, USA

Yuning Wu
Department of Criminal Justice
Wayne State University
Detroit, Michigan, USA

Uri Yanay
School of Social Work
The Hebrew University of Jerusalem
Jerusalem, Israel

Stanley Yeldell
Law and Justice Studies
Rowan University
Glassboro, New Jersey, USA

Terrorism

I

How Nonstate Are Terrorist Groups in Pakistan? Analysis of State Responsibilities and Accountability

1

ASHUTOSH MISRA

Contents

Introduction

In the international system, the role of nonstate actors (NSAs) has gained prominence in recent decades, not only in influencing decision making in multilateral institutions on global issues, but also in shaping regional politics, the foreign policies of states, and international relations, in general. While many NSAs, especially in the fields of environment, international trade, and human rights, have largely operated within the boundaries of civil liberties and freedom accorded under international law, a large number of nonstate armed groups (NSAGs) or terrorist groups have used violence to achieve their ideological and political objectives, sometimes with alleged state support, leading to military conflicts between states. As a result, the activities of NSAGs have caused serious controversies and confrontations between states, confrontations that on many occasions have been referred to international organizations such as the International Court of Justice (ICJ) for dispute settlement. As more and more states (host) employ NSAGs to achieve their foreign policy objectives with little accountability for the NSAGs acts, there has been an increase in preemptive military responses by states (victim/injured) on the grounds of self-defense against the host state. This has necessitated the ICJ looking into several cases of this nature to determine state (host) responsibility and accountability and the rights of the injured states under international law.

The activities of NSAGs based in Pakistan have been the source of diplomatic, military, and political confrontation with India since the 1980s and now with the United States. Since its creation in 1947, Pakistan has played a critical role in regional and global politics due to its strategic location conjoining South Asia, Central Asia, and the Middle East. This geographical centrality made Pakistan a frontline ally of the United States during the cold war, an alliance that deepened militarily, politically, and economically during the Afghan jihad (1979–1989) against the Soviet Union in Afghanistan. During this period, the U.S. State Department and the Central Intelligence Agency (CIA) worked closely with the Pakistani state organs, primarily the Inter-Services Intelligence (ISI) and the military, providing money and weapons to General Zia-ul Haq for the creation of hundreds of madrassas to mentor and train mujahideen to fight in Afghanistan (Haqqani, 2005). The ISI became the frontline agency for raising, training, and weaponizing the mujahideen for the Afghan jihad. Bloated by CIA and Saudi Arabian money, it gradually created a "parallel structure wielding enormous power over all aspects of the government" (Hussain, 2007, p. 17).

Under General Zia's reign, the officer corps was seen to be more "Islamic" than it had been 30 or 40 years ago, and the ISI and army developed close linkages with the influential Islamist party the Jamaat-e-Islami (JI), with other groups, and with many retired ISI officers still working with their former "clients" (Cohen, 2005, p. 112). The jihadi infrastructure that resulted from this United States–Pakistan alliance gradually assumed an autonomous and formidable character, which the Pakistani government and the military has struggled to dismantle even after the loss of over 30,000 lives under the rubric of the ongoing war on terror. The noted Pakistani analyst Hassan Abbas says,

> By the time General Musharraf, a moderate and progressive Muslim, came to the scene, the very scale of religious extremism had reached its climax. When he tried half-heartedly to halt this trend before the tragedy on 9/11, the army found that it was faced with a potential adversary that it was not willing or able to bring to heel. Many of these groups had developed independent channels of financing, giving them increased manoeuverability. This was the beginning of a shift in the power equation away from the army and toward the Jihadist groups, the latter being supported by the Mullah parties acting as their political wings. (Abbas, 2005, p. 13)

Following the Soviet withdrawal in 1989 and the decline in U.S. interest in the region, United States–Pakistan relations turned cold, until the September 11 attacks on the World Trade Center, which led to the U.S. invasion of Afghanistan to overthrow the Taliban regime, which was allegedly harboring Osama bin Laden, for which Pakistan's support again became crucial. But now, certain sections of the military and the ISI felt aggrieved at U.S. indifference during the 1990s toward Pakistan and at the U.S. disowning the mujahideen as solely Pakistan's responsibility. The Afghan jihad had created strong ideological and operational linkages between the jihadist groups and the Pakistani state organs, convincing the latter of its indispensability to achieving foreign policy objectives. The Pakistani military and the ISI now seemed opposed to purging these groups, which they deemed their close allies. The eminent Pakistani scholar Muhammad Amir Rana says,

> As the modern Jihadi culture was created, nurtured and groomed in Pakistan, its effect on the many senior people involved in that process, coupled with the massive public support which was state sponsored, should not be underestimated. The psychological trauma involved in changing sides cannot easily be washed off … The Jihadis have many supporters in the Pakistan's army and secret services. It is extremely unlikely that none of them would be 'helping out' their former friends and allies. (Rana, 2005, p. 47)

According to Fazl-ur-Rehman, leader of the JUI-F, those targeted in the tribal areas were trained, financed, and armed by the Pakistani government against the Soviets.

In the war on terror, as the Taliban casualties increased in the U.S. and Pakistani offensives, anti-Americanism intensified in Pakistan, creating new centers of jihadi resistance and groups in the Federally administered Tribal Areas (FATA) and Khyber Pakhtunkhwa (KP), formerly North West Frontier Province (NWFP), including the Haqqani network in North Waziristan and Quetta Shura in Balochistan. Over 60 local Taliban groups became operational, of which 40 were initially part of the Tehreek-e-Taliban (TTP), the most potent Pakistani Taliban group, now headed by Hakimullah Mehdud, following the death of Baitullah Mehsud in a drone strike in 2009. The Pakistani jihadi landscape is now much more complex and formidable due to the alleged state patronage and operational linkages between the Afghan and Pakistani Taliban groups, having multiple agendas and links with al-Qaeda (Rana, 2012).

As more attacks occur against the U.S. and NATO troops, it is reported that the ISI has been encouraging the Pakistan-based Haqqani network to attack U.S. targets, including the U.S. embassy on September 13, 2011, in Kabul (Reuters, 2011). Senior U.S. officials, including Joint Chief of Staff Admiral Mike Mullen, General John Allen, commander of the NATO-led International Security Assistance Force (ISAF), and leading analyst Vali Nasr have been critical of Pakistan's failure to curb the Haqqanis and have demanded more action against the group (Reuters, 2011). In the meantime, dissatisfied with the Pakistani response, the United States deployed unmanned aerial vehicles (UAVs)—drones—to target militant hideouts inside Pakistan. In connection with these strikes, Pakistani troops and hundreds of civilians have been killed, causing large-scale public demonstrations and a political storm in the Parliament. On March 20, 2012, the all-party parliamentary committee in Pakistan recommended that "The U.S. must review its footprints in Pakistan" and called for an end to the drone attacks, demanding "no hot pursuit or boots" on Pakistani territory and declaring this a violation of its sovereignty.

In a NATO air strike in November 2011, 24 Pakistani soldiers were killed in the Mohmand Agency (a district), a strike that led to the closure of the U.S. drone base at the Shamsi air base in Quetta following the public and political outrage in Pakistan (*The Dawn*, 2012b). According to the Pakistan Institute of Peace Studies, 323 drone strikes were carried out from 2004 to June 2012, killing 2652 militants (including Ilyas Kashmiri, Baitullah Mehsud, Nek Muhammad, Romanullhah, Badar Mansoor, and Abu Yahya Al-Libi) and 227 civilians (Pakistan Institute for Peace Studies, 2012). The corresponding figures for the period as per a New America Foundation study are 302 strikes and 1558–2372 militants including a small percentage of nonmilitants (New America Foundation, 2012). In May 2012, the Pakistani Foreign Office again reiterated that "drones violate international law and its territorial integrity." UN Secretary-General Ban Ki-moon urged states to be more "transparent" about the circumstances in which drones are used and to take necessary precautions under international law to minimize civilian casualties. The UN

High Commissioner for Human Rights Navi Pillay commented, "Drone attacks do raise questions about compliance with international law ... and indiscriminate killings and injuries of civilians in any circumstances are human rights violations" (Mussadaq, 2012). On the other hand, U.S. Secretary of State Hilary Clinton, who officially apologized in July 2012 for the killing of 24 Pakistani soldiers in connection with one drone strike, defended the U.S. policy saying,

> We will always maintain our right to use force against groups such as al-Qaeda that have killed us and still threaten us with imminent attack ... In doing so, we will comply with the applicable law, including the laws of war, and go to extraordinary lengths to ensure precision and avoid the loss of innocent life. (*The Dawn*, 2012a; Mussadaq, 2012)

According to one study conducted on local perceptions toward drone attacks, 58.8% of the respondents in FATA considered them as "never justified," 24.5% as "sometimes justified," and 4.4% as always "justified." In the North Waziristan (which has witnessed the highest number of strikes), 99.3% regarded them as "never justified." However, in the Kurram Agency, where the Haqqani group is currently based, 63.2% regarded drone attacks as "sometimes justified" (Shinwari, 2010 in Nawaz, 2011).

In May 2011, the killing of Osama bin Laden by the U.S. Navy SEALs in Abbottabad, close to the Pakistani Military Academy, was an indication of the collapse of U.S.–Pakistan understanding over the conduct of the war on terror. Apparently, the United States is not very hopeful of the Pakistani military's ability to purge the Haqqanis and other Taliban groups; therefore, while maintaining the pressure on Pakistan to do more, the United States has simultaneously resorted to unilateral strikes inside Pakistan to eliminate militants. Currently, U.S.–Pakistan relations remain deadlocked, with both sides driven by their respective national and strategic interests, posing the conflict between U.S. claims of acting in "self-defense" against the NSAGs and Pakistan labeling this as a violation of its territorial sovereignty.

A similar contestation has been prevailing on Pakistan's eastern front, with India alleging (as discussed in the latter sections) that it has been the victim of cross-border terrorism perpetrated by Pakistan-based jihadist groups in Kashmir and other parts of India. There are countless authoritative works available on Indo-Pakistan relations produced by eminent scholars who have also analyzed the correlation between cross-border terrorism and the Kashmir dispute in depth. One such U.S.-based South Asia scholar, Stephen Cohen, argues that Pakistan, following the success against the Soviets, began contemplating an Afghan jihad-type stratagem in Jammu and Kashmir. Cohen describes how, after having installed Amanullah Khan as the Jammu and Kashmir Liberation Front (JKLF, Pakistan) chief, the ISI created JKLF's India front in 1988 under Ishaq Majid Wani, Yasin Malik, Hamid

Sheikh, and Javed Mir. The aim was, first, to provide a local support base for the militants and Afghan war veterans in Jammu and Kashmir against the Indian forces in Jammu and Kashmir and second, to keep these groups away from causing domestic troubles in Pakistan. The ISI began training the Kashmiri dissidents who opposed New Delhi's policies in Jammu and Kashmir (Cohen, 2003). Indian analysts also claim that following the political unrest and reported electoral bungling in Kashmir in the 1987 elections, Pakistan increased its involvement by providing training to a large number of disgruntled youths from India-administered Kashmir to fight against the Indian military and pressure India to negotiate a final settlement of the Kashmir dispute (Santhanam et al., 2003). Gradually, terrorist groups, allegedly with the support of the ISI, waged a proxy war outside Kashmir and have undertaken bomb attacks in major cities. The attack on the Indian parliament in 2001 and the Mumbai attacks in 2008 remain the high points of cross-border terrorism, which New Delhi claims pushed the two neighbors to the brink of their fifth war. Reportedly, Indian authorities have provided Pakistan with evidence of the involvement of the ISI in supporting terrorist groups, such as Lashkar-e-Toiba (LeT), Hizbul Mujahideen, and Jaish-e-Muhammad, in masterminding several attacks. Pakistan rejected these claims as baseless and unsubstantiated, only to concede later that the attackers were indeed Pakistani citizens (Siddiqi & Baruah, 2009; Agencies, 2010). In June 2012, in cooperation with the United States and Saudi Arabia, the Indian authorities managed to extradite Abu Jundal from Saudi Arabia, in connection with investigations into the Mumbai 2008 attacks. Indian officials claim that Abu Jundal, an Indian citizen, was trained by the Pakistan-based LeT and directed the operation from a "control room" in Karachi along with an ex-ISI man, Sajjid Mir (Baweja, 2012). As Pakistani authorities continue to deny the involvement of state organs in terrorist activities in India, saying that they are as much victims of terrorism as India, public outcry in India following the terrorist attacks has put pressure on the Indian government to respond strongly. After the attack on the Parliament in 2001, India amassed troops on the border (Operation Parakram) with the intention of launching an offensive against these groups, and ever since, India has reportedly been contemplating surgical strikes to eliminate terrorist bases inside Pakistan. In the wake of Operation Geronimo, which killed bin Laden, Indian military officials have been reportedly claiming that India has similar surgical strike capabilities (Gupta, 2011).

In light of the United States–Pakistan and Indo-Pakistan political and military contestations, the recent advances and transformations in modern warfare and military strategy for dealing with NSAs raise new questions. This chapter seeks to answer some of these questions by examining how "non-state" the terrorist groups based in Pakistan are and how accountable the state is toward the wrongful activities of NSAs under international law. The first section provides a brief historical account of Pakistan's alleged support of jihad as a state policy that facilitated the mushrooming of terrorist groups and the creation of the jihadist infrastructure. The second section outlines the current situation, including recent developments in the U.S. and Pakistani offensives, terrorism fatalities in Pakistan and India, and the Islamist discourse on jihad in Pakistan. The third section explores the NSA/NSAGs–state linkages, Pakistan's jihadist policies, major jihadist groups, the profiles of some prominent jihadist generals, and instances of operations with alleged state involvement. The fourth section, based on the discussion in the preceding sections, looks into the provisions of international law to determine to what extent the Pakistani state can be held accountable for the unlawful acts of NSAs. It is necessitated by the ongoing controversy over how lawful are the U.S. drone attacks and commando raids inside Pakistan and whether they violate Pakistan's territorial sovereignty as guaranteed under the UN Charter. This section also explores the rights and limitations of "self-defense" against NSAs, as prescribed under international law for the victim/injured states.

Current Situation

South Asia poses myriad challenges to regional and international security, including terrorism allegedly perpetuated by NSAGs based in Pakistan. The killing of Osama bin Laden in Abbottabad, 50 km from Islamabad, has put the spotlight again on the ISI and the Pakistani military, which has its academy in Kakul, close to the lair where bin Laden had allegedly been living for some years. The Pakistani government's failure to offer a convincing explanation of how it was unaware of bin Laden's existence so close to the military academy has added to the growing mistrust with the United States, compelling the latter to continue with unilateral military strikes against militant hideouts in the tribal areas.

Notwithstanding the U.S. mistrust of Pakistan, the latter today is engaged in a fierce military conflict with the Taliban and other terrorist groups within its own borders, although it has failed to curb their operations completely. Since 2004, over 34,000 people have been killed in Pakistan, including civilians, policemen, and security personnel (Paracha, 2011). In 2011, 7,017 people were killed as opposed to 10,003 people in 2010 and 12,623 in 2009 (Pakistan Institute of Peace Studies, 2011). On June 24, 2012, Pakistani military sources announced that 11 soldiers had gone missing "out of whom seven soldiers have been reportedly killed and then beheaded," and the responsibility was attributed to the Taliban group led by Maulvi Fazlullah, a.k.a. Mullah Radio based in Malakand in the Swat valley (Agencies, 2012). This clearly indicates that Pakistan has itself suffered immensely in its offensive against the Taliban and al-Qaeda, with increasing suicide and bomb attacks in the tribal areas

as well as in other parts of the country. The current spate of relentless suicide attacks and bombings against military and civilian targets has intensified since the Red Mosque crackdown launched by General Pervez Musharraf
in July 2007. The Islamist parties and jihadist leaders have long blamed both
Pakistan and the United States for rising extremism. In 2004, Maulana Fazlur
Rehman, leader of the Jamaat-e-Ulema Islam, bluntly criticized the military
leadership for abandoning the jihadist groups, saying, "The trained ones were
later called terrorists while the ones who trained them were not bothered"
(Raza, 2004).

Emanating from the Afghan jihad, the ideological and operational linkages between the jihadist groups and state organs apparently also encouraged the Pakistani military establishment to nurse, promote, and sponsor
Islamic militancy on the eastern front, which Pakistan itself now struggles
to control (Mir, 2005). Many terrorist training camps belonging to al Badr,
Hizbul Mujahideen, and Harkatul Mujahideen were reopened and resumed
operations in Manshera to engage in jihad in Kashmir, with only a brief suspension following the September 11 attacks (Ali, 2005). Between 1994 and
2010, the country lost over 55,000 people to terrorist violence, but the numbers have declined from a high of 5,839 in 2001 to 1,074 in 2011 (Institute
for Conflict Management, 2011). According to the Indian authorities, the
2008 Mumbai attacks in which 166 people were killed were undertaken by
LeT operatives trained and funded by the ISI, as revealed in the testimonies of Abu Jundal in June 2012 and, earlier, David Coleman Headley, the
Pakistani-born American who is currently in U.S. custody (Siddiqi & Baruah,
2009; Baweja, 2012). Headley has testified in a Chicago court that the ISI
masterminded the entire Mumbai operation (*Hindustan Times*, 2011),
which has raised concerns over the role of Pakistan-based groups. Eminent
scholars, among them Pakistani, have noted that the jihadist infrastructure
in the country has expanded enormously with deeper linkages with global
terrorist networks (Rana, 2005; Haqqani, 2005; Abbas, 2005; Stern, 2000).
In particular, the UN, U.S., and Indian authorities have now focused their
attention on the LeT, which renamed itself *Jamaat-ud Dawa* following its
proscription by the United States and Pakistan in 2001 and 2002, respectively, and *Falah-i-Insaaniyat Foundation* following the Mumbai attacks in
2008. Its chief, Hafiz Saeed, has been listed by the UN 1267/1989 al-Qaeda
Sanctions Committee as an individual associated with the al-Qaeda. In
April 2012, the U.S. State Department authorized a reward of $10 million
for information leading to his arrest or conviction and $2 million for infor-
mation leading to the location of LeT's deputy, Hafiz Abdul Rahman Makki
(U.S. Department of State, 2012). These groups have also received political
patronage from the Islamist parties and former ISI officials in a bid to legitimize their existence. In October 2011, General (retd.) Hamid Gul, a former
ISI chief, is reported to have created a new party called the *Difa-e-Pakistan*

Council (DPC), uniting right wing individuals, leaders, and parties, including Hafiz Saeed. According to Hasan Askari Rizvi, "DPC's formation is a tactic by the military authorities to pressure the civilian government to take a hard stance against the United States and deflect the political discussion on its failure towards the issue of the country's sovereignty" (Farooq, 2012, p. 26). In this context, we now turn to the alleged linkages between the NSAGs and the Pakistani state organs.

NSAs/NSAGs: State Linkages and Jihadist Policy

NSAs refers to a wide range of public and private actors, including intergovernmental organizations, international organizations, non-governmental organizations (NGOs), and any individual or group of individuals (Gordenker & Weiss, 1995). These NSAs can be divided into five broad categories: intergovernmental organizations (IGOs), international non-governmental organizations (INGOs), transnational corporations, epistemic communities, and NSAGs. NSAGs are described by experts as "challenger[s] to the state's monopoly of legitimate coercive force" (Higgot et al., 2000, p. 2; Policzer, 2005, p. 2) and are also referred to as violent nonstate actors (VNSAs) (Thomas et al., 2005). In the Pakistani context, this chapter refers to them as NSAGs that are engaged in terrorist activities in and outside Pakistan.

According to a study conducted by Muhammad Amir Rana, in Pakistan there are 237 Islamic groups belonging to the Hanafi-Barelvi, Hanafi-Deobandi, Ahle-Hadith, and Shi'ite faiths, including 82 sectarian and 24 political groups. There are also 104 jihadist groups and 18 of the Tableeghi persuasion (Rana, 2003). All these groups run their own madrassas to impart Islamic teaching to the poor segment and are considered hatcheries for violent jihad. Jessica Stern, in her seminal work *Pakistan's Jihad Culture*, has shown that there is no dearth of money for terrorist organizations and most of it comes from donations made by both common and wealthy people during religious festivals (Stern, 2000). Jihadist groups include Pashtun, Chechens, Uzbeks, and Arabs, including the TTP (Pakistani Taliban) led by Hakimullah Mehsud, Mullah Omar's Quetta Shura (Afghan Taliban), Jalaluddin Haqqani's Haqqani network, and Mullah Fazlullah's Tehrik-e-Nifaz-Shariyat-e-Muhammadi (TNSM) in the Swat, which is waging jihad in Afghanistan and inside Pakistan. With regard to India and Kashmir, the major jihadist groups include *Jaish-e-Mohammad* (JeM, renamed the Khuddam-ul Islam), *Lashkar-e-Toiba* (LeT, renamed the Dawat-ul Irshad), *Hizbul Mujahideen* (HM), *Harkat-ul-Mujahideen* (HuM), *Al-Umar-Mujahideen* (AuM), *Jammu Kashmir Islamic Front* (JKIF), *Al-Badr*, *Jamiat-ul-Mjahideen* (JuM), and *Dukhtaran-e-Millat* (DeM), which stand declared as terrorist organizations under the Prevention of Terrorism Act

2002 (Government of India, 2003–2004).* All these groups run their own madrassas to impart Islamic teaching to the poor. There are 6761 madrassas in Pakistan Occupied Kashmir (PoK) and of these, 1869 are Deobandi, 1616 Barelvi, 717 Ahle Hadith, and 97 Shi'ite (Rana, 2003). In recent years, new hubs of terrorist recruitment have mushroomed, away from the lawless tribal areas, in South Punjab, where such groups as *Sipah e-Sahaba Pakistan* (SSP), JeM, and LeT are thriving and contributing between 5000 and 9000 militants for jihad in Afghanistan and Waziristan (Siddiqa, 2009).

Jihad as a State Policy

Scholars argue that the proliferation of jihadist groups is a consequence of the state patronage furthered under both civilian and military regimes, to achieve strategic objectives in Afghanistan and India. In 1969, under General Yahya Khan, for the first time the military had joined hands with Islamist groups to counter the nationalists' rise in East Pakistan, which soon seceded to establish Bangladesh in 1971. In 1973, under Zulfiqar Ali Bhutto, extensive Islamic provisions were enshrined in the first democratic constitution to appease the Islamists (Talbot, 2003). The Afghan jihad in the 1980s hastened Pakistan's drift further toward Islamization under General Zia (Dixit, 2002). During this period, Pakistan diverted U.S. financial assistance to create new madrassas and train mujahideen (Haqqani 2005). In the early 1980s, General Zia also allegedly funded Sikh insurgency in the Indian Punjab and by the late 1980s, attention was focused on Kashmir and, as discussed earlier, the alienated Kashmiri youth such as Yasin Malik were mentored and trained and the JKLF was formed to engage in the Kashmir jihad (Santhanam et al., 2003).

Pakistan's preoccupation with Kashmir can be discerned from General Musharraf's much discussed speech on January 12, 2002, in which he alluded to jihad's centrality in Pakistan's foreign policy. He said,

> Kashmir runs in our blood. No Pakistani can afford to severe links with Kashmir. The entire Pakistan and the world know this. We will continue to extend our moral, political and diplomatic support to Kashmiris. We will never budge an inch from our principle stand on Kashmir. (Government of Pakistan, 2002)

The May 1999 Kargil war was another instance of Pakistan's support to jihadist groups and of the involvement of the Force Command Northern Areas (FCNA) and the 10th Corps of the Pakistani military. The operation

---

* LeT and JeM changed their names following their proscription by General Pervez Musharraf in 2002.

was also reportedly supported by the Fourth Northern Infantry Battalion, Gilgit; Sixth Northern Infantry Battalion, Skardu; Fifth Northern Infantry Battalion, Minimarg; and the Third Northern Infantry Battalion, Dansam. During the course of the war, large caches of arms and ammunition with Pakistani markings, identity cards, uniforms, and divisional and battalion patches were recovered from the killed soldiers (Dixit, 2002).

Jihadist Generals

During General Zia's regime, the officer corps had become more "Islamized" than before and more supportive of the jihadi cause in Afghanistan and India. It is believed that 19 retired generals attended the 1991 convention of the JI in Islamabad and even after their retirement, military and ISI officers have remained engaged with their former "clients" (Cohen, 2005). The influence of the Sunni Tableeghi Jamaat (TJ) had also grown in the officer corps in the wake of its entry into the armed forces' premises in order to deliver sermons (Cohen, 2005). Owen Bennett Jones' instructive analysis of the Mullah–army interface showed that the army's growing proximity to the jihadist groups led to some senior generals becoming known for their jihadi mindset. These included Lieutenant General Muhammad Aziz Khan, who was considered more "fundamentalist" than the rest (Jones, 2002), and others identified as "fundamentalist" included Lieutenant General(s) Mehmud Ahmed, Muzaffar Usmani (two key players in General Musharraf's 1999 coup), and Hamid Gul, the former ISI chief.

General Muhammad Aziz Khan

A close confidante of General Musharraf and the leading figure in the Kargil war, General Aziz gained prominence for facilitating the smooth execution of the 1999 coup. Under General Musharraf, all appointments had to be approved by him and every minister and senior government official had to go through the "Aziz channel." He cast a strong influence in shaping Pakistan's policy on Kashmir and Afghanistan and the Comprehensive Test Ban Treaty (CTBT). General Aziz and other like-minded jihadist generals exerted significant control over jihad in Kashmir and influence in Afghanistan under the Taliban. He also reportedly had strong links with the JI (Hussain, 2000). He was elevated to the rank of lieutenant general without ever having commanded a corps, largely due to his influence and links with the hardliners and jihadist groups in Pakistan. General Aziz, being a Kashmiri of the Sudan tribe himself, passionately spearheaded Pakistan's Kashmir policy and was said to have orchestrated jihadi activities in Jammu and Kashmir (Hussain, 2000). His sway among the Kashmiris was such that even after his retirement in 2004, General Musharraf kept a close watch on his links with the Kashmir-oriented jihadist groups and the Taliban (Raman, 2004).

Lieutenant General Mehmud Ahmed

Lieutenant General Mehmud Ahmed was corps commander, Rawalpindi, during the 1999 coup and the ISI chief when the September 11 attacks occurred. Later, he became embroiled in a controversy following his trip to Kandahar on September 17, 2001, at the behest of General Musharraf. The intention of his trip was supposed to have been to persuade Mullah Omar to hand over bin Laden to the United States in order to avert the impending U.S. attack. Instead, he allegedly advised Mullah Omar to stand firm and prepare for war. Following the revelation of his volte-face, reportedly by a cleric of the Binori mosque in the accompanying delegation, he was replaced by Lieutenant General Ehsan ul Haq as the ISI chief (McGirk, 2002). Media reports also suggest that on his instructions, Omar Saeed Shiekh, the person charged with the murder of Daniel Pearl, had transferred $100,000 into the account of Mohammad Atta, one of the main operatives in the September 11 hijacking (*The Dawn*, 2001; Meacher, 2004).

Lieutenant General Hamid Gul

Widely regarded as a hardline Islamist, Lieutenant General Hamid Gul, a former ISI chief, believes that for Pakistan, Islam is the ideology and jihad its instrument. A JI member, General Gul believes that Pakistan must Islamize itself to ward off U.S. pressures on critical issues and be able to stand up against India's hegemony. His views were also shared by the former army chief, General Mirza Aslam Beg and Lieutenant General Javed Nasir, another JI member. Hamid Gul labeled the overthrow of the Taliban regime as a huge "betrayal" by the United States, which intensified his hatred of the United States. He claims that the September 11 attacks were carried out by the Israeli secret service Mossad and its U.S. accomplices and not by bin Laden. He also acknowledges that the chain of events since September 11 have made him more fundamentalist than during the Afghan jihad and enhanced his praise of the Taliban for whom he says,

> They represent Islam in its purest form so far. It's a clean sheet. And they were also moving in the right direction when this crisis was cooked up the by the US. Until September 11, they had perfect law and order with no formal police force, only traffic cops without side-arms. Now in less than two weeks, they have mobilized some 300,000 volunteers to fight American and British invaders if they come. (quoted in de Borchgrave, 2001)

His reputation and ties among the jihadist groups can be measured by the fact that, according to an Afghan news agency, recently, under U.S. pressure, the ISI has approached Hamid Gul to urge Mullah Omar to leave Pakistan for Afghanistan or any third country (Panjwok Afghan News, 2011).

Cases of Suspect State Organ Involvement

The following are some instances of suspect ISI and state involvement in jihadist operations.

JKLF–ISI Linkage

In June 2005, while accompanying the peace delegation to Pakistan aboard the inaugural Srinagar–Muzaffarabad bus service, the JKLF* chairman Yasin Malik said, "Sheikh Ahmed Rashid [the then Information Minister] had played a great role for the Kashmir's liberation. He used to support the frontline Jihadis from Kashmir, but few know of his contribution" (Mir, 2005, p. 44). These supposedly gratuitous remarks triggered a political storm in both countries, leading to a series of denials and clarifications from both Malik and Sheikh Rashid. Reportedly, Rashid had rented his farmhouse to the ISI for the harboring of militants (including Malik himself). In addition, the Pakistan People's Party (PPP) spokesperson also confirmed that the Freedom House in Rawalpindi was a militant training camp and, in 1989, the ISI had been given vast tracts of land without the government's permission for this purpose (Mir, 2005). The PoK-based JKLF chief Amanuallah Khan had once claimed, "We had a gentleman's agreement, an oral sort of agreement. I was given assurances that the ISI was all out for the independence of Jammu and Kashmir" (Mir, 2005, p. 46).

Army–ISI–Taliban Linkage

Prior to the U.S. attack on the Taliban regime, military officials made a clandestine visit to Kandahar in order to help the Taliban build defenses, reportedly without General Musharraf's knowledge, and this threatened the evolving United States–Pakistan cooperation in the war on terror. The renowned journalist Ahmed Rashid told the *Times of India*,

> Senior retired army officers said that General Musharraf was infuriated when informed of the officers' trip because it could have jeopardized Pakistan's relations with the United States and Britain. There is no suggestion that General (Mehmud) Ahmed knew about the trip either, but he nevertheless resigned as ISI chief. (Rajghatta, 2001)

---

* Two factions of the JKLF were born out of the parent organization called the Jammu Kashmir National Liberation Front (JKNLF) founded in 1977 in the United Kingdom. The faction based in Pakistan Occupied Kashmir is headed by Amanullah Khan and the one in Indian Jammu and Kashmir is headed by Yasin Malik. Through the 1990s, the Malik faction spearheaded Pakistan-supported jihad in Jammu and Kashmir until 1996 when Malik renounced violence to pursue the peaceful route to achieve independence for Jammu and Kashmir. Currently, the Malik faction is part of the moderates-led All Party Hurriyat Conference in Jammu and Kashmir, throwing its support behind the India–Pakistan peace process.

Other reports indicated Pakistani army links with the Taliban. Indian intelligence agencies had previously informed the U.S. authorities that military goods, including ammunition and fuel, were being sent to the Taliban with the help of elements in the Pakistani government, from Quetta to the Pakistani border town of Chaman and then to Kandahar, the Taliban stronghold. The supply resumed mostly after sunset when the official monitoring of the border ceased for the day (Staff Correspondent, 2001). According to "Patterns of Global Terrorism 2000," the United States remained concerned with Pakistan's alleged support for Taliban military operations in Afghanistan and for providing material, fuel, funding, technical assistance, and military advisors. The report also said that Islamabad had failed to curb the activities of some of the madrassas as recruitment grounds for jihad (Office of the Secretary of State, 2000). Other reports also revealed that as per the local intelligence sources, the Pakistani authorities provided medical facilities for the ailing bin Laden, including renal dialysis, at an army hospital in Peshawar. The report claimed that without any logistical or other kind of support from Islamabad, the Taliban would not have continued to function the way it had been functioning (Jane's Intelligence Digest, 2001).

Army–Taliban Joint Operation: The Kunduz Case

Another instance of suspected army–Taliban linkage was an airlift in Kunduz, carried out by the Pakistani air force in the middle of the war. According to press reports, in November 2001, amid growing pressure from the coalition forces and the Northern Alliance on the Taliban and al-Qaeda fighters in the northern hill town of Kunduz, the Pakistani army was alarmed, since among those surrounded were Pakistani soldiers, intelligence advisers, and volunteers who were fighting alongside the Taliban against the United States. Subsequent reports revealed that the Pakistani air force performed the airlift after General Musharraf had sought George Bush's agreement for the evacuation on the grounds that these personnel were fighting for the coalition forces and their loss or capture would create a political storm in Pakistan. Later, U.S. officials admitted that the operations undertaken in C-130 planes were thought to be of a limited nature, but eventually evacuated around 1000 pro-Taliban fighters. The CIA believes that in addition to the Pakistani army personnel, hundreds of Taliban and al-Qaeda fighters also escaped to Pakistan, among them several key Taliban leaders (Hersh, 2002).

Ahmed al-Khadir Episode: ISI's Role

In this instance, the ISI and the army, in liaison with the Taliban, are said to have facilitated the escape of Ahmed al-Khadir, an Egyptian associate of bin Laden, to Afghanistan. Tim McGirk reported that Ahmed al-Khadir was the main accused in the Egyptian embassy bombing case in Islamabad in 1995 in which 15 people were killed. Egyptian officials, having found Ahmed in a safe house in Peshawar, surrounded the house and informed the ISI chief general Mehmud Ahmed in order to expedite his capture. As it turned out later, no security operation or arrest occurred; instead, a car with a diplomatic registration carrying Taliban officials arrived and whisked al-Khadir away to Afghanistan through the Khyber Pass. The later official explanation was, "So sorry. The man gave us the slip" (McGirk, 2002). Quoting Ahmed Rashid, McGirk writes that al-Khadir was allowed to escape because he knew too much about ISI's links with al-Qaeda. On another occasion, bin Laden was alleged to have been allowed to slip away when an operation undertaken by a U.S.-trained Pakistani commando unit under ISI supervision did not do "squat" (McGirk, 2002).

Omar Saeed Sheikh and the Daniel Pearl Murder Case

Omar Saeed Sheikh was the mastermind behind the abduction of three tourists, including two British and an American citizen in Jammu and Kashmir in 1994. Fortunately, the hostages were rescued by the Indian security forces and Sheikh was captured. In a turn of events, Sheikh had to be released along with Maulana Masood Azhar, the JeM founder, in a trade-off to secure the release of 178 passengers aboard Indian Airlines flight IC-814, which was hijacked in December 2001 by Sheikh's group, the National Youth Movement for the Sovereignty of Pakistan. In February 2002, Sheikh kidnapped Daniel Pearl, a *Wall Street* journalist, who was investigating the Pakistani connection with the shoe bomber, Richard Colvin Reid. Later, Daniel Pearl was beheaded by his captors, which compelled the United States to pressure Pakistan for Sheikh's arrest. Subsequently, Sheikh surrendered and was sentenced to death by the Terrorism Court on July 15, 2002, but is yet to be executed. He is held in Hyderabad jail under high security as authorities fear his comrades-in-arm may attempt his rescue (Ansari, 2005). Intriguingly, General Musharraf's reaction to Pearl's killing was to say that he had become a victim of "intelligence games" and was "over inquisitive" and "getting involved" in the story (of Richard Reid) (McCarthy, 2002). Musharraf's remarks suggest the complicity of the establishment, especially the top army leadership, in Pearl's murder. It is noteworthy that the demands for ransom from Pearl's captors included expediting the long due delivery of F-16 fighters by the United States. Equally interesting is the allegation that when Sheikh was pressured by the army and ISI to surrender, he made a deal to surrender to the person of his choice with the condition that he not be extradited to the United States, failing which he would expose the establishment's role in the case. The Pakistani government relented and Sheikh surrendered to Brigadier (retd.) Ijaz Shah, a former ISI contact of Sheikh, who at that time was the home secretary of Punjab (McCarthy, 2002). Earlier, in the wake of the 2001 Indian parliament attack, in which Sheikh was reportedly involved as well, a livid Musharraf is said to have barged into the ISI headquarters screaming at the ISI director general (internal security), "Leash in these mad dogs that you have kept" (Hasan, 2005).

2008 Mumbai Attacks and ISI Involvement

On November 26, 2008, 10 LeT terrorists, believed to have been trained by the ISI, carried out a brazen 60-h siege in Mumbai in which 166 people, including security personnel and 26 foreign nationals, were killed (Government of India, 2008–2009). The terrorists attacked the Leopold Café in Colaba, a popular tourist place, the Chatraparti Shivaji Terminus railway station, Cama hospital, Metro Cinema hall, Nariman House (owned by the orthodox Jewish community), and the Taj and Oberoi hotels. They had captured the vessel *Kuber* after killing its navigator Amarsingh Solanki and used an inflatable speedboat to enter Mumbai via the sea route, equipped with automatic weapons, grenades, and explosives (*Indian Express*, May 25, 2009). In the counterterrorist operations, 22-year-old Ajmal Amir Kasab was captured alive. He later confessed to his crime and has been sentenced to death on four counts by the local court in Mumbai (He was hanged to death on 21st November 2012.). He revealed that the objective was to destabilize India and seek the liberation of Kashmir (*Indian Express*, May 25, 2009). Pakistan, after initially denying the nationality of the terrorists, acknowledged that they were indeed Pakistanis (Kamal & Baruah, 2009).

Under intense Indian and international pressure, Pakistani Interior Minister Rehman Malik also admitted that part of the planning had been done in Pakistan. India has provided several dossiers, based on their investigations, to the Pakistani authorities to act upon. The Pakistani authorities later arrested the alleged mastermind, Zaki-ur-Rehman Lakhvi, and five others, including Hammad Amin Sadiq, Zarar Shah, Mohammed Ashfaq, Javaid Iqbal, and Abu Al-Qama. India has maintained that LeT chief Hafeez Saeed is the key accused who must be arrested for perpetrating terrorist attacks in India. In an interview in June 2011, Rehman Malik responded, "We had detained him [Hafiz Saeed, LeT leader]. The law does not go by statement but evidence. If we are provided actionable evidence we will act against him" (*Indian Express*, June 29, 2011).

In a significant development, following his arrest, David Coleman Headley, the Pakistani-born American and an LeT operative, revealed that he had done extensive reconnaissance of the targets and identified entry and escape routes. In a U.S. court, he testified that the ISI had planned the entire Mumbai operation in tandem with the LeT and implicated Major Iqbal of the ISI, Hafiz Saeed, and Tahawwur Rana, a U.S.-based Pakistani Canadian, along with four others in the attacks (*Hindustan Times*, May 24,

2011). Tahawwur Rana, who was later acquitted of the charges, said in his defense that his actions "were done at the behest of the Pakistani government and the ISI, not the Lashkar terrorist organization." Pakistan had reportedly hired the Dallas-based law firm, Locke Lord Bissell & Liddel, to block the lawsuit (by the relatives of the 2008 Mumbai Jewish attacks) in a U.S. court that accused Lieutenant General Ahmad Shuja Pasha, the current ISI chief and his predecessor Nadeem Taj, of complicity in the Mumbai attacks (*Hindustan Times*, May 24, 2011). The testimony of Abu Jundal, mentioned earlier, also points to the involvement of the ISI and the LeT in masterminding the Mumbai operations.

International Law and Accountability of the Pakistani State

The debate over a state's linkage with NSAGs operating from its territory is enmeshed in complexities due to the covert nature of the alleged linkages; the legal requirements under international law to establish the linkage and state accountability based on credible evidence; and, should this linkage be established, the determination of what lawful options (political, diplomatic, and military) are prescribed under international law for the victim states in order to safeguard themselves against the wrongful acts of NSAs. The inherent difficulty, if not implausibility, on the part of the victim states to produce "substantive" and "actionable" evidence to establish the involvement of state organs and their linkage with NSAGs remains a major inducement for many states to employ NSAGs to further foreign policy goals. Intelligence agencies and military regimes may fund NSAs in order to achieve their strategic objectives, which raises concerns over the autonomy of these NSAs from state control (Josselin & Wallace, 2001). International law clearly distinguishes between state and nonstate actors, but this distinction has been eroded in recent decades in several disciplines including *jus ad bellum* (use of force). States have carried out proxy wars and guarded themselves under the principles of territorial sovereignty and nonuse of force in international relations. Any state that engages in such tactics and perpetrates terrorism through terror groups is liable for this international breach of state obligations, as much as are the responsible terrorist groups themselves (Brown, 2002). As shown in the preceding sections, there is considerable evidence that elements connected with the Pakistani military and the ISI have used jihad as a tool of state policy and promoted terrorist groups in order to achieve strategic objectives in Afghanistan and India. In this context, it becomes necessary to go one step further and examine under international law what constitutes an "act of the state" and "state organ" in order to determine how accountable the Pakistani state is for these groups and their wrongful acts.

International Law Commission

In 2001, the International Law Commission (ILC) in its 53rd session adopted draft articles on "Responsibility of States for Internationally Wrongful Acts," which through codification and progressive development sought to formulate the fundamental rules of international law concerning the responsibilities of states for their internationally wrongful acts. It is important to underline that although the legal provisions pertaining to the conduct and responsibilities of NSAs have been recognized, the provisions and law on attributing the acts of NSAs to the state have not been recognized. Nonetheless, there are three key ILC Articles on State Responsibility (ILCASR), which in the Pakistani context are relevant.

Article 1. (*Responsibility of a state for its internationally wrongful acts*):
Every internationally wrongful act of a State entails the international responsibility of that State. (ILC, 2001, p. 32)

Responsibility is defined as "borne by a state for acts which are directly imputable to it, such as acts of its government, or those of its officials or private individuals performed at the government's command or with its authorization" (Jennings & Watts, 1992, pp. 501–502).

Article 2. (*Elements of an internationally wrongful act of a State*):
There is an internationally wrongful act of a State when conduct consisting of an action or omission:
    a) is attributable to the State under international law; and
    b) constitutes a breach of an international obligation of the State. (ILC, 2001, p. 34)

Article 4. (*Conduct of organs of a State*):
    1. The conduct of any State organ shall be considered an act of that State under the international law, whether the organ exercises legislative, executive, judicial or any other functions, whatever position it holds in the organization of the State, and whatever its character as an organization of the central government or of a territorial unit of the State.
    2. An organ includes any person or entity which has that status in accordance with the internal law of the State. (ILC, 2001, p. 40)

Article 5. (*Conduct of persons or entities exercising elements of governmental authority*):
The conduct of a person or entity which is not an organ of the State under article 4 but which is empowered by the law of that State to exercise elements of the governmental authority shall be considered an act of the State under international law, provided the person or entity is acting in that capacity in the particular instance. (ILC, 2001, p. 42)

Article 8. (*Conduct directed or controlled by a State*):
The conduct of a person or a group of persons shall be considered an act of a State under international law if the person or the group of persons is in fact acting on the instructions of, or under the direction or control of that State in carrying out the conduct. (ILC, 2001, p. 47)

Rulings of ICJ

The following cases have been adjudicated by the ICJ and are very instructive in determining what can be considered "an act of the state" and under what circumstances the state can be targeted and to what extent the state can be held accountable for the unlawful acts of NSAs operating from its territory. These cases have been chosen for the purpose of this study because of some similarities with the Pakistan case. The *Genocide* case entails the alleged involvement of the former state of Yugoslavia's linkage in facilitating the acts of the Serbian military, which reportedly carried out genocide against Muslims and non-Serbs. In the *Democratic Republic of Congo (DRC) v. Uganda* case, the DRC alleged that the Ugandan military violated its territorial integrity and committed mass murders and human rights violations, similar to the claims of the Pakistani state against the U.S. and India's claims against Pakistan. In the *Nicaragua v. United States of America* case, the court had to determine whether targeting of the Nicaraguan government and the military by the United States through the Nicaraguan contras was a lawful act. As with the other two cases, in this case also, the ICJ based its judgment on its interpretation of the principles of "attributability," "self-defense," "armed attack," and "proportionality" among others under customary international law, principles that are relevant to the discussion on Pakistan's case.

Genocide Case

In 2007, in a much debated and discussed case, the ICJ determined the contours of state responsibility under the Genocide Convention in the *Genocide* case pertaining to the alleged involvement of Serbia (former state of Yugoslavia, FRY) in the genocide against Bosniaks (Bosnian Muslims) and non-Serb minorities in Srebrenica during the early 1990s. The case was brought to the court by the Republic of Bosnia and Herzegovina. The ICJ declined to attribute genocide to the FRY for lack of evidence that the court deemed was necessary in order to establish direct commission of genocide by the state. Unfortunately, in this case, the ruling of the ICJ has been subject to rigorous criticism by scholars, because of the court's reliance more on the Genocide Convention of 1948, rather than on the provisions of international humanitarian law or customary law, which could have established a greater obligation on the part of the FRY (Birkland, 2009). On the question of "attribution," the court said that the FRY furthered "considerable military and financial support available to the Republika Srpska [Republic of Serbia]" and "had it withdrawn that support, [it] would have greatly constrained the options that were available to the Republicka Srpska authorities" (Birkland, 2009, p. 1642). However, despite this kind of support rendered by the FRY, the VRS (the military of the Republic of Serbia) could not be considered a de jure organ of the FRY as required under international law (Birkland, 2009). On the basis of the reports submitted by the Dutch Military Intelligence Service and the U.S. Intelligence Agency, the ICJ found that the VRS acts were not under the instructions, directions, or control of the FRY (Jiminez, 2007).

The court ruling has also drawn criticism from scholars for constituting a very high and strict attribution test and ignoring circumstantial evidence of intent (Birkland, 2009). At the same time, it must be highlighted that the ICJ also established FRY's clear obligation to rein in the NSAs over which it exercised considerable influence, by broadly interpreting a state's obligation to prevent genocide. In the court's opinion, although there was little evidence to suggest that Serbia exercised "effective control' over the Bosnian Serb forces, there was still satisfactory evidence that Serbia had sufficient control over the VRS, establishing its liability for failure to prevent the genocide (Birkland, 2009). The ICJ ruling on this count has set a precedent of imposing liability upon states for failing in their responsibility to prevent a wrongful act that was not otherwise attributable to them, under the obligation of "duty to prevent" (Birkland, 2009, p. 1649).

DRC v. Uganda *Case*

In the *Democratic Republic of Congo (DRC) v. Uganda* case, the DRC had claimed that the latter's troops had invaded its territory, committing human rights violations, massacring a large number of Congolese, looting property, and causing widespread destruction. In response, in its December 19, 2005 judgment, the ICJ found that Uganda:

   a) violated the principles of non-use of force in international relations and of non-intervention;
   b) violated its obligations under international human rights law and international humanitarian law; and
   c) violated other obligations owed to the Democratic Republic of Congo. (Armed Activities, 2005)

The court ruled that Uganda, by engaging in military activities against the DRC on the latter's territory, by occupying Ituri, and by actively extending military, logistic, economic, and financial support to irregular forces having operated on DRC territory, violated the principle of nonuse of force in international relations and the principle of nonintervention. The court also dismissed Uganda's claims that its actions in the period between 1998 and 1999 constituted self-defense. The court said that Uganda had violated the territorial integrity and sovereignty of the DRC and its actions equally constituted interference in the internal affairs of the DRC. The court did not find any satisfactory evidence to prove the DRC's claims that Uganda created and controlled the Congo Liberation Movement (MLC), led by Jean-Pierre Bemba (Armed Activities, 2005).

The court also found that the DRC, by the conduct of its armed forces, which attacked the Ugandan embassy in Kinshasa, maltreated Ugandan diplomats and other individuals on the embassy premises, maltreated Ugandan diplomats at Ndjili International Airport, as well as by its failure to provide the Ugandan embassy and Ugandan diplomats with effective protection and by its failure to prevent archives and Ugandan property from being seized from the premises of the Ugandan embassy, violated obligations owed to the Ugandan government under the Vienna Convention on Diplomatic Relations of 1961 (Armed Activities, 2005).

The court's decision that since the attacks carried out by anti-Ugandan rebels operating from DRC territory could not be attributed to the DRC, Uganda had no right to use force in self-defense on DRC territory, has triggered severe criticism from scholars (Trapp, 2007). The court had based its decision on the ground that use of force against NSAs in another state's territory is considered a violation of that state's territorial sovereignty under Article 2(4) of the UN Charter, even if the use of force is defensive and is not directed at the state's apparatus. But scholars argue that the court has provided no guidance regarding the circumstances under which legal use of force in self-defense can be used against the NSAs. Scholars argue that Article 51 of the UN Charter, wherein the inherent right of self-defense rests, is an exception to the prohibition of the use of force against the territorial integrity of the state. Article 51 provides,

> Nothing in the present Charter shall impair the inherent right of individual or collective self-defence if an armed attack occurs against a Member of the United Nations, until the Security Council has taken measures necessary to maintain international peace and security. Measures taken by Members in the exercise of this right of self-defence shall be immediately reported to the Security Council and shall not in any way affect the authority and responsibility of the Security Council under the present Charter to take at any time such action as it deems necessary in order to maintain or restore international peace and security. (Charter of the United Nations, 1945)

As far as the use of force against NSAs is concerned, it can be lawfully undertaken under the rubric of customary international law. Under customary international law, an armed attack against NSAs can be reconciled with the territorial sovereignty of the state on the territory of which the use of force is intended, by fulfilling the requirement of "necessity" and "proportionality"

(Green, 2006, p. 480). The element of necessity requires that force should be the last option after all political and diplomatic options have been exhausted to resolve the issue, and proportionality means that the use of force be tailored in such a fashion that it does not go beyond what is necessary to halt or prevent the armed attack in question (Charter of the United Nations, 1945). In the event that the state or the territory in which the NSAs are based is actively doing all that can be done to counter the activities of the NSAs and prevent the launching of terrorist attacks, then the justification for self-defense on the part of the victim or injured state is nullified. However, in the case that the state or the territory in which the NSAs are based is unable or unwilling to prevent such attacks and rein in the NSAs activities, the victim state has few options, and is then forced to either respect the territorial integrity of the other state at its own peril or launch an attack in a targeted fashion against the NSAs as specified under customary international law (Charter of United Nations, 1945).

Nicaragua v. United States of America *Case*

In the case of *Nicaragua v. United States of America*, which related to military and paramilitary activities in and against Nicaragua, the ICJ dealt with the question of whether U.S. assistance to Nicaraguan contras as an act of "self-defense" on behalf of El Salvador amounted to a legitimate right of collective self-defense. The court ruled that the U.S.-supported contras were directly targeting the Nicaraguan government and military, and there was no satisfactory evidence to prove the existence of circumstances under which the United States could have done it. The court rejected the justification of collective self-defense maintained by the United States in undertaking military and paramilitary activities in and against Nicaragua. The court observed that whether self-defense is individual or collective, it can only be exercised in response to an "armed attack." This is to be understood as meaning not merely action by regular armed forces across an international border, but also the sending by a state of armed bands into the territory of another state, if such an operation, because of its scale and effects, would have been classified as an armed attack had it been carried out by regular armed forces. The court rejected the argument that the concept of "armed attack" includes assistance to rebels in the form of the provision of weapons or logistical or other support. In the court's view, the United States, by training, arming, equipping, financing, and supplying the contra forces or otherwise encouraging, supporting, and aiding military and paramilitary activities in and against Nicaragua, had acted against the Republic of Nicaragua in breach of its obligations under customary international law not to intervene in the affairs of another state. The court also determined that the United States had carried out certain attacks on Nicaraguan territory in 1983–1984 and had acted against the Republic of Nicaragua in breach of its obligations under customary international law not to use force against another state. The court ruled that if one state, with a view to the coercion of another state, supports and assists armed bands in that state, the purpose of which is to overthrow its government, this amounts to intervention in its internal affairs, no matter what the political objective of the state giving support may be. Therefore, the support provided by the United States to the military and paramilitary activities of the contras in Nicaragua constituted a clear breach of the principle of nonintervention (ICJ, 1986).

It is pertinent to point out that the court's decision in this case evoked strong criticism from legal experts. In fact, one of the judges on the bench that decided this case, Judge Schwebel, gave a dissenting opinion regarding the judgment. In his opinion, the United States had acted lawfully in exerting armed pressures against Nicaragua, since the scale of Nicaragua's prior and sustained support to armed insurgency in El Salvador was tantamount to an armed attack upon El Salvador, on behalf of which the United States was acting in self-defense. Judge Schwebel stated that "the actions of the United States are strikingly proportionate. The Salvadoran rebels, vitally supported by Nicaragua, conduct a rebellion in El-Salvador; in collective self-defence, the United States symmetrically supports rebels who conduct a rebellion in Nicaragua. The rebels in El-Salvador pervasively attack economic targets of importance in El Salvador; the United States selectively attacks economic targets of military importance" in Nicaragua. He argued that in contemporary international law, the state that first intervenes with the use of force in another state—as by substantial involvement in the sending of irregulars onto its territory—is prima facie, the aggressor. Another dissenting opinion came from Judge Sir Robert Jennings, who viewed that on the use of force, on intervention, and on the question of self-defense, the court lacked jurisdiction. Judges Oda and Ruda regretted that the court had needlessly been brief and hasty in giving its views on collective self-defense and should not have dwelled upon that aspect at all (ICJ, 1986).

The ICJ decisions in the above cases, especially in the *Nicaragua* case, have been subject to intense scrutiny. Scholars and legal experts have taken a strong position on the ICJ's interpretation of "self-defense," "armed attack," "attribution," and "international responsibility." Scholars have questioned the rationale that any action justified by the UN Security Council (UNSC) in self-defense against an NSA cannot be undertaken collectively or individually by states under the rubric of customary international law on self-defense, which is also provided by Article 51 of the UN Charter. The actions that the UNSC deems itself competent to undertake against an NSA under Articles 41 and 42 in accordance with Article 39 cannot become impermissible when taken against the same actor by an attacked state under Article 51 in exercise of a state's inherent right of self-defense. An attacked state has as much right to act in self-defense under Article 51 as does the UNSC under Chapter VII (Frank, 2001).*

For any action to be taken in self-defense by an injured state individually or in cooperation with other states collectively, it is essential that the attack be attributed to the NSA or the state against which the use of force (*jus ad bellum*) is directed. It is absolutely necessary to show that the state or NSA is responsible for that attack and that a breach of international obligation had occurred on the part of the state on the territory of which the NSA in question is based. Under the 1970 Declaration on Principles of International Law Concerning Friendly Relations and Cooperation among States, "Every State has the duty to refrain from organizing, instigating, assisting or participating in ... terrorist acts in another State or acquiescing in organized activities within its territory directed towards the commission of such acts, when the acts referred to in the present paragraph involve threat or use of force"; this is also invoked by the 1994 UN General Assembly Declaration on Measures to Eliminate International Terrorism (Brown, 2003). In the case of an organization providing funding, training, logistical support, and direction to that individual, the organization is also responsible for the attack. The responsible organization, taken as a whole, will be considered to have committed the attack. Based on this rationale, when a terrorist organization is responsible for an attack, a state may use counterforce not only against the individuals, but also against the entire organization. And since terrorist groups are largely based in the territory of states, when they attack other states, they make the state on which they are based liable for the attack (Brown, 2003). As in the case of Afghanistan under the Taliban regime, and arguably of Pakistan that allegedly provided logistical, financial, and training support to

---

* Article 39 of Chapter VII of the UN Charter states, "The Security Council shall determine the existence of any threat to the peace, breach of the peace, or act of aggression and shall make recommendations, or decide what measures shall be taken in accordance with Articles 41 and 42, to maintain or restore international peace and security." Article 40 states, "In order to prevent an aggravation of the situation, the Security Council may, before making the recommendations or deciding upon the measures provided for in Article 39, call upon the parties concerned to comply with such provisional measures as it deems necessary or desirable. Such provisional measures shall be without prejudice to the rights, claims, or position of the parties concerned. The Security Council shall duly take account of failure to comply with such provisional measures." Article 41 states, "The Security Council may decide what measures not involving the use of armed force are to be employed to give effect to its decisions, and it may call upon the Members of the United Nations to apply such measures. These may include complete or partial interruption of economic relations and of rail, sea, air, postal, telegraphic, radio, and other means of communication, and the severance of diplomatic relations." Article 42 states, "Should the Security Council consider that measures provided for in Article 41 would be inadequate or have proved to be inadequate, it may take such action by air, sea, or land forces as may be necessary to maintain or restore international peace and security. Such action may include demonstrations, blockade, and other operations by air, sea, or land forces of Members of the United Nations."

a large number of terrorist groups based on their territory under its control, a state can be considered to have committed an act of aggression and thereby breached its international obligation not to engage in or support terrorist acts (United Nations General Assembly, 1974).*

State responsibility toward an international wrongful act committed by NSAs or its agents can be imputed in three ways: original responsibility, responsibility by endorsement, and vicarious responsibility. *Original responsibility* is borne by a state for acts that are directly imputable to it, such as acts of its government, or those of its officials or private individuals performed at the government's command or with its authorization. It also includes activities of those persons who and organizations which are not organs or employees of the state, but have been acting as its agents, as specified under Article 8 of ILCASR. The limitation of this responsibility is that it does not apply to acts committed by agents or NSAs that are not controlled by the state, although it may have breached its international obligations by enabling the act (Brown, 2003). Under its international obligations, a state has to ensure that it exercises due diligence in not only preventing a wrongful act by those who are not its agents or organs, but also brings them to justice. Failure on these counts will be deemed as an endorsement of those acts by that state, as seen in the Iranian hostage crisis of 1979–1980, and therefore, all acts thereon committed by the NSA would be imputed to the state on the territory of which they are based. The difficulty with this category of responsibility, however, is that the states know well that support for international terrorism is prohibited under international law and therefore they would refrain from directly endorsing the acts of NSAs (Brown, 2003).

Vicarious responsibility provides for a state to be held responsible for the acts committed by NSAs or agents who are not part of its organs or authorized by it, by its failure to prevent the act or bring the culprits to justice (Jennings & Watts, 1992). This category of responsibility can be imputed to Pakistan in the attack on the Indian parliament by JeM in 2001 and the Mumbai siege of 2008 by LeT, for its failure to bring the culprits to justice. Maulana Masood Azhar, the leader of JeM, and Maulana Hafeez Saeed are still at large in Pakistan and engaging in terrorist activities against India, apparently with impunity. The information that India has provided has not convinced the Pakistani authorities enough to take any action, and they have sought "substantive" and "actionable" evidence (Naqvi, 2012).

As ruled in the *Corfu Channel* case of 1946 by the ICJ, a case in which two British warships had been sunk after running into a minefield in Albanian

---

* Definition of "Aggression": "Aggression is the use of armed force by a state against the sovereignty, territorial integrity or political independence of another State, or in any other manner inconsistent with the Charter of the United Nations, as set out in this Definition."

territorial waters, a state that is or should be aware of a terrorist attack against another state, but fails to prevent and warn about it or ignores it, should be held responsible for the attack under the criteria of vicarious responsibility. Also, if the state had been generally supporting an NSA and not necessarily its activities on a case-by-case basis, the linkage between the support and responsibility would be proximate enough to hold the state vicariously responsible for the wrongful act against another state committed by the NSA (Brown, 2003).

Under Article 51 of the UN Charter, nothing prohibits the use of individual or collective self-defense in the wake of an armed attack against a member of the UN, until the UNSC has undertaken any necessary measure to address the situation. In the case of NSAs based in and operating from Pakistan, the United States and other injured states such as India can undertake an act in self-defense because of the Pakistani state's apparent inability to prevent these attacks and its apparent unwillingness for strategic reasons to eliminate terrorist groups such as the Taliban and LeT. The ongoing U.S. military strategy of drone attacks in Pakistan is based on the same rationale under which the United States fired 79 Tomahawk cruise missiles against terrorist training camps in Afghanistan and Sudan on August 20, 1998, in response to the bombings of U.S. embassies in Nairobi and Dar es Salaam. The justification for the missile attacks offered by the then U.S. president Bill Clinton to the Speaker of the House of Representatives and president of the Senate was as follows:

> The United States acted in exercise of our inherent right of self-defence consistent with Article 51 of the United Nations Charter. These strikes were a necessary and proportionate response to the imminent threat of further terrorist attacks against U.S. personnel and facilities. These strikes were intended to prevent and deter additional attacks by a clearly identified terrorist threat. The targets were selected because they served to facilitate directly the efforts of terrorists specifically identified with attacks on U.S. personnel and facilities and posed a continuing threat to U.S. lives. (Quoted in Murphy, 1999, p. 161)

In its notification to the UNSC, the United States said:

> The attacks were carried out only after repeated efforts to convince the Government of the Sudan and the Taliban regime in Afghanistan to shut these terrorist activities down and to cease their cooperation with the Bin Laden organization. That organization has issued a series of blatant warnings that 'strikes will continue from everywhere' against American targets, and we have convincing evidence that further such attacks were in preparation from these same terrorist facilities. The United States, therefore, had no choice but to use armed force to prevent these attacks from continuing.

In doing so, the United States has acted pursuant to the right of self-defense confirmed by Article 51 of the Charter of the United Nations. The targets struck, and the timing and method of the attack used, were carefully designed to minimize risks of collateral damage to civilians and to comply with international law, including the rules of necessity and proportionality. (Quoted in Murphy, 1999, p. 163)

In the ongoing war on terror, the U.S. strategy is based on the right of self-defense enshrined in Article 51 of the UN Charter and continues to target terrorist hideouts inside Pakistan by conforming to the requirements of necessity and proportionality, as mandated by customary international law. Some international law experts also justify drone attacks as perfectly legal under the 2001 U.S. Authorization for Use of Military Force against al-Qaeda (Addicot, 2011). Pakistan's alleged inability and reluctance to wind up its jihadist infrastructure until Afghanistan and Kashmir are settled to its satisfaction can be deemed a violation of UNGA Resolution 2625 (XXV), which proclaims that,

Every state has the duty to refrain from organizing, instigating, assisting, or participating in acts of civil strife or terrorist acts in another State or acquiescing in organized activities within its territory directed towards the commission of such acts...no State shall organize, assist, foment, finance, incite or tolerate subversive, terrorist or armed activities directed toward the violent overthrow of the regime of another State, or interfere in civil strife in another State. (United Nations General Assembly, 1970)

In sum, under customary international law, a victim state can carry out a lawful attack in self-defense against NSAs and the state under the following circumstances: First, the state itself consents to an attack being undertaken by another state against NSAs that are based in its territory (Brown, 2003). An example is the case of Sri Lanka, which had requested the assistance of the Indian Peace Keeping Forces (IPKF) in fighting against the Liberation Tigers of Tamil Eelam (LTTE) in Sri Lanka in 1987. Second, the state on the territory of which the NSAs are based is unwilling to prevent the use of its territory to launch attacks against other states, in contravention of the definition of aggression enshrined in UNGA Resolution 3314. And third, the state on the territory of which the NSAs are based is unable to prevent its territory from being used to launch attacks on other states. In these three exceptional cases, the use of military force against NSAs based in another state is deemed lawful (Brown, 2003).

Conclusion

This chapter discussed the employment of NSAs and NSAGs as instruments of states' foreign policy in order to enhance regional influence and achieve strategic objectives. In the Pakistani context, in light of the discussion based on Pakistani and external sources, it was highlighted how the formidable jihadist infrastructure has been sustained using linkages with the state organs and how it continues to pose a serious threat to Pakistani, regional, and international security. Many of these NSAs and NSAGs appear to continue to have sympathizers in the Pakistani military and the ISI due to the historical links created during the Afghan jihad during the 1980s. The testimonies of Abu Jundal and David Coleman Headley put the spotlight on the alleged role of the ISI in executing terrorist operations in India through NSAGs, including the LeT. The available literature and official reports demonstrate how the alleged NSAGs–state organ linkages have been implicated in attacks on the United States and its allies in Afghanistan. In July 2011, the United States reportedly deferred $800 million aid to Pakistan for expelling U.S. military trainers and for suspect ISI links in the killing of the journalist Saleem Shehzaad, who was investigating the infiltration of extremist elements in the military and the ISI (Schmitt & Perlez, 2011). The jihadist infrastructure comprises a number of NSAGs of different sizes and influence and their affiliated madrassas continue to impart extremist teachings and produce radicalized fighters to fight in Afghanistan and Kashmir, allegedly with the ideological, logistical, and financial support of the Islamist parties and sympathizers in the ISI and the military, both serving and retired. As more NSAGs, including the Haqqani network, Quetta Shura, TTP, and TNSM, entered the scene, the jihadist infrastructure assumed a more formidable character, now threatening even Pakistan's own security and stability. Despite the repeated assurances by the Pakistani military and civilian regimes to prevent Pakistani territory from being used for terrorist purposes, these NSAGs seem to continue to thrive and undertake their operations in and outside Pakistan—and with impunity. As discussed earlier, Pakistani as well as international scholars argue that the unconstrained activities of these NSAGs are facilitated by their alleged acquiescence with state organs. Some analysts argue that the inability or unwillingness of some elements in the military and ISI to purge these groups amounts to a contravention of Pakistan's obligations under UNGA Resolution 2625 (XXV).

In this context, the U.S. frustration in pushing the Pakistani government to do more has compelled the former to target terrorist groups hiding in the lawless tribal areas of Pakistan, using drones and commando raids. The chapter analyzed the political fallout from drone attacks and commando raids, how it has been perceived unfavorably in the tribal areas, and how it has intensified anti-Americanism across Pakistan in public and in political circles. The Pakistani parliament has taken a strong position on the continued U.S. attacks and labeled them as violations of its territorial sovereignty, which led to the closure of the U.S. drone base at the Shamsi air base and the closure of routes for NATO supplies. The United States has continued to pressure Pakistan to do more against the NSAGs targeting NATO, simultaneously justifying the drone strikes under the principles of "self-defense."

On the eastern front, based on the evidence provided by the Indian authorities, the chapter suggests the complicity of Pakistani state organs in providing finances, training, weapons, and infrastructure to terrorist groups operating in Kashmir and other parts of India. The Indian authorities allege that despite years of protesting and providing evidence about the involvement of the ISI in terrorist operations, the Pakistani government has not purged the activities of groups including LeT and JeM. In this context, as the scholars argue in the U.S.–Pakistan case, India can also justify its inherent rights for self-defense as an injured state under law to protect its citizens and interests by targeting these groups based in the territory controlled by Pakistan. In recent years, as the U.S. patience ran out with the Pakistani government's continuing failure to rein in these groups, it chose to target these groups inside Pakistan, unilaterally. Based on the discussion in the preceding section, it can be argued that the Pakistani government can be held accountable for the acts of the NSAGs in light of the evidence that indicates that some elements within the ISI and the Pakistani military continue to maintain links with these groups and provide them with necessary support and training, in breach of Pakistan's international obligation under UNGA Resolution 2625.

The chapter noted three key cases referred to the ICJ involving the role of NSAGs and alleged state involvement. The ICJ decisions shed light on the extent of state responsibility regarding the acts of NSAs; the rights of injured states under international law; the issue of territorial sovereignty of the state on the territory of which the act of self-defense is exercised; and the state's obligation to prevent wrongful acts by the NSAs. The ICJ rulings in the *Genocide* case, the *DRC v. Uganda* case, and the *Nicaragua v. United States* case established several relevant precedents that are very instructive in the U.S.–Pakistan and India–Pakistan contestations. The ICJ stated that any armed attack undertaken by a state in self-defense on behalf of another state is unlawful, unless it is consented to by the state on behalf of which the act of self-defense is undertaken. It will be considered a violation of the state's territorial sovereignty. The court also said that in order to target the state, the wrongful attacks of the NSAs must be attributable to the state, failing which it would be deemed unlawful. However, scholars and legal experts also found that there is an exception available to the state's right of territorial sovereignty under customary international law. UNGA Resolution 2625 clearly establishes state responsibility to refrain from supporting acts of terrorism, failing which the injured states can exercise the right of self-defense to protect its interest and citizens as specified by Article 51 of the UN Charter, and target the NSAGs by complying with the requirements of necessity and proportionality. Pakistan's seeming inability or alleged reluctance to rein in the

NSAGs operating from its territory shows the state's culpability in the attacks undertaken by them against the United States, Afghanistan, and India. While many of these attacks cannot be attributed to the Pakistani state, at the same time Pakistan cannot be absolved of its accountability and must do everything in its capacity to prevent these groups from injuring other states. In the face of noncompliance or the inability of the Pakistani government to purge these groups that have imperiled its own security, the state must act either unilaterally or jointly with the injured states, failing which the United States and India can justify attacks against these NSAGs on the basis of "self-defense" within the boundaries of the principles of "necessity" and "proportionality" under international law.

Acknowledgment

The author wishes to thank Dr. Melanie O'Brien, a research fellow in the Centre of Excellence in Policing and Security (CEPS), Griffith University, Australia, for her comments and research material support in the writing of this chapter.

References

Abbas, H. (2005). *Pakistan's Drift into Extremism: Allah, the Army, and America's War on Terror.* New York: M.E. Sharpe.

Addicott, J. (2011). Anwar al-Awlaqi and the law of war. *Jurist.* Retrieved on June 26, 2012 from http://jurist.org/forum/2011/10/jeffrey-addicott-al-awlaqi.php.

Agencies. (2010). India hands 11th dossier to Pakistan. *The Express Tribune.* June 19. Retrieved on June 22, 2010 from http://tribune.com.pk/story/22381/india-hands-11th-dossier-to-pakistan/.

Agencies. (2012). Seven Pakistani soldiers 'beheaded' by Afghan militants: Military officials. *The Dawn.* June 25. Retrieved on June 29, 2012 from http://dawn.com/2012/06/25/seven-pakistani-soldiers-beheaded-by-afghan-militants-military-officials/print/.

Ali, Z. A. (2005). Back to the camps. *Herald.* July.

Alvarez-Jiminez, A. (2007). International responsibility for acts of non-state actors: The recent standards set by the International Court of Justice in genocide and why the WTO appellate body should not endorse them. *Syracuse Journal of International Law and Commerce, 35*(1), 1–25.

Ansari, M. (2005). The mystery thickens. *Newsline.* April.

Baweja, H. (2012). DNA test, hard bargain with Saudi nets 26/11 prized catch. *Hindustan Times.* June 26.

Birkland, B. H. (2009). Reigning in non-state actors: State responsibility and attribution in cases of genocide. *New York University Law Review, 84,* 1623–1655.

Brown, D. (2003). Use of force against terrorism after September 11; state responsibility, self-defense and other responses. *Cardozo Journal of International and Comparative Law, 11*(1), 1–53.

Cohen, S. P. (2005). *The Idea of Pakistan.* Oxford: Oxford University Press.

de Borchgrave, A. (2001). Interview with Hamid Gul. *Newsweek*. September 14. Retrieved on November 13, 2010 from http://globalfire.tv/nj/c2001/politics/wtc.mossad.htm.

Dixit, J. N. (2002). *India-Pakistan in War and Peace*. New Delhi: Books Today.

Farooq, U. (2012). Politics of defence. *The Herald*, May 26–27.

Franck, T. M. (2001). Terrorism and the right of self-defence. *The American Journal of International Law*, 95, 4. October.

Gordenker, L., & Weiss, T. G. (1995). Pluralising global governance: Analytical approaches and dimensions. *Third World Quarterly*, 16(3), 357–359.

Government of India. (2003–2004). Annual Report. Ministry of Home Affairs.

Government of India. (2008–2009). Annual Report. Ministry of Home Affairs.

Government of Pakistan. (2002). Pervez Musharraf's address to the nation. January 12. Retrieved on April 6, 2004 from http://www.presidentofpakistan.gov.pk/FilesSpeeches/Addresses/1020200475758A Mword%20file.pdf.

Green, J. A. (2006). Docking the *Caroline*: Understanding the relevance of the formula in contemporary customary international law concerning self-defence. *Cardozo Journal of International Law*, 14, 429–480.

Gupta, S. (2011). Surgical strike and India. *Indian Express*, May 3.

Haqqani, H. (2005). *Pakistan: Between Mosque and Military*. Lahore: Vanguard Books.

Hasan, S. S. (2005). The whole truth. *The Herald*, October.

Hersh, S. M. (2002). The gateway. *The New Yorker*, January 21. Retrieved on November 13, 2010 from http:www.newyorker.com/fact/content/?020128fa_FACT.

Higgot, R. A., Underhill, G. R. D., & Bieler, A. (eds) (2000). *Non-State Actors and Authority in the Global System*. London: Routledge.

Hussain, Z. (2000). The hawk at the core. *Newsline*, October.

IANS. (2011). ISI planned, funded 26/11 Sings Headley. *Hindustan Times*, May 24.

Institute for Conflict Management. (2011). India fatalities: 1994–2012. *South Asia Terrorism Portal*. Retrieved on February 12, 2012 from http://www.satp.org/satporgtp/countries/india/database/indiafatalities.htm.

International Court of Justice. (1986). Case concerning the military and paramilitary activities in and against Nicaragua (Nicaragua v. United States of America). Summary of the judgment of June 27, 1986. Retrieved on November 13, 2010 from http://www.icj-cij.org/docket/index.php?sum=367&code=nus&p1=3&p2=3&case=70&k=66&p3=5.

International Court of Justice. (2005). Armed activities on the territory of the Congo (Democratic Republic of the Congo v. Uganda), Press Release (unofficial). No. 2005/26, December 19. The Hague.

International Law Commission. (2001). Draft Articles on responsibilities of states for internationally wrongful acts, with commentaries. *Report of the International Law Commission on the work of the fifty-third session*. United Nations.

Jane's Intelligence Digest. (2001). Overt assistance from Pakistan may bring dire consequences. September 20. Retrieved on March 13, 2006 from http:///www.janes.com/security/international_security/news/jid/jid010920_1_n. shtml.

Jennings, R., & Watts, A. (eds) (1992). *Oppenheim's International Law*. Ninth edition. London: Longman.

Jessica, S. (2000). Pakistan's Jihad culture. *Foreign Affairs*. November–December. Retrieved on March 13, 2006 from http://ksghome.harvard.edu/~jstern/pakistan.htm.

Jones, O. B. (2002). *Pakistan: Eye of the Storm*. New Haven: Yale University Press.

Josselin, D., & Wallace, W. (2001). *Non-State Actors in World Politics*. New York: Palgrave.

McCarthy, R. (2002). Underworld where terror and security meet. *The Guardian*, July 16. Retrieved on March 13, 2006 from http://www.guardian.co.uk/Archive/Article/0,4273,4462107,00.html.

McGirk, T. (2002). Rogues no more? *Time Magazine* (Asia), April 2. Retrieved on March 13, 2006 from http://www.time.com/time/asia/magazine/article/0,13673,501020506-233999,00.html.

Meacher, M. (2004). The Pakistan connection. *The Guardian*, July 22.

Mir, A. (2005). Past imperfect. *Newsline*, July.

Murphy, S. D. (1999). Contemporary practice of the United States relating to international law. *The American Journal of International Law, 93*(3), 628–667.

Mussadaq, M. (2012). Hillary Clinton backs use of unmanned aircraft, despite criticism. *The Express Tribune*, June 8.

Naqvi, S. (2012). Hafiz Saeed issue may test Singh-Zardari talks. *The Dawn*. April 4. Retrieved on April 12, from http://dawn.com/2012/04/04/hafiz-saeed-issue-may-test-singh-zardari-talks/.

New America Foundation. (2012). The year of the drone: An analysis of the US drone strikes in Pakistan, 2004–2011. New York. Retrieved on June 16, 2012 from http://counterterrorism.newamerica.net/drones.

Office of the Secretary of State. (2001). *Patterns of Global Terrorism 2000*. Washington, DC: U.S. Department of State.

Pajhwok Afghan News. (2011). Gul conveys Pakistan govt's message to Mullah Omar. Retrieved on October 15, from http://www.pajhwok.com/en/2011/05/17/gul-conveys-pakistan-govts-message-mullah-omar.

Pakistan Institute for Peace Studies. (2012). Casualties in U.S. drone attacks in Pakistan. Retrieved on June 16, from http://san-pips.com/index.php?action=reports&id=tml3.

Pakistan Institute of Peace Studies. (2011). Pakistan Security Report. Islamabad: Pakistan Institute of Peace Studies.

Paracha, N. F. (2011). Gotcha! *The Dawn*. May 13. Retrieved on June 7, from http://dawn.com/2011/05/02/gotcha/.

Policzer, P. (2005). Neither terrorists nor freedom fighters. *Paper presented at the International Studies Association Conference*, Honolulu, 2–5 March. Retrieved on April 6, 2010 from http:www.armedgroups.org/images/stories/pdfs/policzer_neither_terrorist_nor_freedom_fighters.pdf.

Press Trust of India. (2011). Will act if substantive evidence against him. *Indian Express*, June 29.

Rajghatta, C. (2001). CIA needs ISI more than ISI needs CIA. *Times of India*, October 12.

Raman, B. (2004). Why Musharraf shuffled his generals. Retrieved on April 6, 2004 from http://www.rediff.com/news/2004/oct/05raman.htm.

Rana, M. A. (2003). *Gateway to Terrorism*. London: New Millennium.

Rana, M. A. (2012). The militants' landscape: Pakistan's Islamist organizations and their impact on the body politic. In A. Misra & M. E. Clarke (eds), *Pakistan's Stability Paradox: Domestic, Regional and International Dimensions* (pp. 88–99). London: Routledge.

Rehman, I. A. (2005). Generals and the genie. *Newsline*, April 3. Retrieved on May 26, 2005 from http://www.newsline.com.pk/NewsApr2005/cover3apr2005.htm.

Reuters. (2011). ISI urged attacks on US targets: Officials. *The Express Tribune*. Retrieved on September 27, 2011 from http://tribune.com.pk/story/257842/pakistan-isi-urged-attacks-on-us-targets-officials/?print=true.

Reza, S. (2004). MMA rejects Wana operations. Retrieved on January 15, 2004 from http://www.dailytimes.com.pk/default.asp?page = story_11-1-2004-pg7_37.

Santhanam, K., Saxena, S. S., & Manish. (2002). *Jihadis in Jammu and Kashmir: A Portrait Gallery*. New Delhi: Sage India.

Schmitt, E., & Perlez, J. (2011). US is deferring millions in Pakistani military aid. *New York Times*, July 9. Retrieved on August 12, 2011 from http://www.nytimes.com/2011/07/10/world/asia/10intel.html?pagewanted=all.

Shehzada, R. (2004). No let-up in tribal offensive, says Faisal. Retrieved on May 26, 2005 from http://www.dailytimes.com.pk/default.asp?page = story_19-3-2004_pg7_26.

Shinwari, N. A. (2010). Understanding FATA: Attitudes towards governance, religion & society in Pakistan's Federally Administered Tribal Areas IV, 59-60, cited in Shuja Nawaz (2011). Drone attacks inside Pakistan: Wayang or willing suspension of disbelief? *Conflict and Security*, Summer/Fall, pp. 79–87.

Siddiqa, A. (2009). Terror's training ground. Retrieved on September 27, 2009 from http:www. newslinemagazine.com/2009/09/terror%e2%80%99s-training-ground/.

Siddiqi, K., & Baruah, A. (2009). Our citizens did it, Pak finally admits. *Hindustan Times*, February 13.

Special Correspondent. (2008). Attack on our ambitions: PM. *The Hindu*, December 24.

Staff Correspondent. (2001). Pakistan arms Taliban by the night. *Times of India*, November 1.

Staff Correspondent. (2009). Witness testimony may nail Kasab in the 26/11 case. May 25. At http://www.indianexpress.com/news/witness-testimony-may-nail-kasab-in-26-11-ca/465617/.

Staff Correspondent. (2011). ISI planned, funded 26/11 sings Headley. *Hindustan Times*, May 24.

Talbott, I. (1998). *Pakistan: A Modern History*. New Delhi: Oxford University Press.

The Dawn. (2001). Gen Mahmud's exit due to links with Umar Sheikh. Retrieved on November 13, 2010 from http://www.dawn.com/2001/10/09/top11.htm.

The Dawn. (2012a). Pakistan reopens Afghan supply route after US says sorry. Retrieved on July 5, 2012 from http://dawn.com/2012/07/03/closure-of-nato-routes-harms-us-ties-pm-ashraf/.

The Dawn. (2012b). Pakistan seeks unconditional apology on NATO killings. Retrieved on March 20, 2012 from http://dawn.com/2012/03/20/pakistani-parliament-starts-debate-on-ties-with-us/.

Thomas, T. S., Kiser, S. D., & Casebear, W. D. (2005). *Warlords Rising: Confronting Violent Non-State Actors*. Oxford: Lexington Books.

Trapp, K. N. (2007). Back to basics: Necessity, proportionality, and the right of self-defence against non-state terrorist actors. *International and Comparative Law Quarterly*, 56, 141–156.

United Nations General Assembly. (1970). Declaration on principles of international law concerning friendly relations and co-operation among states in accordance with the charter of the United Nations. United Nations General Assembly Resolution A//RES/2625(XXV), October 24.

United Nations General Assembly. (1974). Definition of "Aggression." United Nations General Assembly Resolution A/RES/3314 (XXIX), 29th UNGA Session December 14. Annexure.

U.S. Department of State. (2012). Media Note. Rewards for justice—Lashkar-e-Tayyiba leaders rewards offer. *US Department of State*, April 3. Retrieved on May 12, 2012 from http://www.state.gov/r/pa/prs/ps/2012/04/187342.htm.

Sea (Maritime) Piracy in the Southern African Development Community Region

2

MOSES MONTESH

Contents

Introduction

Sea piracy is an organized crime. The degree to which it is a threat at any level, from the purely local to the international, depends on the degree to which it is organized effectively. Even with the lowest level of organization, piracy like street crime can be immensely destructive. If not confronted, it can suppress economic activity and distort economic incentives, lower productivity by increasing security and replacement costs, erode confidence in authority, and undermine notions of justice. The Southern African Development Community (SADC) region is a major trading partner to some of the largest economies of the world, including the United States, Europe, China, and the rest of Africa. This means that the transportation of goods via the southern African coastline is of vital importance. Strategically situated along vital sea routes of the world, the South Atlantic, the Indian, and the Southern Oceans, SADC has a coastline of about 3000 km along which its maritime waters are vulnerable to pirate activities. Therefore, it is important for the region to guard against pirates because one cannot predict with absolute certainty when pirates will strike its shores. This chapter seeks to explore the causes, extent, and modus operandi of piracy, as well as proposed strategies to combat it.

Definition

Sea piracy, or piracy as it is widely known, is a crime defined by geography that requires the presence of other factors, such as a permissive political environment, cultural acceptability, and the opportunity for reward, in order to flourish (Murphy, 2005). According to the United Nations Law of the Sea (Article 101) of 1982, piracy consists of any of the following acts:

> (a) any illegal acts of violence or detention, or any act of depredation, committed for private ends by the crew or the passengers of a private ship or a private aircraft, and directed: (i) on the high seas, against another ship or aircraft, or against persons or property on board such ship or aircraft; (ii) against a ship, aircraft, persons or property in a place outside the jurisdiction of any state;
> (b) any act of voluntary participation in the operation of a ship or of an aircraft

with knowledge of facts making it a pirate ship or aircraft; (c) any act inciting
or of intentionally facilitating an act described in sub-paragraph (a) or (b).

In 1982, the United Nations (UN) adopted Article 101 in order to provide
an international legal definition for piracy.

The International Maritime Organization (IMO) conforms to Article
101 of the United Nations Law of the Sea, which restricts piracy to "illegal
acts of violence or detention acts committed on the high seas, or outside
the jurisdiction of a coastal state, for private ends by private ship against
another private ship." The IMO regards acts of violence or detention committed against ships, occurring within the jurisdiction of a state, as armed
robbery at sea. On the other hand, the International Maritime Bureau
(IMB) has a much broader definition of piracy, namely, "an act of boarding or attempting to board any ship with the intent to commit theft or
any other crime and with the attempt to or capability to use force in the
furtherance of that act." For the purposes of this chapter, piracy is simply
defined as "the hijacking of ships in the sea for the purpose of robbing or
asking for ransom."

Causes of Piracy and Maritime Terrorism

The main reason for the increase in piracy and maritime terrorism has
been the collapse of law and order in Somalia. Since 1991, Somalia has been
engulfed in anarchy. Years of peace negotiations between various factions
have been fruitless. In 1991, a breakaway nation, the Somaliland Republic,
proclaimed its independence. Since then, several warlords have set up mini-
states in Puntland and Jubaland (Botha, 2007). As a result of lawlessness, the
Islamic Courts Union (ICU) was established in 2006. The Islamic movement's
growing power base and militancy led to increasingly open warfare between
the Islamists and other factions of Somalia. Since Somalia has no proper
government structures, every warlord fights for control of a territory. Pirates
have taken advantage of this situation. After seeing the profitability of piracy,
since ransoms are usually paid in large amounts of money, warlords began
to facilitate pirate activities, splitting the profits with the pirates. This has led
the pirates to extend their area of operation into the SADC region, especially
the Tanzanian coast and Mozambican channel.

Pirates' Objectives

In addition to the hijacking of ships, the holding of the crew hostage, and
the theft of cargo, other targets of the attackers include the cash in the ship's

safe, the crew's possessions, and any portable ship's equipment (Botha, 2007). Where there has been evidence of tampering with containers, it may be an indication that the raiders may initially have gained access when the ship was berthed in port and then jumped over the side of the ship with what they could carry.

Consequences of Piracy

The threat of piracy has impacts much broader than on maritime trade, placing high costs on whole economies, both directly and indirectly. Any form of piracy and the specter of piracy attacks create uncertainty, which increases the perceived risk and dampens economic activity through several channels and regions (Costs of Maritime Terrorism and Piracy, 2003). Sailors aboard targeted vessels face prospects of weeks in captivity and even death—although relatively few have been killed. The insurance premiums paid by shipping companies have soared since the attacks began in earnest, and anyone sending freight around the east coast of Africa now has to pay about 10 times the previous amounts (Costs of Maritime Terrorism and Piracy, 2003).

This has an inevitable knock-on effect for consumers, with prices bound to rise at the destinations of many cargo ships. Shipping companies might even begin to send their vessels on longer journeys around Africa's west coast, and if that happens, the economic consequences could be considerable (Costs of Maritime Terrorism and Piracy, 2003). Many shipowners are now advised to buy war risk insurance cover for their ships because normal insurance cover excludes losses caused by weapons of war, bombs, or rockets. In addition to obtaining ransoms, pirates are also involved in drug smuggling and human trafficking.

Furthermore, Greenberg et al. (2006) suggest the following summary of the types of consequences of maritime piracy and terrorism that might affect individuals, the private sector, and the public sector. Broadly, these consequences fall into one of three groups: *human, economic,* and *intangible* effects. *Human consequences* refer to the effects on lives caused by fatalities and injuries. It is people who are injured or killed and who suffer debilitating psychological consequences following terrorist attacks. Moreover, the indirect consequences of fatalities and injuries can flow into both the public and private sectors, particularly in terms of economic costs. Again, the costs associated with fatalities and injuries may be transferred, at least in part, through compensatory mechanisms like insurance and civil tort claims, with some of the burdens associated with human injuries borne by the private sector.

Economic consequences are those effects easily quantified in financial terms. Attacks that damage facilities, ships, vehicles, airplanes, infrastructure, or products and raw materials reduce the assets of private firms. In cases in which power is disrupted or computer networks are targeted, loss of data may also reduce a firm's assets that enable future revenues. Damage to infrastructure, facilities, and information systems may propagate into both short- and long-term economic disruptions (Greenberg et al., 2006). Firms may immediately experience delivery delays, loss of revenue from interrupted business, and increased transportation costs. Reduction of demand or supply could eliminate the benefits of economies of scale until facilities and infrastructure can be replaced. As the magnitude and duration of the disruptions to infrastructure, facilities, and information systems increase, the consequences can be more permanent. Firms may experience long-term transportation inefficiencies. *Intangible effects* capture those effects that are difficult to measure in human lives or financial metrics, either because they are measured in metrics that are not easily translated into lives or financial metrics or because the cause-and-effect linkage is not understood well enough to allow a precise estimation and attribution of effects.

According to Gardner (2011), the treatment meted out to victims by the sea pirates in Africa now frequently crosses the line from savagery to torture. Pirates, frustrated when their ransom demands are not met fast enough, have now resorted to inflicting punishments on ordinary seafarers, which include being locked in a ship's freezer, dragged below the hull, or tied up on deck with a gun to their head and subjected to mock executions, sometimes during a forced phone call to their families. Such treatments have resulted in many of the victims suffering lifelong trauma. In some instances, victims are taken up to the bridge deck and tied up with plastic bags, ropes, and nylon ropes for long hours, and sometimes even their genitals are tied up.

Incidents of Piracy within SADC Region from 2009

According to the IMO and the IMB, the incidents shown in Table 2.1 have been reported in the east coast of the SADC countries since 2009. Table 2.1, provided by the IMO and the IMB, shows that there has been a significant increase in vessel attacks by pirates in the east coast of Africa, especially the SADC region. This can be attributed to the increase in the reported incidents of piracy, the ability of the pirates to attack vessels further down the east coast, the fact that they are better armed and organized and also a lack of proper law enforcement in the affected region (Tomberlin, 2008).

Table 2.1   Incidents of Piracy within the SADC
Region from 2009

Country	Year	Number of Attacks
Tanzania	2009	7
	2010	9
	2011	9
Madagascar	2009	3
	2010	1
	2011	1
South Africa	2009	1
	2010	1
	2011	3
Seychelles	2009	1
	2010	2
	2011	3
Mozambique	2009	6
	2010	8
	2011	10
Total		55

Weaponry and Funding

Pirates and maritime terrorists in Africa have little difficulty procuring weapons on the private market, in large part because the region is awash in small and sophisticated arms.

According to Bland (2008), pirates and maritime terrorists get most of their weapons from Yemen, but a significant amount comes from Mogadishu, Somalia's capital. Weapons dealers in the capital receive a deposit from a middleman on behalf of the pirates and the weapons are then driven to Puntland where the pirates pay the balance. Both small arms and heavier weapons, including surface-to-air missiles, can be procured throughout the region. Orders can also be placed with international arms traffickers who fly and ship weapons into remote landing strips and bays undetected. The most common weapons used by pirates are predominantly Russian Kalashnikov (AK-47) assault rifles, rocket-propelled grenades (RPG-7), rocket launchers, and semiautomatic pistols (Menkhaus, 2007).

Additionally, given the particular origin of their weaponry, they are likely to have machine guns and hand grenades, such as Russian fragmentation hand grenades, also known as RGD-5s. These are weapons of war; hence, in many quarters, the pirates' activities are regarded as terrorism. This, in turn, creates opportunities for association with other pirates or terrorist networks. Pirates also use phantom ships to attack their targets. Many of these phantom ships that set off to sea with a cargo and then disappear into dangerous waters are sailed by crewmen with false passports and competency certificates. The false documents are used to escape detection by the port authorities.

Types of Pirate Attacks

Pirates today are armed with global positioning system (GPS) trackers, high-speed boats, grenade launchers, computers, Swiss bank accounts, and machine guns. Subsequently, today, there are many different types of pirate attacks. Most of the attacks prey on the crew and the ships' safes for their on-hand cash. The remaining pirates steal cargo and take hostages, commandeering the whole ship, or they attempt to plant a "stowaway" on the ship before it sails. According to Tomberlin (2008), there are four types of pirate attacks, namely, the hit and run, the cargo heist, the phantom ship, and the stowaway.

Hit-and-Run Robbery

The hit-and-run robberies usually occur early in the morning when the majority of the crew is asleep and the crew standing watch are dozing at their stations. The pirates will stealthily pull alongside the ship, some utilizing poles to scale the sides of the vessel. Once on board, the pirates can easily command the vessel at will (Osterburg & Ward, 1992).

Cargo Heist and Hostage Attacks

A second type of pirate attack is called a cargo heist and hostage attack and involves a larger band of pirates. The pirates rob the crew and make off with the cargo, sometimes taking crew members as hostages. Many of these attacks are organized after the pirates research the manifest of the target vessel through Internet services. Once the ship is targeted, the pirates usually attack the vessel with two or more small, fast crafts. This will help to confuse the helmsman and assist the pirates when boarding (McDaniel, 2007). The Somali pirates commonly use this type of attack in the Indian Ocean and other parts of the world.

Phantom Ship

The act of utilizing a phantom ship begins with the theft of the vessel. The crew is disposed of by sudden death or they are set adrift in the open sea. The ship is then transported to a safe haven and repainted, renamed, and given a fresh set of forged documents. These types of pirates tend to be the most sophisticated and well organized. Organized crime syndicates and government officials are the likely culprits in this type of attack (McDaniel, 2007).

Stowaways

A less sophisticated way for pirates to attack a vessel is from within. This type of piracy plants either a false crew member on board or a hidden stowaway, who waits until the time is right and radios the ship's location and route to the attackers (McDaniel, 2007).

Modus Operandi

Modus operandi is a process that seeks to analyze the ingredients of a crime, and then, by a systematic comparison with analyses of other crimes, to establish the identity of the criminal (Osterburg & Ward, 1992). Pirates and maritime terrorists use sophisticated weapons, such as AK-47s, RPG-7s, satellite phones, and GPS equipment. The satellite phones are used to communicate with the backers inland and the GPS equipment is used to locate the vessels as well as their direction while at sea. In most cases, pirates use the so-called mother ships, which are bigger in size, and then load smaller high-speed boats, which are used to surprise the vessels (Westcott, 2008). The mother ships are able to operate over a longer period of time and in varying weather conditions. These mother ships are also used to broadcast false distress signals, followed by attacks by deployed smaller boats when steaming ships are approaching the mother ship to render assistance (Mahan & Griset, 2008).

Pirates use three kinds of experts, namely, local fishermen, considered the brains of the pirates' operation due to their skills and knowledge of the sea; ex-militiamen, who used to fight for the local clan warlords, for their military skills; and technical experts, who operate high-tech equipment such as GPS (Jordan, 2009). Money paid as ransom arrives in burlap sacks that are sometimes dropped from helicopters or cased in waterproof suitcases and loaded onto tiny skiffs in the rumbling, shark-infested waters (Murphy, 2005). To authenticate the money, the pirates use currency-counting machines, the same technology used at foreign exchange bureaus worldwide. These machines are said to have been purchased from business connections in Dubai, Djibouti, and other areas.

How Vulnerable Is the Rest of the SADC Region?

Tanzania, Mozambique, Namibia, Mauritius, Madagascar, Comoro Islands, The Reunion, Seychelles, South Africa, and Angola pose a serious security threat in the SADC with regard to piracy, first because of their coastlines and secondly because of historical factors. Angola and Mozambique have been affected by long-lasting, full-scale civil wars with a number of weapons still unaccounted for. Namibia and South Africa had internal conflict and it cannot be concluded that that history has no bearing on future events. Tanzania, Mozambique and Madagascar are strategically in the east of the SADC, with Tanzania to the north of the other two countries.

According to the African Union Commission Strategic Plan (2009–2012), concerns have been raised about the lack of effective law enforcement infrastructures in Tanzania, Mozambique, and Madagascar. Furthermore, Jordan (2009) states that piracy has been taking place sporadically along the east coast, including the Mozambican channel. Several ships heading to and from South African ports have been victims, including the product tanker *MV Bow Asir* in March 2009 as it headed for Durban, and the cruise liner *MSC Melody* after it left South Africa bound for Italy. The crew of the *Bow Asir* was held for ransom, while the *MSC Melody* managed to escape the pirates (Jordan, 2009). There is a possibility that similar incidents may occur in the SADC territorial waters. Sporadic piracy and terrorist attacks along the coasts of Tanzania have been reported in the past 3 years already.

Challenges

Geographical Scope of the Offence

Sea piracy may be committed anywhere seaward of the territorial sea of a state. Equally, the jurisdiction and powers granted to states to suppress acts of piracy apply in all seas outside any state's territorial waters. However, the reference in Article 101 to piracy occurring on the "high seas" may be slightly misleading. In terms of Article 86, the United Nations Convention on the Law of the Sea (UNCLOS) prima facie excludes the exclusive economic zone (EEZ) from being part of the high seas. This might suggest that piracy in the EEZ is a matter for the coastal state. However, Article 58(2) provides that Articles 88 to 115 and other pertinent rules of international law apply to the EEZ in so far as they are not incompatible with this part.

This makes it plain that the provisions of the high seas regime (including all provisions on piracy) "apply to the exclusive economic zone in so far as they are not incompatible with UNCLOS provisions on the EEZ." Within the EEZ, the coastal state enjoys sovereign rights "for the purpose of exploring and exploiting, conserving and managing natural resources" and jurisdiction over certain other subject matters (Article 56, UNCLOS). Nothing in Article 56 is incompatible with the UNCLOS provisions on piracy; therefore, under Article 58(2), the general law of piracy applies to all pirate attacks out-side territorial waters. If acting in another states' EEZ, a government vessel engaged in suppressing piracy is obviously obliged to have "due regard" for the coastal state's rights in matters of natural resources, marine pollution, and others in any action it takes.

Limitations within UNCLOS Definition of Piracy

The most obvious limitation within the UNCLOS definition is that it only covers, under Article 101(a)(i) of 1982, attacks committed from a private vessel against another vessel. It therefore does not cover the seizure of a vessel. UNCLOS makes it quite clear that government vessels cannot com-mit piracy, unless the crew mutinies and uses the vessel to carry out acts of violence against other ships (Article 102). Outside of mutiny, any unlawful acts of violence by a government vessel against another craft are a matter of state responsibility, not the law of piracy. Some slight ambiguity is intro-duced by the words "any illegal acts of violence or detention, or any act of depredation" in Article 101(a).

One could ask under what system of law acts must be "illegal"; or whether there is a meaningful difference between the use of the words "acts of violence" (plural) and "act of depredation" (singular). The ordinary meaning, object, and purpose of these words would suggest that a broad approach should be taken. Piracy has always been an international crime enforced by national laws, the exact terms of which have varied between jurisdictions. It may be difficult to give these words the kind of clear and precise meaning that would accord with modern expectations that crim-inal offences should be precisely drafted in advance. It is perhaps better to consider Article 101(a)(i) as setting out the jurisdiction of all states to: (1) prescribe and enforce a national criminal law of piracy and (2) take action to suppress and prosecute piratical acts of violence on the high seas.

Much more controversy has been caused by the words "for private ends" in Article 101(a). It has often been held that the requirement that piracy be for "private ends" means that an act committed for "political" motives cannot be piracy. Thus, some commentators hold that "terrorism" can never be "piracy." An alternative view holds that the relevant distinc-tion is not "private/political" but "private/public." That is, any act of violence on the high seas not attributable to or sanctioned by a state (a public act) is piracy (a private act). These approaches accord both with the drafting of the relevant UNCLOS provisions, which make it clear that a public vessel cannot commit piracy, and with some modern case law indicat-ing that politically motivated acts of protest can constitute piracy. In the Somali context, seizing private vessels in order to demand large ransoms from private companies—without any claim to be acting on behalf of a government or making demands of any government—can only be an act "for private ends."

Exercising Jurisdiction over Pirates: Limitations or Rules of Priority

Article 105 of the UNCLOS of 1982 refers only to the power of *the seizing state* to try a seized pirate. However, as a matter of customary international law, every state has jurisdiction to prosecute a pirate subsequently present within their territory, irrespective of any connection between the pirate, their victims, or the vessel attacked and the prosecuting state (universal jurisdiction). In addition to the existence of universal jurisdiction in public international law, states may also have jurisdiction over suspected pirates on other bases as a matter of national law.

Following the ordinary principles of criminal jurisdiction, the state of the suspected pirate's nationality, the state of nationality of the suspected pirate's victim, and the flag state of any involved vessels may all also have valid claims of jurisdiction over a suspected pirate. An act of piracy, like any number of other offences, may provide a number of states with equally valid claims to exercise jurisdiction over an offence. The law of piracy under UNCLOS does not place any express responsibility upon a seizing state to try an arrested pirate. It simply provides that the seizing state "may" decide upon the penalties to be imposed, including prosecution (Article 105). On its face, this is a discretionary power, not an obligation. However, in exercising this discretion, a state should bear in mind its duty to "cooperate to the fullest possible extent in the repression of piracy." This is contained in Article 100 of the UNCLOS of 1982.

Capacity to Try Pirates

The principle of universal jurisdiction calls for the *domestic* prosecution of apprehended pirates. However, not every country has the capacity to do so while guaranteeing the rights of the accused, and in the process of such prosecutions, countries risk running afoul of international standards of fairness, due process, and human rights. Additionally, there are no uniform procedural standards across the national contexts where a prosecution might occur and domestic legal systems may lack the necessary legislation to prosecute fairly and effectively (Jordan, 2009). Therefore, because not all countries would mete out the same punishment for the crime of piracy, domestic prosecution of piracy could raise issues of legitimacy and accountability. It could be suggested that both the development of model legislation and a reliance on international courts would help domestic legal systems reform their substantive law and prosecute in a manner consistent with international law.

Nexus between Rule-of-Law, the Economy, and Piracy

There is a general recognition that piracy off the coast of Africa represents a unique case. The long-term solution requires rebuilding the collapsed Somali government infrastructure. In the intervening period, building the domestic rule-of-law capacity of other governments in the region willing to prosecute pirates seems a wise idea (Starr, 2008). Such an approach would help to bring regional and domestic legal systems up to international standards. Doing so might have a stabilizing effect in the region. Financing such capacity building may also provide an incentive to states to participate where otherwise they would not. Although effective maritime enforcers might be better equipped to fight piracy, the ultimate solution must be one that deals with the political system ashore, that is, a nation-building solution. One concern though is the international community's ability to intervene in Somalia. Nearly two decades of unsuccessful international efforts directed at Somalia highlight the significant uncertainty and cost of such capacity building (Jordan, 2009). Moreover, recent international events suggest that there are significant, potentially negative consequences to the imposition of law and institutions from without and some caution against this.

Recent Successful Arrests, Prosecutions, and Convictions of Pirates within SADC Region

According to INTERPOL (2011), on July 26, 2011, the Seychelles Supreme Court convicted and sentenced 11 Somali pirates. Eight accused were convicted for acts of piracy, and three others for aiding and abetting an act of piracy. The 11 pirates were each sentenced to 10 years' imprisonment. The offenses took place in the Seychelles EEZ on December 5 and 6, 2009, when a TOPAZ ship was attacked with automatic weapons by the pirates in two different skiffs. The aiders and abettors were found in a mother skiff not very far from the attack. Evidence has revealed that the mother skiff had provided ammunition and firearms to the two attack skiffs before they effected the attack. The conviction of these pirates is a historical milestone as it is the first time that a piracy trial was successfully prosecuted in the Seychelles (United Nations Office on Drugs and Crime, 2010).

Moreover, these convictions will assist in the building of confidence of the countries and institutions supporting Seychelles in efforts in the region, and in doing so, it will serve as a deterrent to prospective Somali pirates who would otherwise have thought that they would have entered the SADC waters with impunity.

Recommendations

Before embarking on any set of measures or recommendations, it is imperative for governmental or other agencies concerned to gather accurate statistics of the incidents of piracy and armed robbery against ships; to collate these statistics under both type and area, to assess the nature of the attacks with special emphasis on the types of attack, the accurate geographical location, and the modus operandi of the wrongdoers; and to disseminate or publish these statistics to all interested parties in a format that is understandable and usable. Advanced intelligence could also prove useful in providing information to governments in order to be able to act in a coordinated manner even before an attack occurs. Therefore, the following approaches are recommended.

Address Underlying Causes

According to Rutherford (2007), addressing the underlying cause means looking at a multitude of social and political factors that drive people to support pirates' activities as a means of furthering their cause. It means recognizing and respecting the grievances that lead a small minority to commit such crimes, more importantly, the causes that lead to broader social support for organizations tied to these crimes. This is a very difficult recommendation. The SADC alone cannot address this aspect. This needs an intervention by the African Union and the UN as well as other role players.

Extend Mandate of Maritime Security Coordination Centre

The Marine Security Coordinating Centre (MSCC) was established in July 2004 in order to facilitate the coordination of South Africa's obligation to the Merchant Shipping (Marine Security) Regulation of 2004 within the framework of the IMO and the International Ship and Port Facility Security (ISPS) Code. The primary function of the MSCC is to ensure the security compliance of South Africa's ports as well as the vessels using them. In terms of this option, South Africa and its counterparts need to second officers from the South African Navy and the South African Police Service's Sea Border Control Unit as well as marine and coastal management (MCM) from the Department of Environmental Affairs and Tourism and the custom services of the South African Revenue Services. This model can be implemented like the Australian Border Protection Command (Tomberlin, 2008). The Australian Border Protection Command not only responds to security incidents in Australia's offshore maritime areas, but also investigates ways to prevent incidents before they occur (Australian Department of Foreign Affairs and Trade, 2003).

Implement Standing Maritime Committee Functions

The establishment of the Standing Maritime Committee follows the mandated decision of the Inter-State Defence and Security Committee (ISDSC) emanating from recommendations of a seminar held in Gaborone in March 1995 and validated at the inaugural meeting of the Standing Maritime Committee in July 1995. It is a subcommittee of the Operations Sub-Sub-Committee (SADC Standing Maritime Committee, 2006). The purpose of the Standing Maritime Committee is to promote peace and prosperity in the region through maritime military cooperation. Its aim is to achieve an optimum degree of maritime military cooperation in the southern African region within the aims and objectives of the ISDSC.

Technology

The South African Maritime Safety Authority has set up a regional, long-range vessel monitoring system as from September 2009. The new system, required by international maritime law, is expected to aid South African neighbors, including Mozambique, Namibia, and Tanzania (Jordan, 2009). The long-range identification and tracking (LRIT) of ships aims to enhance security for government authorities. LRIT provides ship identity and current location information in sufficient time for a government to evaluate the security risk posed by a ship off its coast and to respond, if necessary, to reduce the risk. The LRIT system was set up under the auspices of the IMO. It aims to provide a global system for the identification and tracking of ships that extends the monitoring of ships beyond those areas covered by existing Automatic Identification System (AIS) coastal networks. The LRIT system is mandatory for all passenger ships, high-speed crafts, mobile offshore drilling units, and cargo ships of over 300 gross tonnes. This is good news for South Africa and the SADC as a whole, taking into account that South Africa's territorial waters are about 27 million km^2—almost 25 times the country's land area.

Establish an SADC Standby Brigade

In terms of this recommendation, SADC countries need to contribute a substantial number of navy personnel that can be posted along the coasts of Namibia, South Africa, Mozambique, and Tanzania.

The brigade can operate in the same way as the Combined Task Force 150, which was established by countries such as Canada, Denmark, France, and Germany, to monitor, inspect, board, and stop suspect shipping to pursue the war on terrorism (Mahan & Griset, 2008). In addition to these functions, the brigade can establish a Maritime Security Patrol Area (MSPA) along the coastline from Namibia to Tanzania. The command of such a brigade can rotate among the member countries (South African National Defence Force Military Strategy, 2007).

Counterterrorism and Piracy Strategy

South Africa has legislation that governs piracy and terrorism. However, more needs to be done. It is worth noting that the weapons at the disposal of the world community for combating piracy and terrorism may conveniently be placed under four headings: laws, police agencies, military forces, and legal systems. As concerns laws, the measures for dealing with pirates and maritime terrorists are, by and large, similar in most countries of the world. Legislation governing terrorism in South Africa seems to be fine; however, legislation piracy and maritime terrorism seems to be lacking. When the European Community abolished border controls, it raised many difficult issues relating to the combating of terrorism (Elagab, 1995). However, these have been rectified by the adoption of various international conventions. In most European countries, special antiterrorist units have been established (Elagab, 1995). Ideally, the results of intelligence gathering should be utilized by teams of specialists from various disciplines in order to secure a better understanding of the suspect's movements to be combated and take the initiative away from them.

Establish Prosecutorial Strategy

Although the unprecedented antipiracy naval operations undertaken by the international community have thwarted several hijacking and kidnapping attempts on the high seas, their utility is limited by the lack of political will and the capacity for prosecuting pirates. Regional, domestic, or international courts could address these problems in different ways and with varying degrees of success (Mahan & Griset, 2008). Whichever strategy or combination of strategies involving courts that is eventually pursued, consensus must emerge and it should take account of the following: First, any solution must reflect the reality that piracy is a global, not a local, problem. Pirate attacks occur in areas as far apart as the South China Sea and the coast of Namibia. Moreover, just as states may cooperate to thwart pirate attacks, pirates may cooperate by trading information and pooling resources to reduce the effectiveness of counterpiracy operations. Secondly, there are two tiers of actors executing piratical acts—the perpetrators on the ground and the ringleaders. While pursuit of each may require a different legal or military strategy, any prosecutorial rules or fora developed to try pirates should take into account the importance of holding the "big fish" accountable.

Thirdly, no solution to piracy can ignore human rights concerns (Elagab, 1995). This means that states must ensure that the trials of accused pirates are procedurally fair; articulating a framework for the capture and detention of pirates that is consistent with human rights law; and balancing the need to prosecute against the risk of asylum claims once an accused has served his/ her sentence. Fourthly, a long-term solution to piracy would seem to require capacity building at the domestic level.

Piracy is an extension of land-based violence, itself rooted in weak state institutions, poverty, domestic lawlessness, and corruption. A critical part of developing a strategy for prosecuting pirates should therefore take into account a commitment to supporting local institutions (including courts), promoting a culture of rule of law, and adding value to local economies (Rutherford, 2007). Finally, the issues of cost, capacity, and a lack of political will have conspired to lead many states to regularly decline to accept captured pirates for prosecution in their domestic courts. Since increasing the number of pirates prosecuted is a key part of antipiracy efforts, a future prosecution strategy should include: (1) providing support to those states that have already demonstrated a willingness to prosecute pirates, (2) addressing the concerns of states that have shown an unwillingness to prosecute by working with them to reform national laws to make prosecutions more convenient and less risky, and (3) continued consideration of the major role that a regional or international court could play in antipiracy efforts should domestic prosecutions prove inadequate to suppress piracy.

Role of INTERPOL

INTERPOL's activities in relation to international fugitives have been part of its core business since the organization's creation. SADC countries are members of the Southern African Regional Police Chiefs Cooperation Organisation (SARPCCO), which forms part of INTERPOL within the southern African region (INTERPOL, 2010). INTERPOL circulates internationally, at the request of member countries, electronic diffusions and notices containing identification details and judicial information about wanted criminals. The INTERPOL Red Notice has been recognized in a number of countries as having the legal value to serve as a basis for provisional arrest. The persons concerned are wanted by national jurisdictions or International Criminal Tribunals, where appropriate, and the Red Notice is intended to help police to identify or locate these individuals with a view to their arrest and extradition. Furthermore, INTERPOL has established a Maritime Piracy Task Force, which focuses on three main areas to counter maritime piracy, working closely with the international community:

1. *Improving evidence collection*
   The maritime environment poses unique difficulties for collecting evidence. In this instance, INTERPOL provides advice, training, and equipment to member countries worldwide in order to improve the quality and

quantity of the data collected and to make sure evidence is properly preserved and analyzed. With the creation of a Global Database on Maritime Piracy currently in progress, INTERPOL will soon be in a position to better analyze piracy networks. This will enable it to help member countries identify and arrest high-value individuals involved in Somali maritime piracy—such as piracy leaders and financiers—and to identify their assets.

2. Building regional capabilities

The majority of prosecutions for maritime piracy are conducted in African or Asian countries. INTERPOL is currently working to develop the capabilities of police investigation units on a regional level. By providing specialized training and equipment prior to trial, INTERPOL is in a position to increase the likelihood of successful prosecutions in the future.

3. Working in partnership

Due to the extent and nature of maritime piracy, international and cross-sector partnerships are vital in order to prevent, investigate, and prosecute these crimes. INTERPOL works with the following international organizations:

- UN
- IMO
- Baltic and International Maritime Council
- European Union
- Europol
- Eurojust
- African Union

Criminal Jurisdiction

A person apprehended at sea outside the territorial sea of any state, for committing acts of piracy or armed robbery against ships, should be prosecuted under the laws of the investigating state by mutual agreement with other substantially interested states. A *substantially interested state* means a state:

- Which is the flag state of a ship that is the subject of an investigation or
- In whose territorial sea an incident has occurred or
- Where an incident caused, or threatened, serious harm to the environment of that state, or within those areas over which the state is entitled to exercise jurisdiction as recognized under international law or
- Where the consequences of an incident caused, or threatened, serious harm to that state or to artificial islands, installations, or structures over which it is entitled to exercise jurisdiction or

- Where, as a result of an incident, nationals of that state lost their lives or received serious injuries or
- That has at its disposal important information that may be of use to the investigation or
- That, for some other reason, establishes an interest that is considered significant by the lead investigating state or
- That was requested by another state to assist in the repression of violence against crews, passengers, ships, and cargoes or the collection of evidence or
- That intervened under UNCLOS Article 100, exercised its right of visit under UNCLOS Article 110, or effected the seizure of a pirate/armed robber, ship, or aircraft under UNCLOS Article 105 in port or on land

These recommendations are based on the IMO recommendations to governments for preventing and suppressing piracy and armed robbery against ships, which were adopted on June 26, 2009.

Conclusion

Piracy poses a serious threat to the well-being of the citizens of any country. The above analysis shows that piracy poses a significant threat to the whole world due to the increasing frequency, sophistication, and severity of regional pirate attacks, as well as their knock-on effects. The analysis of the pirates' threat reveals that, on balance, the danger posed by lower-order piracy and the risks associated with higher-order piracy are significant enough to warrant fairly robust regional governmental action. There is a general consensus that piracy consists of a set of traditional crimes that are used to create a climate of terror within a community or a particular region. In most instances, the most common types of crimes in the area include conspiracy, murder, kidnapping, hijacking, bombing, robbery, and extortion. Unfortunately, all these crimes appear throughout the discussion of piracy in this chapter. Hence, in response to these problems, the UN passed numerous resolutions in order to combat piracy and terrorism as well. However, it is very important that member states design strategies to combat piracy. On the other hand, one of the challenges facing the SADC region is the lack of resources and strategies to combat piracy from the member states.

References

African Union Commission. (2009–2012). African Union Strategic Plan. Directorate for Strategic Planning Policy, Monitoring, Evaluation and Resource Mobilisation. Addis Ababa: African Union.

Australian Department of Foreign Affairs and Trade. (2003). Cost of maritime terrorism and piracy and the benefits of working together. Paper Presented to *APEC High Level Meeting on Maritime Security and Cooperation*, Malaki City, Manila, September 8–9, 2003. Retrieved October 12, 2010, from http://wwww.bpc.gov.au.

Bland, A. (2008). The Big Question: Why has piracy exploded off the coast of Somalia, and how can it be stopped? *The Independent*, Wednesday November 19, 2008. Retrieved October 16, 2010, from http://independent.co.uk/news/worl/africa/the-big-question-why-has-piracy-ex.

Botha, A. (2007). Relationship between Africa and International Terrorism: Causes and linkages. Paper prepared for the *Conference on Southern African and International Terrorism*. Dialogue hosted by the Brenthurst Foundation. Tswalu, January 25–27, 2007. Retrieved October 16, 2010, from http://www.iss.co.za/static.

Elagab, O. Y. (1995). *International Law: Documents Relating to Terrorism*. London: Cavendish Publishing Limited.

Gardner, F. (2011). Pirate violence targeted by worldwide campaign. *BBC News*. Retrieved June 5, 2012, from http://www.bbc.co.uk/news/uk-15103818.

Greenberg, M. D., Chalk, P., Willis, H. H., Khilko, I., & Ortiz, D. S. (2006). *Maritime Terrorism: Risk and Liability*. Pittsburg: RAND Corporation.

INTERPOL. (2010). Fact sheet booklet. COM/FS/2010-12/DCO-03. Lyon, France.

INTERPOL. (2011). Fact sheet booklet. COM/FS/2011-11/DCO-01. Lyon, France.

Jordan, B. (2009). High sea outlaws to walk the plank. New Big Brother system will help out during the 2010 World Cup and beyond. Johannesburg: *Sunday Times*, August 23, 2009.

Mahan, S., & Griset, P. L. (2008). *Terrorism in Perspective*. California: SAGE.

McDaniel, F. (2007). Piracy, maritime terrorism and regional interests. Institute of South East Asian Studies. Retrieved October 16, 2010, from http://www.iseas.edu.sg.

Menkhaus, K. (2007). Terrorist activities in ungoverned spaces: Evidence and observations from the Horn of Africa. Paper prepared for the *Conference on Southern African and International Terrorism*. Dialogue hosted by the Brenthurst Foundation. Tswalu, January 25–27, 2007. Retrieved October 16, 2010 from http://www.iss.co.za/static.

Murphy, M. N. (2005). Suppression of piracy and maritime terrorism. United States of America: Naval War College Review.

Osterburg, J. W., & Ward, R. H. (1992). *Criminal Investigation: A Method for Reconstructing the Past*. Cincinnati, OH: Anderson Publishing Company.

Rutherford, C. (2007). Fighting terrorism without terrorizing: A discussion of non-military operations for confronting international terrorism. Thesis submitted to the University of Witwatersrand for the degree of Master of Arts International Relations in the Faculty of Humanities. Retrieved October 16, 2010, from http://wiredspace.wits.ac.za/bitstream/handle/10539/5780/CMRutherford.pdf?sequence=2.

South African National Defence Force Military Strategy. (2007). Application of Maritime Power in the South African Context. Retrieved December 3, 2010, from http://www.mil.za.

Southern African Development Community (SADC). (2006). Standing Committee on Piracy and Terrorism. Pretoria: Department of Foreign Affairs.

Tomberlin, R.L. (2008). *Terrorism's Effect on Maritime Shipping*. Downers Grove, IL: InterVarsity Press.

United Nations (UNLOS). (1982). United Nations Law of the Sea. Pretoria: United Nations.

United Nations Office on Drugs and Crime (UNODC). (2010). Counter-Piracy Programme. Support to the trial and related treatment of piracy suspects. Issue 3, July 2010. Vienna: United Nations.

Westcott, K. (2008). Somalia's pirates face battles at sea. *BBC News*. Retrieved May 2, 2010, from http://news.bbc.co.uk/2/hi/7358764.stm.

The Responsibility to Protect from Terror

Putting an End to Unilateral Misuse of the Precautionary Principle

3

HARJASS SINGH

Contents

Introduction

International law, since the time of Hugo Grotius and the Peace of Westphalia, has been considered the law governing nation states; nation states alone. It is only recently that the role of nonstate actors in shaping international relations, and hence international law, has entered the public consciousness. However, that fateful day of September 11, 2001, shall remain branded in the archives of international law as the day that brought to prominence the most dreadful nonstate actor—the terrorist.

A decade and two major wars later, humanity is still no closer to countering the menace posed by terror. A decade, a few trillion dollars, and countless slogans later, the "war on terror" has borne little fruit. A decade on from that day, humanity is still in search of an answer. Through this chapter, I try to provide some answers that have evaded us with respect to the Bush Doctrine's reinterpretation of the precautionary principle.

First, in declaring a war on terror, it is submitted that there has been a declaration of an unending "war" on an indeterminate body. As Noam Chomsky puts it, terrorism is "what our leaders declare it to be" (Ward, 2009, p. 15). To date, no definition of terrorism has managed to establish a clear consensus among the vast majority of nations, while at the same time addressing the numerous components and threats posed by terrorist acts. Yet, leaders of the only remaining "superpower" nation have launched a preemptive war against this undefined entity. I believe that the practical problem posed by the lack of a clear-cut definition can be solved through reliance on some of the more well-established provisions of the Rome Statute.

The next subsection shall entail a jurisprudential study of Lon L. Fuller's observations regarding the eight ways to fail to make law as well as his hilarious take on the fictitious king Rex's bungling attempts at formulating "good law." In so doing, I will highlight some of the most gaping and fundamental flaws in the practice surrounding preemptive wars.

Back to the Basics: The Morality of Law and Preemptive Wars

Lon L. Fuller, in his restrained departure from the classical natural law approach, managed to string together a compelling jurisprudential understanding of the law. Fuller propounded the idea of the existence of twin moralities: "the morality of duty" and "the morality of aspiration."

The morality of duty, according to Fuller (2009), represents the basic prerequisites of a smoothly functioning society. For example, the long-standing tenet "Thou shalt not kill" would constitute the morality of duty, since it is impossible in today's world to imagine an orderly society that does not espouse this tenet. As Fuller puts it, "[The Morality of Duty] does not condemn men for failing to embrace opportunities for the fullest realisation of their powers. Instead, it condemns them for failing to respect the basic requirements of social living" (Fuller, 2009, p. 6).

The morality of aspiration, on the other hand, represents the quest for excellence. It signifies the requirements of a perfect society. Unlike the condemnation faced for nonobservance of the morality of duty, compliance with the morality of aspiration is looked at as worthy of reward (Fuller, 2009). For example, exemplary bravery displayed by individuals is rewarded by society in the form of honorary distinctions. Ideally, as society progresses, the morality of duty moves toward the morality of aspiration, thereby expecting greater standards of observance from its subjects.

Fuller, in linking morality with law, claims that the morality of duty happens to be the closest sibling of the law. He claims that an inherent feature of this morality of duty is the "rule of reciprocity," that is, one follows certain grundnorms of society expecting that the other members of society shall be subjected to the same scrutiny (Fuller, 2009). This rule of reciprocity is something we all know to be the driving force behind the application of international law. In fact, given the inviolable principle of "sovereignty," it presents us with the only form of checks and balances in international law. The only thing binding a sovereign nation state to fulfill its treaty or customary obligations agreed with another sovereign state is the reciprocal nature of international relationships.

Hence, I submit that this simplistic statement made by Fuller in 1963, at the William L. Storrs Lecture Series, points to the biggest cause for the failure of "preemptive wars," both in countering terrorism, as well as in winning the support of nations around the world. Preemptive wars have worked with utter disregard for that very rule of reciprocity that has sustained international law as a viable system of international governance. In waging full-fledged wars against sovereign nations due to the actions of nonstate actors, the norm of "Judge not that ye not be Judged" (Fuller, 2009, p. 20) stands flagrantly violated.

In addition to this, preemptive wars stand in stark violation of what Fuller describes as "the internal morality of law." In order to explicate the internal morality of law, he embarks on a hilarious, yet stimulating, tale surrounding the fictitious king Rex's attempts at making laws. In doing so, he identifies the following eight ways to fail to make law (Fuller, 2009, pp. 33–39):

1. Failure to make rules at all
2. Failure to publicise the rules one is expected to observe
3. The abuse of retroactive legislation
4. Failure to make rules understandable
5. Enactment of contradictory rules
6. Rules requiring conduct beyond the powers of the affected party
7. Introducing such frequent changes in the rules that the subject cannot orient his actions by them
8. Failure of congruence between the rules announced and their actual administration

I submit that in gauging the rocky relationship between established doctrines of international law and the emerging practice of preemptive wars, a substantial number of these eight techniques of failure to make law stand satisfied.

For instance, the understanding of preemptive wars as a method of self-defense (as has been propagated under the Bush Doctrine) is clearly *retroactive* in nature. Established international law surrounding the concept of self-defense concretely advocates the position that such use of force on the mere apprehension of threat is patently illegal. In addition to this, the implementation of preemptive wars (if accepted as valid customary practice) as well as the doctrine of sovereignty on the global diaspora would be *inherently contradictory.*

Gauging from the practice among those nations that have launched preemptive wars in the recent past, there have been sustained attempts at imposing some form of democratic rule in nations that have never known anything but monarchy. To make things worse, positive results from such actions are expected overnight. If such practices ancillary to preemptive wars were to be accepted as valid international custom, then it would be fair to assume that these would constitute *rules requiring conduct beyond the powers of the affected party* (i.e., the domestic subjects of the occupied territory).

Finally, in blatantly disregarding the tenets of "sovereignty," "sovereign equality," and "the rule of reciprocity," which have long been publicized as sacrosanct doctrines of international law, there appears to be a *marked gulf between the rules announced and their actual administration.*

I am therefore of the belief that a majority of the basic ingredients of good law as identified by Fuller have been tossed out of the equation by nation states looking to promote the practice of preemptive wars. I shall now propose a three-pronged criticism of preemptive wars, owing to the fact that they have been launched as a flawed interpretation of the precautionary principle.

Precautionary Principle: Testing the Three Legs of the Tripod

One of the major foreseeable problems with allowing preemptive wars on terror to continue unchecked lies in the way that international law is formed. Customary international law forms the largest body of law at the international level, and its formation is dependent only on "state practice" and *opinio juris,* that is, the nation state's solemn belief that its state practice was legally obligatory (Shaw, 2007).

It must be noted that the twin requirements of state practice and *opinio juris* have served international law well in the past, and the courts have proved more than competent in dealing with disputes involving international customs (The Lotus Case, 1927). Aggressive reform in the form of the precautionary principle being reinterpreted to support unilateral preemptive wars may, however, trigger a dangerous trend if the law of nations were to embrace such a knee-jerk reaction as customary practice.

I would like to reaffirm the belief that uprooting the global crime of terrorism requires a concerted effort at the international level; yet, as one shall discover through the course of this chapter, the methods being pursued seem flawed at various levels. I propose a three-pronged criticism of the preemptive wars that were launched under the so-called Bush Doctrine's interpretation of the precautionary principle.

Economic Criticism

The precautionary principle, in essence, advocates that regulatory authorities should make efforts to protect against potential harms, even if their causal links are not clearly established and even if we are unsure if the harms will eventually come to fruition. This practice is to be followed until it can be ascertained that the potential harms are nonexistent or too minute to be of major concern (Sunstein, 2005).

A variety of critics state that the most basic condemnation of the precautionary principle lies in the fact that given our limited resources, humanity cannot afford to take extremely costly steps on extremely speculative risks (Sunstein, 2005). Yet, excessively huge losses of life, property, and capital have been caused by various economic and military superpowers relying on limited evidence of threats to national security, as was seen in the trillion dollar war in Iraq. This only serves to reestablish this popular critique based on sound economic principles of "opportunity cost."

The economic "notion" of opportunity cost primarily deals with the efficient use of scarce resources (*Economist*, 2010), which appears to have been grossly contravened by the inefficient use of resources in the preemptive wars launched under the guise of the Bush Doctrine's interpretation of the precautionary principle.

Violation of Established Customs and Basic Tenets of International Law

I agree with the theoretical principle that a very real threat of terrorism needs to be weeded out; however, I find it necessary to submit that the practical implications of the use of precautionary principles in armed conflict scenarios suffer from an inherent defect: it seems to violate some of the most well-established customs and the most basic tenets of international law.

In justifying the use of the precautionary principle in armed conflict situations, proponents of the principle have always stood by their claims of acting in "self-defense." The self-defense argument formed a part of the Bush Doctrine applied after September 11, 2001, in the war against Afghanistan. The United States actually found the support of the international community in their claim that the legitimate aims of self-defense incorporate the right to restore the security of the state after an armed conflict (Gardam, 2006).

However, the origins of the principle of self-defense under international law remain forgotten when such a stance is blindly supported based on hitherto unchecked feelings of sympathy. In fact, it was under the customary laws of war (*jus ad bellum* and *jus in bello*) that the legitimacy of self-defense can first be clearly ascertained. While *jus ad bellum* looks into the moral justification behind waging a war, *jus in bello* concerns itself with the methods employed in waging the war (Coady, 2002).

Jus ad bellum makes it essential to go into a war with a "just cause" and with the "right authority," while *jus in bello* makes it mandatory on the warring party to ensure that the requirements of "proportionality," "last resort," and "reasonable prospects of success" are complied with (Coady, 2002).

In unilaterally carrying out a preemptive war against terror, a nation state may claim to comply with the requirement of just cause. Nevertheless, Article 51 of the United Nations (UN) Charter read together with Chapter VII makes for a sound interpretation of *jus ad bellum* (Gardam, 2006); and in acting "unilaterally," a country not only bypasses the grundnorm of right authority under customary international law, but also violates its duty to comply with the provisions of the UN Charter. This is in gross violation of the doctrine of *pacta sunt servanda* (Shaw, 2007).

Even more disturbing is the fact that all three characteristics of *jus in bello* (now enshrined under the Geneva Conventions and the UN Charter) stand demolished in the case of preemptive wars on terror. First, a terrorist organization is a nonstate actor, and waging a full-fledged war on a nation state and its people in retaliation to a nonstate actor is clearly disproportionate. Moreover, past experience in such cases as Israel's 1981 preemptive strike against the Iraqi nuclear reactor in Osirac, the United Kingdom's preemptive strikes against Argentina after retaking the Falkland Islands, and the United States' preemptive strikes in Afghanistan and Iraq has shown that along with being disproportionate, they are by no means compliant with the requirement of necessity (or last resort), as diplomatic dialogue was still an option in each of these cases (Gardam, 2006). Finally, as has been stated before, with the international community still at loggerheads when it comes to arriving at a clear-cut definition for terrorism, there are no reasonable prospects of success in a war against an unknown entity. *THE ENTITY ISN'T UNKNOWN.*

Sovereign equality, the foundation stone on which the UN stands, is vehemently questioned by preemptive wars. Signatories to the UN Charter, that most sacred of treaties between civilized nation states, may choose to overlook Article 2(4) and 2(7) if they are given a free reign on the use of this principle (Danchin & Fischer, 2010). Acceptance of such a principle could lead to great powers using their economic and military might to "outlaw" smaller states for their own gains. While I agree with the honorable former UN Secretary General Boutros Boutros Ghali that "the time of absolute and exclusive sovereignty ... has passed" (Sinha, 2002, p. 106), I would have to

COMPLETELY FALSE!

contend that sovereign equality still remains and must continue to remain an inviolable principle.

In addition, in order to become a well-established custom, a principle generally needs to enjoy the widespread support of a majority of nations (Shaw, 2007). This is something preemptive wars have always lacked. Whether it was India's self-defense argument while interfering with the situation in Bangladesh in 1971 (Sinha, 2002), Israel's preemptive attack on an Iraqi nuclear reactor (Gardam, 2006), or the most recent use of the argument to defend the U.S. offensive in Iraq (Gray, 2004), widespread support of preemptive wars has been hard to come by historically.

Tracing Historical Application of Precautionary Principle

While gaining an insight into the workings of the precautionary principle, I noticed a trend that is common to almost all applications of this doctrine before efforts were made to incorporate it into the realm of armed conflict.

It is interesting to note that, historically, the precautionary principle has been used by countries to control their own domestic actions, even when the principle was made part of international treaties. For example, the Maastricht treaty on the European Union (EU) adopted in 1992 made it clear that states party to the EU would base enforcement on the precautionary principle with respect to provisions relating to the environment. Now, enforcement of such provisions relating to the environment is clearly within the territorial jurisdiction of the state. Other major instances of the use of such a principle have been with regard to dealing with the problems of climate change, experimenting with genetics, or working with nuclear technology (Sunstein, 2005).

I have no qualms in admitting that the precautionary principle has been used in international treaties in the past and has also formed a part of customary law between nations, especially in Europe.

However, in clear contravention to the customary practice of applying the precautionary principle where scientific uncertainty is cast over the implementation of a domestic policy, the juxtaposition of this principle on the customs relating to armed conflict is set to extend into the jurisdictions of other sovereign nation states; thereby compromising the foundations of international law, as enshrined under Article 2(4) of the UN Charter.

Herein lies the disjointedness of logic in applying the customarily peaceful and domestic use of the precautionary principle to a potentially violent and international scenario presented by armed conflicts.

Therefore, it is clear that on examining the use of the precautionary principle in armed conflicts countering terrorism, as suggested by the Bush Doctrine, there are glaring flaws that not only appeal to one's moral conscience, but may go to the extent of deeming preemptive wars on terror patently illegal under international law.

Living Up to the Responsibility to Protect against Terror

I submit that there are many issues that need to be ironed out in order to ensure adequate protection against the threat posed by terrorism. Just like any major bone of contention at the international level, "definitional challenges" and "problems of jurisdiction" remain the central issues when countering terrorism.

Definitional Challenges

Due to the lack of consensus among nations with respect to a singular, established definition of terrorism, the international community has witnessed a growing pessimism surrounding the whole exercise of countering the threat it presents. Rosalyn Higgins, for example, exclaims that terrorism is a "term without any legal significance," and has become a "convenient way of alluding to activities whether of States or Individuals, widely disapproved of and in which either the methods used are unlawful, or the targets protected, or both" (Ward, 2009, p. 18).

While preemptive wars on terror have bred such pessimism among authorities as high up as the former president of the International Court of Justice, it is essential to try and defy the naysayers and find a solution to the problem at hand. The restrictions of existing legal responses, more specifically the restrictions of existing legal institutions, should in no way imply the need to abandon the cause of justice (Ward, 2009).

The crux of the issue concerning a definition for terrorism lies in the fact that the law governing nonstate actors and the employment of armed force has not kept up with those laws that govern nation states (The United Nations Foundation, 2004).

To this, I feel that there lies a simple yet offbeat solution. The problem with a definition for terrorism seems to be more political than legal, since the Rome Statute has already incorporated most (if not all) of the components that comprise acts of terror under 11 constituents of the article dealing with "crimes against humanity."* The problem lies in the nation states not being willing to compromise on their understanding of the term terrorism. Therefore, I propose that it would be in the best interests of the international community to look for the enforcement of laws relating to terror under the preagreed norms of the Rome Statute. This is an idea that has also gained the approbation of the former UN secretary-general Kofi Annan and the former UN High Commissioner for Human Rights, Mary Robinson (Ward, 2009).

Not only would such a move bypass the recurring problems of consensus, it would also increase the scope of the international community to act positively under the established norms of international criminal law.

---

* Article 7, The Rome Statute of the International Criminal Court.

Problems of Jurisdiction

I submit that the international community would do well to look to the International Criminal Court's (ICC) "complementary jurisdiction" as a viable answer to the predicament surrounding individual criminal liability. In accepting the importance of domestic legal structures, the ICC implemented complementary jurisdiction as opposed to the controversial "universal jurisdiction." This helps respect the important doctrine of sovereignty, while ensuring that the criminal responsible for perpetrating an international crime is brought to justice either by the domestic courts, or if need be, by the ICC (The International Centre for Criminal Reform and Criminal Justice Policy, 2008).

Major criticisms of the ICC have been with respect to the UN Security Council's mandate to bring forth cases pertaining to international crimes and the non-incorporation of certain crimes explicitly under the statute. However, the incorporation of complementary jurisdiction is widely regarded as a masterstroke, which has promoted the signing and ratification of the statute by a large number of nation states. Hence, I submit that individual criminal liability should be subject to complementary jurisdiction as espoused by the Rome Statute.

Having proposed viable solutions to the problems of definition and jurisdiction over terrorism, I further submit that the Responsibility to Protect Doctrine would prove a much more preferable alternative to the use of pre-emptive wars in countering terrorism.

The International Commission on Intervention and State Sovereignty (ICISS) presented a report entitled "The Responsibility to Protect" on the recommendation of the then UN secretary-general Kofi Annan with the aim of addressing the growing discontent among nations due to the lack of consensus on the limits of state sovereignty and the legitimacy of "interventions" (The International Commission on Intervention and State Sovereignty, 2001).

This report soon gained in importance, with its tenets accepted almost unanimously at the World Summit in 2005 and by the high-level panel set up by the secretary-general (The International Centre for Criminal Reform and Criminal Justice Policy, 2008). This points to a change in the world's perception of "collective security" as the Responsibility to Protect Doctrine. The doctrine establishes an inherent duty espoused within a state's right to sovereignty, thereby making states liable to protect their own population (The International Commission on Intervention and State Sovereignty, 2001). Failing to adhere to this responsibility may, in turn, create an *erga omnes obligation* on the international community to intervene. However, military intervention is to be used only as a last resort (The International Centre for Criminal Reform and Criminal Justice Policy, 2008).

The reason I submit such a proposal is simple. The Responsibility to Protect Doctrine, while accepting the importance of countering even legitimately perceived threats of terrorism, stresses on "the international community" having an *erga omnes obligation*. This negates the unilateral use of force, which comes in for great criticism owing to its ambiguous nature. Instead, it focuses on the far more acceptable alternative of collective security, as mandated under Chapter VII of the UN Charter, read together with Article 2(7).*

Also, this doctrine places the first and foremost responsibility on the nation suspected of being unable to "protect" its population from terrorists (and the spread of violent terrorist ideology) within its boundaries. This shows a clearly demarcated respect for the basic international law tenets of sovereignty and sovereign equality.[†]

Finally, it is of utmost importance to note that in urging the international community to act in situations where terrorists are likely to thrive, and aiming at a new collective security regime, the Responsibility to Protect Doctrine lays down three stages of action:

1. The responsibility to prevent
2. The responsibility to react
3. The responsibility to rebuild

In doing so, the doctrine ensures that the international community functions in conformity with the inviolable foundation of international law: the rule of reciprocity. The rule of reciprocity, that is, treat the other as you would expect yourself to be treated, is probably the only norm that ensures the enforcement of international law; and in making provisions for prevention and rebuilding, the commission has looked to ensure progressive action and not merely a vicious armed conflict (The International Commission on Intervention and State Sovereignty, 2001). This, I submit, is in furtherance of the rule of reciprocity.

Conclusion

On evaluating the means and measures at the international community's disposal, I conclude that the world finds itself in a serious predicament due to various problems that are specific to terrorism. However, descending into a state of chaos and lawlessness is not the answer.

---

* The UN Charter, in making provisions for the sovereign rights of nation states, also leaves scope for exceptions where the purposes of the UN may be contravened. This is seen most prominently in Article 2(7) of the charter.
† As espoused under the UN Charter, the Rome Statute of the International Criminal Court, the customary laws of war (*jus ad bellum* and *jus in bello*) as well as the treaty provisions of the four Geneva conventions and the additional protocols.

Harold Koh succinctly describes the flaws in preemptive wars:

> so many lawyers 'seem to have concluded that somehow, the destruction of four planes and three buildings has taken us back to a state of nature in which there are no laws or rules. The very spirit of law appears to have been abandoned; just as the terrorists hoped it would.' (Ward, 2009, p. 11)

The three major flaws in preemptive wars that I have pointed out serve to place the Bush Doctrine in direct conflict with the most sacred of international law principles, such as sovereign equality, the rule of reciprocity, and the laws of war. By contrast, the Responsibility to Protect Doctrine, while respecting these basic grundnorms on which international law is based, furthers the cause of collective security and encourages the enforcement envisioned by the UN Charter; the one treaty to which every civilized nation state pledges allegiance. Through this chapter, I have also tried to elucidate the viable methods that international criminal law presents to countering definitional and jurisdictional problems posed by terrorism.

It is my firm belief that no matter how brilliant and ingenious the methods to counter terrorism are, the challenge the international community faces is one that requires a long-drawn and systematic approach to counter it. However, what the world cannot afford is to descend into a state of nature where laws, rules, and principles that have long been the focal point of affirmative action lose relevance. It is with this belief that I humbly submit that in furtherance of justice, equity, and good conscience, the international community must finally do away with hypocritical methods of countering terrorism and look to more inclusive and just means of countering this evil.

References

Best, G. (2001). *War and Law since 1945*. Oxford: Oxford University Press.

Bowden, B., Charlesworth, H., & Farall, J. (eds.) (2009). *The Role of International Law in Rebuilding Societies after Conflict*. Cambridge: Cambridge University Press.

Coady, C. A. J. (2002). *The Ethics of Armed Humanitarian Intervention*. Peaceworks no. 45. Washington, DC: United States Institute of Peace. Retrieved December 15, 2012, from http://www.usip.org/files/resources/pwks45.pdf.

Danchin, P. G., & Fischer, H. (eds.) (2010). *United Nations Reform and the New Collective Security*. Cambridge: Cambridge University Press.

De Mulinen, F. (1987). *Handbook on the Law of War for Armed Forces*. Geneva: International Committee of the Red Cross.

Economist (2010). Opportunity cost. Retrieved November 10, 2010, from http://www.economist.com/research/economics/alphabetic.cfm?letter=O.

Fuller, L. L. (2009). *The Morality of Law*. Delhi: Universal Law Publishing Co.

Gardam, J. (2006). *Necessity, Proportionality and the Use of Force by States*. Cambridge: Cambridge University Press.

Gray, C. (2004). *International Law and the Use of Force*. Oxford: Oxford University Press.

Shaw, M. (2007). *International Law* (5th edn). Cambridge: Cambridge University Press.

Simpson, G. (2004). *Great Powers and Outlaw States*. Cambridge: Cambridge University Press.

Sinha, M. K. (2002). *Humanitarian Intervention by the United Nations*. New Delhi: Manak Publications.

Sunstein, C. R. (2005). *Laws of Fear: Beyond the Precautionary Principle*. Cambridge: Cambridge University Press.

The International Centre for Criminal Reform and Criminal Justice Policy (2008). The International Criminal Court: Manual for the Ratification and Implementation of the Rome Statute. Vancouver: The International Centre for Criminal Reform and Criminal Justice Policy.

The International Commission on Intervention and State Sovereignty (2001). The responsibility to protect. Ottawa: The International Development Research Centre.

The Lotus Case (1927). Permanence Court of International Justice Series A, No. 10.

The Secretary General's High Level Panel on Threats, Challenges and Change (2004). A more secure world. New York: The United Nations Foundation.

Ward, I. (2009). *Law, Text, Terror*. Cambridge: Cambridge University Press.

Terrorist Financing in Southern Africa
African Commitment to Combating Terrorism

4

VINESH BASDEO

Contents

Introduction

The detection of terror funds is a complicated undertaking due to the size and nature of the transactions involved. Contrary to popular belief, planning and committing a terrorist atrocity do not require much money. If banks are used, the transactions tend to involve small amounts and an uncomplicated layering of funds. The much-cited 9/11 atrocities in the United States provide a classic example. An examination of the hijackers' finances revealed that the individual transactions were small, falling below the reporting threshold for unusual cash transactions, and the funds involved added up to less than half a million U.S. dollars. The 1998 U.S. embassy bombings in

East Africa were estimated to have amounted to an overall cost of less than U.S.$10,000.

Anti-money laundering and combating the financing of terrorism (AML/CFT) regimes have become the key tools in fighting terrorism in the post-9/11 world. The stakes, in what the Bush government in the United States has called a "war on terrorism," have been raised on account of the inevitable friction between the trappings of development on the one hand and the imperative to maintain security on the other. The global and transnational nature and reach of financial institutions, the greater role of intermediaries, and the uneven development, even divergence, of the world's economic systems combine to magnify the challenges of combating money laundering and terrorist financing. Mindful of the differences in the banking and financial systems between the developed and developing worlds, this chapter provides an overview of the international instruments against terrorist financing, the evolving methods of detecting terrorist financing, and the practical problems that they are likely to encounter and, in some cases, have already encountered.

Are the antiterrorist financing mechanisms applied in the developed world appropriate and sufficient in southern Africa? The region comprises Angola, Botswana, the Democratic Republic of Congo, Lesotho, Madagascar, Malawi, Mauritius, Mozambique, Namibia, South Africa, Swaziland, Tanzania, Zambia, and Zimbabwe. These countries' human development index rankings suggest that they will accord priority to speeding up economic development. Considering the limited resources at their disposal, can they afford to implement antiterrorist financing measures?

The informal economic sectors account for a large number of financial and business transactions in southern African countries. With the probable exception of South Africa and Mauritius, the informal economic sectors are far more economically active than the formal sectors. Also known as the "parallel market," "unrecorded trade," or the "cash economy," these sectors provide for the livelihoods of millions of Africans, although their magnitude is undetermined. Direct interaction between the informal sector and the formal financial institutions is insignificant. In Tanzania, which has a vibrant informal economy, a mere 6% of the population use banks for depository purposes, while only 4% of Malawians and less than 1% of Congolese and Angolans are "banked." Figures in other countries are just as low. This chapter is based on findings from field trips and literature studies.

Definitions

How is terrorist financing defined? The financing of terrorism is easily explained as "the financial support, in any form, of terrorism or of those who encourage, plan or engage in terrorism" (Botha, 2006). It is less simple to define "terrorism" because of the political, religious, and national implications that differ significantly from country to country. An all-encompassing and globally applicable definition of terrorism remains elusive, not least in Africa. Legal drafters tend to avoid an outright definition of terrorism, but rather describe an "act of terror" or "terrorist activity."

Terrorist Threat, Vulnerabilities, and Capacity in Southern Africa

Terrorist Financing in Southern Africa

Most financial experts agree that the financing of terrorism can occur in any country in the world, whether or not it has complex financial systems. Since complex international transactions can be abused to facilitate terrorist financing and laundering of money, the different stages of money laundering (placement, layering, and integration) may occur in a host of different countries (Schott, 2004).

Despite the region's apparent vulnerability to terrorist financing, evidence of terrorist funding within or from southern Africa is scanty and mostly anecdotal. Southern Africa has very rich mineral resources, such as gold, diamonds, uranium, and gemstones. Following 9/11, there were allegations that diamonds and gold were being used to support the al-Qaeda terror network.

Clandestine business arrangements involving the diamond trade date back to the days of the Cold War, when the superpowers used African nations as pawns in their geopolitical conflicts. They funneled weapons to what were termed "local proxies." After the end of the Cold War, the superpowers lost interest in Africa, and arms and ammunition became less readily available through direct channels. It was at this stage that the trade in illicit diamonds escalated. Warring factions and even a few governments became reliant on the illegal trade in "conflict diamonds" and "blood diamonds." Notably, the civil war in Angola was prolonged by both the covert support of the UN and the sale of diamonds by the National Union for the Total Independence of Angola (UNITA) terrorist movement (Fletcher, 2003).

African militaries and paramilitary factions may have used diamonds, gold, and other mineral resources to finance their operations, but this would have been impossible without backing from multinational corporations, the international diamond industry, and retail outlets selling blood diamonds (Fletcher, 2003). There is no evidence of a link between the diamond trade or illicit diamond smuggling and al-Qaeda or other terrorist groupings in southern Africa. Furthermore, the Kimberly Certification Process has established a system of warranties, guaranteeing that diamonds are mined and exported legally.

The tanzanite scandal spun by two *Wall Street Journal* reporters has become notorious for its adverse effects on the Tanzanian gemstone industry. The reporters suggested that al-Qaeda controlled a sizable chunk of the trade in the rare blue gemstone mined from a 13 km² patch of graphite rock in northeastern Tanzania. Tanzanian investigators could find no evidence of such a connection. However, the publication of the allegations led major U.S. retailers to drop tanzanite from their sale offerings (Tambulasi, 2006). In February 2002, a Tanzanian delegation assured dealers at a major gem trade show in Tucson, Arizona, that no terrorist group was profiting from the sale of tanzanite. The Tucson Tanzanite Protocol originates from that meeting. Like the Kimberley Certification Process, it established a system of warranties guaranteeing that the gems were mined and exported legally. The United Republic of Tanzania declared the mining site a controlled area where no visitors were allowed without a dealer's license and other identification (Tambulasi, 2006).

Allegations of the abuse of charities to fund terrorism turned out to be unfounded in a case in Malawi. In June 2003, U.S. and Malawian officials arrested five foreign nationals on suspicion of funneling funds to al-Qaeda through various Islamic charities and schools (Tambulasi, 2006). Not only were the arrest and deportation of the suspects in stark contravention of the country's constitutional principles, but the allegations turned out to be false (Hübschle, 2004). No evidence was found that money had been channeled to the terror network.

Another cause for concern is the region's long, porous, and unpatrolled borders. Police forces from several member countries have encountered, and at times arrested, suspects attempting to export huge amounts of U.S. dollars from the region. The apprehension by Mozambican police of four Pakistani nationals on suspicion of attempting to smuggle close to a quarter of a million U.S. dollars out of the country is a case in point (*African Terrorism Bulletin*, 2005). A few months before 9/11, two South African nationals were arrested while attempting to cross the border between South Africa and Swaziland with more than half a million U.S. dollars stuffed into their underwear. Investigators found that the couple had traveled from the South African port of Durban through Swaziland to neighboring Mozambique more than 150 times over an 18-month period. Links emerged between the suspects, an exchange bureau in the Mozambican capital of Maputo, and gold dealers in Dubai (Botha, 2006). Investigators speculated on a possible connection to al-Qaeda. Despite this suggested link, most cases that involve the illegal smuggling of currency across national borders are attempts to bypass or flout tough foreign exchange and currency regulations.

Alternative remittance systems take the form of nonbank institutions that transfer funds on behalf of clients through their own networks. Many of their transactions are paperless. Unregistered lenders in at least two countries move money across borders with no written record. Part of the attraction of this system lies in the fact that there is no proper trail to the source of the funds. It has been alleged that al-Qaeda has exploited the global *hawala* network by using it to transfer funds around the world. The proceeds of drug trafficking were channeled through the network operating between London, the Punjab, and Kashmir to support Sikh and Kashmiri secessionists (Navias, 2002). As for southern Africa, *hawala* operations are said to take place in Malawi, Mozambique, and Tanzania. It is more common for diaspora communities to collect money in the developed world and send it to their poorer brothers and sisters in Africa. Variants of *hawala* are used by the Zimbabwean diaspora in South Africa, Botswana, and Malawi. However, there has been no evidence of links to terrorism. Indeed, African countries are usually at the receiving, not the donating, end of remittances.

State sponsorship of terrorism in the region probably reached its high watermark during the apartheid era, when South Africa perpetrated acts of terrorism against its own citizens and those of neighboring countries such as Namibia and Mozambique. It also sponsored proxy terrorist organizations in Angola, Namibia, and Mozambique over a long period of time. Currently, the Zimbabwean president Robert Mugabe and his associates are accused of using the state machinery to commit acts of terrorism against ordinary citizens (Botha, 2006).

As the international community, with its various protocols, starts cracking down on the trade in conflict diamonds and other mineral resources tainted with innocent blood, a window of opportunity may be opened for warlords and organized criminals to collude with terrorist elements in the largely unknown and unregulated terrain of the informal sector.

Southern Africa's Obligations and Standards on Combating Terrorist Financing

The discourse of risk and globalization is key to the antiterrorist financing debate. Due to the global reach of the international financial network, all countries are vulnerable to money laundering. If terrorist financing follows the same routes as money laundering, it follows that countries are equally vulnerable to terrorist financing. The international community recognizes financial controls as essential antiterrorism tools. A series of measures at national, regional, and international levels have been introduced to deprive terrorists of the means to inflict serious damage. The main sources of international obligations in combating the financing of terrorism are the resolutions of the United Nations Security Council (UNSC), in particular Resolution

1373 of 2001 (referred to here as "the Resolution"), the 1999 International Convention for the Suppression of the Financing of Terrorism (referred to here as "the Convention"), and the nine Special Recommendations on Terrorist Financing (referred to here as "the Special Recommendations") issued by the Financial Action Task Force (FATF). The Convention, which opened for signature on December 9, 1999, stipulated the criminalization of direct involvement or complicity in the financing or collection of funds for terrorist activity. Article 2(1) requires states to create an offence when a "person by any means, directly or indirectly, unlawfully and willfully, provides or collects funds with the intention that they should be used" to commit an act that constitutes a terrorist offence (United Nations, 1999). In southern Africa, it has been ratified by seven states: Botswana, Lesotho, Malawi, Mauritius, South Africa, Swaziland, and Tanzania. The Resolution, adopted in the immediate aftermath of the 9/11 attacks, imposed unprecedented legal obligations on UN member states to comply with measures designed to counter terrorist financing, travel, recruitment, and supply. To monitor the enforcement of these and other antiterrorism measures, the UNSC created the Counter Terrorism Committee. In March 2004, the committee became the Counter Terrorism Executive Directorate and it serves as a professional secretariat for the implementation of counterterrorism strategies.

In October 2001, the FATF adopted eight Special Recommendations on terrorist financing. These included a call for the ratification and implementation of relevant international instruments, the freezing and confiscation of suspected terrorist assets, the reporting of suspicious transactions, the evaluation of alternative remittances and wire transfers, and the revision of laws and regulations related to nonprofit and charity organizations. An additional measure adopted late in October 2004, called on states to stop cross-border movements of currency and monetary instruments related to terrorist financing and money laundering and to confiscate such funds. The recommendation stipulates a limit (U.S.$15,000) for undeclared cash that can be carried across borders. Furthermore, it proposes control over cash couriers through the intervention of national authorities on the basis of intelligence or police information.

Considerable overlap is noticeable among the various obligations and standards. The Convention, the Resolution, and the Special Recommendations each deal with aspects of the freezing, seizure, and confiscation of terrorist assets. The Special Recommendations deal with four topics not covered by the Resolution or the Convention: alternative remittance systems, wire transfers, nonprofit organizations, and cash couriers (IMF, 2003). These topics focus on financial systems other than the formalized banking and financial systems. On the face of it, the four recommendations were informed by conclusions made in respect of the financial sources of al-Qaeda before 9/11. It remains an open question whether the FATF recommendations are pertinent to vulnerabilities within the cash economy or informal sectors in southern Africa.

Of further relevance to the region are antiterrorist financing measures passed in the United States. On September 14, 2001, U.S. president George W. Bush issued Executive Order 13224 entitled "Blocking Property and Prohibiting Transactions with Persons who Commit, Threaten to Commit, or Support Terrorism," which expanded the U.S. list of designated terrorist organizations. Most importantly, the order acknowledges the global reach of terrorists by imposing extraterritorial financial sanctions against all "foreign persons that support or otherwise associate with these foreign terrorists" (U.S. Department of State, 2001).

Another beacon in the U.S. war on terrorist financing is the Uniting and Strengthening America by Providing Appropriate Tools Required to Intercept and Obstruct Terrorism Act of 2001 (also known as the USA PATRIOT Act). Major AML/CFT provisions that have a bearing on foreign jurisdictions include the following:

- U.S. banks are prohibited from opening correspondent accounts for foreign banks with no physical presence, no employees, or no regulatory supervision in the United States.
- Informal money transmitting businesses have to be licensed and report suspicious transactions.

Antiterror measures pose significant dilemmas for developing countries in southern Africa. They are under pressure to either comply with the international obligations or be blacklisted as non-cooperative and risk economic sanctions. There is no evidence that terrorism is considered a significant threat to many of these countries. There is, in consequence, no obvious benefit in adopting the measures stipulated in the antiterrorist financing instruments. Tambulasi (2006) suggests that transnational regulation involves the "persuasion" of "formally independent nation states to adopt similar measures even though there may be no obvious benefit to them in doing so." Terrorist networks and organized criminals threatening the United States and other Western powers may be substantially different from those threatening countries in the developing world, so the "one-size-fits-all" approach may well be inappropriate.

The sentiments of an implicit "persuasion" have been echoed by political decision makers, law enforcement officials, and other bureaucrats assigned the task of implementing the AML/CFT regimes in the region. The political will is low and the perception of bullying is strong in the region.

The World Bank and other international financial institutions (IFIs) have assumed a critical role in persuading developing countries to toe the line. Representing the most influential financial institutions in the world, the World Bank, the International Monetary Fund (IMF), and other IFIs control many billions of dollars in resources, including development aid and foreign direct investments, which are allocated for lending and capital projects around the world. These institutions each have multiple correspondent banking relationships and deposit funds for use in developing or recipient countries in central banks and commercial banks (Schott, 2004). The IFIs declare that they will only do business with commercial banks and other financial institutions that comply with anti-money laundering standards. This, of course, puts international banks and commercial banks with a large turnover at an unfair advantage. A small, local bank in Malawi, Namibia, or anywhere else in the region will struggle to comply with international standards, while its competitor with international ties, or the subsidiary of an international bank, has the capacity and financial backing to do so. Increasingly, smaller and local banks are stigmatized as financial backers to terror financiers, warlords, corrupt bureaucrats, and organized criminals.

Noteworthy in the context of the southern African region is the stipulation in the USA PATRIOT Act that U.S. banks are prohibited from opening correspondent accounts for foreign banks with no physical presence, no employees, or no regulatory supervision in the United States. This means that any financial institution wishing to enter into a trade or banking agreement with a U.S. bank has to open an office in a U.S. territory. For small, local banks in southern Africa, such an obligation presents a serious financial burden. This and other AML/CFT obligations undermine the long-term goal of conducting business with the United States. Small banks struggle to finance and staff such offices. Again, big, international banks or financial institutions command an unfair advantage. Perhaps the question is not how one complies with the international obligations, but who stands to benefit from the AML/CFT regime.

Conclusion and Recommendations

Domestification of International Instruments: Practical Considerations

International bodies such as the UN and the FATF recommend some basic steps toward achieving a reliable AML/CFT regime. It should be noted that these steps, implicit in the Resolution, the Convention, and the Special Recommendations, use as a point of departure the formalized banking and financial sectors of the developed world.

Domestic Legislation

The three key instruments on terrorist financing suggest that domestic legislation should provide the general legal framework and establish the obligations of financial institutions and other providers of financial services. Such legislation should define and criminalize money laundering and terrorist financing, setting penalties. It should cover a wide set of predicate crimes and also define the responsibilities and powers of the various government agencies involved. Commercial banks should be obliged to be especially vigilant, given their role in the payment system (IMF, 2003).

Within the region, Mauritius and South Africa have domestic laws that specifically address terrorist financing. Mauritius lists as key laws in the fight against terrorist financing the International Convention for the Suppression of the Financing of Terrorism Act of 2003 and the Anti-Money Laundering Act of 2002. The main statutes dealing with terrorist financing in South Africa are the Prevention of Organised Crime Act of 1998 (POCA) and the Financial Intelligence Centre Act of 2001 (FICA). With the enactment of the Protection of Constitutional Democracy against Terrorism and Related Activities Act of 2004, the POCA and FICA were amended to accommodate measures against terrorist financing (Hübschle, 2006: 110–111). The Malawian parliament passed the Money Laundering, Proceeds of Serious Crime and Terrorist Financing Act of 2005 in August 2006 after many months of vigorous debate.

As for the rest of the region, most countries are at different stages of developing or implementing anti-money laundering laws. Most are aware that new enforcement agencies and other institutions not only constitute an additional financial burden, but also raise issues around capacity, training, and maintenance. Some officials have suggested that anti-money laundering laws are drafted to satisfy minimum international obligations, but they pay little more than lip service to the international instruments, as their implementation is put on the back burner.

Banking Regulation and Supervision

For primary legislation to be operational, banking regulations and supervision need to be implemented. Ideally, financial institutions should be obliged to institute procedures to avoid dealing with criminal and terrorist elements.

"Know Your Customer"

Banks and other financial institutions should verify the identity and legitimacy of clients, especially new clients and those acting on behalf of others. The "know your customer" (KYC) obligation may involve elaborate background checks.

The KYC obligation poses significant practical challenges to commercial banks in the region. For those banks that can tap into the know-how and financial networks of their foreign parent companies, the KYC obligation, on the face of it, can be implemented with relative ease. However, elaborate background checks involve confirmation of identity and proof of residence, traditionally in the form of utility bills (electricity, water, telephone, etc.), and at this point, no matter how much foreign cash and expertise are available, all banks doing business in the developing countries of southern Africa face certain challenges in this regard. The following are especially pertinent:

- Absence of systems of national identification
- Absence of birth certificates
- Minimal use of passports
- Minimal availability of driving licenses as a means of identification
- Lack of employment credentials or "job cards"
- Unfixed or unmarked residential addresses in informal settlements, undemarcated townships and rural areas (a surprisingly large number of African metropoles and cities only have physical addresses in the city center)
- Low levels of access to utilities and hence to utility bills

When the Basel Committee on Banking Supervision wrote the Basel Statement of Principles and introduced the concept of KYC as a fundamental principle of banking supervision in 1988 (Schott, 2004), little thought appears to have been given to the limitations, in a different setting, of standards that may be viable in the developed world. However, central banks, bankers' associations, and other stakeholders in the region have come up with creative and innovative approaches to circumvent the practical challenges of adhering to KYC obligations. In Tanzania, a bank can carry out a KYC on a customer by contacting two referees. Of great significance are letters of introduction by local authorities. The basic unit of civil administration in Tanzania is a cell, which consists of 10 houses or separate units, and the leader of such a cell may provide proof of identity. But these leaders, who are in a powerful position, are not always unbiased.

The KYC obligation raises another dilemma. Compliance officers from a number of southern African countries have argued that although KYC may lead to compliance with international obligations, in reality it discourages the vast majority of "unbanked" citizens of the region from entering the banking system. Uncomfortable questions and requests for documentation may put off prospective customers. Banks may do business with international investors and multinational corporations, but the people sleep with their money under the mattress.

Of further concern in South Africa is that banks are reluctant to allow asylum seekers and refugees to open accounts. Upon arrival, asylum seekers are furnished with an asylum-seeker permit until they receive official refugee status. The processing of applications can take months, and the backlog is huge. In the meantime, banks will not allow asylum seekers to open bank accounts, as the temporary permits do not provide a 13-digit identity number as required by the FICA regulations. Increasingly, criminals have targeted asylum seekers (especially the Somali community), as they are known to keep their money on their business premises or in their homes (Botha, 2006).

"Fit and Proper"

The Convention calls for measures to ensure that criminals and terrorists do not set up or gain control of financial institutions. The question is how to do this effectively in a free market. Shareholders and senior managers in financial institutions should demonstrate that they are fit and proper to hold these positions of control and oversight. This applies to the initial licensing stage, but regulators should also scrutinize management turnover and changes in shareholdings.

The Finance Bank in Malawi provides an excellent example of what can happen if no fit and proper test of senior managers is conducted. The Finance Bank's banking license was revoked on January 27, 2006, after several acts of operational malpractice and noncompliance with banking regulations were discovered. More specifically, senior managers had not complied with foreign exchange regulations and had created "ghost accounts," apparently in order to externalize foreign currency. Furthermore, the branch manager in Lilongwe had failed to provide the Anti-Corruption Bureau with information on clients who contravened the foreign currency transaction regulations. Corrupt government officials were found to have hidden their ill-gotten gains in accounts at the Finance Bank, while 12 bank employees had created an intricate net of transactions that effectively drained the bank's coffers of close to U.S.$200,000 (Tambulasi, 2006).

Unusual Transaction Reporting

Financial institutions are advised to establish systems of identifying and reporting unusual transactions. Bank officials have pointed out that what constitutes an unusual or suspicious transaction in one country may be perfectly "normal" in another. Bank regulators may not bat an eyelid if an amount of U.S.$20,000 is transferred in a developed country, but the same mount transferred in a developing nation could constitute an unusually large amount. The unusual transaction threshold may be linked to the KYC obligation. This would be unusual, for example, if a civil servant transferred amounts in excess of his/her monthly income.

Record Keeping

Linked to KYC and the reporting of unusual transactions, is the need for adequate record keeping. When a suspicious transaction is investigated, a financial institution needs to be able to help authorities establish an audit trail going as far back as 5 years. The laundering of funds controlled by General Sani Abacha of Nigeria demonstrated the need for financial institutions to focus more attention on the "layering stage," where laundered funds or terror finances are already in the system and the audit trail is disguised, often with numerous transactions used to move the funds around (Botha, 2006).

An anti-money laundering officer for one of the big banks in Tanzania cynically remarked that even though banks were keeping records of transactions, tracing them was still problematic. Finding the record of a specific transaction in a storeroom was like looking for a needle in a haystack. Paperless and computerized transaction record keeping is not that well established. In this regard, local subsidiaries of banks and financial institutions in developed countries may have an edge over smaller indigenous banks.

Establishment of a Supervisory Institution

Linked with banking regulation and supervision is the need for government to establish a supervisory institution to ensure that commercial enterprises comply with the laws and regulations and that suspected cases of money laundering or terrorist financing can be monitored. Typically, such financial sector regulators are responsible for supervising AML/CTF procedures followed by financial institutions and for checking that their managers, owners, and shareholders meet the fit and proper test. Many countries have also set up specialized FIUs.

The mandate of FIUs includes investigating, analyzing, and passing on to the appropriate authorities financial and related information concerning suspected proceeds of crime or terror funds. A key component of an FIU's mandate is to share information about suspicious transactions across borders. The Egmont Group, set up in 1995, serves as an association of FIUs and promotes best practice among its members. International cooperation between FIUs in terrorist financing or money laundering cases is encouraged and based on mutual trust. Part of the mandate of FIUs is to ensure that national legal standards and privacy laws are not formulated in a way that inhibits the exchange of information. Thus, FIUs should be able to exchange information freely on the basis of reciprocity or mutual agreement and consistent with procedures understood by the requested and requesting parties.

Here again, the recommendation raises concerns for some countries. It is not only a costly exercise to establish an FIU, but also competent staff has to be recruited and trained. Mauritius, South Africa, and Zimbabwe are the only countries in the region with FIUs in place.

The Financial Intelligence Bill before the Namibian parliament will, if passed, allow the central bank, the Bank of Namibia, to collect, access, and analyze financial intelligence data and to freeze and seize the assets of suspicious institutions under investigation. This initiative exemplifies a bone of contention as regards the independence of FIUs. Ideally, an FIU should be a stand-alone institution, because links with the regulator (the central bank), a law enforcement agency (a general or specialized police agency), or the line ministry (finance) may constitute a conflict of interests. Yet, such a conflict of interests may be preferable to not creating an FIU at all. Considering the financial and developmental status of most countries in the region, this may be the lesser of two evils. At least the central bank, the police agency, or the line ministry may be able to provide financial resources, equipment, staff, and institutional memory to undertake financial intelligence work.

The FIU in Mauritius and South Africa's Financial Intelligence Centre (FIC) have received thousands of suspicious transaction reports. Data on how many of the reported cases have led to successful prosecutions are not available. Furthermore, it remains unknown whether there have been cases involving terrorist financing, as there have been no prosecutions for financing terrorism.

In addition to the reality that terrorism presents a direct and indirect threat to international, regional, national, and human security, international and regional bodies, with the assistance of civil society, also have an additional responsibility. This includes preventing draconian counterterrorism policies and legislation from provoking and legitimizing terrorism. In all political systems, whether liberal democracies or totalitarian regimes, force, coercion, and repression are double-edged swords. The prevailing challenge to all governments will therefore be to balance the protection of state security with the equally vital safeguarding of basic human rights. In addition to this, the protection of the right to free association and speech reflected in the legitimate dissent that preceded the formation of organizations, whether influenced by ideology, religion, or culture, is of prime importance. Governments need to be able to distinguish between political opposition and terrorism as a criminal act to be dealt with in a criminal court.

Excessive counterterrorism legislation and initiatives in themselves directly threaten democracy, particularly as they often criminalize and punish legitimate dissent, which might have the following two consequences: (1) forcing individuals and organizations still within the framework of legitimate dissent to resort to illegitimate violence (including terrorism) and (2) limiting the development of a healthy political system that allows political opposition. In other words, the challenge to governments and security forces is not to gather information in the name of counterintelligence operations only to protect the political order of the day; rather, they should focus on the primary role of intelligence and security agencies, which is to gather information on all activities that undermine human security.

What is self-evident is that without a functioning, nationally recognized central government, failed and weak African states provide a safe haven for domestic and international terrorism alike. No military operation can make these countries safe if it is not linked with a process ultimately aimed at reconciliation and reconstruction of a functioning state with a government in control of its territory, including its land, sea, and aerial borders. Above all, strong engagement to bring internal peace and to reconstruct failed, weak, and undemocratic states is the strategic challenge facing Africa and the international community. Civil society has a responsibility to assist our governments and their security forces to implement these initiatives. Information sharing can be a proactive strategy in building trust between governments, their security forces, and their citizens.

References

African Terrorism Bulletin. (2005). Mozambique detains Pakistani nationals with huge stash of cash. 4 (September). Pretoria: Institute for Security Studies. Retrieved on December 6, 2006, from http://www.iss.co.za/pubs/Newsletters/Terrorism/0405.htm.

Botha, A. (2006). Africa's vulnerability to terrorism and its ability to combat it. In A. Botha & W. Okumo (eds), *Understanding Terrorism in Africa: In Search of an African Voice*. Seminar report, Institute for Strategic Studies. Pretoria: Institute for Security Studies.

Fletcher, B. (2003). Deadly trade: Diamonds are an African's worst friend. *Charleston Gazette*. February 16.

Hübschle, A. (2004). Unholy alliance. Assessing the links between organised criminals and terrorists in Southern Africa. *ISS Occasional Paper 93*, Pretoria: Institute for Security Studies.

Navias, M. S. (2002). Finance warfare as a response to international terrorism. *The Political Quarterly*, 73(s1), 57–79.

Schott, P. A. (2004). Reference guide to anti-money laundering and combating the financing of terrorism (2nd edn). Washington, DC: World Bank [online]. Retrieved on July 26, 2010 from http://www1.worldbank.org.

Tambulasi, R. (2006). Research report on the vulnerabilities of NGO's, charities and schools to terrorist financing in Malawi. Unpublished.

United Nations. (1999). International Convention for the Suppression of the Financing of Terrorism, United Nations General Assembly Resolution 54/109, December 9. Retrieved on December 6, 2006, from http://daccessdds.un.org/doc/UNDOC/GEN/N00/251/28/PDF/N0025128.pdf?OpenElement.

U.S. Department of State. (2001). Patterns of global terrorism. U.S. Department of State. http://www.state.gov/j/ct/rls/crt/2001/html/index.htm

Cyber Crimes and Victimization

Use of Electronic Evidence in South African Law
Embracing Technical Change

5

FAWZIA CASSIM

Contents

Introduction

A common feature of the virtual age that we live in is the use of written communication between individuals by way of e-mails, text messages, and other written communication media rather than by way of conventional letters (Eversheds International, 2011). This has resulted in numerous documents being created, transmitted, and signed electronically. In the context of litigation, the existence of an electronic document such as an e-mail in a party's possession may well be relevant to the outcome of the case. The purpose of discovery is to ascertain from other parties to the action what information or documentation is in existence that might be relevant to the action. This enables a party to properly prepare for trial and prevents the party from being taken by surprise at the trial. The question thus arises whether parties have discovered relevant electronic documents in their possession. Such failure may be harmful to the other party's case.

Documentary evidence is required to be relevant and admissible, its authenticity must be proved, and the original document must be produced (see *inter alia, Seccombe v. AG* [1919] TPD 270 at 277; *S v. Mpumlo* [1986] 3 SA 485 (E) at 489). However, exceptions to this rule arise in the following instances: where the original document is destroyed, it cannot be located, or its production is illegal and secondary evidence is thus admissible (see *inter alia, Ex parte Ntuli* [1970] 2 SA 278 (W)). This has now changed as a result of the Electronic Communications and Transactions Act 25 of 2002 ("ECT"), which addresses electronic discovery. South African e-discovery obligations arise from the ECT read together with the Uniform Rules of Court (which were promulgated during 1965). Section 15 of the ECT creates a rebuttable presumption that data messages and printouts are admissible in evidence.

Definition of Electronic Discovery

Electronic discovery refers to the discovery of electronically stored information. This includes e-mail, web pages, word processing files, computer databases, and any information that is stored on a computer or other electronic device. Electronically stored information is said to be electronic if it exists in a medium that can be read through the use of computers or other digital devices. Such media may include cache memory, magnetic disks such as DVDs or CDs, and magnetic tapes. On the other hand, paper discovery refers to the discovery of writings on paper (printed words) that can be read without the aid of electronic devices.

According to rule 35(15) of the Uniform Rules of Court, a tape recording includes a sound track, film, magnetic tape, record, or any other material on which visual images, sound, or other information can be recorded (Rules of the High Court of South Africa, 1965; Faris & Hurter, 2010). This definition was found to be wide enough to include all electronically stored information in the case of *Le Roux v. The Honourable Magistrate Mr Viana* (Case 494/06, dated November 30, 2007). However, this decision does not state further whether such electronically stored information must be in readable format or not.

Problems with Electronic Discovery

Electronic discovery can be regarded as a complex and expensive exercise because of the following factors:

- The huge volume and number of messages.
- The difficulty of erasing electronic data from hard drives.

- The problem with metadata (information that is contained in electronic documents). For example, e-mail data elements include the dates the mail was sent, received, replied to, or forwarded.
- The contents are forever changing. The metadata elements also change each time a spreadsheet or word-processed document is copied. The question of which is the best "document" for discovery creates problems for discovery.
- Electronic data cannot be separated from its environment. To illustrate this, information in a database requires an application for interpretation, so an application is necessary.
- Upgrades and technological changes may also impact on the recovery of data. The necessary personnel or technological infrastructure may not be available when the data need to be accessed.
- Different locations of electronic data: while documents can be boxed or stored in filing cabinets, electronically stored information can reside in many locations, such as desktop hard drives, laptop computers, network servers, floppy disks, CDs, and backup tapes, and have similar copies.
- It could also be an expensive exercise to engage the services of computer forensic experts (Cilliers et al., 2009).

Relevant Legislation

The ineffectiveness of the South African common law to combat cybercrime led to the promulgation of the ECT (Burchell, 2002). The advent of the ECT has impacted on electronic discovery. The traditional requirement for documentary evidence was that it must be relevant and admissible, its authenticity must be proved, and the original document must be produced (*Seccombe v. AG* [1919] TPD 270 at 277; *S v. Mpumlo* [1986] 3 SA 485 (E) at 489). The admissibility of a printout in court in terms of the old Computer Evidence Act 57 of 1983 provided much legal uncertainty (Snail, 2009). This has now changed as a result of the ECT. Section 15 of the ECT provides that the rules of evidence must not be used to deny admissibility of data messages on the ground that it is not in its original form. The ECT thus creates a rebuttable presumption that data messages and or printouts are admissible in evidence. This is commendable.

Section 1 of the ECT defines a data message as data generated, sent, received, or stored by electronic means (Snail, 2009). A data message will not infringe the best evidence rule on the ground that it is not in its original form (Snail, 2009). The question arises as to what constitutes best evidence. The argument has been advanced that a data message produced in the form that it was originally created retains the metadata and would therefore constitute the best evidence of that message (Hughes, 2008). Hughes maintains that the "integrity" of a data message or electronic document (as required by section 14 of the ECT) can only be assessed by having regard to its metadata (Hughes, 2008). It thus appears that lawyers may insist on the production of an electronic copy containing the document metadata during court proceedings. Therefore, it is suggested that documents should be produced in their original form to ensure their integrity (Hughes, 2008).

The case of *SB Jafta v. Ezemvelo KZN Wildlife* (Case D204/07) concerned an e-mail that was used to accept an employment contract. This e-mail was regarded as conclusive proof of the acceptance of the employment contract. In *S v. Motata* (Johannesburg District Court, Case 63/968/07—now concluded), electronic information, that is, data in the form of images and sound from a cell phone, was admitted into evidence in a trial within a trial. In this case, Judge Motata allegedly drove into a wall of a private home while under the influence of liquor. The owner of the home made an audio recording of the accident on his cell phone. The judge had challenged the admissibility of cell phone recordings in his trial for driving under the influence. The recording was copied onto a computer and the issue arose whether this constituted real or documentary evidence. The judge was subsequently found guilty of drunken driving and fined R20,000 or 12 months' imprisonment (news24, 2011; *Motata v. Nair NO and Another* [2009] 1 SACR 263 (T)).

Recent Case Law Addressing Admissibility of Electronic Evidence

In *Ndlovu v. Minister of Correctional Services and Another* ([2006] 4 All SA 165 (W)), the court had to consider *inter alia* whether a computer printout, which was a copy, complied with the best evidence rule and whether it could not be admitted into evidence unless properly proved. The court found that the plaintiff's failure to object to the evidence during the trial precluded him from relying on the best evidence rule during argument. The plaintiff had also referred extensively to the printout during evidence without objecting, with the result that this amounted to a tacit waiver of the best evidence principle. The court also found that as the printout was generated by a computer, it was governed by the ECT. Thus, it examined section 15 of the ECT, and found that section 15(1)(a) prohibits the exclusion from evidence of a data message on the mere grounds that it was generated by a computer and not by a natural person, and section 15(1)(b) on the mere grounds that it is not in its original form. However, the printout was admitted into evidence not in terms of section 15 of the ECT, but rather in terms of the court's statutory discretion to admit hearsay evidence in terms of the Law of Evidence Amendment Act 45 of 1988. This case has been criticized for its failure to provide clarity on the impact of section 15 of the ECT on the authenticity rule and the hearsay rule (Collier, 2005).

In *S v. Ndiki and Others* ([2008] 2 SACR 252), the state sought to introduce certain documentary evidence consisting of computer-generated printouts, designated as exhibits D1 to D9, during the course of a criminal trial. The court found that if a computer printout contained a statement of which an individual had personal knowledge and which was stored in the computer's memory, then its use in evidence would depend on the credibility of an identifiable individual and this would therefore constitute hearsay. On the other hand, where the probative value of a statement in a printout depended on the "credibility" of the computer, then section 3 of the Law of Evidence Amendment Act 45 of 1988 would not apply. Section 3 gives the court a discretion to admit hearsay evidence if it is in the interests of justice. However, the court found that because certain individuals had signed exhibits D1 to D4, the computer had been used as a tool to create the relevant documentation. Therefore, these documents constituted hearsay. Exhibits D5 to D9 had been created without human intervention and therefore such evidence constituted real evidence. The admissibility of this evidence depended on the reliability and accuracy of the computer and its operating systems and processes. The duty to prove such accuracy and reliability was found to rest with the state. The court's progressive approach in regarding part of the computer-based evidence as real evidence has been lauded (Van der Merwe et al., 2008). It is submitted that I agree with the learned professor's comments.

It is encouraging to note that judges are admitting electronic evidence in recent criminal cases. In one case (not yet reported), cell phone evidence was allowed in a murder trial (Legalbrief, 2011), whereas in another case, the presiding officer instructed an investigating officer to find crucial CCTV camera footage in a case involving claims of police brutality (Legalbrief, 2011). In another high-profile case, Sheryl Cwele, the wife of State Security Minister Siyabonga Cwele, along with her co-accused, a Nigerian, were both found guilty of one count of dealing in dangerous dependence-creating drugs or conspiring to do so and two counts of incitement of dealing in dangerous dependence-creating drugs. The charges related to allegedly recruiting one Tessa Beetge, who is presently serving an 8-year prison sentence in Brazil for trafficking cocaine, and trying to enlist another state witness to commit a similar crime. The outcome of the trial depended on the state's submission of intercepted text messages and phone calls between the accused and Beetge (Legalbrief, 2011).

The above discussion demonstrates that our courts are following a progressive approach in e-discovery cases. The discussion demonstrates that courts are admitting electronic evidence more readily. Nevertheless, it is submitted that more clear and concise judicial guidance on the admissibility and evidential weight of electronic evidence is required in future cases.

Shifting the Costs of Electronic Discovery

The traditional position is that the costs of discovery and the costs relating to the production of documents for inspection and their production at the trial are initially borne by the party making discovery (Coumbe, 2004). However, in the United States and New Zealand, cost shifting to the requesting party is considered when an electronic discovery imposes an undue burden or expense on the producing party. The following factors are considered: the purpose of the request (whether it is specifically tailored to discover relevant information), the availability of such information from other sources, the total cost of production versus the amount in dispute, the total cost of production versus the resources available to each party, and the relative ability of each party to control costs and the related incentive (Coumbe, 2004).

The question arises whether South African courts should consider these factors in the exercise of their discretion in terms of rule 35(7) of the Uniform Rules. It has been found that circumstances should dictate the exercise of the court's discretion. The courts should either refuse to order discovery if the request is not specifically tailored to discover relevant information, or shift the cost to the requesting party when an electronic discovery imposes an undue burden or expense on the producing party (*Rubico (Pty) Ltd v. Paywell (Pty) Ltd* [2001] 2 All SA 671 (W)). This appears to be a fair approach to follow in future cases.

Role of European Convention on Cybercrime: ETS No. 185

South Africa has adopted the European Convention on Cybercrime (ECCC) but has not ratified it. South Africa is the only African country to have done so. The treaty contains important provisions to facilitate criminal investigations or proceedings and to assist law enforcement and the judiciary in their fight against transborder cybercrime. The main objective of the treaty is to pursue a common criminal policy aimed at the protection of society against cybercrime, by adopting appropriate legislation and fostering international cooperation. States are encouraged to adopt appropriate legal measures to prevent attacks on computer networks and electronic information. Therefore, South Africa needs to ratify the cybercrime treaty to avoid becoming an easy target for international cybercrime.

Way Forward: Conclusions and Recommendations

Personal computers are an important source of evidence. The differences that exist between the mechanisms of physical and digital evidence collection compound the problems of discovery, for example, home searches are conducted by physical entry while computer searches occur offsite on a government computer that stores a copy of the suspect's hard drive (Kerr, 2005/2006). Although an adequate legal framework is important for effective action against cyber criminals, such action can be frustrated by antiquated procedural laws that only authorize the issuance of warrants to search for and seize tangible evidence. This omission has serious consequences for investigators because the prosecution of cybercrime usually requires the collection and analysis of intangible evidence. Therefore, it is advocated that countries must evaluate their procedural laws governing evidence and amend them (Goodman & Brenner, 2002). Brenner also suggests that countries should evaluate their procedural laws governing the collection and analysis of evidence to include intangible evidence that is covered by cybercrime as opposed to traditional crimes that deal with tangible evidence (Brenner & Clarke, 2005). However, courts also need to understand the technical characteristics of the Internet and develop well-settled precedents to address the question of electronic discovery and the admission of electronic evidence in an intelligent and logical manner.

As we move further into the digital age, lawyers must adapt and keep abreast with changing technology. To this end, lawyers must also change the way they practice law. However, they must be mindful of maintaining a balance between the interests of effective law enforcement and fundamental human rights. South Africa needs to take the following steps to combat the growing scourge of cybercrime in the country and improve electronic discovery measures:

- Introduce specialized law enforcement and training skills.
- Improve personnel and technical infrastructure. To this end, the police and the judiciary should also become more cybercrime savvy.
- Improve computer forensic capabilities through the appointment of competent and experienced staff.
- Build regional partnerships and enter into multilateral agreements with other countries to counteract Internet crime and protect computer networks.
- Initiate support and training within government, with the help of the private sector and international organizations.
- Ratify and accede to the ECCC as the ECCC is open to accession by nonmember states.

References

Brenner, S., & Clarke, L. L. (2005). Distributing security: Preventing cyber crime. *John Marshall Journal of Computer and Information Law, 23,* 659–709.
Burchell, J. (2002). Criminal justice at the crossroads. *South African Law Journal, 119,* 579–585.

Cilliers, A. C., Loots, C., & Nel, H. C. (2009). Discovery, inspection and production of documents. In: *Herbstein & Van Winsen: The Civil Practice of the High Courts of South Africa and the Supreme Court of Appeal of South Africa* (5th edn, Vols 1 and 2). Juta.

Collier, D. (2005). Evidently not so simple: Producing computer print-outs in court. *Juta's Business Law,* 13(1), 6–9.

Coumbe, G. (2004). E-Discovery. *The New Zealand Law Journal,* 130–134.

Council of Europe Convention on Cyber Crime ETS No 185. Retrieved on June 30, 2011 from http://conventions.coe.int/Treaty/EN?treaties/html/185.htm.

Electronic Communications and Transactions Act 25 of 2002.

Eversheds International. (2011). Discovery in the Digital Age: South Africa. Retrieved on June 30, 2011 from http://m.hg.ord/law-articles/area-litigation.

Faris, J., & Hurter, E. (2010). *The Student Handbook for Civil Procedure.* Durban: Lexis Nexis Butterworths.

Goodman, M. D., & Brenner, S. (2002). The emerging consensus on criminal conduct in cyberspace. *International Journal of Law and Information Technology,* 10(2), 139–223.

Hughes, M. (2008). Electronic litigation. Paper presented at *Cyber Crime Africa 2008 Summit,* November 13, 2008, Monte Casino, Johannesburg.

Kerr, O. S. (2005/2006). Searches and seizures in a digital world. *Harvard Law Review,* 119(1–3), 532–585.

Legalbrief. (2011). Cyberfocus [online]. Retrieved on May 11, 2011 from http://www.elaw@legalbrief.co.za.

news24. (2011). Judge loses appeal [online]. Retrieved on June 29, 2011, from http://www.news24.com/South Africa/news/Judge-Motata.

Snail, S. (2009). Cyber crime in South Africa: Hacking, cracking, and other unlawful online activities. *Journal of Information, Law and Technology, 1.* Retrieved on June 30, 2011 from http://go.warwick.ac.uk/jilt/2009-1/snail.

Van der Merwe, D., et al. (2008). *Information and Communications Technology Law.* Durban: Lexis Nexis Butterworths.

Hacking and Fraud
Qualitative Analysis of Online Offending and Victimization

6

ALICE HUTCHINGS

Contents

Introduction

This research relates to computer crimes that compromise data and financial security, namely, hacking and online fraud, focusing on offenders' perceptions of victims. Very little is known about those who commit computer crimes. This is despite the increase in offending rates that have corresponded with the wider availability of computers to the general public from the 1980s and the introduction of the World Wide Web in 1991 (Moschovitis et al., 1999). These technological advances have increased the reach of offenders as well as the vulnerability of potential victims. Cybercrime offenders constitute a hidden and hard-to-access population. This qualitative analysis draws from interviews with self-identified offenders, law enforcement officers who investigate these offenses, and court documents.

The aim of this study is to examine the factors relating to online victimization. Rational choice theory and techniques of neutralization have been identified as suitable theoretical frameworks to achieve this aim. Therefore, areas that are explored in this analysis include: offenders' motivations; people or organizations that are targeted; rationalizations for offending based on victim characteristics; whether physical distance from the victim helps alleviate feelings of guilt; whether offenders believe that those who do not secure their systems or information deserve to be taken advantage of; and potential targets that are avoided due to an increased likelihood of detection or for other reasons. This work contributes to the literature relating to online victimization, providing insight through the lens of offenders, law enforcement officers, and the judiciary.

Nature of Hacking and Fraud

Hacking, for the purpose of this research, is defined as unauthorized access to a computer system, regardless of the motive, or misuse of legitimate access to a computer system. Misuse of legitimate access to a computer system, or insider abuse of access, occurs when hackers abuse the trust they have been given, such as an employee or contractor accessing or altering an employer's data (Shaw et al., 1998). Computer fraud refers to the use of information and communication technology to manipulate others into providing money or identity information.

Some of the activities pursued by computer enthusiasts have been labeled as criminal. One example is "hacking," an umbrella term that, these days, encompasses a variety of pursuits that compromise computer security but overall refers to gaining unauthorized access to a computer system with or without a further criminal motive (Brenner, 2007; Wall, 2007). Once access has been gained, hackers may obtain confidential information, such as credit card details, or "deface" websites. Hackers may employ social engineering techniques as well as technical methods to gain access to computer systems.

A number of studies have examined the hacker subculture. For example, Meyer (1989) found that hackers had an extensive social network, which was used for expertise and skill advancement. Holt (2007) examined how hackers learned, through these online social networks, as well as through trial and error, the use of forums, and offline connections. Perceived and reported motivations for hacking and computer fraud offenses are many and varied, and hackers may be motivated by more than one factor. Table 6.1 summarizes some of these motivations, drawn from the relevant literature.

Computer fraud, for the purpose of this research, involves a large number of frauds that are conducted in the online environment. Online fraud may be conducted to manipulate others into providing money or identity details, using a variety of mediums, including e-mail, social networking sites, such as chat or dating websites, and online trading sites (Brenner, 2007; Finch, 2007).

Table 6.1 Motivations Reported in the Literature

Motivation	Key Cited Literature
Curiosity and self-education	Barber (2001); Chantler and Broadhurst (2006); Jordan and Taylor (1998); Standing Committee on Communications (2010); Taylor (1999)
Ecological, political, and ethical activism ("hactivism")	Australian Institute of Criminology (2005); Barber (2001); Chantler and Broadhurst (2006); Furnell (2002); Standing Committee on Communications (2010); Taylor (1999)
Financial gain, such as through extortion, espionage, or fraud	Australian Institute of Criminology (2005); Barber (2001); Chantler (1995); Chantler and Broadhurst (2006); Coleman (2006); Furnell (2002); Shaw et al. (1998); Standing Committee on Communications (2010)
Feelings of power	Australian Institute of Criminology (2005); Jordan and Taylor (1998); Taylor (1999)
Damage other countries or political parties, such as through information warfare	Barber (2001); Berson and Denning (2011); Standing Committee on Communications (2010)
Demonstrate, test, and challenge skills	Australian Institute of Criminology (2005); Chantler (1995); Furnell (2002); Goode and Cruise (2006)
Obtain social status	Australian Institute of Criminology (2005); Chantler (1995); Jordan and Taylor (1998); Standing Committee on Communications (2010); Taylor (1999)
External pressure, such as from terrorism organizations or organized crime groups	Chantler and Broadhurst (2006)
Anonymize future attacks	Australian Institute of Criminology (2005)
Settle personal grievances	Australian Institute of Criminology (2005); Chantler and Broadhurst (2006); Coleman (2006); Furnell (2002); Shaw et al. (1998)
Use system resources for personal use	Australian Institute of Criminology (2005); Taylor (1999)
Fund terrorist activities or attack critical infrastructure for terrorism	Australian Institute of Criminology (2005); Furnell (2002); Smith et al. (2010)
"White hat" hacking, such as testing computer and network security	Australian Institute of Criminology (2005); Barber (2001); Jordan and Taylor (1998)
Addictive compulsion	Chantler (1995); Furnell (2002); Jordan and Taylor (1998); Taylor (1999)
Be free from, or escape from, the real world	Chantler (1995); Taylor (1999)
Fun, excitement, enjoyment, or pleasure	Chantler (1995); Furnell (2002); Jordan and Taylor (1998); McQuade (2006)

There are many types of online computer frauds, including identity fraud, card-not-present fraud, Internet auction fraud, investment fraud, advance fee fraud, and phishing.

There is a relationship between the two types of offenses considered in this study as hacking may facilitate fraud. For example, hacked web servers may result in compromised credit card details. Web forums provide a marketplace for malware (malicious software) and stolen data, as well as services such as the distribution of spam, web hosting, and proxy services, which may be used for fraudulent purposes (Chu et al., 2010; Franklin et al., 2007; Holt & Lampke, 2010; Motoyama et al., 2011). Similarly, hacked e-mails or social media profiles may be used to disseminate spam promoting fraudulent pharmaceuticals or other products and for the purposes of advance fee fraud.

Multiple victims may be involved in scams, such as an individual whose identity or account details have been stolen and the financial institution, government agency, or service provider that has been duped. The cost of online fraud extends beyond the direct financial loss to include loss of consumer confidence, lost time, and the emotional impact on victims.

Theoretical Perspectives

Two criminological theories provide the main framework for this analysis. Rational choice theory assumes that offenders calculate the perceived costs and benefits of crime with the assumption that they seek some type of advantage from their actions, be it "money, sex or excitement" (Cornish & Clarke, 1987, p. 935). Rational choice theory looks at how offenders in particular situations make these calculations (Vold et al., 2002). The theory acknowledges that offenders' perceptions of costs and benefits can be subjective, "constrained as they are by time, the offender's cognitive abilities, and the availability of relevant information" (Cornish & Clarke, 1987, p. 933), and therefore may not be rational at all (Akers & Sellers, 2004). Other "choice-structuring properties" (Cornish & Clarke, 1987, p. 935) are offense-specific. For example, when offenders weigh up the type and amount of benefit likely against the perceived risk of detection and punishment, they take into consideration their skills and the skills needed to successfully commit the offense and the availability of the necessary equipment or situations (Cornish & Clarke, 1987). In addition, each of these considerations may not have equal weight. For example, a high likelihood of detection may be more influential in deterring crime than harsh punishments (Clarke, 1997).

According to the second theory, Sykes and Matza's (1957) techniques of neutralization, offenders learn to use techniques to justify or neutralize acts that might otherwise produce feelings of shame or guilt and distinguish between "appropriate and inappropriate targets for ... deviance" (Sykes &

Matza, 1957, p. 666). Matza (1990) maintained that those who commit crime are not fundamentally different from those who do not; in fact, they spend most of their time behaving in a law-abiding way. Matza's (1990) claimed that most delinquents drift in and out of crime, enabled by the loosening of social control. The conditions that make this drift to criminal behavior possible include the use of the techniques of neutralization. These techniques are: to deny responsibility; to deny injury; to deny the victim; to condemn the condemners; and to appeal to higher loyalties (Sykes & Matza, 1957).

McQuade (2006, p. 141) states that "there has been extremely little empirical testing of established theories to explain in explicit terms why cyber crimes occur." Some exceptions are Skinner and Fream (1997), who applied social learning theory to music piracy and unauthorized computer access by a student population; Rogers (2001), who applied social learning theory and moral disengagement to hackers; and Patchin and Hinduja (2011), who applied general strain theory to cyber bullying. Digital piracy has also been examined using low self-control and social learning theory as frameworks (Higgins, 2004), as well as the techniques of neutralization (Higgins et al., 2008).

Turgeman-Goldschmidt (2009) interviewed Israeli hackers and identified their use of the techniques of neutralization. Walkley (2005) discussed how the techniques of neutralization may explain computer crimes, but she did not conduct an empirical test of this theory. Interestingly, Turgeman-Goldschmidt (2009) and Walkley (2005) came to quite different conclusions about the applicability of some of Sykes and Matza's (1957) proposed neutralizations. For example, Turgeman-Goldschmidt (2009) found no evidence that offenders engage in denial of responsibility, which was the technique of neutralization that Walkley (2005) argued had the greatest support. Pontell (2002, p. 319) has called for more "explanation and theory testing and ethnographic and descriptive study" into these types of crime in order to strengthen criminology as a discipline, particularly in its understanding of emerging deviant and criminal behaviors.

Research Questions

Rational choice theory and techniques of neutralization provide frameworks for thinking about how offenders may go about victim selection, particularly who might be targeted or avoided. For example, rational choice theory examines the likelihood of detection, the level of technical skills required, or the level of anticipated benefit. The costs to offenders are not limited to the punishments meted out by the criminal justice system, but could also include feelings of guilt or shame, which may be mediated by the Internet as offenders are not in physical contact with their victims. The techniques of neutralization may also inform target selection, as the characteristics of some potential victims may be more conducive to neutralization than others. Therefore, with these theories in mind, the areas explored in this study include:

1. What are offenders' motivations?
2. What people or organizations do offenders target?
3. What people or organizations do offenders avoid?
4. Do offenders rationalize their actions based on victim characteristics?
5. Does physical distance from the victim help alleviate feelings of guilt?
6. Do offenders believe that those who do not secure their systems or information deserve to be taken advantage of?

Method

A qualitative research design was selected for its ability to provide a deep understanding of the offending behavior. This study involved three stages. The first stage was a qualitative analysis of court documents, in particular sentencing remarks and court judgments relating to prosecutions and extraditions involving computer fraud and unauthorized access in Australia, the United Kingdom, the United States, and New Zealand. A systematic review of legal databases was conducted to identify relevant cases. Only documents available on public databases were identified and retrieved. Although this resulted in a selected sample, it provides an illustration to explore the issues pertinent to this research. Of the 54 cases included in this stage, 12 were female offenders, while the remaining 42 were male. The mean age of the sample, where known ($n = 35$), was 32.7 years, ranging from 18 to 50 years. When sorted by type of offense, 44.4% ($n = 24$) had committed a fraud offense, 27.8% ($n = 15$) had committed a hacking offense, and the remaining 27.8% ($n = 15$) had committed offenses that could be classified as both hacking and fraud.

Stage two consisted of interviews with law enforcement officers within computer crime or fraud specialist units from four policing agencies in Australia, namely, the Australian Federal Police, the Queensland Police Service, Western Australia Police, and Victoria Police. These interviews focused on officers' experiences with, and perceptions of, offenders who have been identified by the criminal justice system. The interviews were one-on-one, open-ended, and semi-structured. The interviews were broadly structured as follows:

- The background of the interviewee, such as how long they had been with the policing agency, and their overall experience with these offense types
- Offender characteristics, including age, gender, family status, and employment status

- Offenders' skill, expertise, and time dedicated to offending
- Involvement in other offense types
- Involvement with other offenders
- Initiation into, and desistance from, offending
- Target selection
- Motivations
- Offenders' reactions to law enforcement

The 15 law enforcement officers interviewed in stage two included 14 males and 1 female. The interviews ranged from 32 min to 1 h and 16 min, with a mean time of 51 min.

Stage three consisted of face-to-face interviews with active and former offenders. Participants were recruited within Australia using snowball sampling, a nonrandom, purposive method. Initial recruitment used informal networks. Those known to the researcher who worked and/or studied in the IT industry were encouraged to source participants. The benefit of such an approach is that such recruiters are able to assure potential participants that the researcher is legitimate (Wright et al., 1992). Participants were also encouraged to approach additional potential participants. Recruitment consisted of advising potential participants about the research and what it entailed and providing the contact details of the researcher. In this way, participants self-identified as being members of the target population and because the participants had to contact the researcher, they were in control of the amount of personal information that they provided. The interviews were one-on-one, open-ended, and semi-structured based on a modified version of McAdams' (2008) Life Story Interview. Additional questions enquired about the following topics:

- Relationships with family members, friends, significant others, and other offenders
- Employment and living arrangements
- Time involved in offending
- Involvement in other illegal behavior
- Experiences with the police and the criminal justice system
- Age when started offending
- How the decision to start offending was reached
- How targets were chosen and what was gained
- Perceptions of getting caught and penalties
- Feelings before, during, and after offending
- People or organizations that would not be targeted
- The best and worst parts of offending
- Self-perceptions
- How skills were obtained and improved

- The extent that offending interferes with participation in other activities
- When is it okay to offend and when is it not
- Why they stopped offending and at what age (for former offenders)
- Opinions of those who do not secure their systems or information
- How morally wrong/serious hacking/fraud is
- Whether hacking/fraud should be against the law
- Friends' involvement in hacking/fraud and other types of crime
- How serious do police officers consider hacking/fraud to be and respect for police
- Opinion of school and education level

Of the seven offenders who participated in stage three, five identified as hackers and two as both hackers and online fraudsters. Five were active offenders and two identified themselves as former offenders. All participants were male, aged between 18 and 49, with a mean age of 29.7 years at the time they were interviewed. The interviews ranged from 45 min to 2 h and 18 min, with a mean time of 1 h and 39 min.

All interviews were transcribed verbatim. Data from the three stages were analyzed together to identify the themes that related to victimization and target selection. Coding of the data was mainly "concept-driven" (Gibbs, 2007, p. 44), in that the codes used primarily arose from the literature relating to the theories examined. However, "data-driven coding" or "open coding" (Gibbs, 2007, p. 45) was also utilized when other key themes arose during the analysis. NVivo, a qualitative data analysis program, was used to classify and sort the data according to the codes applied, to see how the data represented the theoretical frameworks.

Results

Question 1: What are offenders' motivations?

Many motivations for offenders were identified in the data. Financial gain appeared to be the logical motivation for fraud, whereby victims are persuaded to part with their money. However, Braithwaite (1993) prompts us to question whether financial gain, in turn, is motivated by need or by greed. To distinguish between the two, offenses motivated by need are committed by those living in poverty, but offenses that are motivated by greed or "insatiable wants" (Braithwaite, 1993, p. 222) are crimes of the wealthy.

In order to establish whether financial gain was motivated by greed or need, how the money was applied was considered. It is noted that this is a subjective measure, as what may be considered luxurious to some, may be a necessity to others. However, it was clear that in some instances, financial gain was used to meet basic needs:

He admitted that he had received the complainant's money and said that he had spent it on living expenses ... That the proceeds of the fraud were used to meet expenses including child support payments. (Case #21, male fraudster, age unknown)

However it seems clear that you committed these crimes because you were unable to get any money from any other sources. (Case #43, female fraudster, aged 45 at time of court appearance)

However, there were other instances where it appeared that the gain was not used to meet the necessities of daily life:

The moneys were spent on furniture ($12,000.00), motor vehicle repairs following two accidents ($10,000.00) and the remaining sums on personal expenditure such as restaurants, clothing and other items. (Case #30, female hacker and fraudster, aged 22 at time of court appearance)

At interview with the police you said you had no idea why you had stolen the money. You were not in financial need. You paid lump sums off mortgages, assisted your parents and bought things for yourself and gifts for others. (Case #49, female fraudster, aged 32 at time of offence)

On one occasion, the fraud commenced as the offender was in a difficult financial situation; however, it appeared that the offending continued beyond the rectification of this state:

In June 2006, after two years in this position, [he] was in financial difficulties as a result of over-spending on credit card purchases ... By the end of September 2006, after five such transactions, he had defrauded his employer of over $68,000, and was no longer in financial difficulty. In fact he had been able to spend a lot of money modifying his new partner's home and purchasing items for it. He ceased offending for about 15 months because he had all the money he wanted ... He resumed offending in late December 2007. (Case #46, male fraudster, aged 43 at time of offence)

Law enforcement officers advised that hackers and fraudsters often differed in terms of motivation. While fraudsters were always seen as being motivated by financial advantage, this was not always the case for hackers, although this appeared to be changing as hackers were identifying ways to utilize their skill sets for illicit gain:

Is suppose, what they're trying to achieve, um, yeah, typically I'd think, if it's going to be an online fraud it's going to be money based, if it's going to be hacking it's not, not financially based ... I think, probably the most, with the hacking I would say they're most likely to target their previous employment. (Law Enforcement Officer #4)

It depends what fraud you're going into. With hacking you might have an IT skill; you might want to prove yourself. You might want to get even with some-one at school, so you work out how to hack someone's, you know, a person you don't like, you hack into their account, get their email, take their email, depends what your motivation is. The financial scammers, obviously they're in it for money. People go from never having committed a criminal offence in their life to full time online scamming without any hesitation at all. Really there's a distinction between the hacking and the socially engineered crimes. (Law Enforcement Officer #9)

As was identified above, one motivation for hackers was retribution or revenge against an employer or former employer (Case #7, male hacker, aged 26 at time of court appearance; Case #19, male hacker, age unknown; Case #25, male hacker, aged 24 at time of court appearance; Case #42, male hacker, age unknown) or as the result of being unsuccessful with a job application (Case #11, male hacker, aged 28 at time of offense). Other instances of hack-ing were motivated by retribution against perceived wrongdoing by someone known to the offender, for example:

But, um, besides that, I have targeted a few people, not a few, just like one or two. Um, mainly because I didn't like them, and there was some other stuff that, um, caused a bit of shit between us. And I was quite upset with these people, so I thought, well, this is what I can do, they will never catch me. (Interview #6, male former hacker, aged 18)

One law enforcement officer recounted an investigation whereby the offender, initially motivated by changing their university grade, had then targeted those who had realized the error, as revenge:

... and he's changed his marks from fails to passes and then of course, once he's learnt that's so easy, he's been prolific ... and what's happened in this spe-cific case is he's obviously been caught, because they realised that marks had been changed because the administrators gone hang on, that student failed, why is his mark all of a sudden a pass mark. And of course, that led to report-ing to the police and we investigated it and then we charged him. You know, he saw that as the professor's fault. You made me; it's because of you I got charged ... So then he started stalking the professor. So he started stalking all the professors that had given evidence and all the staff that have given evi-dence in relation to this case, and to facilitate the stalking he compromised more accounts ... And he's using facilities like that to ring up and socially engineer the details of the professors, and once he's got that, arrange for their phones to be disconnected and their power to be disconnected, so, that whole revenge motivation then comes into play and it's in full swing. You know, and he's compromised people's accounts, he's reading all their emails, he's sending emails, setting up dodgy gmail accounts in the professors' names, signing up to websites, sending them emails purporting to be a professor to gain access into other sites, it just blew out of control. (Law Enforcement Officer #8)

Parker (1998) claimed that some hackers have extreme political views, including anarchist, Nazi, or extreme right wing associations. However, while law enforcement officers advised that there were hackers targeting sites for political reasons, they also indicated that this was a small minority:

Um, look, I think it's a couple of things. I think it's mainly for money, you do see the occasional hactivist group, but it very much tends to be monetaris-ing that skill set. Um, so, and, yeah, so that's the main cause that they come to, it's about getting the money out of the system as much as you can. (Law Enforcement Officer #13)

Yeah. Look, there's not many that's political … you might get the odd one for political motivation that, you know, that send something to the government or do something to affect the government, or some other agency, body, they'll do that for that sort of a gain. (Law Enforcement Officer #7)

It appeared that political ideology was overrepresented in the media compared to hacking for other purposes:

Yeah. I'd say there are political reasons. Targeting sites … So we don't have a lot of those here. Besides what we see in the media. (Law Enforcement Officer #4)

Of the motivations identified in the literature, the data from these stud-ies supported (1) to demonstrate, test, and challenge skills; fun, excitement, enjoyment, or pleasure; curiosity and self-education; feelings of power; espio-nage; (2) to obtain social status; and (3) to anonymize further attacks. Many offenders obtained more than one benefit from their offending.

A number of unique motivations were identified in this research, namely, righting perceived unfairness, to commit further offenses, and for sexual gratification. In the following case, the offender had granted members of the public relief from taxation due to perceived unfairness:

There was no financial gain to the appellant in taking this course. He did so because of a desire to expedite the process, a heavy workload and concern about suggested inconsistencies in determinations of applications for relief. (Case #1, male hacker, age unknown)

One of the hackers and fraudsters interviewed also claimed that he first started offending due to apparent injustice:

Oh. One of the network admins at school had, what's it called, one of the network admins at school had Mist on his computer, or on his account. School children aren't allowed games on their computers. That's not fair, you're playing it! We can play it at lunchtime. No, you're not allowed it. That's for me. Right. No, it's for everyone, it's not fair. That was the first bit … That was ah, yeah, that was the first time I think. The first time I ever did something dodgy with a computer. And then I committed fraud on his computer, signing him up to a whole bunch of stuff. (Interview #5, male hacker and fraudster, aged 22)

A law enforcement officer advised how identity fraud was used to commit further offenses, namely, drug trafficking:

Oh, yeah, I'd say drug trafficking … Well, it helps support their operation, those particular deceptions were used, um, more so for travel arrangements. Interstate and overseas … Yeah, so the online fraud was used to purchase tickets to travel interstate for the purposes of trafficking. (Law Enforcement Officer #4)

Motivations relating to sexual gratification included hosting child exploitation material on compromised servers, as well as obtaining access to photographs and impersonating another for erotic purposes:

He hacked in to someone's MSN and then pretended to be the guy, pretended to be that person, and then was chatting to that person's girlfriend, and basically it got quite lurid and stuff like that. And the girl realised it wasn't her boyfriend and backed out sort of thing. (Law Enforcement Officer #11)

No, they would, I suppose almost stalk, they were sending out emails from that account, or uploading photos or contacting other people requesting sexual favours. And, even putting it politely to start with, yeah, it was bizarre. (Law Enforcement Officer #4)

Question 2: What people or organizations do offenders target?

Six main themes arose when analyzing the data in relation to types of people or organizations that would be targeted, namely, systems known to or accessible by the offender; companies perceived as undertaking questionable activities or offending ideological reasoning; those that are perceived as having wronged the offender; those who have known vulnerabilities or are perceived as being easy targets; indiscriminate targets, based on chance; and targets providing a high reward.

Ease of access appeared to be a factor that explained why systems known to or accessible by the offender were targeted. In some instances, offenders acted on opportunities presented to them, for example:

The accused was formerly a police officer and as such had authorised access to the […] computer system. (Case #32, male hacker, age unknown)

Denial of the victim was apparent when offenders targeted companies perceived as undertaking questionable activities or offending ideological reasoning:

> I suppose you've got anything from ideology, you know, people who want to stop animal testing will purposely target sites, you know, pharmaceutical companies and things like that. Sort of along the same vein, if people who don't believe in shooting animals, you know, will target a deer hunting website and graffiti that. (Law Enforcement Officer #5)

Law enforcement officers also stated that offenders were targeting those that they perceived had done them wrong:

> As far as hacking, unauthorised access, we've had a few where they've been ex-employees, in general the disgruntled employee's been dismissed for whatever reason, uses those privileges that they have, the company sometimes fails to secure the network after that person leaves and they just access it without authority later on. Either using their own credentials or using someone else's. (Law Enforcement Officer #2)

Some targets were selected because they had known technical vulnerabilities, thereby lessening the effort required to gain unauthorized access:

> You can target an SQL database with credit card details. And they target those because they can run exploits and they can scan vulnerable, say, SQL database targets. (Law Enforcement Officer #1)

Offenders also admitted that they chose their targets based on the likelihood that their activities would go undetected:

> When you go with the bigger companies it's easier to get what you want because, for the most part, they're busier, their policies and procedures overlook everything. Where smaller companies tend to have more of a wire tooth comb policy. You know, they go through everything a little further. So it's easier to deal with something big or something like that. (Interview #1, male hacker and fraudster, aged 27)

Some targets were obtained by chance, with the Internet allowing offenders to obtain a large number of targets with little cost in terms of time or involvement:

> I think, what we find online is that they target so many people and so rapidly and economically, it doesn't cost you any more to hit one than to hit thousands, it's almost a scattergun approach. You look at, like, bot herding and bot cultivation, which is the biggest risk on the internet bar none, that's very much

a scattergun. They write their bot code and put it on YouTube and Facebook and MP3s. And then they just spread it online and see what comes back. (Law Enforcement Officer #1)

Finally, some targets were selected due to the amount of the perceived benefit to the offender:

Yeah, basically I like to put it in the terms of a return on investment. Um, you know, we've seen countless times in logs and so forth, where they talk about this account has only got ten thousand dollars in it, I need accounts with forty thousand dollars in it. So, basically there's a cost for them to move the money and the corresponding cost if you will, the opportunity cost to exposing themselves to that risk of offending, so they are looking for a certain dollar value before they'll undertake those activities. (Law Enforcement Officer #13)

Question 3: What people or organizations do offenders avoid?

Just as some targets were selected because they were seen to be deserving of victimization, there was evidence that some targets were avoided if there was the potential for innocent parties to be harmed:

I've definitely come across a couple of cases where I've spoken to people and they've said that they'd never do that. You know, I suppose things like hacking into hospitals or medical centres, where people's lives may be affected by the data, you know, medication and things like that. (Law Enforcement Officer #5)

Likewise, potential targets were spared if they were seen to be undeserving of victimization:

It's not fair to kick them while they're down though. [...] you don't have a deaf person that's just had five people die and given their credit card number out to the funeral home and then say oh, I need a CD player, and then, you know, try and jack that person for it. Um, it's really really bad ethics to do it in the first place, but there's still, there's at least a little bit of honour to it. (Interview #5, male hacker and fraudster, aged 22)

One law enforcement officer advised that offenders were not likely to victimize those who could potentially retaliate against them:

I don't think they would target you know, anything that could really hurt them. You know, like Russian organised crime or the Chinese government. (Law Enforcement Officer #12)

Similarly, another officer advised that offenders were not likely to target government or military sites:

I'm pretty sure that most would steer away from.gov or.mil sort of things. You know, if they knew what they were doing. If they saw a target come up and it was like .gov or a .mil site they'd probably much prefer to go off to the you know, the Swedish web shop rather than the government installation, so there probably is a bit of self-preservation in there. (Law Enforcement Officer #14)

As mentioned above, one offender advised that he selected large businesses as fraud targets as they were less likely to detect abnormal transactions. Conversely, one hacker advised that he avoided large businesses as they were more likely to try and identify who he was:

I would never target the government or big businesses or, I never really target people who know about that stuff as well, and could actually track me down. Like, I wouldn't target a big business because they obviously have the power to do something about it. (Interview #6, male former hacker, aged 18)

Question 4: Do offenders rationalize their actions based on victim characteristics?

Offenders reportedly rationalized their actions if they perceived that there was little or no loss to individual victims:

Because they know, if they rip someone off generally the banks will reimburse them or if they're ripping someone off on an online auction site there's Paypal. Paypal will reimburse them. All the big organisations will cop the hit, not so much the individual. We've had some of them say in regards to those types of offences, they actually think they're excuses, that they picked that site because they knew that site had a policy that if people would be reimbursed, so they didn't want to actually target the particular victim, they just wanted the money out of the site, they knew the site would reimburse the money. (Law Enforcement Officer #2)

Well, for a lot of credit card fraud it's, you know, the banks have got lots of money, the banks will give the customers the money back anyway so, yeah, they try to make out as if it's a victimless crime. (Law Enforcement Officer #12)

Another rationalization related to the neutralization technique of "appeal to higher loyalties," particularly where it was seen that the offenders' actions were for the common good, such as instances where there was a lack of transparency on behalf of the victim:

I think the reality is that the people, the perpetrators of the problem, in this particular instance, the climate change debate, was the university. [...] there was no free speech, [...] if you've got something to hide, you know, there's a problem there. (Interview #4, male former hacker, aged 49)

Offenders also appealed to higher loyalties by claiming that their behaviors revealed vulnerabilities that would ultimately make the Internet a safer place, for example:

> Sometimes you get that in the hacker space, i.e. yes, I committed an offence, but I only did it to show the world that, you know, these people should be more secure in the way they're doing their business kind of thing. (Law Enforcement Officer #13)

Another rationalization was to condemn the condemners for the harm that they had allegedly caused. This rationalization was usually ideological in nature, such as the following instance:

> He stated that his targets were high level US Army, Navy and Air Force computers and that his ultimate goal was to gain access to the US military classified information network. He admitted leaving a note on one army computer reading: 'US foreign policy is akin to government-sponsored terrorism these days…'. (Case #28, male hacker, aged 40)

However, one officer maintained that high-level offenders operating in criminal syndicates did not rationalize their actions:

> Um, to be honest, most of the organised crime guys, they're not really looking for any justification, they're there to commit fraud to make money. It's a business. Your whole justification thing is more when you're moving into that kind of grey hat, you know, I'm a social activist who operates online kind of thing. (Law Enforcement Officer #13)

Question 5: Does physical distance from the victim help alleviate feelings of guilt?

There was substantial evidence that offenders were able to resolve their feelings of guilt or remorse as they were not physically near their targets. For example:

> A lot of the extortions and threats that you get online in the social networking sites, the way people talk to each other and those sorts, they wouldn't say it to the person's face. But, because, yeah, there is that element of being removed. […] they do tend to be removed from what they're doing, removed from the consequences of their actions as well. (Law Enforcement Officer #2)

Question 6: Do offenders believe that those who do not secure their systems or information deserve to be taken advantage of?

The belief that victims who do not secure their systems or information deserve to be taken advantage of relates to the neutralization technique "denial of the victim." Offenders particularly mentioned that people or organizations that had lax password management, such as not changing default passwords, were deserving of victimization. The overall consensus of offenders could be summed up as:

> There's no defence really, if you're too stupid to secure your information then you don't deserve to be the custodian of that information. (Interview #4, male former hacker, aged 49)

Discussion

While fraudsters are mainly motivated by financial gain, hackers enjoy a variety of benefits from their activities. The data supported a number of benefits previously reported in the literature, as well as righting perceived unfairness, to commit further offenses such as drug trafficking, and sexual gratification.

There was little evidence that hacking was committed for purposes such as information warfare. By contrast, it was found that hackers would avoid government and military targets in order to avoid focus on their activities. While this may appear to contradict the wider literature that identifies these as potential targets (Barber, 2001; Berson & Denning, 2011), the sample included in this research may reflect more mainstream offenders, representing the majority rather than a minority of offenders with the appropriate skill, expertise, and relevant motives for such attacks.

One component of rational choice theory is that when offenders weigh up the type and amount of benefit likely against the perceived risk of detection and punishment, they take into consideration the skills and equipment needed to successfully commit the offense (Cornish & Clarke, 1987). This analysis identified that the types of people or organizations that were deemed to be suitable targets included systems familiar to or accessible by the offender and those that had known vulnerabilities. This indicates that cybercrime offenders are targeting systems that are easily accessible and well known to them. Many offenders also took steps to conceal their activities by removing or changing evidence that they had accessed particular systems. There was some indication that offenders are calculating the risks of detection and punishment when selecting victims. For example, other targets included those who did not have systems in place to detect fraudulent activities, further reducing the likelihood of detection.

The data indicated that offenders are employing the techniques of neutralization, particularly denial of the victim. Companies perceived as undertaking questionable activities or offending ideological reasoning were perceived to be fair game. Revenge or retribution was also a common theme that emerged in cases where targets were selected because they were alleged to have wronged the offender. However, offenders avoided targets if they were undeserving of victimization or if they were aware of the potential harm arising from their actions that would impact innocent parties. Other targets were selected indiscriminately, based on chance. The rationalizations for offending based on victim characteristics were ideological in nature, including the loss impacting major corporations rather than individual victims. Some offenders appealed to higher loyalties when hacking in order to obtain information where it was seen that the victim lacked transparency and the release of that information was in the public's interest. Consistent with Turgeman-Goldschmidt's (2009) findings, there was little evidence that offenders engaged in denial of responsibility.

This study also found that physical distance from the victim does help alleviate feelings of guilt and that offenders do believe that those who do not secure their systems or information deserve to be taken advantage of.

Reliability, Validity, and Reflexivity

This section will address some of the pertinent issues relating to reliability, validity, and reflexivity. In relation to reliability, it is possible that the data obtained is not an accurate depiction, that is, that the information provided is not truthful or valid. This may occur because the participant had trouble with recollection, misinterpreted the question, or preferred not to give an honest answer. It may be asked how the researcher can believe the accounts of those who, due to the subject matter, may be untrustworthy. However, Wright and Bennett (1990) have examined the literature relating to the truthfulness of accounts given by offenders during qualitative interviews. They conclude that much of the information provided during interviews agrees with official records, and that, after agreeing to be interviewed, offenders perceive lying to be pointless, as they may as well not have consented at all. In addition, during the interviews with active and former offenders, time was spent checking for distortions and exploring the participants' responses with them to seek clarification. Some questions were also asked in more than one way in order to compare the responses. For example, the questions "how did you choose the targets that you did" and "what type of target do you avoid" are both aimed at examining the applicability of rational choice theory in relation to risk, reward, and difficulty levels.

Another problem with reliability may be "definitional drift" (Gibbs, 2007, p. 98), where the meanings of codes may change over time. Notes were made on all the possible meanings of each code to enable a more reliable and stable coding system.

The validity of the research design was improved by triangulation (Gibbs, 2007). The different sources of data and theories tested allowed for two types of triangulation, namely, "triangulation of measures," as there are different methods of data collection, and "triangulation of theory," as multiple theoretical perspectives have been utilized (Neuman, 2006, pp. 150–151).

Reflexivity refers to the preconceptions and effects that the researcher brings to the study, for example, preconceived notions of what the research will find, which may affect how questions are asked, or biases and experiences toward the subject being researched (Gibbs, 2007). Reflexivity has gained much attention in qualitative studies; however, this challenge to objectiveness may also be applied to quantitative research designs (Gibbs, 2007). Reflexivity may also change during the research project, as the researcher's interpretations and understandings adjust to the phenomenon studied. Gibbs (2007, pp. 92–93) provides some suggestions for "reflexive good practice," including critically assessing the data and biases held by the researcher, being explicit about any theoretical models and the assumptions that these may hold in relation to broader values, discussing what decisions were made and why, and avoiding oversimplification of the data.

Conclusion

Offender techniques are constantly evolving, as are the technologies that present the opportunities to offend. Therefore, it is argued that a strategic approach to crime prevention should be implemented. This can include technical countermeasures, such as firewalls, antiviruses, and other target-hardening techniques. However, in many instances, the vulnerabilities exist at the user level, with offenders using social engineering tactics to gain access to systems. Therefore, educating potential victims about computer security is also essential. However, there is a large pool of susceptible targets, and offenders are constantly changing their methods. Thus, it is important to know more about these types of offenses so that alternative deterrence strategies can be developed.

Limitations

It is noted that limitations may arise due to biases within the research design. For example, as noted by Smith et al. (2004), the limitations of using court documents include the fact that many matters are heard in the lower courts where judgments may not be published and that it is difficult to determine which matters involve computer crime due to the classification of offenses. Another limitation that is relevant to stage one is that cases brought before the courts are unlikely to be representative of the larger population of hackers and online fraudsters who are not apprehended or prosecuted. Interviewing active and former offenders mitigated this limitation.

However, the sample of active and former offenders was not chosen at random; therefore, it may be argued that the participants are not representative of the offender population. In addition, those who agree to be interviewed may differ from the typical offender. Nonetheless, although this sample is not likely to include offenders who have worked for, or are part of, a terrorist organization or organized crime syndicate, it may include more mainstream offenders who, collectively, may cause significant damage or fear of victimization. Again, this limitation was minimized by including offenders who have been identified by the criminal justice system and those who have not.

Acknowledgments

I would like to thank those who participated in this study and the assistance provided by the Australian Federal Police, the Queensland Police Service, Western Australia Police, and Victoria Police. I also appreciate the support of my supervisors, Dr. Hennessey Hayes, Associate Professor Janet Ransley, Professor Simon Bronitt, and Professor Peter Grabosky.

References

Akers, R. L., & Sellers, C. S. (2004). *Criminological Theories: Introduction, Evaluation and Application* (4th edn). Los Angeles, CA: Roxbury.

Australian Institute of Criminology. (2005). Hacking motives. *High Tech Crime Brief,* 6, 1–2.

Barber, R. (2001). Hackers profiled: Who are they and what are their motivations? *Computer Fraud & Security,* 2(1), 14–17.

Berson, T. A., & Denning, D. E. (2011). Cyberwarfare. *Security & Privacy, IEEE,* 9(5), 13–15.

Braithwaite, J. (1993). Review: Crime and the Average American. *Law & Society Review,* 27(1), 215–231.

Brenner, S. W. (2007). Cybercrime: Re-thinking crime control strategies. In Y. Jewkes (Ed.), *Crime Online* (pp. 12–28). Devon: Willan Publishing.

Chantler, A., & Broadhurst, R. (2006). *Social Engineering and Crime Prevention in Cyberspace: Technical Report.* Brisbane: Queensland University of Technology.

Chantler, A. N. (1995). Risk: The profile of the computer hacker. PhD thesis submitted to Curtin University.

Chu, B., Holt, T. J., & Ahn, G. J. (2010). Examining the creation, distribution and function of malware on-line. Technical Report for National Institute of Justice. NIJ Grant No. 2007IJCX0018.

Clarke, R. V. (1997). Introduction. In R. V. Clarke (Ed.), *Situational Crime Prevention: Successful Case Studies* (2nd edn). Monsey, NY: Criminal Justice Press.

Coleman, J. W. (2006). *The Criminal Elite: Understanding White-Collar Crime* (6th edn). New York: Worth Publishers.

Cornish, D. B., & Clarke, R. V. (1987). Understanding crime displacement: An application of rational choice theory. *Criminology, 25*(4), 933–947.

Finch, E. (2007). The problem of stolen identity and the Internet. In Y. Jewkes (Ed.), *Crime Online* (pp. 29–43). Devon: Willan Publishing.

Franklin, J., Paxson, V., Perrig, A., & Savage, S. (2007). An inquiry into the nature and causes of the wealth of internet miscreants. Paper presented at the *ACM Conference on Computer and Communications Security (CCS)*, October 2007, Alexandria, VA, pp. 375–388.

Furnell, S. (2002). *Cybercrime: Vandalizing the Information Society*. London: Pearson Education.

Gibbs, G. (2007). *Analyzing Qualitative Data*. London: Sage.

Goode, S., & Cruise, S. (2006). What motivates software crackers? *Journal of Business Ethics, 65*, 173–201.

Higgins, G. E. (2004). Can low self-control help with the understanding of the software piracy problem? *Deviant Behavior, 26*(1), 1–24.

Higgins, G. E., Wolfe, S. E., & Marcum, C. D. (2008). Music piracy and neutralization: A preliminary trajectory analysis from short-term longitudinal data. *International Journal of Cyber Criminology, 2*(2), 324–336.

Holt, T. J. (2007). Subcultural evolution? Examining the influence of on- and off-line experiences on deviant subcultures. *Deviant Behavior, 28*(2), 171–198.

Holt, T. J., & Lampke, E. (2010). Exploring stolen data markets online: Products and market forces. *Criminal Justice Studies, 23*(1), 33–50.

Jordan, T., & Taylor, P. (1998). A sociology of hackers. *The Sociological Review, 46*(4), 757–780.

Matza, D. (1990). *Delinquency & Drift*. New Brunswick: Transaction Publishers.

McAdams, D. P. (2008). The Life Story Interview. Retrieved November 12, 2009, from http://www.sesp.northwestern.edu/docs/LifeStoryInterview.pdf.

McQuade, S. C. (2006). *Understanding and Managing Cybercrime*. Boston, MA: Pearson Education.

Meyer, G. R. (1989). The social organization of the computer underground. Unpublished Masters Thesis, Master of Arts, Northern Illinois University.

Moschovitis, C. J. P., Poole, H., Schuyler, T., & Senft, T. M. (1999). *History of the Internet: A Chronology, 1843 to the Present*. Santa Barbara, CA: ABC-CLIO.

Motoyama, M., McCoy, D., Levchenko, K., Savage, S., & Voelker, G. M. (2011). An analysis of underground forums. Paper presented at the *2011 ACM SIGCOMM Conference on Internet Measurement*, Berlin, Germany.

Neuman, W. L. (2006). *Social Science Research Methods: Qualitative and Quantitative Approaches* (6th edn). Boston, MA: Pearson Education.

Parker, D. B. (1998). *Fighting Computer Crime*. New York: Wiley.

Patchin, J. W., & Hinduja, S. (2011). Traditional and Nontraditional Bullying Among Youth: A Test of General Strain Theory. *Youth & Society, 43*(2), 727–751.

Pontell, H. (2002). 'Pleased to meet you … Won't you guess my name?': Identity fraud, cyber-crime, and white-collar delinquency. *Adelaide Law Review, 23*, 305–328.

Rogers, M. K. (2001). A social learning theory and moral disengagement analysis of criminal computer behaviour: An exploratory study. PhD Dissertation submitted to University of Manitoba.

Shaw, E., Ruby, K. G., & Post, J. M. (1998). The insider threat to information systems: The psychology of the dangerous insider. *Security Awareness Bulletin, 98*(2), 1–10.

Skinner, W. F., & Fream, A. M. (1997). A social learning theory analysis of computer crime among college students. *Journal of Research in Crime and Delinquency, 34*(4), 495–518.

Smith, R. G., Grabosky, P., & Urbas, G. (2004). *Cyber Criminals on Trial*. Cambridge: Cambridge University Press.

Smith, R. G., McCusker, R., & Walters, J. (2010). Trends & Issues in Crime and Criminal Justice No. 394: Financing of Terrorism: Risks for Australia. Canberra: Australian Institute of Criminology.

Standing Committee on Communications. (2010). *Hackers, Fraudsters and Botnets: Tackling the Problem of Cyber Crime*. Canberra: The Parliament of the Commonwealth of Australia.

Sykes, G. M., & Matza, D. (1957). Techniques of neutralization: A theory of delinquency. *American Sociological Review, 22*(6), 664–670.

Taylor, P. A. (1999). *Hackers*. London: Routledge.

Turgeman-Goldschmidt, O. (2009). The rhetoric of hackers' neutralisations. In F. Schmalleger & M. Pittaro (Eds.), *Crimes of the Internet* (pp. 317–335). Upper Saddle River, NJ: Pearson Education.

Vold, G. B., Bernard, T. J., & Snipes, J. B. (2002). *Theoretical Criminology* (5th edn). New York: Oxford University Press.

Walkley, S. (2005). Regulating cyberspace: An approach to studying criminal behaviour on the internet. PhD thesis submitted to The Australian National University.

Wall, D. S. (2007). *Cybercrime: The Transformation of Crime in the Information Age*. Cambridge: Polity Press.

Wright, R., & Bennett, T. (1990). Exploring the offender's perspective: Observing and interviewing criminals. In K. L. Kempf (Ed.), *Measurement Issues in Criminology* (pp. 138–151). New York: Springer-Verlag.

Wright, R. T., Decker, S. H., Redfern, A. K., & Smith, D. L. (1992). A snowball's chance in hell: Doing field research with residential burglars. *Journal of Research in Crime and Delinquency, 29*(2), 148–157.

Cyber Victimization in India
Preliminary Study*

7

DEBARATI HALDER
K. JAISHANKAR
E. ENANALAP PERIYAR
R. SIVAKUMAR

Contents

* Parts of this chapter were published earlier in Halder, D. & Jaishankar, K. (2010). Cyber victimization in India: A baseline survey report. Tirunelveli, India: Centre for Cyber Victim Counselling. Published with permission.

Introduction

In India, the use of cyberspace for professional as well as personal communications has increased since the beginning of the new millennium. However, cyber usage is a double-edged weapon. On the one hand, it has brought a new era of communications; on the other hand, the perils of the misuse of private information are more pronounced.

In India, cybercrime and victimization in cyberspace is a subject of great concern, but lacks awareness. A bizarre combination of the nature of attacks, ever-changing trends of victimization, limited knowledge about direct laws that address cybercrimes in India, and the rights of victims in cases of cyber attacks contribute greatly to the contemporary cyber victimization scenario. Today, millions of Internet users in India are frequenting cyberspace on a regular basis for professional, commercial, social, and educational purposes. Since the boom in the IT sector in India in the 1990s (which still continues), almost every household in the moderate- to high-income groups has Internet access at home and people in the age group of 13–70 years who belong to these clusters regularly use the Internet either at home, in the workplace, at educational institutes, or at cybercafes. However, along with Internet dependency, the victimization of "cyber citizens" and those who are not on the "Internet" has grown at an alarming rate, despite India's exclusive legislation dedicated to information technology, e-governance, e-commerce, and also e-socialization to a certain extent, which has hardly helped in curbing the ever-increasing victimization of individuals in cyberspace in India.

Regrettably, less awareness means more victimization and cyberspace victimization is no exception. In India, awareness of cyber victimization has remained limited to several informative and useful tips on how to save one's personal computer and personal data from identity fraud, emotional blackmailers, and so on. A comprehensive empirical survey on this issue is needed at this time.

Review of the Literature

An international survey conducted by Norton among 7066 adults aged 18 and over across 14 countries, including Australia, Brazil, China, Germany, India, Japan, New Zealand, the United States, and the United Kingdom, found that 76% of Indians are victims of cybercrime. Virus and malware attacks affected the majority of the victims (60%).

The gravity of the problem of interpersonal cybercrime victimization could be vouched from the 2009 report released by the Mumbai police (HT Correspondent, 2010), which stated that the Mumbai police had received around 268 complaints from women regarding the misuse of cyberspace, including social networking sites. In India, the phrase *cyber victimization* has become limited within the four conceptual pillars of cyber terrorism, phishing, defamation, and pornography. This study points out that cyber victimization of individuals in India may not be limited to phishing, defamation, or pornography, but may also include adult bullying, stalking, cyber hatred, and cyber flaming.

Despite the lacunae in research on cybercrime victimization, it has become the focal point of some contemporary criminologists (Alshalan, 2006; Desai & Jaishankar, 2007; Halder & Jaishankar, 2008, 2009, 2010; Kumar & Jaishankar, 2007; Roberts, 2008, 2009; Umarhathab et al., 2009), and further research work in this area is currently underway (Halder & Jaishankar, 2011). Much research has been carried out on individual cyber victimization cases, such as *cyberbullying* (Berson et al., 2002; Burgess-Proctor et al., 2010; Campbell, 2005; Finn, 2004; Halder & Jaishankar, 2011; Hinduja & Patchin, 2007, 2008, 2009, 2012; Jaishankar, 2009a; Jaishankar & Shariff, 2008; Juvonen & Gross, 2008; Kennedy, 2000; Li, 2006, 2007; Patchin & Hinduja, 2006, 2010, 2012; Shariff & Hoff, 2007; Smith et al., 2004, 2008; Spitzberg & Hoobler, 2002; Tolga Aricak et al., 2008; Vandebosch & Van Cleemput, 2008; Wolak et al., 2006; Ybarra, 2004; Ybarra & Mitchell, 2004; Ybarra et al., 2007), *cyber stalking* (Bocij, 2003, 2002; Bocij & McFarlane, 2002; McFarlane & Bocij, 2003; Medlin, 2002), *cybercrimes against women* (Halder & Jaishankar, 2008, 2011), and *sexting* (Halder & Jaishankar, in press; Ito et al., 2008; Jaishankar, 2009b; Lenhart, 2009; The National Campaign to Prevent Teen and Unplanned Pregnancy, 2009).

In the international arena, a number of statistical reports have been published on cyber stalking victimization, including Working to Halt Online Abuse (WHOA) in the United States, cyber victimization on high school students and young adults in Australia (Roberts, 2008), and cybercrimes against English users (Fafinski, 2008). While the WHOA statistics mainly reveal the year-wise growth/decline of stalking victimization of U.S. citizens and people from other countries such as Canada, England, and Australia, and South Asian countries such as Korea and Malaysia, who approach WHOA for help, Roberts' (2008) study analyzes cyber victimization in Australia from multidisciplinary aspects, such as psychology, law, and victimology. This study divided cybercrimes into two main compartments, namely, property cybercrimes such as identity theft, scams, and phishing e-mails, and interpersonal cybercrimes such as cyber harassment, cyberbullying, and cyber stalking.

The Garlik report, on the other hand, analyzed the concept of cybercrime from criminological perspectives. This report mainly concentrated on identity theft and identity fraud, financial fraud, and offenses against the person, such as cyber harassment, defamation, computer misuse, and sexual offenses. It pointed out that cybercrime is a "pressing and prevalent social problem." This report also emphasized issues such as less reporting by the victims and legal loopholes. There are little or no studies dealing with cyber victimization in India. Barring one study (Halder & Jaishankar, 2010), until now, a holistic study on interpersonal cybercrime victimization has not been done in India. The current research work tries to fill the gap in the literature in this area.

Preliminary Study on Cyber Victimization in India

On behalf of the CCVC, we conducted a preliminary survey with a sample size of 73 respondents (60 respondents were female) from all over India on cyber victimization of women and the related awareness among women and men in India (Halder & Jaishankar, 2010).

The goals of the current survey are:

- To examine the level of awareness of adult Internet users of modern cybercultures, the trends of victimization and common legal rights
- To spread awareness about the various trends of cyber victimization of adult Internet users

The objectives of the study are:

- To examine the trends of individual victimization
- To analyze the level of awareness about the victimization that occurs in cyberspace
- To know about the respondents' awareness of common legal principles and legal rights regarding Internet crimes

Methodology: Research Tool, Samples, and Data Collection

The research tool used for this study is a structured questionnaire. This survey is designed with the purpose that the sample selection should closely represent the characteristics of the target population, that is, the general adult Internet users of India, who may or may not be aware of the nature of their victimization in cyberspace.

The target population consists of 73 respondents (including 13 male and 60 female) from different regions of India, who are computer literate and Internet savvy and use social networking websites for virtual hanging out.

These respondents belong to different economic and social strata and they may or may not have personal computers at home. The researchers contacted 100 respondents by e-mail and 73 responded. Several of these 73 respondents also gave specific feedback, which helped us to frame our observations more accurately.

Results and Discussion

Cyberculture

Cyberculture could be defined as a compact term that expresses the norms and cultures that are followed in cyberspace or on the Internet. Often, the word cyberculture is used in context with varied meanings, including the culture of hacking or computer revolution or cybercultural issues like cyber topics, cyber organization (see Macek, 2005), etc. Clarke (1997) has significantly associated the term *cyberculture* with authorities in cyberspace, such as Internet service providers (ISPs), e-news groups, and cyber communities. For the purpose of this chapter, we construe the term *cyberculture* as "a conglomeration of cyber rules, norms, cultures, and principles generally provided by the Internet service providers (inclusive of website hosts, chat line providers, and e-mail providers) and those rules and cultures which may or may not have legal sanction, but which are generally expected to be followed by the common internet users."

Hence, in this context, cyberculture may mean the following:

1. Knowledge of minimum age to join any cyber community
2. Personal information-sharing activities
3. Use of the freedom of speech

Knowledge of Minimum Age

It is evident from Table 7.1 that among the 73 respondents, 56.2% are aware of the basic age limit for joining any cyber community/groups/social networking sites. It is to be noted that these 73 respondents are adults and the majority of them are "Internetting" for more than 5 years. This particular assessment was necessary as many of these respondents have children who are either preteens, teenagers, or young adults. The majority of the respondents felt that only mature users should use cyber communities, social networking sites, and chat rooms. These respondents are also aware that impersonating as a child (when the user is an adult or a young adult and camouflages as a preteen or teenager to groom women and children for cyber nuisances including sexual crimes) in chat rooms or social networking sites and trapping other children or women especially, is ethically wrong and can lead to serious legal problems.

Table 7.1 Awareness of Cyberculture among Indian Internet Users

	Yes (%)	No (%)
1. Knowledge of minimum age to join cyber communities, such as Facebook, Orkut, and Myspace	56.2	43.8
2. Allow others to use one's own e-mail ID/profile ID/passwords, etc.	46.6	53.4
3. Use safety tips, such as filtering e-mails, locking personal albums and information, personal walls of social networking sites, and so forth	69.9	30.1
4. E-mail back to unknown senders of spam/pornographic/erotic/ phishing e-mails	37.0	63.0
5. Share personal information/emotions with virtual friends/ chat-room partners, and so forth, whom one does not know in real life	74.0	26.0
6. Believe in controlling free speech while communicating in cyberspace	37.0	63.0
7. Read policy guidelines of social networking sites, ISPs, etc.	28.8	71.1
8. Use pseudo names	45.2	54.8

Allowing Others to Use One's Own ID and Password

Of the respondents, 46.6% allow others, such as their spouse, children, or intimate partner, to use their ID and passwords. Surprisingly, this 46.6% also includes a fraction of those who belong to the 56.2% of the respondents who are aware of the minimum age for joining cyber communities. These respondents primarily allow their spouse or intimate partner to use their IDs and passwords to check any e-mails or messages that they may have received during their absence from cyberspace. They feel comfortable knowing about such "vacation messages" from their spouse or intimate partner and they trust that their spouse or intimate partner will not misuse these IDs. When asked about children who use their parents' IDs, these respondents gave a cumulative answer that the children use their parents' IDs for communicating with their parents when they are away from them or communicating with friends of their own age (who are probably using their parents' IDs in the same fashion) and this is done under the strict vigilance of the parents.

Using Safety Tools and E-mailing Back to Unknown Senders

Of the respondents, 69.9% are aware of the various self-protection tools on the Internet, for example, filtering e-mails, blocking unwanted persons, and locking one's personal walls, albums, and information in the social networking sites. These individuals have used such options either by learning from their own mistakes or from various safety tips available on the Internet. Of the respondents, 30.1% do not believe in restricting their e-mails/chat boxes/social networking sites only to known friends and they do not use the safety options; 37% e-mail/message back to any e-mails/messages that they receive from unknown sources, including strangers and spammers. These respondents communicate with such strangers more out of curiosity than necessity. Of the respondents, 74% share personal information, such as their home address, telephone numbers, personal favorites, personal pictures, mood swings, opinions about other friends, political parties, nonpolitical events, cinemas, holiday places, children's school details, and information on spouses' workplaces and other related information with virtual friends in social networking communities, chat partners, and so on, whom they have never seen in real life, but are in regular contact through e-mails, messages, and phone calls.

On Exercising Free Speech for Communicating in Cyberspace

An awareness of cyberculture also includes the typical way of exercising the right to "free speech" in cyber communications. These communications may include e-mails, chats, the language used for writing on others' message boards, and writings on community walls or bulletin boards. We found out that only 37% of the respondents believe in exercising the right to free speech in a controlled and measured way. Some of these respondents also exercise similar communicative language when they express their feelings through blogs. Many of these respondents felt that informal communications should be limited to those whom they have known for a long time in real life or close relations, such as siblings and cousins. It is to be noted that the concept of free speech in India* differs from that in the United States and other countries. This stands true even for cyber communications. What could be "free speech" in the United States† may not be "decent," "wanted" speech or way of expression in India. However, it should also be noted that 63% of the respondents felt that there is no need to be formal or control speech or expressions in the written form while in the cyber social networking sites or chat rooms or even in e-mails. Some felt that this is an extended version of friendship and a growing relationship and hence the communication should be as informal as it would be in real life between two friends or a group of close friends, even if they do not know each other in real life. Some felt that

---

* As has been guaranteed under Article 19(1)(a) of the Constitution of India; Article 19(2) of the Indian constitution lays down the grounds for restrictions on the freedom of speech and expression, which are as follows: sovereignty and integrity of India, security of the state; friendly relations with foreign nations, public order, decency of morality, contempt of court, defamation, and incitement of an offense.

† Freedom of speech is guaranteed by the First Amendment to the Constitution of the United States, which says "Congress shall make no law respecting an establishment of religion, or prohibiting the free exercise thereof; or abridging the freedom of speech, or of the press; or the right of the people peaceably to assemble, and to petition the government for a redress of grievances." For more information, see http://topics.law.cornell.edu/constitution/first_amendment.

using harsh/teasing/rude/criticizing words will never wound the sentiments of the recipient(s).

Reading Policy Guidelines

The policy guidelines of various cyber communities and ISPs significantly contribute to the cyberculture. Many of these cyber communities have adopted their own policy guidelines to prevent hacking and related economic and sexual crimes, verbal abuse through cyber communications, child abuse, and so forth. The majority of these cyber communities have followed U.S. laws and may take precautionary actions when dealing with any complaints of abuse. In India, several U.S.-based and some Indian ISPs and cyber communities have become highly popular. The majority of the respondents of this study have indicated ISPs such as Yahoo, Gmail, Rediff, and Hotmail and networking communities such as Orkut, Facebook, Myspace, Yahoo groups, Twitter, and Zorpia as their favorite cyber hangout spaces. Notably, 71.1% of the respondents do not read any policy guidelines before joining cyber communities. It is interesting to note that many of this 71.1% belong to the group of 63% respondents who feel that communication and speech need not be restricted in cyberspace. On the contrary, 28.8% have read the policy guidelines and feel that these policy guidelines are enough to create awareness about cybercrimes, cultures, and norms.

Using Pseudo Names

Of the respondents, 45.2% prefer to use pseudo names especially when socializing through social networking communities or chatting, for various reasons including protecting their own identity; 54.8% do not use pseudo names and do not feel that protecting their privacy or identity by using pseudo names is needed.

Frequency of Cyber Networking

The second part of these findings includes research on the frequency of cyber networking among Indian Internet users. Some of these responses may be included in the first part of these findings, namely, awareness of cyberculture. However, we intend to list them under the title "frequencies" to show how often individuals hang around in these web hubs and how frequently they befriend other chat-room/social networking site partners. Table 7.2 describes the frequency of cyber networking.

The statistical data in Table 7.2 show that among the 73 respondents, 83.6% are highly active in networking through e-mails and social networking sites such as Orkut and Facebook; 15.1% of the respondents are moderately active in socializing through e-mails and networking sites; and 1.4% are least active in cyber socializing. We found that the latter two groups of

Table 7.2   Frequency of Cyber Networking

	High (%)	Moderate (%)	Low (%)
1. Frequency in cyberspace (including e-mailing, socializing through social networking sites, and cyber communities)	83.6	15.1	1.3
2. Frequency in chat rooms	71.2	28.8	—
3. Frequency in interacting with unknown chat partners	27.4	71.2	1

respondents (moderate and low) use e-mails and social networking sites mainly for business/academic/professional purposes and do not feel as comfortable socializing through cyberspace as those who form the first category (highest). Of the respondents, 71.2% are highly active in chat rooms, whereas 28.8% are moderately active in their preferred chat rooms. These respondents prefer to chat in chat rooms provided by ISPs, such as Gmail, Yahoo, Rediff, and AOL, and through online chats available on social networking sites such as Facebook and Orkut. However, we found that only 27.4% take the risk of chatting with unknown chat-room participants; 71.2% felt that it was risky to chat with unknown people and they often give a cool response to unknown persons when such persons start a conversation with the said respondents. These respondents, however, feel comfortable chatting with familiar chat-room participants, whom they may have known either in real life or previously through social networking sites; many of them prefer to chat only when such "virtual friends" through social networking sites are known for a minimum of 2–5 months, and these virtual friends have already shared their thoughts and information on community walls and previous e-mail introductions. Of the respondents, 1.4% do not chat with unknown persons.

Knowledge of Being Victimized

We preferred the title "knowledge of being victimized" to illustrate the extent to which these respondents are aware that they have become victimized. Table 7.3 describes the victims' knowledge of their own victimization.

Table 7.3 shows a mixed response to the awareness of cyber victimization. The survey aimed to cover victimization in e-mails, social networking sites, chat rooms, blogs, and search engines as a whole. It can be seen that 61.6% of the respondents had bad experiences in the social networking sites that they regularly visit to hang out and 78.1% had received obscene/abusive e-mails from known/unknown senders. These groups of respondents had opined that even if they used filters and safety measures, somehow they had been attacked through their e-mails or social networking sites; they also felt

Table 7.3 Knowledge of Being Victimized

	Yes (%)	No (%)	No Awareness (%)
Has had a bad experience in social networking sites	61.6	38.4	—
Has received abusive/obscene e-mails from known/ unknown sources	78.1	21.9	—
Has experienced hacking (either directly or indirectly)	46.6	43.8	9.6
Has experienced cyber stalking	37.0	49.3	13.7
Has experienced phishing attacks	50.7	42.5	6.8
Has been impersonated by e-mail account/social networking profiles/websites, etc.	28.3	60.3	11.4
Has seen their "cloned" profile/e-mail IDs	41.1	46.6	12.3
Has been a victim of defamatory statements/activities involving himself/herself in cyberspace	68.5	23.3	8.2
Has received hate messages in their in-boxes/message boards	42.5	47.9	9.6
Has seen morphed pictures of themselves	31.5	57.5	11.0
Has been bullied	39.7	50.7	9.6
Has experienced inflammatory messages from others	43.8	46.6	9.6
Has been victimized by their own virtual friends	45.2	53.4	1.4
Has reported incidents to the authorities	37.8	47.3	14.9
Feels women are prone to cyber attacks	74.0	26.0	—

that they had become accustomed to the idea that cyberspace is a vulnerable place and users are prone to be attacked.

Hacking, Stalking, and Phishing

Table 7.3 shows that 46.6% of the respondents had experienced hacking and they understood that their profile/e-mail ID/web page, etc., had been hacked; 43.8% had never experienced hacking as they continuously take precautionary measures to prevent hacking; 9.6% are not aware if their account has been hacked or how their accounts can be hacked; 37% felt that they have experienced cyber stalking; 49.3% had never experienced cyber stalking; and 13.7% were not aware of cyber stalking. Notably, those belonging to this 13.7% failed to understand the true nature of stalking. Indian laws do not describe cyber stalking. It is unfortunate that the term *cyber stalking* continues to be neglected in the laws of India. This particular term is not defined or explained in the Indian penal code or the Information Technology Act. Many respondents construed the term as harassment, like pornography. This misleading conception about cyber stalking arose because in the few reported cases on cyber stalking in India, the accused was booked under section 509 of the Indian Penal Code (Duggal, 2009). Section 509 speaks mainly about the harm to women's modesty and privacy and related harassments.

But stalking is not necessarily harassment alone and cyber stalking does not happen only to women, even though women may form the majority of victims of cyber staking. Duggal (2009) rightly pointed out that the said section does not cover cyber stalking fully. If we analyze the U.S. laws on stalking, the nearest explanation of cyber stalking can be found in the Violence Against Women and Department of Justice Reauthorization Act of 2005, which amended the Communications Act of 1934 (47 U.S.C. 223(h)(1)) through section 113 to include *the use of* any device or software that can be used to originate telecommunications or other types of communications that are transmitted, in whole or in part, by the Internet for the purpose of "stalking," annoying, and harassing others as a penal offense. This U.S. provision attempts to explain cyber stalking as follows:

> Cyber stalking = following the victim's internet activities + using digital device, software to create harassing, threatening, abusing mails/messages, etc. + transmitting the said mail to the victim's in-box and/or victim's friends or relative's in-boxes + successfully creating fear, annoyance, irritation harassed feeling in the victim.

In one word, when "following" is added by mens rea to commit harm and it is successfully digitally carried out, we can say that cyber stalking has occurred. Further, this study shows that 50.7% of the respondents understood that they had been victims of phishing attacks; 42.5% stated that they have never been victims of phishing attacks; and 6.8% stated that they were not aware of such attacks. The 50.7% respondents have seen phishing attacks through e-mails. The most common method is being asked to help in acquiring a lump sum of money from a deceased customer/relative, or lottery prize money. The other method is sending fake "Google/Yahoo warnings," whereby the recipient is asked to provide their name, date of birth, password, country of residence, and so forth, with a warning that if these details are not sent, their Gmail/Yahoo account will be closed. Apparently, these sorts of e-mails had arrived in the respondents in-boxes and they had opened them for further clarification. But this study does not show how many of the respondents had been victims of a phishing attack, thereby losing their money. Those respondents who were never aware of such phishing attacks had not communicated with the sender once they checked the originality of the e-mails from the Internet and also from friends and acquaintances. Of the respondents, 42.5% were already aware of such phishing e-mails and they marked them as "spams" whenever they received such e-mails. These 42.5% never opened these e-mails and from the subject header they understood that these e-mails were "phishing mails." Of the respondents, 6.8% were never aware of these phishing e-mails and they claimed that they had never received such e-mails or knew anything about phishing.

Impersonation and Related Attacks

Table 7.3 shows that 28.3% of the respondents are aware of being victimized by impersonated profiles. Impersonated profiles are fake profiles made by an individual using the screen name, personal information, or even a picture of another. The impersonator may use this profile to cheat others. Our respondents either have directly encountered such impersonated profiles through e-mails and social networking websites, or have heard about them from their friends and acquaintances. In their feedback, the respondents stated that these impersonated profiles came up either in the course of socializing through public chat rooms, social networking forums, or even in the guise of fake e-mail IDs, whereby creators of the impersonated e-mail account had taken the name of their friends or even the name of the respondents' friends. Of the respondents, 60.3% have not encountered such impersonated profiles (even though they know such pranks could be played by others) because they are rarely in cyberspace, they do not use chat options, or they use cyberspace only for professional purposes and do not allow anyone to chat or send any private e-mails/messages or entertain anyone unknown in their personal mailing list; 11.4% have never heard of impersonated profile attacks.

We also surveyed the respondents' awareness of "cloned profiles." While in the previous paragraph, we noted the awareness of impersonated profiles of others, this particular statistic shows how many respondents have seen their own impersonated or cloned profiles whereby the harasser misuses the victim's personal information and contacts. Of the respondents, 41.1% have seen their own cloned profiles in the form of either a social networking profile or an e-mail ID profile or a chat room ID profile. Apparently, these profiles may have been made either by simply creating fake profiles or using the original screen names or even sometimes by data mining from social networking sites. These respondents either saw their cloned profiles themselves or were made aware of them through friends or acquaintances. In much of their feedback, these respondents have also indicated that they had e-mails from cloned e-mail IDs. Apparently, these are proxy e-mail IDs that are often received by e-mail users, with obscene advertisements and so forth. These respondents felt uncomfortable when they first received or saw cloned or proxy profiles; 46.6% of the respondents have never seen or encountered any such cloned or proxy profiles; and 12.3% are unaware of such occurrences on the Internet.

Defamatory Statements/Bullying and Flaming Messages/ Hate Messages/Morphed Images

Of the respondents, 68.5% had seen defamatory statements about themselves in e-mail messages or community discussions or public chats; 23.3% had not seen such defamatory messages; and 8.2% responded that they were unaware of such messages. Interestingly, many of these respondents' responses were affirmative in receiving bullying and flaming messages and hate messages about themselves in their public profiles or community discussion boards and, as such, they felt that this too added to the defamatory activities against them. Of the respondents, 39.7% have received bullying messages and 43.8% have received flaming messages either in their in-boxes or in their public profiles; 42.5% have seen hate messages either in their in-boxes or in their public profiles; and 31.5% have seen their morphed pictures. Of the respondents, 23.3% indicated that they have not received or seen any such defamatory messages and would not be bothered by such occurrences and 8.2% indicated that they are unaware of any such occurrences. We presume that those who were negative in their response to receiving or seeing such messages/ images and so forth, are well aware of cyberspace culture and they feel this is normal in cyber life and hence do not worry about such cyber-generated disturbances.

Victimized by Virtual Friends

Of the respondents, 45.2% felt that they had been victimized by their virtual friends in either or all of the aforementioned ways. These respondents may have befriended these friends-turned-harassers without knowing them in real life or maybe these "friends" never bothered to abide by cyber ethics and have upset the respondents in one or many ways. Of the respondents, 53.4% indicated that they were not victimized by their virtual friends and 1.4% indicated that they have no knowledge of it. We noted that many of those who indicated that they were not victimized by their virtual friends had practiced safe cyber practices, such as not accepting everybody as a friend and accepting only those who are recommended by the respondents' existing friends; keeping a safe distance from virtual friends; and not exhibiting too much personal information.

Reporting to the Authorities

Among the respondents who are aware of cyber attacks or who have been victims themselves, 37.8% have reported such incidents to the authorities of Gmail, Yahoo, Orkut, or Facebook; 47.3% never bothered to report such incidents; and 14.9% indicated that they do not know how to report and where to report such incidents. We understand that those who reported and those who have not bothered to report may have read the "how to report" columns and other policy guidelines of service providers and those who indicated that they do not know how to report may have never read any policy guidelines regarding reporting. Of these respondents, 74% think that women are prone to attack in cyberspace. We will discuss the victimization of women in cyberspace in a later section.

Awareness of Legal Rights and Reporting Behavior

In this section, we cover the legal awareness and the reporting behavior of the respondents. Table 7.4 shows the data on the legal awareness of the respondents.

As this section deals with the awareness of cyber laws, we need to expand a little on the Indian cyber laws. India is governed by the Information Technology Act 2000 (which was amended in 2008) for cyberspace-related issues, including several cybercrimes such as hacking, computer-related offenses, offensive communications, violations of privacy, cheating by impersonation, identity theft, cyber terrorism, obscenity, child pornography, transmitting or publishing sexually explicit materials, and breach of confidentiality, and also by the Indian Penal Code. In this section, our aim is to establish how aware laypersons are of certain cyber behaviors that are deemed illegal under both Indian laws and international covenants/rules and regulations and general cyber ethics.

Table 7.4 shows that 80.8% of the respondents are aware that hacking and the creation and distribution of pornographic material are illegal, and 78.1% of the respondents are aware that they have a right to privacy in cyberspace. Only 19.2% of the respondents are aware that cyberbullying, stalking, sending annoying messages, and so forth, can be penalized. This gives the impression that as hacking and pornography-related cybercrimes are often spoken about in the newspapers, on news channels, and by the audiovisual media, including modern IT-related cinemas and daily soaps, many have become aware of these types of illegalities. On the other hand, stalking, adult bullying, sending offensive messages, and so on, are rarely spoken about in public and hence awareness about the illegalities of these types of cyber behaviors is comparatively poor. This survey also shows that when cybercrime happened, 9.6% of the respondents had opted to report the matter to the police. We noted that the reporting behavior of victims improved after cybercrime police stations became functional in almost all the major cities of India. However, 90.4% of the respondents still feel that reporting cybercrime to the police may bring more victimization and hence they prefer not to report such crime to the police.

Table 7.4   Awareness of Rights and Reporting Behavior

	Yes (%)	No (%)
Aware that hacking, creating/distributing pornography, distributing obscene material, and so forth, are criminal offenses	80.8	19.2
Aware of the legal right to protect their privacy in cyberspace	78.1	21.9
Aware that cyberbullying, cyber stalking, sending annoying, defamatory messages, and so forth, can be penalized	19.2	80.8
Has reported incidents of cyber victimization to police/lawyers/courts	9.6	90.4

Cyber Victimization of Women and Awareness

This section is dedicated to research on cyber victimization and awareness of the same on the female respondents. Table 7.5 elaborates the findings.

Table 7.5 shows that among the 60 female respondents, 11.7% had had bad experiences of some sort in cyberspace; 85% had received abusive and obscene messages from known or unknown senders and 16.7% had received repeated e-mails from the same individual/individuals asking to befriend them.

Of the respondents, 50% have received threatening e-mails/messages from ex-partners/husbands and 75% have received sexually teasing remarks in their social networking profiles and/or associated e-mail in-boxes; 48.3% have been victims of hacking; 40% have been victims of stalking; and 43.8%

Table 7.5   Cyber Victimization of Women and Reporting Behavior

	Yes (%)	No (%)	Not Aware of (%)
Experienced bad incidents on the Internet	11.7	88.3	—
Received abusive e-mails with sexual images and obscene messages from known/unknown senders	85.0	15.0	
Received repeated e-mails from the same individual/ individuals asking to befriend him/them	16.7	83.3	
Received threatening e-mails from ex-boyfriends/ husbands	50.0	50.0	
Received sexually teasing remarks/images in her social networking profile/associated e-mail/message box	75.0	25.0	
Has been the victim of hacking	48.3	41.7	10.0
Has been the victim of cyber stalking	40.0	46.7	13.3
Has experienced phishing attacks	43.8	48.3	7.9
Has been the victim of impersonation	61.7	26.7	11.6
Defamed in cyberspace/in real space due to the cyber activities of others	71.7	18.3	10.0
Has received hate messages	41.7	46.7	11.6
Has been targeted because of her sexuality/feminist ideologies	45.0	53.3	1.7
Has been the victim of morphing	33.3	58.3	8.4
Has been bullied	33.3	56.7	10.0
Has been victimized by her virtual friend/friends	40.0	58.3	1.7
Has seen her cloned profile	50.0	40.0	10.0
Feels women are prone to victimization in cyberspace	76.7	23.3	—
Feels women's communities/groups and so on are safe to discuss women's issues	38.3	60.0	1.7
Has reported victimization	35.0	46.7	18.3
Has reported incidents to police/lawyers	8.3	91.7	—

have experienced phishing attacks. The survey further shows that 61.7% of the respondents had been victims of impersonation; 50% had seen their cloned profiles; 71.7% had been defamed in cyberspace and also offline due to cyber defamation; 41.7% had received hate messages from various persons; and 45.5% had been targeted because of her sexuality and/or feminist ideologies. Of the respondents, 33.3% had been bullied and 33.3% had seen their morphed images; 40% had been victimized by their virtual friends; 76.7% feel that women are prone to victimization in cyberspace and 38.3% feel online women's communities are safe for discussing women's issues; 35% had reported cyber victimization to ISPs, etc.; and 8.3% preferred to report the incident to the police.

Major Findings

- The majority of the respondents do not feel that it is necessary to read the policy guidelines or the terms and conditions of ISPs and social networking websites before entering into a contract with these sites and opening their accounts.
- The majority of the respondents do not mind sharing their profile/account and password with their spouses and children.
- The majority of the respondents like to participate in virtual socializing; however, many are not aware of spams/phishing e-mails, etc., and often reply to these e-mails out of curiosity.
- Many of the respondents dislike chatting with complete strangers in public chat rooms and they are aware that such chat friends may be fraudulent; many dislike sharing their personal secrets with chat friends. Many of the respondents prefer to chat with people whom they have met and know through the social networking sites and have followed their responses in various posts. Regardless of whether these people have met in real life or not, such chat partners may even exchange their personal e-mails for professional as well as personal purposes.
- Several Internet users feel that in cyberspace they need not follow a strict formal rule of communication when in a group or a forum; many such Internet users are unaware of basic cyber ethics.
- The Indian social value system differs from that of the United States and European countries. Serious problems arise in cyberspace when Indian users try to adopt the Western cyberculture into the Indian social value system; glaring examples are the attack on the modesty of women in typical cyber ways, the use of abusive or harsh language in groups or forums attacking the core social/religious sentiments of other users, and the treatment of the same by Indian laws.

- Cyber defamation, sending threatening messages, and so forth, are rampant in India. Sexual crimes on the Internet are growing.
- Using bullying words in cyberspace by Indian Internet users is becoming rampant.
- Social networking sites, such as Orkut (maximum) and Facebook, are used to harass women by putting up fake profiles with or without morphed pictures, obscene descriptions, and so on.
- The majority of the respondents do not understand the true nature of stalking.
- The majority of the respondents are aware of hacking but few know how to protect themselves from hacking.
- Impersonating, emotional and financial cheating, victimizing by making cloned profiles in cyberspace, taking revenge through cyberspace for breach of romantic commitments, and so on, are growing in India.
- Many are aware that hacking, sexual crimes on the Internet, economic scams, sending threatening messages, and so forth, can invite legal problems; however, the majority of Indian Internet users are not aware that stalking is an offense that can be prosecuted. Similarly, bullying, sending annoying messages, impersonating and cheating, posting defamatory messages, and so on, are also offenses that can be prosecuted.
- Many Indian users are aware that they have a right to protect their privacy in cyberspace. However, we understand that this "privacy" may indicate their personal lives, financial information, and so forth, and may not include the awareness of the right to privacy and the right to protection against misuse of already exhibited information in their profiles, and so on.
- Very few respondents, especially women, favor reporting victimization to the police as they feel this may bring further victimization; however, many are aware of the reporting options provided by ISPs and social networking websites and some users use these options.
- In cyberspace, women are more prone to victimization than men.
- The majority of women receive e-mails from unknown men with disturbing contents, requests for friendship, and so forth, and such e-mails may be the result of data mining.
- Many women are victims of several types of harassment meted out by their former partners, including former boyfriends.
- The majority of women receive hate messages, sexual/nonsexual teasing remarks, offensive comments, and so forth, because of their feminist perceptions expressed both in blogs and on forum walls; and because of their marital status, profile pictures, profile statements, and so on, which they exhibit on their main profile page.

Recommendations

Based on the aforementioned findings, we suggest the following recommendations:

1. An awareness campaign must be launched from a grassroots level, such as in schools and colleges, about cyber ethics and probable cybercrimes, such as economic cheating, stalking activities, defamatory activities, and misusing e-mail and social networking websites.
2. The police, social workers, lawyers, and NGOs must be invited to educational institutes, corporate offices, clubs, social awareness campaigns, workshops, and seminars to talk about the legalities and illegalities of cyber conduct among adults of both genders. Reporting of cyber victimization must be encouraged at all levels directly to the police and also to NGOs working for the cause.
3. More stringent laws must be enacted to curb individual victimization in cyberspace. The present Information Technology Act only includes a few sections on cybercrimes; hence, a separate law on cybercrimes should be created.
4. Seminars and workshops must be arranged for police personnel to better understand cyberspace victimization and ensure prompt responses toward the complainants. Legal and academic experts and NGOs working for this cause must be encouraged to participate in such seminars and workshops.

Conclusion

The scenario of cyber victimization in India needs to be studied in detail. It is ironic that even though cyber victimization includes the abuse of fundamental rights and gender harassment, hardly any steps have been taken to curb such victimization. The majority of ISPs and social networking sites adhere to Western cybercultures and cyber rules and regulations, which may give rise to opportunities to experiment with personal freedoms, especially the freedom of speech and expression and the right to privacy. In the Indian social value system, some cybercultures may give rise to severe abuse of the fundamental rights guaranteed under our constitution. Mature adult Internet users must understand that what is offensive in real space is also offensive in cyberspace. Cyber socializing has opened the gateway to a global village, which may form its own culture, rules, and ethics. But that in no way should encourage the abuse of personal rights and freedom.

Limitations

This survey does not intend to cover cyber-generated or cyber-assisted attacks on governments and corporate bodies and child sexual harassment through the Internet. This survey is meant to analyze only the individual victimization of adults and the awareness among adult Internet users about cyber victimization. Due to time limitation, a purposive sampling method was adopted. This study is only a preliminary study; a full fledged study is planned and no generalizations should be inferred on the findings of this chapter.

References

Alshalan, A. (2006). Cyber-crime fear and victimization: An analysis of a national survey. PhD dissertation submitted to Mississippi State University.

Berson, I. R., Berson, M. J., & Ferron, J. M. (2002). Emerging risks of violence in the digital age: Lessons for educators from an online study of adolescent girls in the United States. *Journal of School Violence*, 1(2), 51–71.

Bocij, P. (2002). Corporate cyber stalking: An invitation to build theory. *First Monday*, 7(11). Retrieved on February 15, 2007, from http://firstmonday.org/issues/issue7_11/bocij/index.html.

Bocij, P. (2003). Victims of cyber stalking: An exploratory study of harassment perpetrated via the Internet. *First Monday*, 8(10). Retrieved on February 15, 2007, from http://firstmonday.org/issues/issue8_10/bocij/index.html.

Bocij, P., & McFarlane, L. (2002). Online harassment: Towards a definition of cyber stalking. *Prison Service Journal*, 139, 31–38.

Burgess-Proctor, A., Patchin, J. W., & Hinduja, S. (2010). Cyberbullying and online harassment: Reconceptualizing the victimization of adolescent girls. In V. Garcia & J. Clifford (eds), *Female Crime Victims: Reality Reconsidered* (pp. 162–176). Upper Saddle River, NJ: Prentice Hall.

Campbell, M. A. (2005). Cyber bullying: An old problem in a new guise? *Australian Journal of Guidance and Computing*, 15(1), 68–76.

Clarke, R. (1997). Encouraging cyber culture. Retrieved on July 2, 2010, from http://www.rogerclarke.com/II/EncoCyberCulture.html.

Desai, M., & Jaishankar, K. (2007). Cyber stalking victimization of girl students: An empirical study. In The Second International Conference on Victimology and Sixth Biennial Conference of the Indian Society of Victimology, Chennai, India, February 9–11, 2007.

Duggal, P. (2009). India's first cyber stalking case. Retrieved on July 2, 2010, from http://cyberlaws.net/cyberindia/2CYBER27.htm.

Fafinski, S. (2008). UK Cybercrime Report. Garlik. Retrieved on December 3, 2012, from http://www.garlik.com/press/Garlik_UK_Cybercrime_Report.pdf.

Finn, J. (2004). A survey of online harassment at a university campus. *Journal of Interpersonal Violence*, 19(4), 468–483.

Halder, D., & Jaishankar, K. (2008). Cyber crimes against women in India: Problems, perspectives and solutions. *TMC Academy Journal, Singapore, 3*(1), 48–62.

Halder, D., & Jaishankar, K. (2009). Cyber socializing and victimization of women. *Temida—The Journal on Victimization, Human Rights and Gender, 12*(3), 5–26.

Halder, D., & Jaishankar, K. (2010). Cyber victimization in India: A baseline survey report. Tirunelveli, India: Centre for Cyber Victim Counselling.

Halder, D., & Jaishankar, K. (2011). *Cyber Crime and Victimization of Women: Laws, Rights, and Regulations.* Hershey, PA: IGI Global.

Halder, D., & Jaishankar, K. (in press). Sexting among teens: An analysis on the questions of legalities and illegalities. In S. McQuade (ed.), *Cybercrime: Issues, Practices and Responses.* Lanham, MD: Rowan and Littlefield.

Hinduja, S., & Patchin, J. W. (2007). Offline consequences of online victimization: School violence and delinquency. *Journal of School Violence, 6*(3), 89–112.

Hinduja, S., & Patchin, J. W. (2008). Cyberbullying: An exploratory analysis of factors related to offending and victimization. *Deviant Behavior, 29*(2), 129–156.

Hinduja, S., & Patchin, J. W. (2009). *Bullying Beyond the Schoolyard: Preventing and Responding to Cyberbullying.* Thousand Oaks, CA: Sage.

Hinduja, S., & Patchin, J. W. (2012). *School Climate 2.0: Preventing Cyberbullying and Sexting One Classroom at a Time.* Thousand Oaks, CA: Sage.

HT Correspondent. (2010). Victim of a cyber crime? Report it. *Hindustan Times,* Mumbai, May 26, 2010. Retrieved on December 3, 2012, from http://www.hindustantimes.com/India-news/Mumbai/Victim-of-a-cyber-crime-Report-it/Article1-548604.aspx.

Ito, M., Horst, H. A., Boyd, M. B., Herr-Stephenson, B., Lange, P. G., Pascoe, C. J., & Robinson, L. (2008). Living and learning with new media: Summary of findings from the Digital Youth Project. The John D. and Catherine T. MacArthur Foundation Reports on Digital Media and Learning, November 2008. Retrieved on January 26, 2010, from http://digitalyouth.ischool.berkeley.edu/report.

Jaishankar, K. (2009a). *Cyber Bullying: Profile and Policy Guidelines.* Tirunelveli, India: Department of Criminology and Criminal Justice, Manonmaniam Sundaranar University.

Jaishankar, K. (2009b). Sexting: A new form of victimless crime. *International Journal of Cyber Criminology, 3*(1), 21–25.

Jaishankar, K., & Shariff, S. (2008). Cyber bullying: A transnational perspective. In F. Schmallager & M. Pittaro (eds), *Crimes of the Internet* (pp. 66–83). Upper Saddle River, NJ: Prentice Hall.

Juvonen, J., & Gross, E. F. (2008). Extending the school grounds?—Bullying experiences in cyberspace. *Journal of School Health, 78*(9), 496–505.

Kennedy, T. (2000). An exploratory study of feminist experiences in cyberspace. *Cyberpsychology and Behavior, 3*(5), 707–719.

Kumar, A. R., & Jaishankar, K. (2007). Cyber bullying using mobile phones: A study on victimization and perpetration among school students. In the Second International Conference on Victimology and Sixth Biennial Conference of the Indian Society of Victimology, Chennai, India, February 9–11, 2007.

Lenhart, A. (2009). Teens and sexting: How and why minor teens are sending sexually suggestive nude or nearly nude images via text messaging. Washington, DC: Pew Internet & American Life Project. Retrieved on January 26, 2010, from http://www.pewinternet.org/Reports/2009/Teens-and-Sexting.aspx.

Li, Q. (2006). Cyberbullying in schools: A research of gender differences. *School Psychology International, 27*(2), 157–170.

Li, Q. (2007). New bottle but old wine: A research of cyberbullying in schools. *Computers in Human Behavior, 23*(4), 1777–1791.

Macek, J. (2005). Defining cyber culture (V.2) (translated by Monika Metyková and Jakub Macek). Retrieved on July 2, 2010, from http://macek.czechian.net/defining_cyberculture.htm#_edn2.

McFarlane, L., & Bocij, P. (2003). An exploration of predatory behavior in cyberspace: Towards a typology of cyberstalkers. *First Monday, 8*(9) (September 2003). Retrieved on February 15, 2007, from http://firstmonday.org/issues/issue8_9/mcfarlane/index.html.

Medlin, A. N. (2002). Stalking to cyber stalking, a problem caused by the Internet. Law and the Internet. Fall 2002 papers, Georgia State University College of Law, Atlanta, GA. Retrieved on February 15, 2007, from http://gsulaw.gsu.edu/lawand/papers/fa02/medlin/.

Patchin, J. W., & Hinduja, S. (2006). Bullies move beyond the schoolyard: A preliminary look at cyber bullying. *Youth Violence and Juvenile Justice, 4*(2), 148–169.

Patchin, J. W., & Hinduja, S. (2010). Changes in adolescent online social networking behaviors from 2006 to 2009. *Computers in Human Behavior, 26*, 1818–1821.

Patchin, J. W., & Hinduja, S. (2012). *Cyberbullying Prevention and Response: Expert Perspectives.* New York: Routledge.

Roberts, L. (2008). Cyber-victimisation in Australia: Extent, impact on individuals and responses. TILES Briefing Paper No. 6.

Roberts, L. D. (2009). Cyber-victimization. In R. Luppicini & R. Adell (eds), *Handbook of Research on Technoethics* (pp. 575–592). Hershey, PA: IGI Global.

Shariff, S., & Hoff, D. L. (2007). Cyber bullying: Clarifying legal boundaries for school supervision in cyberspace. *International Journal of Cyber Criminology, 1*(1), 76–118.

Smith, P., Mahdavi, J., Carvalho, M., & Tippett, N. (2004). An investigation into cyberbullying, its forms, awareness and impact, and the relationship between age and gender in cyberbullying. A report to the Anti Bullying Alliance. Unit for School and Family Studies, Goldsmiths College, University of London. Retrieved on February 15, 2007, from http://www.anti-bullyingalliance.org.uk/downloads/pdf/cyberbullyingreportfinal230106_000.pdf.

Smith, P. K., Mahdavi, J., Carvalho, M., Fisher, S., Russell, S., & Tippett, N. (2008). Cyberbullying: Its nature and impact in secondary school pupils. *Journal of Child Psychology and Psychiatry, 49*(4), 376–385.

Spitzberg, B. H., & Hoobler, G. (2002). Cyberstalking and the technologies of interpersonal terrorism. *New Media & Society, 4*, 71–92.

The National Campaign to Prevent Teen and Unplanned Pregnancy. (2009). Sex and Tech: What's Really Going On. Retrieved on January 26, 2010, from http://www.thenationalcampaign.org/sextech/PDF/SexTech_Summary.pdf.

Tolga Aricak, T., Siyahhan, S., Uzunhasanoglu, A., Saribeyoglu, S., Ciplak, S., Yilmaz, N., & Memmedov, C. (2008). Cyberbullying among Turkish adolescents. *CyberPsychology and Behavior, 11*(3), 253–261.

Umarhathab, S., Rao, G. D. R., & Jaishankar, K. (2009). Cyber crimes in India: A study of emerging patterns of perpetration and victimization in Chennai city. *Pakistan Journal of Criminology, 1*(1), 51–66.

Vandebosch, H., & Van Cleemput, K. (2008). Defining cyberbullying: A qualitative research into the perceptions of youngsters. *CyberPsychology and Behavior*, *11*(4), 499–503.

Wolak, J., Mitchell, K. J., & Finkelhor, D. (2006). *Online Victimization of Youth: 5 Years Later*. Alexandria, VA: National Center for Missing & Exploited Children.

Ybarra, M. L. (2004). Linkages between depressive symptomatology and Internet harassment among young regular Internet users. *Cyberpsychology and Behavior*, *7*(2), 247–257.

Ybarra, M. L., & Mitchell, J. K. (2004). Youth engaging in online harassment: Associations with caregiver–child relationships, Internet use, and personal characteristics. *Journal of Adolescence*, *27*(3), 319–336.

Ybarra, M. L., Mitchell, J. K., Finkelhor, D., & Wolak, J. (2007). Internet prevention messages: Are we targeting the right online behaviors? *Archives of Pediatrics and Adolescent Medicine*, *161*, 138–145.

Arabic Muslim Hackers
Who Are They and What Is Their Relationship with Islamic Jihadists and Terrorists?

8

ALAELDIN MANSOUR MAGHAIREH

Contents

Introduction

In recent years, the world has witnessed the rapid growth of Middle Eastern terrorist organizations combined with hacking activities and other online offences. Jihadist and terrorist organizations have invested heavily in cyberspace to radicalize and recruit Muslim youth as well as to legitimize their cause and atrocities. Hezbollah, Hamas, and al-Qaeda have established a significant presence online (Shay, 2005; Weimann, 2006). For example, al-Qaeda has maintained its presence in cyberspace pre- and post-September 11 and reinforces that presence by publishing e-journals, e-magazines, and newsletters on different topics in different languages. This has led some commentators to believe that al-Qaeda is the first web-directed guerrilla network (Atwan, 2006). The danger of influencing or/and recruiting Muslim youth by terrorist and jihadist organizations in the Middle East and beyond is increasing daily as the number of Arabic Muslim netizens increases. Every day, thousands of people in the region join cyberspace. As of June 2010, there were more than 70 million online Arabic users (http://www.internetworldstats.com). A significant number of these people either create or participate in online hacking forums that inspire their followers to exercise hacking activities and other online offenses. Therefore, the cyber world faces what I have coined *hactwer* to describe Rambo Arabic Muslim hackers (AMHs). The new term *hactwer* is composed of the initials of the following five words: hacker, activist, criminal, terrorist, and warrior. Hactwers hack websites for glory and leave political messages, break laws, and cooperate with terrorists to wage cyber war against enemy websites.

It is important to distinguish hactwers from AMHs who are not interested in fighting a cyber war or taking part in any kind of hacking activities that are waged in the name of religion or nationalism and other AMHs who are willing and desirous to commit multiple cyber offenses in the name of either Arabism or Islam. Thus, not every AMH is a hactwer as there are a number of hacking forums that prohibit their members from misusing hacking tools or waging attacks on non-Muslim websites. Thus, the term *hactwer* will be used to distinguish between AMHs who commit or attempt to commit or participate in or facilitate the commission of cyber offences and non-offenders who are members of the Arabic hacking forums, but they abstain from involving themselves in hacking activities.

Psychologists and other social scientists have investigated the white hackers and cyber terrorists' characters and motivations; however, hactwers and their relationship with jihadist and terrorist organizations, particularly Hamas and al-Qaeda, have received no attention in the literature of cyber criminology. Although several studies have been carried out on Muslim hackers associated with al-Qaeda, none of these studies focused specifically on AMHs and their relationship with jihadist or terrorist groups. In most studies on cyber terrorism, cyber jihad, or terror on the Internet, the main focus is on professional hackers who are either full-time terrorists or hackers recruited by terrorist organizations.

This study has located as many as 154 AMH forums, though many of these are temporary, and they may close down or relocate their operation. The study identifies and examines nine prominent hacking forums. These nine forums are the most popular and populated hacking forums. This chapter focuses on whether and to what extent hactwers cooperate with the known jihadist and terrorist organizations, particularly Hamas and al-Qaeda. Is it fair to say that hactwers are increasingly waging coordinated cyber attacks alongside the real violence conducted on the ground by terrorists? What is the relationship between hactwers and terrorist organizations? What is the influence of the fatwas issued by Muslim clerics on the AMHs?

I visited a number of Arabic hacking websites and subscribed to several hacking forums in order to observe and conduct a survey examining the links and affiliations of the Arabic hackers with the jihadist and terrorist organizations. The survey includes questions about the hackers' political and religious perspectives, hacking experience, and fatwa influence. Additionally, I examined face-to-face interviews with hactwers conducted by Arabic journalists.

The observation, questionnaire data, and interviews advance the following hypotheses about the Arabic netizens and AMHs and the conversion to hactwer.

H1: Political and religious tensions are significant factors converting AMHs to hactwers.

H2: Cyber users who are more religious or have higher levels of religious involvement are more likely to establish jihadist hacking forums.

H3: Cyber users who have a more negative view of non-Muslim websites and their effects on Muslim youth are more likely to be involved in hacking activities and become a hactwer.

H4: Cyber users who hold negative views about the United States are more likely to be involved in hacking activities.

H5: A powerful council of muftis or a scholar is more likely to influence Arabic hackers than unpopular muftis.

The chapter first examines the white hacker's history and pinpoints the emergence of the AMHs. It divides the hacking community into two different schools, an old and a new school, and shows that the AMHs belong to the second phase of the new school. The next section identifies AMHs and hactwers and discusses the implications of the conversion of AMHs into hactwers. I then probe the nexus between AMHs and jihadist and terrorist organizations. In the last section, the chapter examines the influence of two contradicting fatwas on AMHs' hacking activities.

White Hackers and Emergence of AMHs

Historically, the hacking phenomenon can be divided into two different schools, an old and a new school of hackers. The ideologies and behaviors of the hackers in each school are different.

The old school of hackers was informally formed in the 1950s by small, well-known groups of students and professors affiliated to technological institutions in the United States, who acted for nonprofit purposes (Arrieta, 2000; Ross, 2000). In the early days of hackers, the computing and programming industry was not completely integrated into public services or considered a phenomenon worthy of mention in the mass media.

Nevertheless, commentators on the hacking phenomenon have described the first stage of hacking as a "golden era of hacking" (Levy, 1984) and these hackers as "computer virtuosos" (Baase, 2003). Hackers engaged in decoding intricate programs and analyzing computer puzzles. They spent long, lonely hours in front of a little screen learning more about a computer system and then developing it by using their own ideas and techniques (Baase, 2003).

They were fascinated by the computer system and unintentionally observed an implicit ethical code (Levy, 1984). During this era, a written ethical code of conduct for hackers describing permissible online acts was published in Levy's (1984) book titled *Hackers: Heroes of the Computer Revolution*. The hackers' code of ethics demonstrated an independent set of principles as well as the first brick in the construction of the hackers' subculture (Thomas, 2002a; Turkle, 1995). However, hackers' ethics are not recognized by law enforcement agencies, because they appear to be a virtual code written to justify illegal hacking activities. Nevertheless, most importantly, the old school of hackers did not show any sign of malicious intentions to destroy or interrupt computer systems. They were driven by intellectual challenge and curiosity. Moreover, none of its members were ever accused of or prosecuted for any criminal offences. On the contrary, most of them have crafted a vast array of software programs, sparking the proliferation of information technologies and Silicon Valley start-up companies. However, the old school of hackers is no longer active.

The new school of hackers, on the other hand, can be divided into two phases, each a new kind of hacker. The first stage of the new school of hackers, spanning from the 1970s to the mid-1990s, was triggered by the widespread use of the PC in developed countries and later by the creation of cyberspace (Young & Aitel, 2004). The transition of hacking from the innovative exploration of computer systems to unauthorized intrusions and other types of illegal activities motivated by self-interest* was a fundamental shift in the hackers' subculture (Skorodumova, 2004). The ethical code gradually deteriorated, but in many cases, hackers were applauded by the mass media and described as "white hat" hackers or "heroes of digital culture" (Taylor, 2001). For example, a hacker who trespassed onto computer systems belonging to wealthy individuals and large corporations and then transferred money to poor individuals and small organizations was depicted as a "digital Robin Hood" (Tavani, 2004). As more people joined the hacking community, the term *cracker* was coined by the old school of hackers to distinguish themselves from the criminal hackers (Goodman, 1997).† Scholars and computer experts have described the latter as the dark side of hackers (Lilley, 2002). It is worth mentioning that there is a growing recognition of the crackers'

---

* The first hacking activity motivated by self-interest was reported in the early 1970s, when an American student hacked into the Pacific Telephone Corporation's central computer (Sieber, 1986).
† A *white hat* hacker is a term used by hackers and the computing community to describe a hacker who is interested in computer security and illegally exploring system vulnerabilities and who would impart information and cooperate with the owner before divulging it to the public. In contrast to a white hat hacker, *black hat* hackers do not handle security holes sensitively. A cracker, on the other hand, is a controversial term used by computer experts and hackers to describe a hacker with a malicious intent (Tavani, 2004; Young & Aitel, 2004; Yar, 2005).

own subculture. The majority of hackers do not show a malicious intention to destroy or interrupt a service, but crackers are driven by malevolent incentives. Crackers believe that cracking activities should not be illegal or immoral (Baird et al., 1987), while hackers walk a delicate line between immoral and ethical hacking (Reid, 1995).

During this era, the political motivations of hacking also began to take new shape. For instance, an American group established the Youth International Party Line (YIPL), the first American hackers' organization to adopt a political agenda for cyberspace.* Nonetheless, this phase of hacking witnessed waves of legislation and criminal procedures against the phenomenon (Taylor, 2001). For example, in 1984, the United States enacted the Computer Fraud and Abuse Act (CFAA). Moreover, several notorious hackers were arrested and brought to trial. In 1987, for instance, 18 hackers from New York were arrested on charges of illegally reprogramming memory chips in their mobile phones in order to make free calls and, in 1990, Operation Sun Devil was launched in 14 U.S. cities to crack down on illegal computer hacking activities. This stage in hacking culminated with the maturation of a complete virtual world: websites, organizations, magazines, hacking tools, books, conferences, and the Bulletin Board System (BBS), all supporting various agendas and motivations (Forester & Morrison, 1994).

The second phase of the new school is the new millennium hackers' school or the hackers of the twenty-first century or the *global hackers*. The participation of developing countries in this cyberspace world has enriched the hacking subculture. Vast numbers of hackers from the third world have joined the hacking community. They have created innovative hacking techniques, for instance, the "love bug" or "I LOVE YOU" virus was launched from the Philippines (Broadhurst & Grabosky, 2005). However, this new generation of cyber attacks has significantly turned the world's view against hacking activities. For example, the recent waves of cyber attacks against eBay, Yahoo, CNN, Amazon, and other prominent websites were enough to revise the media and public attitudes to hacking activities.†

The Arabic Muslim hacking phenomenon is in its infancy compared with the established Western hacking community. From observation and the accumulation of facts, it can be presumed that the AMHs' first emergence was in 2003. They spontaneously started creating their own websites

---

* In 1973, the YIPL changed its name to the Technological American Party (TAP). It published a newsletter and information about *phone freak* or *freaking*—a type of computer-related crime that is perpetrated by a hacker to exploit telephone systems for the purpose of making free long-distance calls; after TAP terminated, the hacker magazine *2600* was launched.

† In 2000, an inept young hacker, known as MafiaBoy, launched DoS attacks against prominent websites including CNN, Yahoo, and eBay, using malware available online (Schell & Martin, 2004).

from scratch while mimicking the more established white hackers' websites, but after gaining more experience and sophistication, hacking forums have become a common place to interact, socialize, and, most importantly, to propagate and defend Islam. In fact, the use of these hacking forums goes way beyond simple socializing, to establishing powerful hacking fronts, and political and religious fronts.

The political front of the AMHs is not a struggle between left- and right-wing tendencies in politics, but spontaneously formed online groups to defend Arabic issues such as the Palestinian case and, recently, to protest against dictatorial regimes in the Middle East and support the Arabic revolutions. They come together, recognize their potential, explore their connectedness, and define their joint associations, and all are interested in working collaboratively to wage cyber attacks against their adversaries.

The religious front takes two forms. The first involves creating and designing websites, blogs, and other web-based application websites, designed and optimized specifically to defend Islam from its enemies. All the prominent hacking forums contain religious sections that teach the members of the group different issues about shariah and some have a jihadist section where the main focus is to wage cyber attacks against non-Muslim websites that pose a threat or are a source of substantial harm to the religion of Islam. The second form is hacktivism and cyber attacks. It is aggressive and is meant to cause harm as well as to protect from harm. It defaces websites and perpetrates different forms of cyber attacks against ideological enemies to revenge or protect Muslims from websites containing harmful materials.

Cyberspace has witnessed a noticeable increase in the number of attacks by Muslim hacker groups who are either associated with terrorist organizations or share a similar ideology with al-Qaeda and other jihadist groups. The following two sections identify AMHs and hactwers and probe into the relationships between hackers and jihadist and terrorist organizations.

AMHs versus Hactwers

AMHs can be defined as hackers who speak Arabic, believe in Arabism, have Islam as their religion, present themselves as experts on hacking techniques, and are members of a hacking forum. Meanwhile, a hactwer is an AMH who commits cyber vandalism and hacktivism in the name of religion. I have coined the word "hactwer" to describe these aggressive, politicized Middle Eastern hackers. "Hactwer" is composed of the initials of the following five words: hacker, activist, criminal, terrorist, and warrior. It is not necessary that the AMHs and hactwers only inhabit the Middle East and Northern Africa; many are operating in various parts of the world and they range from inexperienced newbies who are keen to learn from hacking websites and find out how to defend Islam to highly technical individuals who create hacking forums and direct AMHs to hack non-Arabic websites.

AMHs and hactwers are distinguished from the white hackers in that they are directly impacted not only by political events, such as the war between Israel and Hamas, but also by sectarian clashes and religious tensions. Hence, it is not uncommon to find Arabic Islamic hacking websites designed and optimized specifically to defend Islam from its enemies. For example, the website http://eljehad.netfirms.com was established to defend Muslim websites, particularly Palestinian websites against Israeli hackers (see Table 8.1; Maghaireh, 2008). The founder and supervisor of the website, in promoting cyber jihad, writes (translated by the author):

> I built this website for my Muslim brothers around the world. It is a gift to everyone willing to devote himself for Jihad and E-Jihad. It is a present to every decent Muslim who attention is only to use the Internet to raise the religion and to fight the enemies of Allah ... this website will guide you to the E-Jihad options.

The observation and survey of the AMHs' forums clearly demonstrate that a significant number of the members are ready to dedicate their time, effort, and devotion to hacking non-Arabic websites, particularly Israeli websites, because they strongly believe that Hamas is a legitimate organization fighting Israeli occupation. For example, a Saudi hacker who was jailed in Egypt for hacking and defacing an Israeli website showed no remorse and even planned for more attacks (http://forums.soqor.net). Also, they are willing to defend Islamic websites. Al-soqor, a hacking forum (see Table 8.1; Maghaireh, 2008), houses more than 149,000 members who show extreme eagerness to defend Islamic websites and the Prophet of Islam against European newspapers' publication of cartoons lampooning the Prophet or against offensive websites. For example, an Arab journalist for Garednet, an Arabic online journal, interviewed a notorious Saudi hactwer known as Al-Janah (الجانح) for a major profile of his hacking activities. The hactwer proudly admitted that he had hacked non-Muslim websites posting inflammatory materials against Islam (http://forum.z7mh.com/t68709.html).

From the aforementioned, it can be seen that a significant number of the hacking community members can be labeled as hactwers who have committed cyber offences—including criminal access, cyber terrorism, cyber jihad, and cyber war—in the name of Islam and Arabism. However, on the other hand, a great number of hackers are not involved in hacking activities and abstain from involving themselves in illegal hacking activities. They cannot be labeled as hactwers, but can be labeled as AMHs as long as they do not get involved in offensive hacking activities. For example, Pirates Hacking Forum and Arabic Thunder Network prohibit their members from involving themselves in unacceptable hacking activities against others (see Table 8.1).

Table 8.1 Most Prominent AMH Forums and Their Hacking Orientation

Name	Total Members	Active Members	Web Address	Supports Hamas	Supports al-Qaeda	Hacking Activities
International Hacking Forum منتدى الاختراق العالمي	165,000	600	http://www.vbhacker.net	Yes	No	Prohibits cyber-sectarian
Pirates Hacking Forum القرصان	51,000	4,400	http://www.alkrsan.net	No	No	Prohibits hacking non-Muslim websites
The Storm Hacking Forum العاصفة	244,000	No data available	http://www.3asfh.net	Unknown	Unknown	Prohibits hacking Arabic websites
Proponent of Electronic Jihad انصار الجهاد الالكتروني	No data available	No data available	http://www.al-ansar.virtue.nu	No data	Yes	Hacking is a sort of Jihad
Arabic Hacking Organization منظمة الهاكر العربي	27,000	No data available	http://www.arhack.net	No	No	Prohibits cyber-sectarian
Arabic Thunder Network شبكة الصاعقة العربية	161,000	54,000	http://www.sa3eka.com	No	No	Prohibits cyber-sectarian, no indication that it supports attacks against Israeli websites
Black Scorpion Forum منتدى العقرب الاسود	5,500	539	http://www.n-0-n.com	Unknown	Unknown	Hacking anti-Muslim websites
Falcon Hacking Forum منتدى الصقر للهكر	149,000	No data available	http://www.soqor.net	Yes	No	Hacking Israeli and anti-Muslim websites
Egyptian Hacking Intelligence Agency (EHIA) الجهاد الالكتروني	No data available	No data available	http://www.eljehad.netfirms.com	Yes	No	Hacking Israeli and anti-Muslim websites

Relationship between AMHs and Jihadist and Terrorist Organizations

Two types of relationships between hackers and jihadist and terrorist organizations can be differentiated: a direct relationship in which a terrorist organization coaxes hackers to join its cause and wage cyber attacks, propaganda, and other psychological operations; and an indirect relationship in which the AMHs work either individually or together to help and support terrorists and jihadist causes. Both the observation and questionnaire approaches revealed that none of the prominent hacking forums maintain a direct relationship with Hamas or al-Qaeda, except one, the Proponent of Electronic Jihad forum, which maintains some sort of direct relationship with al-Qaeda as its members expressly engage to dedicate their time and effort to support al-Qaeda online. Meanwhile, seven of the prominent hacking forums, except Pirates Hacking Forum and Arabic Thunder Network, sustain an indirect relationship with Hamas. These forums condone cyber attacks and use significant portions of their sites to teach and ignite members to hack Israeli websites and proudly post tens of stories of cyber attacks against Israeli and Western websites. However, none of these forums has posted messages of sympathy or support for al-Qaeda. I have noticed that none of the AMHs who responded to the questionnaires are sympathetic to al-Qaeda.

The members of these groups are more likely to establish a direct relationship with cyber terrorists or be more susceptible to recruitment by jihadist and terrorist organizations. Hence, it is possible that the indirect relationship observed between the AMHs and terrorists might develop into an intimate and interactive collaboration. Thus, there is a great likelihood that terrorists might recruit or coerce hackers to carry out a part of their activities online (Serio & Gorkin, 2003). Recent history has provided several examples of how AMHs become affiliated with terrorist organizations. For example, Irhabi 007, meaning Terrorist 007, Younis Tsouli, hacked into American university computers, propagandized for the Iraqi insurgents led by Abu Musab al-Zarqawi, and taught other online jihadists how to wield their computers for the cause (von Knop, 2008).

However, in general, the relationship between the AMHs and terrorist organizations is weak and uncertain. In most cases, they do not share the same ethical values as the terrorists, although they do share the religion, ethnicity, and some general principles of the jihad duty. For example, different hackers' forums are decorated with Islamic motifs and jihad slogans and some hackers use jihadist photos as their profile pictures. However, the vast majority of AMHs are sympathetic to the Palestinian cause and are willing to work hard to shut down or deface Israeli websites. For example, the Moroccan Hacking Organization website provides its members with comprehensive instructions on how to hack and sabotage Israeli websites (http://www.h4ck-mks.co.cc/vb/showthread.php?t=1840). In a similar manner, the Egyptian Hacker Intelligence Agency (EHIA) has established a website encouraging AMHs to join the EHIA to defend Islam and wage e-jihad against Israel (http://eljehad.netfirms.com). The EHIA has set as a priority to unite the AMHs groups with the objective of forming an army of hackers to attack Israel and protect Palestinian websites. The observation and survey have come to support the conventional viewpoint that "numerous cyber attacks have been attributed to hackers affiliated with terrorist organizations or sympathetic to terrorist cause" (Himma, 2007).

AMHs and Fatwas

A fatwa is a religious verdict, given by a knowledgeable (qualified) person (mufti), a council of muftis, or a scholar of distinction on subjects connected with shariah (Hasan, 2006), on a troubling religious issue that has only recently emerged in Muslim society (Kamrava, 2006). For this reason, every Muslim country has a mufti or a council of scholars who is appointed by the government to issue a fatwa on an emerging matter and to consider whether the matter is Islamically acceptable or not. For example, in Egypt, the Al-Azhar Al-Sharif is responsible for issuing fatwas. In Saudi Arabia, the official Council of Senior Scholars headed by Sheikh 'Abd Al-'Aziz Ibn 'Abdallah Aal-Sheikh issues fatwas. However, it is worth mentioning that not all fatwas are issued by authorized muftis or scholars. Several notorious fatwas have been issued by illegitimate authorities. In 1998, for example, a fatwa issued by Bin Laden and four other Islamic radicals called on Muslims to kill Americans and steal their money whenever and wherever they find it. Although this fatwa has been rejected by the majority of the Muslim community, it has ignited acts of terror that have resulted in massive loss of life. However, when a respectable mufti council, such as the Al-Azhar Al-Sharif in Egypt, issues a fatwa, this fatwa is greeted both in Egypt and among Muslim communities throughout the world.

In July 2008, the Al-Azhar Al-Sharif issued a remarkable fatwa condoning cyber attacks against infidels' websites. The fatwa stated that "Cyber Jihad is religiously permitted because it is a digital weapon used against the enemy of Islam who are defaming Islam, the prophet Mohammad, and Muslims ...." According to this fatwa, hacktivism is legitimate and perceived as a sort of jihad against the enemy of Islam (Maghaireh, 2011). This fatwa is too broad and motivational a tool for Muslim youth because it includes any website that a Sunni Muslim hacker might consider an adversarial website. Indeed, because the fatwa was issued by a powerful mufti, the fatwa converted thousands of AMHs to hactwers as four forums condoned cyber attacks. The fatwa of Al-Azhar Al-Sharif may have ignited what can be termed *cyber-sectarian conflict*. For example, in September 2008, Sunni hackers attacked more than 300 Shia websites, including the main website of the Grand Ayatollah Ali al-Sistani (http://news.bbc.co.uk/hi/arabic). A group of Shia hackers called the "Shia Digital Security Team" responded by attacking more than 77 Sunni websites (translated from http://www.saudiyatnet.net). The fatwa also motivated a Saudi hacker, known as "snipper Haks," to hack and bring down more than 55 Dutch websites, responding to a video defaming the Prophet of Islam produced by Geert Wilders (translated from http://www.arabianbusiness.com/arabic/516279), a Dutch politician and the leader of the Party for Freedom (http://en.wikipedia.org).

The AMHs continuously attack nonbelievers' websites, such as the Arabic atheist website http://www.ladeenyon.net, which has been repeatedly attacked. A member of the Arabic atheist "ladeenyon" commented that,

> Al-Mujahedin cyber attacks against our website didn't stop since it was built, killing and sabotage on the earth and Internet, they are not professional but to kill and corrupt, they believe themselves to be intellectually superior, but they are not because they use what they believe to be the tools of the infidels, hacking programs … the website will survive. (Translated by the author from http://www.forum.3almani.org)

In April 2009, Sheikh Saleh Al Fozan, a member of the Saudi Higher Council of Clerics, issued a contradictory fatwa against hacktivism, forbidding hacking activities against Israeli websites (http://www.lojainiat.com). Although, his fatwa has been the subject of intense debate on Arabic cyber world blogs and has been condemned by the majority of cyberspace users, the fatwa is of enormous importance within a particular small group of the AMHs and Internet users because it was issued by a higher religious figure who plays a significant role in the Saudi Arabian community. For example, two hacking groups, Pirates Hacking Forum and Arabic Thunder Network, have been affected by the fatwa. However, this fatwa contradicts several previous fatwas issued by different scholars permitting and praising Muslim hacking activities against Zionist and missionary websites as well as against the Al-Azhar Al-Sharif's fatwa.

The harmful effects of the first fatwas are twofold: They radicalize the AMHs and encourage Muslim Internet users to learn hacking techniques, and commit different forms of cyber vandalism, cyber terrorism, cyber jihad, and cyber crimes, such as hacking; the distribution of viruses, Trojans, and worms; cyber defamation; and denial of service (DoS) attacks (Andrews, 2005). The fatwa creates a new platform that then creates fertile ground for cyber extremist fundamentalist individuals (hactwers) and groups.

Conclusion

Cyberspace creates a unique environment for the AMHs and terrorists to interact, work directly or indirectly together, and learn from each other. The risk of recruiting hackers to work with terrorist organizations is growing remarkably fast. The Islamic world has populated cyberspace and opened up websites propagating Islamic rhetoric and ideology. Some of these websites are established to defend Islam and teach hacking techniques to Muslim youth. Unfortunately, the growing Muslim presence in cyberspace has been accompanied by contradictory fatwas, a prevailing fatwa that has affected cyberspace negatively and incited the AMHs to commit cyber vandalism, and an unpopular fatwa that condemned cyber vandalism against Israeli websites. Thus, it is not uncommon to find that Islamic and non-Islamic websites have been hacked and vandalized by the AMHs. The problem does not stop here; the attacked websites retaliate by counterattacking and may increase their activities, which are abhorred by Muslims and create a hostile environment.

Cyberspace requires the Arab world to enact comprehensive and rigorous anti-hacking strategy policies and regulations, and the government must restrict and observe the religious fatwas. Furthermore, traditional laws must be evaluated and adjusted as required, to facilitate law enforcement efforts to prevent the growing link between the AMHs and terrorist organizations.

References

Andrews, J. (2005). Understanding TCP reset attacks. http://kerneltrap.org/node/3072 (accessed March 7, 2011).

Arrieta, S. (2000). *Hacker Categorized*. MSC Institute of Technology.

Atwan, A.-B. (2006). *The Secret History of Al-Qa'ida*. London: Abacus.

Baase, S. (2003). *A Gift of Fire: Social, Legal, and Ethical Issues for Computer and the Internet*. Upper Saddle River, NJ: Prentice Hall.

Baird, B. J., Baird Jr., L. L., & Ranauro, R. P. (1987). The moral cracker? *Computer & Security*, 6(6), 471–478.

Broadhurst, R., & Grabosky, P. (2005). Computer-related crime in Asia: Emergent issues. In R. Broadhurst & P. N. Grabosky (eds), *Cyber-Crime: The Challenge in Asia* (pp. 1–9). Hong Kong: University of Hong Kong Press.

Forester, T., & Morrison, P. (1994). *Computer Ethics: Cautionary Tales and Ethical Dilemmas in Computing*. Boston, MA: Massachusetts Institute of Technology.

Goodman, M. D. (1997). Why the police don't care about computer crime. *Harvard Journal of Law & Technology*, 10, 465–469.

Hasan, N. (2006). *Laskar Jihad: Islam, Militancy, and the Quest for Identity in Post-New Order*. Ithaca, NY: Cornell Southeast Asian Studies Program.

Himma, K. E. (ed.) (2007). *Internet Security: Hacking, Counter Hacking, and Society*. Sudbury, MA: Jones and Bartlett.

Kamrava, M. (2006). *The New Voices of Islam: Reforming Politics and Modernity: A Reader*. London: I. B. Tauris.

Levy, S. (1984). *Hackers: Heroes of the Computer Revolution* (1st edn). New York: Nerraw Manijaime/Doubleday.

Lilley, P. (2002). *Hacked, Attacked, and Abused: Digital Crime Exposed*. London: Kogan.

Maghaireh, A. (2011). Fatwa chaos ignites cyber vandalism: Does Islamic criminal law prohibit cyber vandalism. In K. Jaishankar (ed.), *Cyber Criminology: Exploring Internet Crimes and Criminal Behavior* (pp. 347–357). Boca Raton, FL: CRC Press.

Maghaireh, A. M. (2008). Shariah law, cyber-sectarian conflict and cybercrime: How can Islamic criminal law respond to cybercrime? *International Journal of Cyber Criminology*, 2(2), 337–345.

Reid, K. (1995). Computer Hackers Wrestle with Often Ambiguous Morals of Cyberspace. *Knight Ridder/Tribune News Service*, August 23, 1995.

Ross, A. (2000). Hacking away at the counter-culture. In D. Bell and B. M. Kennedy (eds.), *The Cybercultures Reader*. London: Routledge.

Schell, B. H., & Martin, C. (2004). *Cybercrime: A Reference Handbook*. Santa Barbara, CA: ABC-CLIO.

Serio, J. D., & Gorkin, A. (2003). Changing lenses: Striving for sharper focus on the nature of the 'Russian Mafia and its Impact on the Computer Realm'. *International Review of Law Computers*, 17(2), 197.

Shay, S. (2005). The radical Islam and the cyber jihad. In M. Last and A. Kandl (eds.), *Fighting Terror in Cyberspace*. World Scientific.

Sieber, U. (1986). *The International Handbook on Computer Crime*. New York: Wiley.

Skorodumova, O. (2004). Hackers as information space phenomenon. *Social Sciences*, 35(4), 105–113.

Tavani, H. T. (2004). *Ethics and Technology: Ethical Issues in an Age of Information and Communication Technology*. Hoboken, NJ: Wiley.

Taylor, P. (2001). Hacktivism: In search of lost ethics. In D. S. Wall (ed.), *Crime and the Internet* (pp. 59–73). London: Routledge.

Thomas, D. (2002a). *Hacker Culture*. Minneapolis, MN: University of Minnesota Press.

Thomas, D. (2002b). New ways to break the law: Cybercrime and the politics of hacking. In Y. Jewkes & G. Letherby (eds), *Criminology: A Reader* (pp. 387–398). London: Sage.

Turkle, S. (1995). *Life on the Screen: Identity in the Age of the Internet*. New York: Simon & Schuster.

von Knop, K. (2008). Institutionalization of a Web-focused, multinational counter-terrorism campaign—Building a collective open source intelligent system—A discussion paper. In Centre of Excellence Defence Against Terrorism, Ankara, Turkey (ed.), *Responses to Cyber Terrorism* (pp. 8–23), *NATO Science for Peace and Security Series—E: Human and Societal Dynamics* (Vol. 34).

Weimann, G. (2006). Virtual disputes: The use of the internet for terrorist debates. *Studies in Conflict and Terrorism*, 29, 623–639.

Yar, M. (2005). Computer hacking: Just another case of juvenile delinquency? *Howard Journal of Criminal Justice*, 44(4), 387–399.

Young, S., & Aitel, D. (2004). *The Hacker's Handbook: The Strategy behind Breaking into and Defending Networks*. New York: Auerbach.

Additional Arabic Sources

http://www.lojainia http://kerneltrap.org/node/3072 (accessed November 23, 2007).

هاكر سعودي خطير يحاكم في مصر [A dangerous Saudi hacker prosecuted in Egypt]. Retrieved on December 11, 2010, from http://forums.soqor.net/a-t9958.html.

منظمة الاختراق المغربية [Moroccan Hacking Organization]. Retrieved on March 3, 2011, from http://www.h4ck-mks.co.cc/vb/showthread.php?t=1840.

حصرياً مقابلة مع ثاني هكر عربي [An exclusive interview with the second prominent Saudi hacker]. Retrieved on March 3, 2011, from http://forum.z7mh.com/t68709.html.

Sexual Harassment over Cell Phones
A Survey of Women in Dhaka City

9

UMMEY QULSUM NIPUN

Contents

Introduction

The cell phone has become an integral part of our daily lives. It reduces the need to travel, helps us to better manage our time, and makes all types of transactions smooth and easy. This small device brings the world closer to us so that everything is within our grasp. With the advent of new technologies in mobile communications, the cell phone is now being used for e-mailing, chatting, and blogging. Various multimedia options are now being installed in cell phones, such as music players, 3D games, and video players.

Nevertheless, we can probably all agree that pros and cons go hand in hand. Apart from offering endless benefits, the cell phone also creates opportunities to commit crimes. Hence, it is of the utmost importance that we become aware of the risks associated with cell phones. These risks range from irritating calls or blank calls to blackmail or even virtual sexual assault. These types of harassment have an appalling impact and repeated sexual harassment using cell phones remains under the cover of a virtual web network of communications. It can affect victims' physical and mental health and make their personal, social, and professional lives uncomfortable. This situation has underscored the urgency of taking bold steps toward preventing the use of cell phones for sexual harassment. Unfortunately, in Bangladesh, this area is still off the political radar and, to date, no comprehensive study has been done on this issue. While analyzing this issue from a research perspective, this chapter asks (a) Who is using cell phones unethically? (b) Who are the victims of sexual harassment via cell phones? and (c) What are the adverse impacts of cell phone sexual harassment on a victim's social life? The answers to these questions address the situation through appropriate case studies that have been collected by an extensive field survey.

The harassment of women by making sexually explicit advances through cell phone conversations or any other communication tool has become common in the Western world. It has not yet been reported on a great scale in the Asian region and it is lowest among the countries of South Asia and beyond. Such intimidation can start when a girl picks up a phone call and becomes worse if the caller delivers sex-related jokes and words after hearing the girl's voice over the phone. The caller often uses swear words and is gratified if the girl slams down the phone. The caller may keep calling until the girl picks up the phone again or switches it off. However, this is not the end of the incident as odd messages and pictures of sexual organs may start to reach the girl's cell phone and she may be too embarrassed to tell anyone. Someone who faces such intimidation may go through severe psychological agony. This is also a very sophisticated area, where there is a need for more basic data and case study material on how girls and women suffer from the adverse impact of sexual harassment over cell phones, on the differential impacts of such activities, and on the possible ways of helping them through the trauma caused by it. This chapter advises the creation of more comprehensive awareness on this sophisticated issue through extensive research to explore ways of providing a sound basis for policy implementation as an effective solution.

Defining Sexual Harassment

Business & Legal Reports Inc. (2005) described sexual harassment as unwelcome sexual advances or requests for sexual favors, or verbal or physical conduct of a sexual nature, or the display of material perceived as unwelcome. The Department of Social Development, South Africa, in their *Sexual Harassment Policy, 2008*, defined sexual harassment as unwanted or unwelcome sexual tendencies, and a request for sexual favors that have a negative effect on the recipient. It can range from inappropriate gestures, innuendos, advances, suggestions or hints, to touching, comments, statements and/or remarks without consent and, at worst, rape. Sexual harassment creates an intimidating, hostile, and offensive environment (Department of Social Development, 2008). The International Trade Union Confederation (April, 2008) defines sexual harassment as unwanted, unwelcome, and unasked-for behavior of a sexual nature. It can occur either on a one-time basis or as a series of incidents. Sexual harassment is coercive and one-sided, and both males and females can be victims (ITUC, 2008). The U.S. Supreme Court defined sexual harassment precisely as a form of sex discrimination (Ford & Donis, 1996). It was defined as unwanted and unwelcome verbal or nonverbal behavior of a sexual nature that links academic or professional status to sexual favors or that hinders the work or learning process (Wood, 1997).

With technological development or other changes of the modern era, the modes of and approaches to sexual harassment have acquired new dimensions. Apart from eve-teasing, harassment can also be carried out through the Internet and cell phones. According to the Supreme Court of Bangladesh High Court Division, Special Original Jurisdiction (2010), the definition of 'Eve teasing', is as follows: "Eve teasing is a euphemism used in India, Pakistan, Bangladesh and Nepal for public sexual harassment or molestation of women by men." This chapter focuses on the various ways of sexual harassment using cell phones. Text messages containing sexually explicit words, picture messages with nudity, prank calls, and, most importantly, blackmailing via cell phones are considered as sexual harassment in this study.

Sexual Harassment Using Cell Phones: Talking, Text Messages, Picture Messages, and Voice Messages

The cell phone is now frequently used for talking, sending text messages/short message service (SMS), taking pictures, sharing information and documents (as a substitute for the flash drive), entertainment, Internet browsing, and much more. All of these functions create opportunities for the misuse and abuse of this small device of communication as it can be used to send messages of a sexual nature, sex jokes or to make blank calls and take pictures for future communications. All these behaviors come under the definition of sexual harassment because all are unwelcome, unasked for, and unwanted by any cell phone user.

Then come the issues of call charges, bonuses, tariff-free options, and cash-back offers that promote the infraction of cell phone etiquettes. All mobile companies operating in Bangladesh offer the lowest call charge after midnight. Surprisingly, they also offer some ridiculous options to increase the sales of their SIM cards. For example, if you purchase a SIM card from company "X," you will get 500 SMS free or 150 min free talk time or even 150 Taka (Bangladesh currency) instant cash back. These types of offers encourage offensive behaviors. This seems to be the main reason that sexual harassment via cell phones has become very common. Most cell phone users hold more than one number in order to take advantage of the minimum call rate of particular companies. Additionally, cell phone companies' registration systems are not sophisticated enough to trace the subscriber or monitor a particular subscriber for future reference. Lenhart (2010) explained that teenagers are the group who usually send and receive nude picture messages.

Who Are the Abusers and What Is Their Motivation?

Rape is considered a sexual offense, but in reality the issue of treating someone in a way that they are not comfortable with should also be considered sexual harassment. Promoted by the thinking of Katherine Franke (1997), it can be said that sexual jokes, flirting, dating, and teasing playfully in sexually explicit ways can also be considered sexual harassment. In addition, some verbal exchanges, such as discussions on conjugal life and relationships, sexual dissatisfaction, regret, etc., are not always welcome and this is a good example of the kind of sexual harassment that falls outside its regular definition (Franke, 1997). The cell phone is a means of conducting all of these behaviors without effort, which can be disseminated easily to hurt others. In this regard, Franke raised the vital question of whether anyone should be held accountable for sexual harassment because he/she created an unpleasant situation or uttered sexually suggestive words (Franke, 1997). So, observing the appalling consequences of harassing behaviors using technological tools that never keep any evidence, this should be considered a criminal offence.

All of these give society good reason to consider the intent and effects of sexually harassing behavior over cell phones. It is obvious that the "Sexual Harassment Law," "Gender Equity Policy," and so on, have not been very successful in preventing this harmful behavior. Considering all of this, MacKinnon proposed the dignity theory to redefine the term *harasser* from the gender perspective. This theory exaggerated the causal significance of sexual conduct in explaining the subordination of women, thereby discouraging coercion, threat, intimidation, insult, humiliation, etc., through different activities, attitudes, and gestures toward a female. MacKinnon termed this *dignitary injuries*, harmful to an individual's identity (MacKinnon & Siegel, 2004).

Kinnear (2007) discovered certain visible, clinical identifications of abusers: denial, sexual arousal, sexual fantasy, social skills, cognitive distortions, and other psychological and social problems. According to Kinnear (2007, p. 7),

> Many perpetrators deny that they are abusing anyone or deny that what they are doing is sexual abuse. Most perpetrators also are sexually aroused by children. Sexual fantasies have been suggested as a behavior characteristic of abusers; although its significance remains unclear, many researchers believe that the role of sexual fantasy should be considered.

It can therefore be said that women are raped and sexually harassed because of gender inequality and the institutions that support the notion (Conte, 2002). Sexual harassment is a behavior that is perpetrated by those who have reason to believe that they are unlikely to suffer any negative consequences for their crime. Most scholars and activists agree that rape and sexual harassment are crimes of power and domination. While most power relations in our society are gendered (i.e., men as a class have power over women as a class), there are powerful people in both genders—the power dynamics and consequences are similar regardless of the victim's gender, race, ethnicity, social class, sexual orientation, age, or ability/disability (Rozee, 2000).

Driving Forces To Consider This Issue around the World

The cell phone provides people with the excellent option of virtual communication. With this device, one can always be in touch with his/her family and maintain regular communication. In Bangladesh, the total number of cell phone active subscribers reached 75.484 million by the end of May 2011 (BTRC, 2011). This shows the rapid growth in the rate of cell phone usage in the country.

As in other countries around the world, the younger generation of Bangladesh is strongly fascinated with this technology. Most of them now own a cell phone or have access to a cell phone and consider it a fashion accessory. The cell phone has also changed the communication pattern of our young generation, that is, text messaging. Additionally, the cell phone is highly appreciated by parents as they can easily trace their children when they are not at home. Children also feel much safer and secure as they can communicate with their parents as and when necessary. Therefore, it is equally important that parents acquaint their children with the use of cell phones in their daily activities.

The Harris Interactive study (2008) found that in the Western world, the young generation carry their cell phones to access friends, family, and current events, and their activities range from text messaging to talking and logging on to social networking sites (Facebook, Twitter, Messenger, etc.). This study explored the fascination of the younger generation in using a cell phone. From this study, it has been found that in the Western world, the cell phone is an active instrument for exposing the personality of teenagers and establishing their social status (Harris Interactive, 2008). In addition to the cell phone, operating companies are now trying to attract the young generation with many lucrative offers, such as cash back on cell phone recharge and all-night zero call charges. Thus, youths are inspired to carry more than one cell number to attain all the free services and facilities offered by the cell phone companies. Eventually these extra services or free offers from the cell phone service providers allow a group of people to execute their sinister plans to harass girls and women. Additionally, such motives are responsible for creating social tensions and sexual harassment over cell phones. Marion (2010) rightly mentioned that new technology opens up opportunities for new crimes.

Such incidents are now being increasingly covered by the media in South Asia as several have taken place in recent times (*South Asia Times*, 2009; AsianFanatics Forum, 2009). For example, Asia Media Forum of Karachi, Pakistan, reported an incident involving the Pakistani journalist Maheen Usmani, who explored the reasons for considering a telephone call as sexual harassment. From her perspective, sexual harassment over the phone started when her superior called her late at night and launched into "suggestive talk" and lots of "innuendoes and told her to give him a call any time of the day or night." After that, she had no option but to resign from her job. Thus, sexual harassment in the workplace turned to sexual harassment over the cell phone. According to South Asian Women in Media (SAWM)-Pakistan, a network of female media professionals, sexual harassment via a cell phone had never been reported in Pakistan until the incident with Maheen came to light and no one could even imagine this type of victimization, which is unlike the usual forms of sex crime (*South Asia Times*, 2009). SAWM-P has received four or five such complaints and found a group of people in Pakistan who did not consider such behavior (sexual harassment through telephone conversation) important enough to report. Rather they tried to accuse women, arguing that a decent woman should not receive phone calls from unknown callers, especially objectionable calls (South Asia blog, 2011). But these people failed to perceive that these situations cannot be anticipated. Regarding this situation, the head of the Alliance Against Sexual Harassment (AASHA), Fouzia Saeed, said that the alliance is determined to raise sexual harassment as an issue to seek policy and legislative protection and "turn the tables on harassers and put them under the spotlight, rather than the women getting the stigma" (AASHA, 2010).

In Egypt, sexual harassment via a cell phone is not an unusual phenomenon (*The New Egypt*, 2010). The calls range from minor inconveniences to persistent, threatening behavior that becomes a major source of frustration for Egyptian women. In frustration, they do switch off their phones, but the perseverance of the harasser takes the form of love messages, persistent calls, and so forth. Victims of such behavior also informed their guardians but they seemed helpless in tackling this psycho-social problem. It has been found that the age of the victims in Egypt ranges from 20 to 50 years and the forms of such harassment are very similar to those in other regions of the world, which proves that the cell phone has become the most common tool for sexual harassment.

In addition to, similar incidents have been reported by victims in Hong Kong and, in some cases, it was possible for law enforcers to take immediate action. The Asian Human Rights Commission (2011) also reported that they received complaints about sexual harassment at the workplace in South Korea, but such harassment was not committed using a cell phone.

In Bangladesh, this issue is now being considered more seriously by society. Harassment over cell phones is a frequently discussed topic in Bangladesh. Several reports, articles, and letters have been written in newspapers, blogs, and many other public forums about young people's entanglement with these technologies (Raisa, 2011). Selim Mahbub, an engineer, commented in an editorial about *e-stalking* published in *The Daily Star* (2010):

> Mobile phone has been playing a vital role in the development of communication systems in the country. Nevertheless, some are using this technology in unethical way as a suitable and safe media to fulfill their evil desire. It is a kind of violence against women and in most cases, victims do not or cannot disclose it to others. As a result people having lustful desire to take the benefit of the mobile technology.

It has been observed that there is a great similarity in sexually explicit behavior over cell phones between Bangladesh and other countries, including Western countries. In addition to the alluring offers of cell phone service providers, handset manufacturers are also coming up with new technologies and facilities for the youth of Bangladesh. These smart phones make it very easy for youngsters to indulge in sexual harassment through cell phones. Handset manufacturing companies like Nokia, Samsung, LG, Sony Ericsson, and many more are now competing with each other to attract the younger generation by installing such devices as video cameras, Bluetooth, and Internet services. These multidimensional facilities may also result in some negative outcomes and can create certain risks if not used responsibly. It has also been considered that building virtual relationships among teenagers has become very common only due to the ease of mobile communication. Therefore, it can be said that as girls are the direct victims of bullying through cell phone, mostly in the form of sexual harassment, this must be treated as a sexual offence. This most pressing issue needs to be empirically analyzed and the current study is an effort in this direction.

Methods

The target group of this study were women from Dhaka city. This study extensively analyzes the experiences shared by the respondents, who were of different age ranges, marital statuses, and educational backgrounds. This research has tried to investigate the extent of sexual harassment over the cell phone, how it varies among the different age groups, and what the apparent impacts of this issue are. The analysis was concentrated on females as they are the prime victims of such harassment. For this purpose, a survey was conducted on three different age groups, namely school-going girls (age group 13–16), college/university female students (age group 17–24), and young professionals (age group 25–30). The respondents were from different socioeconomic backgrounds: students, housewives, and office workers.

Study Area, Sampling, Tools, and Respondents

The study area for this research was Dhaka city and according to the *Statistical Yearbook 2001*, the total population of Dhaka district is about 8.5 million (8,511,228), of which 45% is female (about 3,798,898) (Bangladesh Bureau of Statistics, 2010). If we consider the area under the jurisdiction of Dhaka city corporation (urban and semi-urban zone), its population is about 5.4 million (5,327,306) of which the female population is about 2.3 million (2,308,176). As no census has been taken of the adult female population of Dhaka city, it was not possible to cover the minimum percentage of the total female population for this research.

The simple random sampling method seemed to be the most convenient method to use, considering this huge population. In choosing the respondents, the age groups were presumed on the basis of the problem statement. Marital and occupational statuses were also considered, while the respondents were randomly selected from 10 schools, 10 colleges/universities, and 10 different institutions, that is, banks, public service offices, life insurance companies, corporate houses, international and national organizations, research institutions, and so on. Girls studying in schools were selected both from public and privately owned institutions. In choosing schools, the medium of study instruction (Bengali and English) was also considered as it has been perceived that, in Bangladesh, students from English-medium schools are much more technology oriented and mainly use cell phones to maintain an active social network. To own a cell number rather than using the family number is considered a token of status to some of the students. It has also been perceived that most victims of virtual harassment are young girls and women rather than older women. That is why this research assumed that the selected respondents of different age groups would represent the rest of the females in Dhaka city (Table 9.1).

An open-ended questionnaire was designed on the basis of the research questions stated earlier. Twenty-eight questions were asked regarding the problem statement. After an introductory discussion on this issue for rapport building, respondents were asked about cell phone behavior and about their feelings while receiving harassing calls both from known and unknown numbers. They were asked about the following details: Do you have your own cell number? Why do you carry more than one cell number? What are the possible ways of getting your personal number publicly disseminated? When do you feel harassed through cell phone behavior (message content or caller's talk)? How frequently do you receive odd/blank messages and phone calls? For how long have you been receiving such calls or messages (weeks/months/years)? Could you ever find out the identity of the caller? How do you react to such calls and messages? How do you feel after experiencing blank calls and obscene messages? Have you ever made a complaint? If yes, then to whom? Have you ever noticed someone trying to harass others over the phone? Could you determine the age range or social or family status of the person making such obnoxious calls over the cell phone? How can this type of behavior be controlled? Do you have any suggestions for actions that can be taken by the authorities to mitigate this problem? Answers to these key questions have established the background of this research and provided much information about this current problem in society.

To answer these questions, face-to-face interviews were carried out during the research period. School-going and college-going girls were interviewed at home with their parents and siblings present because they too were very interested in the issue. They also shared their experiences and suggestions for solving the issue in the long term. Most of the respondents from the age group of 17–25 years and above preferred to respond to the questionnaire through telephone conversations and sometimes through e-mails, not only for convenience but also to preserve their anonymity when they shared the nature of their experiences. It took a maximum of 40–45 min to complete the face-to-face survey after the rapport building. The telephone conversation

Table 9.1 Marital Status of Respondents According to Age Group

Marital Status	13–16 Years	17–24 Years	25–30 Years
Married	0	50	50
Unmarried	100	50	50
Total	300	300	300

was much easier and took 30 minutes to 1 hour depending on the issues to be covered by both the respondent and the interviewer. The response rate was 100% for this research because of its focus on a regular phenomenon that is a menace to our society and the lack of attempts to solve this problem.

Although the respondents were very cooperative in answering the questionnaire, some of them preferred to skip some questions, such as "Could you highlight the behavior in a little more detail (message content or picture details, etc.)? Do you maintain any restrictions in disseminating your contact number?"

Quantitative Analysis and Results

A quantitative analysis was made by calculating the correlation using a one-way ANOVA, the most reliable statistical tool for social science. The analysis for this particular study has been made on the basis of primary data. The data were collected through a questionnaire survey. Table 9.2 shows the patterns of cell phone behavior that caused a sense of sexual harassment in the respondents. Regarding the correlation analysis, we can measure the justification of this research in addressing a social problem. During the survey, school-going girls demonstrated how they got involved in a network of friendship and subsequently suffered from the intimidation of their so-called friends. College girls explained how they had been blackmailed by their boyfriends and their male friends. Professional women faced similar types of harassment and, in

Table 9.2 Ways of Sexual Harassment through Cell Phones (Call, SMS, Picture Messages, etc.)

Oral	Nonverbal
1. Sexual comments/remarks about person's appearance, body, or clothing	1. Sending sexually explicit pictures, wallpaper, cartoons, etc.
2. Telling sex-related jokes	2. Sex-related music, lyrics as ringtone
3. Asking about sexual fantasies	3. Taking photos
4. Insulting comments on someone's sex and conjugal life	4. Editing personal photos and disseminating them
5. Discussing sexual issues	5. Using camera phone, Bluetooth for data transfer without someone's consent
6. Asking for sexual support and continued pressure for dates	
7. Sexually suggestive signals and whistling on call	
8. Direct sexual proposition	

some cases, their reactions were very complex. Some of them became daring enough to be vocal in making their experiences public while many of them have never raised their voices or have even denied that they have ever been harassed at all.

We know that correlation analysis determines the degree of the relationship between two or more variables using a scattered diagram, Pearson's correlation coefficient, and so forth. A correlation coefficient lies between -1 and $+1$. Symbolically, $-1 < r < +1$. When $r = +1$, it means there is a perfect positive correlation between the variables. When $r = -1$, it means there is a perfect negative correlation between the variables. When $r = 0$, it means that there is no correlation between the variables. But no such relationship has been presented in the analysis section or can be detected in the data tables.

Table 9.3 shows that the correlation coefficient r is 0.131 for this analysis and thus denotes a perfect positive correlation between these two variables. It can be said that respondents from different occupations face sexually harassing behavior over a cell phone that affects their psychosocial life. Here, the types of sexual harassment were reported as blank or continuous phone calls, odd SMS or messages containing nude pictures, voice recordings, and blackmailing through previous communication history or photos taken and edited without permission.

An analysis of the survey information has been summarized in Table 9.4:

1. In the case of school-going girls, the rate of harassment through text messages, picture, and voice message is very high.
2. In the case of college/university-going female students, they are receiving sexually explicit behavior through phone calls and text messages, picture and voice messages. Surprisingly, the rate of blackmailing via a cell phone is higher in the case of college/university female students, which is significantly different from those of school-going girls and professional women.
3. In the case of young professional women, the rate of harassment through phone calls and texts, picture and voice messages is also very high. They are the main victims of sexual harassment from their colleagues, who call them after office hours seeking sexual favors or to share sex-related jokes.

Table 9.3   Correlation Analysis

Groups of the Respondents and their Occupations	Correlation Coefficient	Types of Sexual Harassment
School-going, college/ university-going, young professional	Pearson Correlation	0.131[a]
	Sig. (2-tailed)	0.023
	N	300

[a] Correlation is significant at the 0.05 level (2-tailed).

Table 9.4 Survey Findings

Respondent Groups	Phone Calls (X)		Text, Picture and Voice Message (Y)		Blackmailing (Z)		X + Y		Y + Z		Z + X		X + Y + Z	
	f	%	f	%	f	%	f	%	f	%	f	%	f	%
School-going	60	20	84	28	45	15	63	21	12	4	9	3	3	1
College/university-going	36	12	66	22	51	17	90	30	36	12	12	4	9	3
Young professional	30	10	60	20	15	5	105	35	45	15	24	8	21	7

n = number of respondents, 300; f = frequency.

During the survey, statements of the victims about the SMS content were recorded to measure the intensity of the harassment and were analyzed accordingly. A summary is given in Table 9.5.

From the SMS content, it can be said with full confidence that the cell phone now plays a vital role in disseminating threats to the life of a female and it is very easy to embarrass them using this sophisticated weapon. The degree of harassment may vary according to the persistence of the abusers, but the abused female has no control over such intimidation.

Table 9.6 depicts the frequency of offensive behavior exhibited by perpetrators over cell phones and its duration, which affects a girl's normal life.

This research has aimed to ensure the representation of females from school, college/university, and young professionals to explore the extent of

Table 9.5 Statement from the Victim (SMS Content)

Target Group	SMS Content	Incident Shared/Disclosed to (Prioritized)
School-going girls	• "What's your bra size? I know it's pink" • "Are you VIRGIN?" • Picture of sex organs/nude couple	1. Classmate friends 2. Parents 3. Cousins/siblings
College/university-going	• Physical measurement • Expressed sex desire and favorite places to meet • Picture of having sex • Quote from romantic novels	1. Fiancé 2. Siblings 3. Classmate friends 4. Senior friends/roommates 5. Parents 6. Teachers
Young professionals	• Asked for sex favor • Asked for meeting at night after work • Offered money	1. Friends 2. Husbands 3. Parents 4. Colleagues

Table 9.6 Frequency and Duration of Incidents

Incident	Time Limit	Frequency (f)	Percentage
Frequency of blank calls/ SMS/picture SMS/voice message	Once a day	48	16
	Twice a day	108	36
	Several times	144	48
Number of respondents, $n = 300$			
Duration of sexually harassing behavior over cell phone	<6 months	63	21
	6–12 months	159	53
	>1 year	78	26
Number of respondents, $n = 300$			

this social problem in Dhaka city by measuring the duration of its occurrence and thus they have been taken as the respondents of the target group of this research. All of the participants reported that they had experienced irremissible behavior over their cell phones that made them feel they were being sexually harassed. They had received at least one blank phone call or SMS containing nudity or voice messages a day, sometimes reaching several in 24 h. Moreover, it was found that all the respondents had suffered from these types of behavior for more than 6–12 months.

The ANOVA table (Table 9.7) predicted that all respondents (students and young professionals) are equally harassed by such behaviour and the significant level is 0.004, which is very low in the case of relating the extent of harassment with the status of the girl. This research has also found that there is no significant reason that tempted the abusers to harass girls through SMS or phone calls containing sex jokes.

To find out the answer to research question number 3, which queried the adverse impacts of sexual harassment over a cell phone on the respondents' social lives, some critical questions were asked of the school/college/university-going students and young professionals in order to depict the situation. This part of the research questionnaires covered the psychosocial condition of girls and women who felt they had been sexually assaulted, though it was only over their cell phones (Table 9.8).

Table 9.7 One-Way ANOVA (Duration of Harassment through Blank Calls/SMS from a Particular Number)

ANOVA	Sum of Squares	df	Mean Square	f	Significance
Between groups	5.193	2	2.597	5.653	0.004
Within groups	135.951	296	0.459		
Total	141.144	298			

Table 9.8 Effect and Impact of Such Behavior on Cell Phone Users

Effects	Impacts of Cell Phone Sexual Harassment on Social Life
Social stress	Elimination from socialization and co-curricular activities
	Missed deadlines
	Increased suspicion
	Difficulties in conjugal life
Psychological stress	Becoming introverted
	Increased hiding tendency
	Over-consciousness
	Lacking concentration on studies
	Poor performance in studies
	Disappointment
	Lower self-esteem
Physical stress	Physical strain
	Numbness, depression, fear, shame, and guilt
	Change in appetite
	High temperament

Qualitative Analysis and Results

While conducting the survey, some notable cases were found, which have been presented here:

CASE A

I got a phone call from a complete stranger and after getting the female voice, they started to send me chain messages. I have the phone number and the name of the person who called. I got the most disgusting messages which literally had me in tears. I showed those messages to my husband, and became angry that why I have received unknown phone calls. Even If you heard the messages you would cringe! It is absolutely disgusting. This person doesn't even know me. After that I have received hundreds of messages from that number and even calls at midnight. I personally have requested for not calling me but it did not work. When I stopped receiving that number, then they keep calling me from several numbers and spread out my numbers among group of peoples. I was crashed being tortured with the sex related voice calls and messages. The only solution was changing my number that I did at last.

CASE B

I was gifted with my touch screen, multifunction cell phone for my unpredictable result in SSC. I was so excited that I disbursed my phone number to all my friends and relatives. Even though I was controlled by my parents with the limited recharging of my cell phone, I was capable to keep it active in maintaining my newly established friend circle. Thus, I was so acquainted with unknown, unseen matters and subjects that insist me to build up an emotional relationship and I did that. I was eager to get his call, sms and so on. And I felt that I was getting addicted to that I seem LOVE. Though it has not last long, but several of my SMS, pictures, etc. have been shared with him in some weak moments. I discovered my photos on some of my classmates' cell phone and feeling unbearably trashed.

CASE C

I used to work with male colleagues and suddenly I found someone of them sending me filthy pictures of himself to cell phone but the face was not clear. After sometimes, he started to call and directly offers money for sex, then tries to blackmail me with it, as I said no. As well as he claimed that he recorded my voices over phone and will attach them with some others videos.

As it is tough to get the actual identity of the person on the other side of the phone and also cannot be proven. This has to stop, and I was in need to complain to the authority accused him for sexual harassment might impair my reputation among colleagues. I was not sure what I might do. But he was driving me crazy! I have changed my number twice but he keeps finding people I know and getting the new one. This can't continue!!!

Other Significant Findings

a. *Possible ways of making a cell phone number widely known*: As experienced by the respondents, the most recurrent medium through which a cell number is made widely known is the recharge center. School-going girls who are dependent on others to recharge their numbers are the common victims.
b. *Extent of monitoring*: It is quite obvious that school-going girls will have to be monitored by their parents and this study found that some of the married, young professionals were also being monitored by their husbands.

c. *Actions taken*: Guardians/parents attempted to resolve this sensitive issue when they noticed the harassment causing serious threats to the girls. The most common and possible actions are changing the number, call blocking, and complaining to the authorities.

d. *Precautions*: All of the respondents have felt helpless in answering the questions regarding their protection from such harassment. Most of the victims opted for controlling the dissemination of their cell numbers and switching off their mobiles at night as the final precaution. In regard to this issue, it was found that the parents of school-going girls took care of this issue and professional young women chose to switch off their cell phones at night.

School Teens: Prime Victims

Parents usually give a cell phone to their school-going daughters in order to have constant communication and to ensure their safety. Through the cell phone, she can communicate with her friends as and when necessary. In some cases, parents keep track of their school-going daughter so that they are aware of what she is doing in the absence of a guardian and whether she is being disturbed by the cell phone.

However, it has generally been observed that the cell numbers of young female users are usually spread among friends, relatives, and now mostly from the recharge centers. Nonetheless, a young girl in Bangladesh always hesitates to receive an unknown caller in the presence of her parents. Girls remain under pressure if their cell phone use is monitored by their parents and monitoring becomes strong while such harassment takes place. Such monitoring sometimes makes girls hide the harassing incidents from guardians, as there is a chance they will confiscate their cell phones.

School girl X: Once I got a phone call from an unknown caller while I was in coaching center. I thought it might be my uncle as I didn't have numbers of my all relatives. But I was wrong as I picked up the call and just said HELLO but the caller said nothing … … …..

Interviewer: Then what happened? What was the wrong?

School girl X: It was wrong as they got my voice; they started to call me again and again as well as texting. My parents always warned me not to receive the unknown calls. But I could not stop myself … … … …..

Interviewer: What do you think? How they got your number?

Girl: I gave my phone number only to some of my close classmates and my family members. Not to my cousins even. I thought it's from the recharge center as I never go to recharge my cell phone number, my younger brother used to do this for me. May be they tried my number and when they found a girl's voice, they started calling and texting. Though I don't pick the calls now, but it keeps ringing and I got threatened. If that continued, my parents will take it away from me. But what should I do ... ...??

College/University Students: Courageous Ones

This research survey found a praiseworthy situation due to the bold attitude of college and university students. They are the most frequent users of cell phones, and they are not monitored as closely as school-going girls. Above all, they are capable of maintaining the cost of cell phones. However, a college-going or university-going girl has to swap her cell number with her classmates, friends, and teachers. This study has found that the cell numbers of college-going and university-going girls are distributed through their friends of friends.

College-going girls face the most awful situation when they get involved with an admirer who subsequently blackmails them. Additionally, such blackmailing can also take place when a misunderstanding occurs within groups of friends. The cell phone can become an active tool creating opportunities for misunderstanding, blackmailing, and taking revenge. It has been found that girls have to be very cautious when using cell phones, to protect themselves from suffering the humiliation of unwanted behavior.

College-going and university-going girls received many obscene texts and pictures via their cell phones and it has been found that the suspected person was much respected by the victim. Though it is very easy for university students to handle such situations, as they have access to technology-aided precautions such as call blocking, SMS alerts, missed calls alerts, and so on, their gender sensibility bugged them and they continued to feel threatened, even after solving the problem. Survey discussions have found that friends often support the victim to trace the caller, thereby taking positive action. A young university-going woman shared her experience:

It was in the very beginning of my university life, I started to get messages describing my beauty in a very poetic manner. Numbers of SMS were coming even while I am in class, it seemed someone was following me. I was amazed to find myself being admired in this way but I was really annoyed at this. That is why I was trying to find out to whom I swap my number with. As a newcomer of my university, I was not so known to all my university mates. After a certain period, that particular person started to call me at midnight and then I showed those to my senior roommate and she helped me to recognize the sender. The sender was identified as one of my senior classmate and nobody showed courage to protest against such behavior.

Young Professionals: Vulnerable Ones

Professional women are the most frequent users of cell phones as they make business calls over the phone when they are at home and busy with other aspects of their lives. Cell phones are the most comfortable and supportive way for women to manage their responsibilities both at home and work. Usually, their numbers are disseminated among business clients and office colleagues, and they may receive phone calls, voice mails, and so forth, throughout the day and into the night. The situation is similar for both married and unmarried women, even from different perspectives as the form of calls, the timing and the content of these communications vary. Married women suffered mental agony when they discovered that they were being monitored by their husband.

Unmarried girls also faced the same situation. They found that some of their male colleagues/professional friends, both married and unmarried, tried to lure them into relationships beyond a working relation and would make requests for sexual favors during phone conversations. Sometimes, colleagues recorded their friendly conversations with female colleagues for unethical purposes and made reference to them for future blackmailing. This research found that professional women are harassed over the cell phone mostly by their colleagues/professional friends and then by outsiders, unlike school-going and college-going girls. So, females always feel frightened when using cell phones; they keep receiving unwanted phone calls, messages, and so on, while waiting to attend to calls that pertain to their job.

Impact of Victimization

Cell phones are frequently used to deliver sexual threats and insults, thereby causing severe harassment to a girl and affecting her personal, social, professional, and conjugal statuses. The fear of being humiliated again haunts them all the time. Girls are also found to be indirectly harassed behind their back when others spread rumors about their activities and relationships. It is particularly difficult for them to escape from such harassment when it happens over their cell phone. Dr. Israt Jahan Bithi, a psychologist in the Bangladesh Rehabilitation Centre for Trauma Victims, says, "Harassment over cell phones has now become a social problem. It might have a long-term influence on one's psychology" (Madhuri, 2010). Dr. Mahmudur Rahman, head of the Department of Psychology at Dhaka University, says, "Filthy words and ugly comments over cell phones create mental pressure on a person for which she can later even decide to commit suicide. The cell phone operators need to pay attention to this serious issue and must take necessary measures sooner than later" (Madhuri, 2010).

A particular group of cell phone users makes uninhibited contact with females of all ages through cell phones and thus cause virtual sexual exploitation and hence embarrassment in many respects, which are as follows:

a. *Affected social life*: Young girls considered text messaging as the most widely used facility provided by a cell phone, helping them to maintain contact with their peers, thereby coordinating their social life. Sexual bullying through cell phones makes females feel so threatened that they are reluctant to answer even important calls and check SMS content and sometimes they never answer calls from unknown numbers. Continuous monitoring, control over recharging, number swapping, and so forth, has led the female cell phone users to feel themselves imprisoned. Certainly, all this never brings vital positive changes to the lives of victims and prevents them from socializing and participating in family activities. Students stop talking and sharing their feelings even with their close friends. Thus, most of their personal problems remain untreated due to their introvert nature and this reluctance may lead to fatal outcomes.

b. *Education/institutional/professional status*: Female students have to change their regular cell phone number to eliminate this harassment. Parents can confiscate the phone to reduce the risk fatal incidents later. Young cell phone users are also afraid of being disconnected from their friends' network and consequently they tend to hide calls or messages. All of this distract them from their studies and other co-curricular activities, causing poor performance and so on. Sometimes victims become too frustrated to deal with their life goals. In addition to students, young professionals' performance was also affected due to missing deadlines for reporting, losing concentration at work, and so forth. Receiving phone calls or SMS at night, which keeps them awake, puts them under so much pressure that their productivity and creativity are reduced.

c. *Physical disorder*: The survey results revealed an influx of blank callers sending messages during the night and this behavior caused a deterioration in the health of the abused girls. Continuous phone calls/missed calls and chain messages from the cell phone perpetrators kept the user awake at night, causing fatigue and a consequent inability to perform regular work efficiently. Being threatened by the content of messages, they started to suffer from appetite changes and physical pain and the continuous disruption of their sleep led to numbness, depression, intense fear, shame, and so forth. Severe brain damage and irritability may also occur in women suffering from such fearful situations for a long time.

d. *Mental/psychological disturbance*: Sexual exploitation over cell phones demoralized the victims and they suffered from lower self-esteem, suicidal ideation, and a variety of emotional responses, including the fear of being harassed again, frustration, anger, and depression. All these disappointing behaviors lead the young school girls to discover the harshness of their surroundings, which is very unlike their familiar environment. Sometimes they felt humiliated when sharing their experiences of harassment with friends and family members and also thought of committing suicide. Although such fatal cases have not yet been filed in Bangladesh, it could occur any day.

e. *Conjugal life*: Sexual abuse via a cell phone has a dreadful impact on conjugal life. It causes misunderstanding and suspicion for couples and weakens their bond, sometimes causing the relationship to end. Dr. Israt Jahan Bithi says "continuous harassment not only causes annoyance, but also invites troubles in a conjugal life. Members of the family blame a girl for the harassment, which casts a negative impact on one's mind. Mobile operators must take measures against harassment over cell phones" (Madhuri, 2010).

Discussion and Conclusion

The cell phone now seems to be the most successful weapon in aiding perpetrators to indulge in sexual harassment, unlike other visual ways of committing such crimes. As well as the regular use of cell phones for communication, they are now being used to commit virtual social crimes. It has been found that the cell phone is the most useful tool to harass females as no evidence remains. Thus, women are in a constant dilemma about using cell phones as they are the victims of this virtual offense. As discussed earlier, policies regarding this issue have not been very effective in most countries, especially in Bangladesh. In addition to ineffective policies, the social structure of Bangladesh is not very favorable toward complaints from women about sexual harassment over the phone. Victims as well as their families are not interested in bringing such offenses to the notice of the authorities or state-led justice.

Some steps have been taken by the Bangladeshi government and other authorities to reduce such victimization. Persons below 18 years of age will not be able to purchase cell phone cards under new rules that are being enforced by the Bangladeshi government (*The Times of India*, 2010). Over 1.2 million unregistered SIM (subscriber identity module) and RUIM (removable user identity module) cards have so far been blocked. There are authoritarian rules on obtaining certificates to cell phone SIM cards. A minimum education to secondary school certificate is required to apply for this business and the person would have to go through police verification (Rahman, 2011). In addition to the call-blocking service offered by all telecommunication service providers, Robi, a growing cell phone service provider, introduced the pin recharge system in which there is no need to disclose the user's phone number in order to recharge it at the center.

Vodafone has developed an "Offensive Content Policy" to control offensive content on their network to ensure the security of their subscribers. It does not detect the person's communication details but it has control over the level of information exchange among subscribers (Yates, 2003). As a cell phone service provider, Vodafone has performed their corporate social responsibility with great success by controlling the content of web messages through their policy.

Now we will discuss the effectiveness and the extent of the present laws and regulations to tackle cell phone sexual harassment in Bangladesh. In this regard, Bangladesh Legal Aid and Services Trust (BLAST) deputy director and a Supreme Court lawyer Farida Yasmin said, "Section 509 of the Penal Code of 1860 states, a person may be sentenced to one year imprisonment or fined or be punished by both, if he makes any offensive comments or undignified gesture or shows any object that can harm a woman's dignity. There are some other laws, too and the Metropolitan Police Ordinance deals with this issue" (Madhuri, 2010). Although in Bangladesh, there are well defined laws and regulations with proper amendments to support law enforcers, these incidents are not being made public. To bring such harassment to public notice is considered more an insult to the dignity of the girl and her family. As a result, such cases remain undiscovered and unpunished (Madhuri, 2010).

Section 10(2) of the Women and Children Repression Prevention Act, 2000, and amendment, 2003, Bangladesh, explain that if a man sexually assaults or makes indecent gestures for his sexual gratification, this will be considered as sexual harassment and the person is liable to receive up to 7 years' imprisonment and a fine (Madhuri, 2010). Cell phone operators need to take more responsibility in applying these laws and regulations through their effective policies.

"Such types of harassment caused by a subscriber cannot be solved by the mobile phone operators only," an Airtel marketing executive said. He exclaimed that it is not even possible to reduce this harassment by disconnecting the accused subscribers. He also added that "we acknowledge that sexual harassment over cell phone is a problem. We receive several complaints every now and then. Legally we cannot do much. We only can request the accused subscriber not to do so. Yes, we are ready to cooperate with the law enforcing agencies if there is any legal step taken for this" (Rahman, 2011).

Thus, in the present context, cell phone operators in Bangladesh are hardly taking any legal action as they also need to look after their business.

Regarding this critical point of marketing, the deputy director of Bangladesh Telegraph and Telephone Board (BTTB), Mir Mohammad Morshed, said, "Bangladesh Telecommunications Regulatory Commission (BTRC) has been set up for development of telecommunications, improvement of services provided by different companies and regulating the industry. It's the responsibility of BTRC to look into the subscribers' problems" (Madhuri, 2010). Here he addressed The Bangladesh Telecommunications Act, 2001, which all cell phone service providers need to observe in order to take care of harassed subscribers. BTRC also maintains a "complaint cell" to support such victims (Madhuri, 2010).

As it is impossible to trace the cell phone perpetrator who is exhibiting sexually exploiting and embarrassing behavior toward a female, I propose the following recommendations to execute the redemption process to eliminate social tension.

1. Stop offering bonus talking time and unlimited SMS service.
2. Strictly follow the registration methods while selling and buying SIMs.
3. Mandatory submission of birth certificates and national identification numbers to issue SIMs.
4. Incentives to the owners of recharge centers to keep the confidentiality of the user's number.
5. Promote users to identify their abusers through awareness-building campaigns.
6. Proper counseling to encourage young girls to share the incidents that threatened them.

Bangladesh is still lagging behind in taking bold steps to prevent such harassment.

Nevertheless, it is a matter of hope for us that "Over 200,000 mobile phone connections have so far been cancelled following allegations of various criminal offences, including extortion, issuance of threats, and other forms of harassment," said Ms. Sahara Khatun MP, Honorable Minister, Ministry of Home Affairs.

As evidence of such an attempt, the court also asked the government to properly define "sexual harassment" under the law and replace the term *eve teasing* with "stalking" as a sexual offence in the Women and Children Repression Prevention Act. There is also an order to form a cell in every police station to supervise activities in the prevention of sexual harassment of women. This initiative can also be an effective approach in reducing sexual harassment over cell phones, if cell phone service provider companies take greater responsibility for maintaing records for future reference, thereby helping in judicial activities. They may also take responsibility for collecting reports of such occurrences and taking further action to prevent this. Hence, we can see the light at the end of the tunnel. In conclusion, it can be said that there should be a massive campaign against sexual harassment via mobile phones. The government should enact more specific laws to prevent such incidents. The NGOs can also play a significant role in mobilizing the mass population against harassment via cell phones. The Asian Human Rights Commission suggested writing blogs, newspapers, networking websites, and so forth, about cases that appear in any form.

References

Alliance Against Sexual Harassment. (2010). Retrieved February 5, 2012, from http://www.aasha.org.pk/about_aasha.php.

AsianFanatics Forum. (2009). Sherming Yiu was sexually harassed over the phone, reports to the police Monday May 25, 2009 Hong Kong. Retrieved February 4, 2012, from http://asianfanatics.net/forum/topic/656185-sherming-yiu-was-sexually-harassedover-the-phone-reports-to-the-police/.

Asian Human Rights Commission. (2011). South Korea: Dismissal of a female worker after complaining about sexual harassment at the workplace. Asian Human Rights Commission—Urgent Appeals Programme. Retrieved February 4, 2012, from http://www.humanrights.asia/news/forwarded-news/AHRC-FUA-017-2011.

Bangladesh Bureau of Statistics. (2010). http://www.bbs.gov.bd/WebTestApplication/userfiles/Image/SY2010/Chapter-02.pdf. Retrieved January 31, 2012.

Bangladesh Telecommunication Regulatory Commission (BTRC). (2011). Mobile phone subscribers in Bangladesh. Retrieved June 22, 2011, from http://www.btrc.gov.bd/newsandevents/mobile_phone_subscribers/mobile_phone_subscribers_may_2011.php.

Business & Legal Reports Inc. (2005). Sexual harassment essentials of prevention and response, p. 2. Retrieved May 20, 2011, from http://books.google.com/books?id=fB5AdFYn6q0C&pg=PA46&dq=sexual+harassent+over+cell+phone&hl=en&ei=OILNTcuYFMeCOquj7JcN&sa=X&oi=book_result&ct=result&resnum=3&ved=0CEsQ6AEwAg#v=onepage&q&f=false.

Conte, J. R. (2002). *Critical Issues in Child Sexual Abuse: Historical, Legal, and Psychological Perspectives.* Thousand Oaks, CA: Sage.

Ford, C. A., & Donis, F. J. (1996). The relationship between age and gender in workers' attitudes toward sexual harassment. *Journal of Psychology, 130,* 627–633.

Franke, K. M. (1997). What's wrong with sexual harassment? *Stanford Law Review.* 691–772. Retrieved May 20, 2011, from http://www2.law.columbia.edu/faculty_franke/Whats_Wrong_With_Sexual_Harassment.pdf.

Harris Interactive. (2008). *Teenagers: A Generation Unplugged: Research Report.* Retrieved May 22, 2011, from http://files.ctia.org/pdf/HI_TeenMobileStudy_ResearchReport.pdf.

ITUC. (2008). *Stopping Sexual Harassment at Work—A Trade Union Guide.* ITUC: International Trade Union Confederation. p. 9.

Kinnear, K. L. (2007). *Childhood Sexual Abuse,* 2nd edition. Santa Barabar, CA: ABC-CLIO.

Lenhart, A. (2010). Teens, cell phones and texting: Text messaging becomes center-piece communication. Pew Internet & American Life Project. Retrieved May 10, 2011, from http://pewresearch.org/pubs/1572/teens-cell-phones-text-messages.

MacKinnon, C., & Siegel, R. (2004). *Directions in Sexual Harassment Law*. New Haven, CT: Yale University Press.

Madhuri, S. (2010). Steps needed to stop sexual harassment over cellphone. *The Financial Express*. Vol. 10, No. 235. Retrieved May 10, 2011, from http://www.thefinancialexpress-bd.com/more.php?news_id=108038.

Marion, N. E. (2010). The Council of Europe's Cyber Crime Treaty: An exercise in symbolic legislation. *International Journal of Cyber Criminology*, 4(1&2), 699–712.

Rahman, A. (2011). Interviewed by the author. May 15, 2011, Dhaka.

Raisa, A. (2011). Virtual space real crime. *The Daily Star*. Vol. 10, Iss. 23. Retrieved June 23, 2011, from http://www.thedailystar.net/magazine/2011/06/03/cover.htm.

Rozee, P. D. (2000). *Issues in the Psychology of Women*. New York: Kluwer Academics/Plenum Publishers.

Sexual Harassment Policy. (2008). Department of Social Development, Province of the Eastern Cape. p. 4.

South Asia blog. (2011). Sexual Harassment Instead of Eve Teasing in Bangladesh. South Asia blog on social economic situation. Retrieved February 4, 2012, from http://thesouthasia.blogspot.com/2011/01/sexual-harassment-instead-of-eve.html.

South Asia Times. (2009). e-Pak scribe pursues sexual harassment case. Retrieved February 4, 2012, from http://www.southasiatimes.com.au/news/pak-scribe-pursues-sexual-harassment-case/.

The Daily Star. (2010). E-stalking: Stop the faceless menace in its strides. Retrieved May 10, 2011, from http://www.thedailystar.net/newDesign/news-details.php?nid=153468.

The New Egypt. (2010). Egypt: Battling sexual harassment on the phone. Retrieved February 4, from http://bikyamasr.com/7619/egypt-battling-sexual-harassment-on-the-phone/.

The Supreme Court of Bangladesh High Court Division, Special Original Jurisdiction. (2010). Writ Petition No. 8769, pp. 11–12. An application under Article 102 of the Constitution of the People's Republic of Bangladesh and Bangladesh National Women Lawyers Association (BNWLA). Retrieved on January 1, 2012, from http://www.bnwlabd.org/wp-content/uploads/2011/08/Judgment-to-prevent-eve-teseasing1.pdf.

The Times of India. (2010). Bangladesh to ban sale of SIM cards to youths under 18. Retrieved May 10, 2011, from http://articles.timesofindia.indiatimes.com/2010-07-08/south-asia/28296883_1_sim-cards-cell-phone-telecommunications-regulatory-commission.

Wood, J. (1997). *Gendered Lives: Communication, Gender and Culture*. Belmont, CA: Wadsworth.

Yates, C. (2003). *Mobile Phone Issues—What Risks Are Associated With Their Use By Our Youth*. Retrieved May 1, 2011, from http://www.netsafe.org.nz/Doc_Library/netsafepapers_colinyates_mobile.pdf.

Marginality and Social Exclusion III

Community Reentry from Jail for Mentally Ill Offenders

10

Challenges of Program Implementation

DALE K. SECHREST
GISELA M. BICHLER
DON A. JOSI
DAVID SHICHOR

Contents

Introduction

The principal objective of this chapter is to report on the problems of implementing a state-funded, county-implemented, short-term intervention program for mentally ill offenders reentering the community from a large jail. The purpose of the program was to reduce jail returns and jail days subsequent to mental health program intervention, as well as to reduce the need for psychiatric in-patient services. The findings for enhanced-treatment (experimental) subjects showed that they did not manifest significant reductions in returns to jail or jail days in comparison to randomly selected treatment-as-usual (control) subjects during 1 year after their release from the jail. Significant reductions in the cost of caring for these individuals were not realized. We provide a brief literature review, a description of the program and its goals, the research methodology used, and findings from the experimental-control group study for male participants. This is followed by a presentation of some of the reasons the program was not successful, with some lessons learned.

Prisoner Reentry

For a long time, the problem of prisoners returning to the community was an important topic for criminal justice in the United States, and "reintegration" was highlighted in the President's *Task Force Report Correction* (1967). It became a pivotal concern in the wake of the mass imprisonment policies following the 1970s' and 1980s' campaigns of "war on crime" and "war on drugs" (see, e.g., Mauer, 2001), prompted by the conservative turn in the sociopolitical atmosphere. Prisoner reintegration resurfaced as reentry during the late 1990s and has become a major issue in criminological research and literature. Petersilia (2003, p. 3) defines prisoner reentry as "all activities and programming conducted to prepare ex-convicts to return safely to the community and to live as law abiding citizens."

About 93% of prison inmates eventually return to society (see Petersilia, 2003; Travis, 2000); this roughly quantifies to 600,000 prison inmates each year (Travis, 2000). This massive reentry of inmates into society has attracted the attention of politicians, public officials, and social scientists. The main issues are public safety, the management of the release by formal agencies, cost-effectiveness, and the capacity and readiness of communities to absorb and reintegrate these individuals into social environments that will facilitate their becoming law-abiding citizens. Serious questions were raised about the potential increases in crime, meeting the challenge of supervision in the community, and finding resources to increase the community's capacity to absorb the returnees. These concerns seemed to be valid, since funding for effective supervision did not keep up with the growing number of returnees to the community and there were problems in finding jobs for unskilled or low-skilled individuals (Lynch & Sabol, 2001).

So far, the record in this respect is not very promising because about two-thirds of the released prisoners reoffend and return to confinement either by committing new offenses or by violating the conditions of their release (Petersilia, 2003). Within California, recidivism rates for parolees are generally at 70% (Little Hoover Commission, 2003). Higher rates of release coupled with comparable levels of recidivism suggest that the effectiveness of reentry programs is of vital concern, particularly for those individuals with mental illness—approximately 16% of all inmates (Ditton, 1999)*—who face even greater community reintegration challenges.

Reentry of Mentally Ill Substance Abusers

Upon release, inmates with mental illness require more formal monitoring and aftercare arrangements by mental health staff. Many of the mentally ill in the criminal justice system also have substance abuse problems that adversely affect their adjustment in the community (see Drake et al., 1998). Furthermore, criminal justice policies tend to place greater emphasis on surveillance rather than on social service support (see Seiter & Kadela, 2003). This tendency serves to increase the likelihood of recidivism: more than 75% of mentally ill inmates incarcerated in 1998 had at least one prior conviction resulting in prison, jail, or probation (Ditton, 1999).

Jails serve only as a stopgap measure, providing temporary "psychiatric inpatient care" within ill-equipped facilities with staff who often do not have sufficient training in recognizing or managing mentally ill individuals. One report showed that:

> On average, mentally ill inmates spend nine months in jail before release or transfer; disciplinary problems were more common among mentally ill inmates ... more than 24 percent of the mentally ill inmates were charged with breaking jail rules, compared with 16 percent of the general population; and only 41% in the local jails report receiving some sort of treatment (counseling, medication, etc.). (Gallemore, 2000: 67)

---

* These populations include the case of an inmate with schizophrenia in the Denver County Jail, who was incarcerated for the 100th time, charged with creating a nuisance in the community. In Memphis, Tennessee, a mentally ill woman was incarcerated for the 258th time on an assault charge. In Orange County, California, in 1998, 300 mentally ill offenders were rearrested three times and 119 were rearrested four times (Torrey, 1999). For example, when the mental hospital (Agnews State) was closed in Santa Clara County, California, the jail population increased 300% (Izumi et al., 1996). A detailed report provided ample evidence that mental illness was a costly problem for California's prisons and jails and was probably a driving force in the legislation creating the MIOCR grants (Izumi et al., 1996).

Further complicating treatment is that most of the mentally ill inmates have co-occurring disorders (or are dually diagnosed). According to the National GAINS Center (Peters & Bartoi, 1997), between 25% and 50% of all people with mental health disorders also have a substance abuse disorder. Abram and Teplin (1991) report that both male and female detainees with severe mental disorders have a 72% rate of co-occurring substance abuse disorders. In criminal justice populations, the rates for mental health disorders (four times higher) and alcohol/drug disorders (four to seven times higher) are significantly higher than in the general population. For example, after controlling for demographic differences between Cook County jail detainees and five-city samples, Teplin (1990) found that the jail prevalence rate of severe mental disorder was still two to three times higher than that of the general population.

In the spring of 2002, the National GAINS Center for People with Co-Occurring Disorders in the Justice System reported on the prevalence rate of co-occurring disorders in the jail population. Based on Diagnostic Interview Schedule criteria (version III and III R), they found that among male detainees, at intake, 2.7% met the criteria for schizophrenia/schizophreniform disorder, 1.4% for mania, and 3.9% for major depression. Among female detainees, they found that 2.0% met the criteria for schizophrenia/ schizophreniform disorder, 1.4% for mania, and 10.5% for a major depressive episode (National GAINS Center, 2001). More significantly, 2-week substance use disorder prevalence rates were much higher than the severe mental disorder rates for both male and female detainees entering jails, 29% and 53%, respectively (National GAINS Center, 2001).

Not unexpectedly, offenders with a mental illness and a substance abuse disorder experience a high rate of recidivism. Research conducted by the Federal Bureau of Prisons found that recidivism rates are higher among individuals who have a pre-prison history of drug or alcohol abuse (Harer, 1994). These individuals then become part of a revolving-door syndrome because they do not receive the proper services and support necessary to allow them to integrate successfully back into the community. Hartwell (2004) underscored this by referring to it as the "triple stigma" of mental illness, substance abuse, and criminal justice system involvement.

Mentally Ill Offenders

Many mental health professionals observed that the treatment needs of this clientele were not satisfactorily met in correctional institutions that were not established or equipped for that purpose. According to several studies, very few reentry programs have special mental health components included or available. Even when they are available, many of the released mentally ill inmates refuse services, fearing reinstitutionalization (Petersilia, 2005). These concerns were amplified by the fact that the funding for effective mental health supervision and monitoring of the returnees is inadequate (Lynch & Sabol, 2001). Thus, efforts to arrange their reentry into society and to treat them in the community became a major criminal justice concern, and several programs were launched with the purpose of mainstreaming these people into the community.

One of the most significant factors is the way the mental health system is set up. Research indicates that this population is extremely vulnerable to arrest due to a lack of coordination between systems and a lack of proper treatment facilities (Abram & Teplin, 1991; Laberge & Morin, 1995). Abram and Teplin (1991) state, "Although a complex array of services is available, each subsystem designs its programs to fit a specific need, and many programs are managed as if clients were pure types" (p. 1036). Often, the system is not set up to deal with dual diagnosis patients, especially in a correctional setting.

It is also essential for the criminal justice program to include mandatory treatment elements. For example, Broner et al. (2005) reported on a reentry program for jail inmates with alcohol, drug, and mental health disorders. The authors compared offenders who were mandated by the court to participate in a program involving treatment, mandatory case management reporting, and sanctions for noncompliance, versus those who were released without court involvement or any sanctions. As expected, mandated diversion in the community was more effective than nonmandated diversion in reducing the subsequent incarceration and drug abuse of mentally impaired jail inmates. This result indicates the importance of monitoring and aftercare of mentally ill jail inmates after their release.

SPAN Project

In September 1998, the California legislature provided funds for a select group of counties to develop demonstration projects aimed at keeping non-violent mentally ill offenders in the community. In line with concerns about cost-effectiveness in the public sector, one of the main concerns was the reduction of the estimated annual cost of U.S.$315 million spent on keeping mentally ill inmates in jails in California (Linden, 2000). One of the programs developed in response to this initiative was the San Bernardino Partners Aftercare Network (SPAN). Following the "collaborative model," a multiagency body (the Sheriff's Department and the County Mental Health Department) was charged with linking inmates diagnosed as mentally ill to community services upon their release.* In doing so, the SPAN program was intended to serve as a bridge between the custodial setting of jail and life in the free community, thereby reducing the returns to jail and the related criminal justice costs.†

The criteria for client admission included the following: current resident of San Bernardino County; criminal charges that excluded extensive violence or sex crimes; client's current mental illness or history indicating that their mental illness was manageable without inpatient services; client able and willing to pursue voluntary treatment; client able to live safely in the community; client to be released into the community; and client was medically stable. While the focus of admissions for the SPAN program was mental illness, it was recognized that co-occurring disorders were present for about the proportion stated by Abram and Teplin (above 70%–80%). At the beginning, the program was intended to assist the lower-functioning, persistently mentally ill (those with schizophrenia and major mood disorders). Later, the program was expanded to include dually diagnosed/co-occurring disorder individuals, as well.

Aside from the initial SPAN assessment and an evaluation of their medical condition, treatment plan development and medication services were the only prerelease services offered to SPAN clients. Candidate evaluations were assigned to line staff of the Jail Mental Health Services (JMHS) Division and were organized around an inmate's release date. For example, it was common that a new referral would have a potential release date within a few days of

---

* The San Bernardino County Sheriff's Department houses a substantial number of mentally ill offenders. Estimates produced by the Jail Mental Health Services (JMHS) indicate that between 10% and 12% of the total jail population served by the San Bernardino County Sheriff's Department are mentally ill (San Bernardino County Sheriff's Department, 1999). In terms of volume, JMHS provide in-custody treatment to about 450 mentally ill inmates (average daily census). Preliminary analysis found that this population averaged about 9 returns to jail over a 4-year period (median of 7 returns). Moreover, about 50% of the mentally ill served by this system also suffer with a substance disorder.
† The program goals were: (1) to reduce the use of illicit substances and alcohol; (2) to reduce the costs of arrest, incarceration, and adjudication; and (3) to promote barrier-reducing system change. The program objectives included: early discharge planning at booking to assess mental health status, postincarceration housing, and community service needs; family support services to include notification, reunification, and community resource education to assist families and significant others in accessing services; financial advocacy to obtain employment, social security, medical, and other benefits; housing advocacy in locating independent living settings or residential placement; 14 days' supply of medication until contact with a community mental health treatment resource; identification cards to alert treatment providers, law enforcement personnel, and others that the individual is part of the treatment program; release from custody during days and hours when community services are accessible; medical condition review by a public health nurse and referral for follow-up medical care to ensure that all health-care needs are being addressed; substance abuse assessment and treatment referral; transportation to community mental health clinics, residence, or placement facilities (Grant Proposal, Section 5, Abstract).

receiving the referral, while others were to remain incarcerated for several months. Consequently, those referrals with the most immediate date were interviewed first.

Aftercare plans were negotiated during the initial assessment while the individual was incarcerated. The assigned staff ensured that the service plan was implemented upon release. If needed, other team members assisted the assigned case manager in the transportation and placement of a client. The public health nurse oversaw the ordering of medications and ensured that the medications were given to the client. This meant placing the medications in the inmate's personal property, but if needed, they were delivered to the client immediately following release. Program clinicians monitored the participants once they were released from the jail facility. They contacted them by telephone and made appointments for them prior to their release. They were given monthly bus passes to enable them to attend their appointments with clinicians.

The evaluation of a participant's success or failure in the program was based on several criteria. The goal was to ensure that upon release, inmates/clients successfully transitioned into the community. Achieving a successful transition required that the client's basic needs of food, clothing, and shelter were met, along with their behavioral health and ancillary support. Objectives for behavioral and ancillary support included: family support services including reunification; financial advocacy to obtain social security, medical, and other benefits; and referrals for follow-up medical care. Regardless of the response to the program, case management services usually terminated within 3 months from the date of the initial release into the community.

Findings

To evaluate the impact of SPAN, the research examined client success (outcomes) and program fidelity (process evaluation). The primary objective of the outcomes assessment was to determine whether this short-term intervention program reduced arrests and bookings into jail, and ultimately, the entire cost of handling nonviolent mentally ill offenders suitable for community reentry under certain conditions. The second research component focused on program fidelity in order to assess whether SPAN was implemented as intended.

Outcomes Assessment

Methodology

To gage the effectiveness of SPAN, inmate referrals who met the program criteria and were considered suitable for the services (1278 individuals) were randomly assigned* to either of two groups: the treatment-as-usual group (control)—clients who, upon discharge, pursued treatment without the assistance of the jail staff but were eligible for the standard services provided through the Department of Behavioral Health (DBH); or the enhanced-treatment group (experimental)—clients who were eligible for standard departmental services and received the additional services provided by the SPAN program. If the client was assigned to the control group, the intake worker discussed the methods for pursuing treatment through the normal DBH referral channels. If, however, the client was placed in the experimental group, the intake worker negotiated a service, treatment, and discharge plan. The experimental group of 636 individuals was compared to a group of 642 individuals who received standard treatment and services provided before the introduction of SPAN.

The data collection focused on three main areas: background data, offense history data, and program delivery data (process). The admission/baseline data were retrieved from existing information systems in the DBH and the jail information management system, and the offense data were collected for the project by the Sheriff's Department. Background characteristics included age, gender, ethnicity, education, family, and work history. Legal variables were coded, such as the criminal offense leading to incarceration, sentence length, custody level, classification information, and prior criminal history. The data for prior criminal history and offenses in the year after release into the community were collected by the Sheriff's Department and forwarded to the evaluation team.† Mental health status was documented, to include mental health history, diagnoses, treatments and medications, reported substance abuse history, and social services received.

For the purposes of establishing comparability between the experimental participants and members of the control group, the demographic backgrounds and the mental health/behavioral characteristics of the two groups were reviewed. The two groups were compared statistically on seven key background variables using the chi-square significance test, as shown in Table 10.1. There were no statistically significant differences at the .01 level between the two groups. Thus, the experimental and control groups were equivalent for evaluation purposes.

Similar to the demographic comparison, the mental health and behavioral problems of the members of the two groups were compared. As in the previous comparison, among the background variables, six variables indicating mental health and behavioral problems were compared, as shown in

---

* Inmates were preselected and assigned to a group by a computer-generated random number based on the inmate's date of birth.
† Only the sheriff's staff was authorized to retrieve these data.

Table 10.1 Demographic Characteristics of Program Participants

| | Study Group | | |
Variable	Enhanced-Treatment Percent (n)	Treatment-as-Usual Percent (n)	Total (n = 1278) Percent (n)
Male	57.7 (367)	57.2 (367)	57.4 (734)
Age			
Up to 29	27.2 (173)	28.5 (183)	27.9 (356)
30–39	31.1 (198)	33.3 (214)	32.2 (412)
40–49	31.6 (201)	29.4 (189)	30.5 (390)
50 and over	10.1 (64)	8.7 (56)	9.4 (120)
Ethnicity			
Caucasian	49.4 (314)	50.8 (326)	50.1 (640)
Hispanic	22.0 (140)	22.6 (145)	22.3 (285)
African-American	25.0 (159)	22.4 (144)	23.7 (303)
Other	3.6 (23)	4.2 (27)	3.9 (50)
Has dependent children	35.5 (226)	38.6 (248)	37.0 (474)
Education level			
Lowest to 12 grade	77.3 (490)	78.4 (502)	77.9 (992)
13–16 years	19.9 (126)	19.1 (122)	19.5 (248)
17 years to highest	2.8 (18)	2.5 (16)	2.7 (34)
Living arrangement (housing)*			
House/apartment	81.7 (519)	75.4 (483)	78.5 (1002)
Homeless	18.3 (116)	24.6 (158)	21.5 (274)
Unemployed at arrest	80.3 (508)	77.8 (499)	79.0 (1007)

*Significant at the .01 level.

Table 10.2. Noteworthy, the self-reported problems of addictive behavior (alcohol and drugs) were high in both groups: around 65% of the participants in each of the two groups reported that they had problems with drugs. Again, both groups were generally equivalent during the pretest with one exception; the number of jail bookings during the 12-month period prior to the SPAN project was different. The overwhelming majority in both groups (about 98%) were booked into jail at least once in the 1-year period prior to the program. However, the comparison group had a statistically higher percentage of members (62.4%) who had two or more bookings in the prior program year than did the experimental group (55.6%, $p < .03$).

Results

Follow-up of the participants' offending behavior during the first year after release is considered to be a measure of the effectiveness of a program. In this case, such an analysis was mandated by the funding source. Of the 1278 individuals who entered the SPAN program, 12 months of follow-up data

Table 10.2 Personal Background Characteristics of Program Participants

| | Study Group | | |
Variable	Enhanced Treatment Percent (n)	Treatment-as-Usual Percent (n)	Total (n = 1278) Percent (n)
Primary mental health disorder			
Substance abuse related	3.6 (23)	4.0 (26)	3.8 (49)
Schizopsychotic	26.1 (166)	28.4 (183)	27.2 (349)
Mood disorder	41.9 (267)	42.1 (271)	42.0 (538)
Bipolar disorder	16.5 (105)	16.0 (103)	16.2 (208)
Anxiety disorder	5.3 (34)	4.2 (27)	4.8 (61)
Other	6.6 (42)	5.3 (34)	5.9 (76)
Problems with alcohol	41.8 (266)	40.5 (261)	41.1 (527)
Problems with drugs	65.5 (414)	64.0 (412)	64.5 (826)
Perceived family support			
Weak	36.5 (229)	37.2 (238	36.9 (467)
Moderate	25.5 (160)	23.6 (151)	24.5 (311)
Strong	38.1 (239)	39.1 (250)	38.6 (489)
Age at first arrest			
Up to 17	15.4 (98)	13.2 (85)	14.3 (183)
18–20	31.1 (198)	34.0 (219)	32.6 (417)
21 and over	53.5 (341)	52.8 (340)	53.2 (681)
Prior bookings (past 12 months)			
None	2.4 (15)	1.9 (12)	2.1 (27)
One	41.9 (266)	35.7 (229)	38.8 (495)
Two	28.2 (179)	30.8 (198)	29.5 (377)
Three or more	27.6 (175)	31.6 (203)	29.6 (378)

were available for 1204 (94%) participants. Seventy-four participants did not receive a full 12-month criminal justice follow-up because their release dates from custody were past the data collection deadline. (For the 6-month period, criminal justice follow-up data were available for 1262 individuals, or 98.7% of admissions.) The 12-month comparison required aggregating (adding) the data for the 0–6-month and 7–12-month periods of the common data elements specified by the Board of Corrections to create a return rate for the entire 12-month period. Jail returns over this 12-month period ranged from none (0) to 32 times, and jail days returned ranged from none (0) to 356 days; 49.5% did not return to jail in this period—49.2% enhanced treatment, 49.7% treatment-as-usual.

The comparison between the experimental and control groups on returns to jail, as shown in Table 10.3, did not show any statistically significant difference in the rate of returns to jail at 1 year post-release. The data for just the first 6 months after release were examined (1262 persons); 63.5% did not return to jail in that period (62.2% enhanced treatment, 64.8% treatment-as-usual).

Table 10.3   Mean Jail Bookings Pre-SPAN and Post-SPAN Program

| | Study Group | | | | | |
| | Enhanced Treatment | | Treatment-as-Usual | | Total | |
Jail Bookings	Mean (SD)	n	Mean (SD)	n	Mean (SD)	n
Preprogram (months)						
25–36	0.61 (1.05)	635	0.50 (1.09)	644	0.55 (1.07)	1279
13–24	0.95 (1.47)	633	0.85 (1.63)	644	0.90 (1.55)	1277
0–12	2.15 (1.93)	635	2.24 (1.48)	642	2.19 (1.72)	1277
Postprogram (months)						
6	0.62 (1.09)	555	0.64 (1.50)	546	0.63 (1.31)	1101
12	1.09 (1.58)	385	1.12 (2.18)	385	1.11 (1.91)	770

There were no statistically significant differences between the enhanced-treatment and the treatment-as-usual groups in the return rates (returns, $n = 1270$, $U = 197{,}321$, $p = .44$; days, $n = 1238$, $U = 186{,}494.5$, $p = .34$).

For the 1-year postprogram admission, no statistically significant differences in jail returns and jail days were found (for cases on whom follow-up data were available for the 12-month period). Using the Wilcoxon–Mann–Whitney U test, the enhanced-treatment group was not significantly different from the treatment-as-usual group (days, $n = 1152$, $U = 164{,}891$, $p = .85$; returns, $n = 1207$, $U = 180{,}834$, $p = .82$). Therefore, the short-term intervention provided by SPAN did not appear to produce significant reductions in returns to jail or reductions in time in jail at 6 or 12 months following admission.

In order to see if offense patterns changed for either group postprogram, we were able to examine 255 male participants on whom these offense data were available preprogram and postprogram (see Table 10.4). The changes between the preprogram and postprogram charges were compared within

Table 10.4   SPAN Males Type of Offense 12 Months Preprogram and Postprogram ($n = 255$)

| | Study Group | |
| | Enhanced Treatment | Treatment-as-Usual |
Offense Type	($n = 139$) (%)	($n = 116$) (%)
Drug	22.3	16.4
Other felonies/misdemeanors	14.4	22.4
Property offenses	28.1	39.7
Violent offenses	35.3	21.6
Percent total	100.0	100.0

Note: Data are presented only for participants on whom preprogram and postprogram offense data were available.
Chi-square = 10.03, $df = 3$, $p = .018$.

each group for the four major offense categories—drugs, property, violent, and other felonies and misdemeanors. There were no statistically significant differences. Both groups showed declines in reoffending in the 1-year post-program. Comparison of the two groups showed a decline in the proportion of postprogram booking charges for property and other offenses for the experimental subjects and an increase in drug and violent offenses. These offense patterns preprogram and postprogram are not favorable to the program of short-term intervention. They raise questions about the effectiveness of this type of reentry program for these individuals, many of whom have had significant interactions with the criminal justice system over an extended period of time.

Program Fidelity

Methodology

In order to focus on the issues of program implementation for individuals with co-occurring disorders who are involved in the criminal justice system, a process evaluation was carried out over the 5 years of the project. Data triangulation was relied on to construct a thorough assessment of the program development, implementation, maintenance, and completion. Information obtained from structured interviews with current and past staff members was supplemented with observations of staff interaction,* a review of 3 years of interoffice memorandums and intraproject correspondence (150+ documents),† interviews with jail personnel (deputies, health services, and administration), and 30 interviews with participants returning to jail.

---

* Two instruments were developed to interview staff about their involvement with SPAN: a survey of training and general opinions about the project and in-depth interviews about their roles, responsibilities, concerns, and suggestions for improvement. Staff members forwarded a copy of these materials prior to setting an interview time. They were interviewed alone in their workspace; interviews were tape-recorded and transcribed. The responses were examined collectively to identify themes. These materials were then provided to a second researcher independent of the project and the evaluation staff to verify the reliability of the coding scheme. The information collected through the survey was examined through conventional qualitative means; the small sample size limited a statistical analysis. Following the interview, the evaluation staff worked with the project staff on a file reorganization project for 3 days. This project involved a number of staff meetings and enabled the evaluation staff to witness the interaction between staff members as participant observers.
† Interoffice communications and correspondence between the project staff and other agencies were collected for the duration of the project (including the start-up period). These documents were sorted in chronological order and reviewed to examine the development and management of SPAN. Key program dates, implementation difficulties, and goal achievement were identified through these artifacts. These items proved invaluable in reconstructing the program development. Several program reports and documents were reviewed.

Themes

Program implementation involved a number of different agencies, which entailed coordination with the SPAN staff, correctional staff, court, district attorney, public defender, the DBH, and the Board of Corrections (grant monitor). The program faced a number of challenges that affected its timely implementation. Several themes emerged from this research component, raising serious concerns about the fidelity of the SPAN program: program management failure, program disintegration, and aftercare linkage variability.

Program Management Failure

The county DBH dedicated human resources to staff the program. The DBH hired clinical supervisors and staff and provided administrative oversight. Structured interviews with the project staff provided limited information about the completion of start-up tasks due to the turnover in a number of key positions throughout the duration of the program, including the position of clinical director. The internal office documents were unable to shed light on exact dates and the project manager's computer records system crashed midway through the first year.

The dates provided reflect initial hiring and periods of high levels of staff turnover. Following the initial recruitment of staff between September and December 1999, many staff members were replaced between April and August 2001. The supervising clinical therapist II position was never filled, instead a clinical therapist I was used to manage the program. Personnel turnover continued to be a challenging issue for the program at all staff levels.

Interviews conducted with the staff showed that most were provided with limited information about the program when they were drafted or recruited to the position. The staff felt that job descriptions were nonexistent and worked on a "learn as you go" basis. There was no formal training program for program staff, because each position was uniquely structured based on employees' diverse backgrounds and varying expertise within the correctional field. This confusion was compounded by procedural changes— a by-product of staff turnover and programmatic adjustments to satisfy the grant requirements mandated by the Board of Corrections—that produced numerous changes to job duties.

As a team, the SPAN personnel displayed a wide range of experience and expertise. Comparing staff experience to their programmatic functions revealed that a few did not have prior experience working in a correctional setting; however, many had experience with prior demonstration projects or research. Disjunction between expectations and program realities caused many of the project staff to become frustrated. The project staff expected that they would be working with inmates toward their rehabilitation on a more therapeutic level rather than providing networking to community services upon release. This resulted in staff turnover in crucial positions. Moreover, estimates of the personnel needed to accomplish all of the program's objectives were grossly under target. This contributed to a management crisis, untenable work conditions, and ineffective case management.

Program Disintegration

Data and records management was poor until late in the project, when steps were taken to improve record keeping. The facilities constraints exacerbated the problems with information management. One area of concern was the cramped staff workstations and general meetings areas, which were often shared with another co-occurring program, forcing staff members to literally crawl on top of one another to complete their daily tasks. During many phases of the program, the growth of the client list exceeded the resources on hand, contributing to a file storage crisis that reduced operational efficiency, resulting in lost, duplicated, and incomplete files. An information system overhaul in 2002 radically improved operations. However, it was not possible to recapture some of the records produced by a staff member who was found to be fabricating data on follow-up contacts: this produced a loss of cases.

Deficiencies in the county jail information management system, a data system relied upon by SPAN to identify potential referrals, generated continual issues resulting in four modifications of the referral process to increase the number of participants. The system was simply not equipped to satisfy the programmatic needs. For example, about 30.6% of referrals were excluded following assessment because the subjects did not satisfy all of the admission criteria—usually the person was sentenced to prison (41.5% of ineligibilities) or the person had a violent record or the current offence was for a violent crime (25.6%) (Bichler & Gabriel, 2002). In the end, the clinical director reviewed new bookings on a daily basis and then assigned cases to staff members; this served to even out the caseloads and added consistency in participant identification.

Client assessment proved to be challenging throughout the duration of the project for a number of reasons: potential participants were released prior to the completion of their assessment; the assessments were conducted as early as possible leading to the possibility of confounding symptoms of mental illness with substance abuse withdrawal; and a formal assessment tool was never implemented. Additionally, the substance abuse component was a much bigger problem than estimated. Substance abuse counselors appeared to be worked beyond their capacity. Some assessments of potential program participants may have been conducted when the subjects were still "high." This raised critical concerns regarding the data quality on all self-reported items.

Aftercare Linkage Variability

Individualized, community-based treatment plans were intended to enable clients to integrate successfully back into the community after serving jail time. Early discharge and family support plans, coupled with financial and housing advocacy and mental health support (i.e., a 14-day supply of medications), were intended to act as a bridge linking inmates back into the community. One of the major concerns was the poor follow-up of participants leaving the program, limiting full implementation of the treatment required. Often, the 14-day supply of medications provided prior to local clinic contact was not enough. The SPAN staff could not provide the family support services required. Meetings were called but no families turned up. The participants were referred to community clinics for family support services, as were the control subjects. Other areas of family advocacy, such as financial support, were difficult to implement. Finding housing for the participants was also difficult due to various local restrictions on such facilities. In short, the treatment integrity was significantly compromised. This is the most damaging problem raised through the program fidelity assessment.

Discussion

The SPAN program was designed to provide short-term intervention, treatment, and essential services for jail inmates with serious mental problems, upon their release into the community. Based on this evaluation, these efforts did not appear to be more effective in terms of reoffending than regular release, which did not provide the additional services stipulated in SPAN. Other forms of more intensive and longer-term interventions may be necessary to achieve more promising results. In general, the high proportion of inmates diagnosed as mentally ill, whose prior official records and self-reports emphasize substance abuse problems, indicates that alcohol and drug rehabilitation should be a very high priority when dealing with this kind of population. Future programs aimed at mainlining mentally ill inmates into the community should provide more intensive aftercare. It is paradoxical that jail inmates diagnosed as mentally ill, or having mental impairments, are expected to take care of their medication, keep their appointments, sign up for government documents, apply to various social service agencies for benefits, and generally function satisfactorily in the community without substantial aftercare arrangements. Performing all these tasks requires not only effective surveillance, but also substantial help and guidance from the program staff, which may not have been as intensive as necessary for this population due to grant restrictions.

Also, the question of how much independence and responsibility could be expected from inmates diagnosed as mentally ill after their release should be reevaluated. The immediate post-release period is the hardest for prison or jail inmates in making adjustments in the community and withstanding the hardships, challenges, and temptations involved in a negative social atmosphere that might influence their reoffending. It is not encouraging that the experimental group, which received more extensive services, did no better in terms of recidivism than the control group. On the other hand, it is feasible that the clients in the experimental group, most of whom received more services than the control clients, may be more visible to the service providers and agency personnel who could more easily detect their law violations. If the latter is the case, then we may arrive at the common sense conclusion that more visibility and surveillance leads to more detection of infractions, which in turn may lead to more arrests. This is a hypothetical conclusion that cannot be supported by the available data, but would be worth exploring in future research.

It should be recognized that many of the program participants were institutionalized several times and some of them even for extended periods in the past. Thus, it appears that most of them went through the well-known "institutionalization" process, which might exacerbate their mental impairments. Some of these participants may have become even more dependent than the general group of inmates on the institutional arrangements and on available authority figures to function and organize their everyday lives. This phenomenon is characteristic, to various degrees, of all inmates of "total institutions," including jails, and it might be even more relevant in the case of mentally impaired individuals than in the case of other inmates (Clemmer, 1940; Goffman, 1961; Garabedian, 1963).

In addition, while interagency cooperation is an ideal model for the implementation of this type of reentry program, in this instance there were certain operational problems involved with it. The release from the custodial setting to the community under the guidance of the DBH may have been difficult to manage for many participants and agency personnel. For example, because 70% of the participants did not go voluntarily for mental health treatment after their release, which was considered an integral component of the program plan, it is suggested that this kind of clientele requires either another form of intervention or a viable aftercare arrangement that was not a part of the program plan.

Public opinion regarding the release of mentally impaired inmates into the community is not completely clear. While there is a concern with institutional costs at times of severe budget cutting in social services, there is also great anxiety about having mentally ill offenders in the community, especially when there is no firm evidence that they are sufficiently supervised. This anxiety has historical roots, for example, in the nineteenth-century decarceration movement of the mentally ill into the community. One reason for citizens' objection to this trend was that it was disturbing for many to see "lunatics" in their midst (Scull, 1977). The fact that these individuals were previously kept in closed institutions reinforced the public perception that they may constitute a danger to the community.

As indicated, the behavioral characteristics of both groups showed that the populations studied had severe problems with alcohol abuse, and even more so with drug abuse. These figures lead to the conclusion that reentry efforts aimed at jail inmates assessed as mentally ill should make sure that they are "truly" mentally ill, and not simply substance abusers, although the difference may, at times, be difficult to determine. Moreover, since a large proportion of the population were dual diagnosis cases, it would seem appropriate to target the addiction problems of all jail inmates by devising treatment programs in the community that could facilitate their reintegration.

Within the experimental group, 73% self-reported a problem with alcohol and/or substance abuse while 79% did so in the control group. Additionally, 38 (12%) "denied" chemical abuse problems despite being arrested for such crimes. Consequently, it was concluded that 88% of the experimental group and 88% of the control group were arrested or acknowledged substance abuse problems, as noted above.

To confirm this, the sheriff's booking information was evaluated. Of the experimental group, 77% had alcohol-substance abuse or related arrests and a corresponding 66% in the control group had such arrest histories. For both groups, the arrest histories included charges such as driving under the influence of alcohol or drugs; injury caused while driving under the influence; repeat public intoxication; open alcoholic beverage containers; disorderly conduct under the influence; and the various health and safety codes that cover substance-related violations.

Regardless of the research group, when examining the correlation of diagnosis to alcohol/substance abuse arrests, mood/affective disorders stood out as the predicting diagnosis, not the psychotic diagnoses. Another pattern was that of the participants who self-reported alcohol/substance abuse problems, 76% did, in fact, commit such crimes. Given these data, it is fair to conclude that this sample largely contains substance abusers rather than mentally ill clients. Some may conclude, however, that this merely shows that there are a lot of dually diagnosed clients who are being rearrested and unnecessarily reincarcerated. Another possible conclusion is that these are mentally ill/dually diagnosed clients who would respond and benefit from treatment once it is offered. To address these possibilities, other data pertaining to inmates' medical benefits and medication services were examined.

As to be expected, problems arose that impacted the delivery of services. These issues involved symptomatic issues with the clients, short release time, and departmental community service limitations. By definition, the target population was one of the most difficult to clinically engage. Many clients lacked any true motivation or desire to change; this is especially true for substance abusers who did not want sobriety. Some wanted to avoid law enforcement or mental health staff, fearful that illegal activities might be discovered. Many of the homeless mentally ill lacked the most basic social skills necessary to engage in sustained and meaningful relationships. As a result, these low-functioning clients abandoned the program, preferring to sleep under bridges and in fields. Family members may have also been a factor blocking the delivery of services. In some instances, families protected and temporarily supported their loved one to the point of negating further services. Other families were less supportive, resulting in the client abruptly leaving the program, hence reducing the opportunity for any follow-up services. Finally, there were the traditional barriers to successful treatment with these clients: paranoia, inability to comprehend, poor judgment, labile moods, and responding to psychotic processes.

Referrals in which the potential candidates were arrested and released within a couple of days presented special problems. The short lead-time made it difficult to evaluate the client and set up a necessary discharge plan. Discharging clients with medications was difficult due to the time it took to order, process, and receive medications. It was difficult to negotiate a placement on short notice because of the limited beds available in the community.

Impacting the interventions and treatment plans were not only the scarcity of placements and affordable housing, but also the scarcity of clinical and community support services. It must be noted that San Bernardino County Behavioral Health, like many other county mental health departments, was hit hard with budget cuts. Outpatient, day treatment, and medication clinics operated over capacity. In some instances, the SPAN clinic clients did not get the full array of services simply because the department was serving other highly needy clients. Another factor was that participants usually had neither funds nor Medi-Cal benefits to pay for services. Filing for social security disability and Medi-Cal was done, but the results took a minimum of 6 months. The result was that some clients received minimal services and left the program, preferring to stay with friends or revert to their familiar homeless lifestyle.

Conclusion

The major hypothesis was that at reentry, providing short-term case management and linkage to community resources would assist mentally ill offenders in avoiding reincarceration, hence reducing continued detention and the related system costs. Another hypothesis was that key variables would show statistically significant differences between the experimental group members who receive the continuum of services and members of the control group.

Based on the foregoing research and input by program staff, it was found that the basic hypothesis that jail recidivism would be reduced as a result of the services provided by the DBH was not supported. Seventy percent of all subjects (combined) never used mental health services in the community. One of the likely reasons for this appears to be that instead of serving the persistently mentally ill, the program served substance abusers that were highly unwilling to change their drug-related lifestyles. Eighty-eight percent of all subjects were substance abusers as defined by their own self-reports and official records.* Of the 30% of clients who did follow up with services after release, the experimental group fared no better than the comparison clients. There was no positive correlation between being eligible for monetary benefits and following up for services. For those who had benefits, just as many pursued aftercare services as did not. In contrast to the larger group of patients, a separate study (subgroup) of 120 patients who were placed on probation as mental health court participants, 70% did go for mental health treatment in the community, a rate directly opposite nonprobation patients, a finding that raises questions about compulsory treatment for these populations.

It appeared that in lieu of addressing the needs of the persistently mentally ill, the SPAN program served individuals who had a sustained history of substance abuse and who were unwilling or unable to change their lifestyles. Eighty-eight percent of this population had a history of sustained substance abuse as defined by their own self-reports and criminal history (see San Bernardino County Department of Behavioral Health and Sheriff's Department SPAN Program Final Report, 2005). On the basis of the self-report, the review of the arrest records, and the general observations of staff members, it seems that substance abuse among the SPAN program participants was widespread and might have contributed, in some cases, to the diagnosis of mental illness.

Future demonstration programs of this type should make an effort to differentiate between subjects whose major problem is mental illness and those whose major problem is substance abuse. This may require training and educating program staff in substance abuse, while de-emphasizing traditional, psychiatrically oriented mental health approaches. Greater care must be taken to screen inmates to determine those who legitimately need medications versus those who want medications to mask their drug habit or avoid the problems of being detained. Current mental health treatment programs within detention centers may need to reevaluate the population and type of services offered. As the bulk of the inmates being served are substance abusers, clinical services may need to be reorganized to reflect substance abuse models rather than psychiatric mental health models.

Changes in treatment models may also need to be considered once inmates are discharged into the community. Again, instead of emphasizing a

* These data were generated, in part, by program staff evaluation of client records.

psychiatric mental health model, these clients may warrant and respond better to the inclusion of a substance abuse recovery continuum of care. Finally, to ensure the availability of services, it is recommended that a comprehensive service system devised for this target population be created. Many private providers are hesitant to work with offenders, fearing the ramifications to their staff and other clients. These clients seem to be a low priority when compared to serving the lower-functioning, persistently mentally ill, especially at a time of limited services and budgetary restraints. By creating programs for these individuals, they may receive adequate services designed to reduce their recidivistic behavior and enable their successful reentry into the community. Therefore, in the future, the emphasis should be placed on long-term programs with continuous efforts to improve the quality of the existing services, and especially the development of meaningful aftercare services, which should include both surveillance and helping functions. The report concluded by noting several specific areas of organizational and structural change needed to improve programs of this type.

Acknowledgments

This study was completed under a grant from the California Board of Corrections (now the Correctional Standards Authority), with the cooperation of the San Bernardino Sheriff's Department and the county Department of Behavioral Health. Ray Liles conducted initial staff interviews. Araseli de la Rosa assisted in the compilation of data for the chapter. David Sechrest edited the chapter. Christie Gabriel assisted with the process evaluation by conducting staff interviews and surveys, as well as examining intraoffice communications and interoffice correspondence.

References

Abram, K. M., & Teplin, L. A. (1991). Co-occurring disorders among mentally ill detainees: Implications for public policy. *American Psychologist, 46*(10), 1036–1045.
Bichler, G., & Gabriel, C. (2002). San Bernardino Mentally Ill Offender Crime Reduction Grant (MIOCRG) Program: San Bernardino County, CA Process Evaluation Report. Center for Criminal Justice Research, California State University, San Bernardino.
Broner, N., Mayrl, D. W., & Landsberg, G. (2005). Outcomes of mandated and non-mandated New York City diversion for offenders with alcohol, drug, and mental disorders. *The Prisoner Journal, 85*(1), 18–49.
Clemmer, D. (1940/1958). *The Prison Community*. New York: Holt, Rinehart, & Winston.
Ditton, P. M. (1999). *Mental Health and Treatment of Inmates and Probationers*. Washington, DC: Bureau of Justice Statistics, Department of Justice.

Drake, R. E., McHugo, J. G., Clark, R. E., Teague, D., Gregory, B., & Xie, H., et al. (1998). Assertive community treatment of patients with co-occurring severe mental illness and substance abuse disorder: A clinical trial. *American Journal of Orthopsychiatry, 68*(2), 201–215.

Gallemore, J. (2000). Strategies for success: Addressing the needs of mentally ill inmates. *American Jails, 14*(March/April), 67–71.

Garabedian, P. G. (1963). Social roles and processes of socialization in the prison community. *Social Problems, 11*, 139–152.

Goffman, E. (1961). *Asylums.* Garden City, NJ: Anchor.

Harer, M. D. (1994). Recidivism among Federal Prisoners Released in 1987. Washington, DC: Federal Bureau of Prisons, Office of Research and Evaluation.

Hartwell, S. (2004). Triple stigma: Persons with mental illness and substance abuse problems in the criminal justice system. *Criminal Justice Policy Review, 15*(1), 84–99.

Izumi, L. T., Schiller, M., & Hayward, S. (1996). Corrections, criminal justice, and the mentally ill: Some observations about costs in California. Retrieved on February 20, 2012, from http://www.pacificresearch.org/issues/health/mental hlth.html.

Laberge, D., & Morin, D. (1995). The overuse of the criminal justice dispositions: Failure of diversionary policies in the management of mental health problems. *International Journal of Law and Psychiatry, 18*(4), 389–414.

Linden, D. (2000). The mentally ill offender: A comprehensive community approach. *American Jails, 13*(January/February), 57–59.

Little Hoover Commission. (2003). *Back to the Community: Safe and Sound Parole Policies.* Sacramento, CA: Author.

Lynch, J. P., & Sabol, W. J. (2001). *Prisoner Reentry in Perspective.* Washington, DC: Urban Institute.

Mauer, M. (2001). The causes and consequences of prison growth in the United States. *Punishment & Society, 3*(1), 9–20.

National GAINS Center for People with Co-Occurring Disorders in the Justice System. (2001). The prevalence of co-occurring mental illness and substance use disorders in jails. Fact Sheet Series. Delmar, NY: National GAINS Center.

Peters, R. H., & Bartoi, M. G. (1997). *Screening and Assessment of Co-occurring Disorders in the Justice System.* Delmar, NY: The GAINS Center.

Petersilia, J. (2003). *When Prisoners Come Home.* New York: Oxford University Press.

Petersilia, J. (2005). From cell to society. In Travis, J. & Visher, C. (eds), *Prisoner Reentry and Crime in America* (pp. 15–49). New York: Cambridge University Press.

San Bernardino County Department of Behavioral Health and Sheriff's Department SPAN Program Final Report, for the California Board of Corrections, October 1, 2005.

Scull, A. T. (1977). *Decarceration.* Englewood Cliffs, NJ: Prentice-Hall.

Seiter, R. P., & Kadela, K. R. (2003). Prisoner reentry: What works, what does not, and what is promising. *Crime & Delinquency, 49*(3), 360–388.

Teplin, L. A. (1990). The prevalence of severe mental disorder among male urban jail detainees: Comparison with the Epidemiologic Catchment Area Program. *American Journal of Public Health, 80*(6), 663–669.

The President's Commission on Law Enforcement and Administration of Justice. (1967). *Task Force Report: Corrections*. Washington, DC: U.S. Government Printing Office.

Torrey, E. F. (1999). How did so many mentally ill people get into America's jails and prisons? *American Jails, 13*(November/December), 9–13.

Travis, J. (2000). *But They All Come Back: Rethinking Prisoner Reentry.* Washington, DC: Office of Justice Programs, National Institute of Justice.

Locked In and Locked Out

Global Feminist Perspectives on Women and Imprisonment

11

HELEN CODD

Contents

Introduction

This chapter brings together the emerging literature on global feminist perspectives on women's imprisonment with the rapidly expanding body of research exploring the impacts of imprisonment on women and girls as members of prisoners' families and as members of urban communities where imprisonment is common. Research on women's imprisonment is considered alongside research documenting and analyzing the needs and experiences of women and girls as members of the families of both male and female prisoners, focusing on three key themes and identifying global commonalities and differences. The chapter concludes with a discussion of the need for further research and activism, which links work on women, girls, families, and criminal justice with critical perspectives on punishment and the expansion of the prison-industrial complex, to develop radical, critical, and global feminist perspectives that challenge the power of the prison.

Research from many countries has documented the experiences of imprisoned women, who are always a minority within the criminal justice and penal systems created and dominated by men. This increasingly substantial research literature has identified the challenges and difficulties faced by women prisoners, many of whom are separated from their children, and has documented the manifold difficulties experienced by women on release and afterward (O'Brien, 2001). Some of these studies have documented not only women's difficulties in the prison environment but also their strategies of coping and resistance, many researchers adopting qualitative methodologies that prioritize women prisoners' own voices (Bosworth, 1999; George, 2009; Quinlan, 2010; Lawston & Lucas, 2011). A number of important edited collections, such as those by Cook and Davies (1999) and Sudbury (2005), have encouraged perspectives on women's imprisonment that consider the issues not only through an international lens but also, especially in Julia Sudbury's work (Sudbury, 2005), endeavor to interweave questions of global trends in the incarceration of women with global capitalism.

It is important to remember that imprisonment affects women and girls not only as prisoners but also as the partners, parents, children, and family members of prisoners, especially of men (Codd, 2008). However, attempts to consider imprisonment from a global perspective have, on the whole, not extended to women's and girls' roles as members of prisoners' families even though criminology is already developing and assessing global and not merely transnational perspectives on a range of phenomena. Just as the globalizing world has been described as "a world in motion" (Inda & Rosaldo, 2002), so is the criminological world (Aas, 2007).

In parallel to this, with a few exceptions, most research into prisoners' families has been based on, and focused on, countries or particular geographical locations. That said, the Quaker United Nations Office (QUNO) has published a number of detailed reports that are global in their scope, and the recent international report edited by Sharff-Smith and Gampell (2011) draws on sources from many countries, even though its case studies are all European countries.* The published research into imprisonment and its consequences for families has tended to be jurisdiction focused and there is a huge amount of potential for research that brings together themes on a global level and links prisoners' families' issues with broader questions of globalization and capitalism. After all, wherever prisons exist, there are prisoners' families, both in geographical and historical terms. No real attempts have been made to explore international and global perspectives on prisoners' families or to move outside the traditional jurisdictional boundaries that have dominated the research, even though people migrate and some crimes are transnational in their scope and method. There are important international questions to be explored, such as the needs of families of foreign national prisoners; prisoners'

---

* See Murray and Farrington's (2007) comparison of Sweden and the United Kingdom. The Quaker United Nations Office (QUNO) has also been active in researching, promoting, and disseminating international perspectives on prisoners' children (see Robertson, 2007, 2008).

children; provision for mothers and babies; and problems of family contact. Although much of the recent literature on prisoners' families has focused on single jurisdictions, the impacts of imprisonment on families and communities go beyond narrow jurisdictional boundaries. There are many potentially significant avenues for future research and this chapter will focus on three issues. First, the impact of having a family member in prison. Second, the needs and experiences of imprisoned mothers, babies, and children. Finally, the question of the experiences and needs of women in semipenal and quasipenal confinement will be explored.

Impact of Having a Family Member in Prison

It is undeniable that for some families, especially where interactions with an imprisoned family member or members are characterized by abuse, violence, a chaotic lifestyle, substance abuse, and criminal behavior, imprisonment offers respite and many benefits for the nonimprisoned family members (Mills & Codd, 2007). However, even where such perceived benefits exist, the partners and other close family members of prisoners experience a range of hardships, challenges, and difficulties (Morris, 1965; Fishman, 1990; Codd, 2008). In U.K.-based and U.S.-based research, it is commonplace to consider how families cope, especially with the imprisonment of men, and very often the prison sentence prompts changes in accommodation and often, for children, multiple changes in caregivers. Research since the 1980s has generally suggested that parental imprisonment is usually associated with negative outcomes for children, often linked to increased chances of delinquency and criminal behavior, aggression, social exclusion, and problems at school (Murray, 2007; Johnson & Easterling, 2012). The published research has documented how children of prisoners are highly likely to experience emotional and behavioral difficulties, including eating disorders, anxiety, depression, and enuresis. It is commonplace in the literature from the United States, the United Kingdom, and Australia to find that the imprisonment of a family member (usually male) can lead to other family members experiencing financial hardships and poverty; housing changes; emotional and mental distress; and sometimes stigmatization and harassment (Codd, 2008).* Alongside the children affected by parental imprisonment, many more children and family members are affected by the imprisonment of siblings, grandparents, aunts, and uncles (Scharff-Smith & Gampell, 2011).

However, these questions play out differently across the world. For example, in the San Pedro prison in La Paz, Bolivia, entire families go to live in the

---

* For a detailed and meticulously referenced assessment of the impacts of parental imprisonment on children, see Scharff-Smith and Gampell (2011).

prison, or live in temporary, hastily built, accommodation around the prison, because they could not survive otherwise (Luna, 2004; *Wall Street Journal*, 2007). The prison allows prisoners to earn money—indeed, they have to as they have to buy all their basic needs—and without these earnings, the family would be destitute. The impact of imprisonment on the family varies according to cultural norms. In the United States and the United Kingdom, the media and members of the public often stigmatize prisoners' partners and, to a lesser extent, their children, especially where the offense involved is perceived as extremely serious or otherwise shocking; women, in particular, falling prey to media assumptions that they must have collaborated in, or at the very least condoned, the wrongdoing of their male sons and partners (Condry, 2007; Codd, 2008). In some cultures, the shame and stigma are far greater. For example, it is sometimes argued that the imprisonment of fathers has its greatest impact on sons, but in some countries, such as Jordan, the imprisonment of the father brings shame and stigma on the family such as to make any daughters subsequently unmarriageable (Al Ghairabeh, 2008). By contrast, in India where a high proportion of women prisoners are incarcerated for completed or attempted homicide linked to the dowry system, imprisoned women and their families may not experience stigmatization or hostility as they may be seen to be upholding familial honor and accepted gendered social norms (Cherukuri et al., 2009).*

Facilities and opportunities for families to maintain contact may vary, as is vividly illustrated in relation to family or conjugal visits. Some countries, such as England and Wales, do not permit in-prison private or conjugal visits at all. In Germany, the emphasis is on family visits over an extended period, as in some U.S. states where overnight visits may take place in designated bungalows or trailers; by contrast, in some Scandinavian countries the emphasis is squarely on sexual activity, with the visit taking place in small cubicles with a bed and little else. Conjugal visits tend to be between a prisoner and their partner (Smith, 2006). In some jurisdictions, this must be a marital partner (Bandele, 1999). Linked to this is the variation in the recognition of same-sex relationships. In Brazil, male prisoners are allowed same-sex visits whereas all conjugal visits for female inmates are tightly regulated. In the United States, officially approved conjugal visits began in Mississippi in the early part of the twentieth century and, at the time, were aimed at black inmates as an incentive to work harder (Hopper, 1969). There is much, however, to criticize about the aims, implementation, and inherent racism of this early program, which involved access to prostitutes and assumptions that black inmates were less able to control their sexual urges than white inmates. Then, as now, these private visits became a tool of behavior management,

---

* For further discussion of the needs and experiences of imprisoned women in India, see Kaushik and Sharma (2009) and Kaushik (2010).

although more recent family visitation programs in the United States have tended to stress the preservation of family ties as their key aim. These visits tend to focus on sexual activity and operate as a form of incentive for prisoners to behave well and conform to prison rules.

Some countries are moving toward family visits, which focus on maintaining family ties. These family visits vary in length and location; for example, in France, the Unités Expérimentales de Visite Familiale en France (UEVFs) have been operating at the Centre Pénitentiaire de Rennes since September 2003. Since then, the scheme has been expanded to three prisons. The UEVFs scheme allows prisoners and their families weekend-long private visits with several family members. Sentenced prisoners can see their family members for 6–48 hour, and are allowed a 72-hour visit once a year. It is interesting to note that the scope of the potential visitors is wider than simply close family members or members of the extended family; rather, individuals for whom several factors provide evidence of a legitimate emotional bond to the offender can also be included. The scheme offers a means of family contact for those who are ineligible for other family contact schemes such as leave (Eurochips, 2006). In Ireland, the children of imprisoned mothers are able to stay overnight with their mothers when staffing permits and this is useful in the absence of other programs. These programs of extended visits strengthen family relations and improve the probability of successful reintegration after release (Eurochips, 2006).

Issues of culture and gender may dictate who visits prisoners; although it is usually said in the Western research literature that "regardless of the gender of the inmate it is women who visit" (Girshick, 1996), this may not be the case in cultures where women are viewed as belonging in the private sphere and where prison is seen as an unsuitable and inappropriate environment for a woman (as in the anecdotal accounts given by my female Asian students, of British Muslim families where wives, sisters, and daughters of prisoners are not allowed to visit prisoners as visiting is viewed as a male activity). There are numerous accounts in the literature of the female partners of male prisoners worrying about how their men are coping or how they are being treated in prison; these worries are compounded if they know that their family member is likely to be tortured or otherwise mistreated and abused (Djaba, 2008). It is also commonplace in the literature to discuss the challenges of prisoner return and reentry, involving negotiating family reintegration; there are additional challenges posed when the returning prisoner has been tortured or even maimed during their incarceration. Families also find themselves part of the "web of punishment," when family members may themselves be incarcerated due to their association with an offender, or risk torture and abuse themselves in an attempt to encourage them to testify against the detained offender, especially in the case of political dissidents or leaders of failed military governmental takeovers. The consequences of imprisonment can be compounded for families of prisoners who are detained outside their country of origin or residence. The families of foreign national prisoners may not have access to information, even as to the location of their family member, and may have to negotiate language difficulties, distance, and poverty in an attempt to maintain relationships. Indeed, the challenges faced by foreign national prisoners are common across jurisdictions.

Across all jurisdictions, there are many commonalities in the strategies employed, particularly by women, to cope with the offender's incarceration. Other family members and friends can offer practical help, as demonstrated in Codd's study (2000) where the father of an offender's wife added her to his own car insurance so that she could continue to drive, which she otherwise could no longer have afforded. Families and friends can offer emotional support, especially at key times in the sentence, assisting, for example, in explaining the crime and sentence to children, or offering childcare so a woman with children is able to visit her partner alone. Around the world, sources of formal support for prisoners' families vary. Technological developments, where they can be accessed, have seen an expansion in social networking pages for prisoners' families, and blogs, and these can allow members of prisoners' families to engage in mutual support and sharing in the virtual environment, anonymously if necessary. A common theme around the world, however, is that formal state agencies, such as correctional authorities and prisons themselves, often do not do enough to support prisoners' family ties throughout the sentence, family members often having to travel long distances to visit, in poor facilities. Prison visitors can feel intimidated by searches and security requirements, feel humiliated by or fearful of prison staff, and feel unfamiliar with the myriad of rules and regulations that govern visits, gifts, letters, and telephone calls. That is not to say that the picture is uniformly negative. Some prisons have well-funded visitor centers, for example, and excellent extended visits schemes for prisoners' children, such as that run at Bedford Hills high security prison in upstate New York (Johnston, 2012). However, in most countries, prisoners' family members rely first on their own families and friends for support, and then they look to nonprofit community and voluntary organizations. Non-governmental organizations (NGOs) of varying sizes, significance, scope, and spread offer a range of support and services, such as telephone help lines and counseling. In China, for example, "Morning Tears" runs a network of children's homes for the children of prisoners, including the children of executed prisoners, and their staff work with prisoners who are about to be put to death and run final "goodbye" visits for their children.* These nonstate agencies can literally mean the difference between

* See www.morningtears.org.

life and death for prisoners' family members, especially children, who may find themselves vulnerable, homeless, and destitute as a consequence of the imprisonment of a parent. As one interviewee in Wing Hong Chui's study of prisoners' partners and their children in Hong Kong said, if she had not received help from a center run by an NGO, she "might have had to steal and live on the streets" (Chui, 2010, p. 202). The non-governmental nature of these organizations is significant, as family members may be unwilling to access state-based formal sources of support if they are distrustful or suspicious of the legal system and criminal justice agencies, or if they perceive the services as inappropriate. In Northern Ireland, for example, the families of men imprisoned for terrorist offenses during "the Troubles" did not access services aimed at prisoners' families, as they perceived their imprisoned men not as criminal prisoners but as prisoners of war, and sought and received support from the terrorist groups themselves, rather than accessing projects aimed at helping prisoners' families (McEvoy et al., 1999).

Academics, policy makers, and activists in a number of countries have become increasingly concerned with the collateral consequences of imprisonment. These collateral consequences vary from jurisdiction to jurisdiction and can include disenfranchisement, welfare disqualifications, social stigma, financial problems, and difficulties finding employment, among many others.* In addition, significant recent research in the United States, the United Kingdom, and Ireland has begun to explore the impact of imprisonment on communities, especially in urban areas (Braman, 2004; Braman & Wood, 2003; Breen, 2008). This research has highlighted the gender imbalance emerging in many urban communities and the disruption of family relationships (Travis, 2005). Although much of this work has been based on and published in the United States, there are important implications for other countries (Mauer & Chesney-Lind, 2002; Travis & Waul, 2003). Although in the United States the mass imprisonment epidemic has been extreme and highly visible, predominantly focused on African-Americans and other minority groups, those living and working outside the United States cannot be complacent and take the view that this is simply "American exceptionalism." After all, in England the origins of electronic tagging, sex offender registration, and mandatory minimum sentencing guidelines can be traced back to American initiatives and penal policies, which flow across the Atlantic to the United Kingdom far more than penal policies flow across the English Channel from the rest of Europe. In some American cities, the ratio of males to females has become one male to every seven females, as a consequence of drugs, guns, HIV and AIDS, and mass imprisonment, and has led to a lack of accountability for the few

* For a detailed discussion of these impacts, see Codd (2008).

men who are left (Travis, 2005). These communities have become essen-
tially matriarchal, and are now being affected even more by the increased
imprisonment of women, which means that many children lose "the only
anchor they have left" (Golden, 2005).

Mothers, Babies, and Children

Children may live in prisons not because they have been accused or convicted of a crime, but as a consequence of the imprisonment of a parent,
usually their mother. In England and Wales, debates are ongoing about the
appropriateness or otherwise of babies remaining with their imprisoned
mothers, and recent court cases have questioned the appropriate timing
of when a baby or toddler should leave the prison (Munro, 2002; Codd,
2008). The balancing act is between the benefits to the child of bonding
with the mother, and the negative consequences of growing up in the
prison setting.

In some continental European countries, children live in specialist
homes with their mothers and leave the prison to go to community nursery
schools (Eurochips, 2006). In some countries, the question becomes thorn-
ier because if mothers are not allowed to keep their children with them, then
their children may end up begging on the streets, have to drop out of school,
and may experience rape, physical abuse, and neglect by other caregivers, or
die (Tibatemwa-Ekirikubinza, 1999; Bhana & Hochfeld, 2001; Musungezi &
Staunton, 2003), but in prison there are no specialist facilities for children.
They may share their mothers' dormitories, as in Jamaica and India (Henry-
Lee, 2005; Pandey & Singh, 2006); and their beds, as in Nigeria (Amnesty
International, 2008); share their food; not have access to health care including immunization and not have any play, education, or social activities
appropriate for them (Bharucha, 2007). Vetten (2008), highlights a number of issues relating to pregnancy, birth, and children in prison in African
countries. These concerns range from poor nutrition and health care for
pregnant women, to women giving birth in their cells in Mozambique and
Zimbabwe; however, it is important to remember that women have given
birth in their cells in U.K. prisons too, and poor care for pregnant women
is not simply the preserve of so-called developing countries. Children are
imprisoned with their mothers in Benin, Ethiopia, South Africa, Zimbabwe,
Sudan, and Uganda. In Uganda, the state has to provide clothes to women
prisoners but not their children (Tibatemwa-Ekirikubinza, 1999). The food
situation is a key issue; for example, in Sudan, children beyond breastfeed-
ing age do not have ready access to food and the only way their mothers can
obtain food for them is to work as water carriers for vendors in the local
market in return for food. In other countries, prisoners are allowed, or even

expected, to work outside the prison during the day, usually in return for food.

Thus, whereas in England campaigners and policy makers discuss keeping mothers and babies together up until an appropriate time to send the baby or child out, in many countries, including India, the emphasis of prison reformers has been on getting children out of the prisons. In Aranjuez in Spain, the Centro Penitencario has a unit for the children of parents where both parents are imprisoned, where children can stay with both parents until they are 3 years old (Fair, 2009). As far as the author is aware, currently there are no "father and baby" or "father and child" units, reflecting the social reality that women tend to be the primary caregivers of babies and small children, and when men go to prison, childcare responsibilities tend to fall on female relatives and friends.

Women in Semipenal and Quasipenal Confinement

There are other forms of less formal semipenal confinement, which affect women and girls. One of the most underresearched areas is that of the confinement of women in institutions, situations, or conditions that are prison-like in nature and effect. Rather as in European countries in the past, when so-called deviant women found themselves detained in institutions such as Ireland's Magdalen laundries (Finnegan, 2004), in other countries, women may find themselves confined in religious premises such as temples in order to appease the gods.

One of the most significant, but often overlooked, examples of this form of confinement is that of the practice of trokosi as operated by certain ethnic groups in areas of Ghana, Togo, and Benin.* A child, who is usually female and a virgin, is selected to serve in a shrine as reparation or atonement for crimes committed by other members of their family and in order to please the gods (Ameh, 2004a; Vetten, 2008). These crimes can include adultery, stealing, failing to redeem a pledge to a deity, or having sex with a trokosi. The word *trokosi* can be loosely translated from the local dialect as "wife to the gods" or "slave to the gods (or deity)" (Botchway, 2007–2008). The girl and her family may not be told what the crime is and the priests act as "proxies" for the gods (Bilyeu, 1999).

This practice thus renders women and girls responsible for a wrongdoing that they themselves have not perpetrated (Ameh, 2004a,b; Bilyeu, 1999;

---

* Nobody is sure how many "trokosi" there are and the way they are treated varies widely. For example, some are forced into sex as soon as they arrive, whereas other priests follow the "rule" that girls cannot be forced into sex until after their third menstruation. Some reports have suggested that there are around 4,000 girls and women bound to shrines in Ghana, along with their 16,000 children (Wing & Murray Smith, 2003).

Boaten, 2001; Botchway, 2007–2008).* This is vividly described by Botchway (2007–2008):

> Imagine that you had a different childhood. You wake up on your eighth birthday and your family takes you to a remote village and leaves you with a strange man who does not take care of you financially or emotionally. Thus, your formal education stops at age eight. You are forced to clean and do daily chores for the man. When you reach puberty one of your 'chores' will be having sex with this man. You *might* be released in three years, 20 years or you may *never* be released. If you die before you are released your family may have to send another child. *If* you are eventually released, you will have lost your innocence, your youth, and possibly your sanity. You may have lost contact with your family. To top everything, you will have nowhere to live and no employable skills. When you ask why you were sent to live with the man, you are told it is because of something that someone else, probably a male relative, did over *700 years ago!* No one knows exactly what happened, but you are still being punished for it, at age eight. Happy Birthday! (If you are a male-not to worry-this fate is not likely yours.

Although the children are only meant to remain at the shrine for short periods of between 3 months and 6 years, in reality they become stigmatized and their families become reluctant to have them released, meaning that they may stay there for their whole lives. Trokosis offer domestic, agricultural, and sexual services to the priests, having their movements confined to the shrine and having to wear distinctive clothing.[†]

The practice is based on a belief system that sees justice and punishment as communal and thus an individual with no connection to a crime may be punished to spare others. Similarly, when one person's offense goes unpunished, "vengeance may be wreaked upon the entire community" (Bilyeu, 1999). Some reports suggest that children as young as 2 have been given to shrines for crimes committed by relatives (French, 1997). This may promote wrongdoing rather than deter it, as wrongdoers know that they themselves never have to be punished (Botchway, 2007–2008), and indeed they may never have been found guilty or the nature of the alleged "crime" may never be clear or notified to the family.

---

* "Punctured Hope—A Story about Trokosi and Young Girls' Slavery in Today's West Africa" is a recent Canadian film that tells the real-life story of a girl who becomes a temple slave under the trokosi system. It was first shown at the Montreal Film Festival in August 2009 and went on limited U.S. release in late 2011.
† It is most often discussed in relation to the Ewe people of the Volta Delta in Ghana, but has been linked to similar practices in Benin, Togo, and Nigeria (Botchway, 2008; Boaten, 2001). That said, some Ewe people argue that it is not common to all the Ewe in the region and is only practiced in a few villages (Ghanaweb, 2010).

The common view in the literature is that this practice has operated for hundreds of years, although some writers (Woods, 2000–2001) argue that this has, in fact, only been the usual practice for around 100 years, after a family was unable to raise the money to donate cattle and instead offered one of their virgin daughters; "This offer was gratefully accepted, and a new tradition was instantly born" (Woods, 2000–2001, p. 876). Some writers have viewed it as a uniformly negative practice, whereas others suggest it was seen initially as akin to the reasons that girls entered convents, as a way of creating elite women (fiasidi) (Quashigah, 1999). Other items, such as alcohol (apoteshe) and rolls of calico, can also be given. For some priests, the ritual of making the girl a trokosi is purely spiritual and symbolic and she returns to live with her family after a feast, but this version is barely mentioned in the literature. As wives and servants to the gods, they undertake domestic duties such as cooking and cleaning, they do farm work, and they can also act as mistresses and sex slaves to the priests. To all intents and purposes, they are slaves. They are supposed to stay there for some years and then return home, but many do not and sometimes even lifelong servitude is held not to be enough to settle the debt to the gods. The burden of providing a slave to appease the gods passes from generation to generation and if a trokosi dies, the family have to provide another daughter as a replacement, which means that girls can be slaves to the priests long after the relevant wrongdoing has been forgotten. It is not uncommon for trokosis to be the fifth or more generation in the shrine, and any babies born to trokosis take on the status of their enslaved mothers. The fear is that unless a young girl is given, other misfortunes will befall the family, such as diseases and death. It is important to note that even if they are allowed to leave, they become stigmatized and their families may not have them back and they may become outcasts. The girls and women themselves are not happy; some accounts in the literature talk of their weariness, depression, and despair and some talk of wanting to kill themselves with poison (Bilyeu, 1999).

It is important to note that the practice of trokosi is no longer legal in Ghana, as a law was passed in 1998 outlawing ritual servitude,* but it has proved difficult to eradicate and has been enmeshed in debates around human rights and, by contrast, safeguarding cultural and religious practices.† Of course, it also contravenes a number of international legal instruments. A huge anti-trokosi campaign and some mass liberations of trokosi slaves have taken place, the first in October 1996, and by 2004, it was estimated that

---

* The Criminal Code (Amendment) Act 1998 (Act 554).
† For a critical discussion of the intersection between protecting human rights and promoting culture, in the context of the marginalized girl-child, see Amoah (2007).

less than a couple of hundred trokosis were still held;* however, this figure has been disputed as many trokosis returned to the shrines after experiencing extreme social and economic hardship after their "liberation."

Research and campaigning around trokosi and the girls affected have focused on human rights issues, antislavery activism, and campaigns against harmful inheritance practices (Hauser, 2003). However, no published research, to my knowledge, has focused on the intersection between gender and punishment and sought to place the practice of trokosi within a feminist penological context, even though punishment is a key element of the practice as it is experienced by those who are affected and, to some extent, an underpinning justification by those who engage with it.

It is tempting to argue that the practice of trokosi is some kind of strange practice adopted by a small number of people, and to adopt a kind of imperialistic distancing, which says that these are outdated tribal practices that have nothing to do with so-called civilized nations. However, the trokosi system forms part of a broader continuum of attitudes to women and girls, which manifests itself in its most essential and visible form in the trokosi system, but which can be seen in less extreme forms in attitudes to women and girls in relation to offending in other parts of the world. Rather, as in the 1970s and 1980s, when feminist writers began to define the rape and murder of women as part of a continuum of patriarchal and sexist attitudes, which also include low-level sexual harassment and sexualized comments, trokosi can be interpreted as the extreme and ultimate manifestation of other tendencies to render females responsible for male wrongdoing. An obvious objection to this link is that in the trokosi system the girls are children so they cannot be assumed to have had any real awareness of or responsibility for the offense, but in a way this is simply female-blaming taken to its ultimate conclusion; females can be held responsible even if they are too young and "innocent" to have actually played any part in the crime.

It could be argued that, unlike under the trokosi system, women or girls are not imprisoned for the crimes of the males in their family unless they are conspirators, codefendants, or otherwise complicit, but it must be recognized that women are utilized in penal policies, as "instruments of resettlement" after release and also as stabilizing influences during the sentence, ideally acting as providers and supporters.† The news media tends to look toward adult women to explain shocking or extreme offending by men. For mothers, it is not so much a case of "she must have known," which is often said of

---

* For a discussion of the reform campaign, and the work of Walter Pimpong and others, see Ameh (2004b).
† For example, Rumbelow (2009) in an article in the *Times* about Internet pedophiles, entitled "Mothers, don't be blind to the threat of paedophiles," argues that women should not be naïve, implying that women could and should watch over their children and male partners to a far greater extent.

wives and partners, as a case of "she must have been responsible."* Girls often experience stigmatization, hostility, and negative social reactions as a consequence of their familial link to an offender. We can see global commonalities in women's and girls' experiences, an underlying theme being that of rendering women responsible for male wrongdoing, with women bearing the burdens of caring "from the outside" and suffering harm and stigma as a consequence.

Conclusion

When women's imprisonment is considered globally rather than locally, the number of commonalities is striking. Women form a minority in all prison systems and, as a consequence, they find themselves enclosed within a predominantly male-focused setting, where women's needs are either invisible or ignored. It is striking how women's own accounts of imprisonment, which can include experiences of neglect and abuse, echo the same recurring themes, often regardless of whether the country in which they are imprisoned is a "Western" or "developing" country. For example, the contrast between the existence of legal prisoners' rights and entitlements, but women prisoners' own powerlessness to challenge breaches and enforce these rights, is visible in Indian research (Kaushik, 2010) and also in research from the United States.[†] It is also striking how little has been done around the world to improve women's experiences of imprisonment, despite a range of visible reports, research projects, and grassroots campaign initiatives.

Alongside this, women continue to be blamed and deemed responsible for male wrongdoing (and for male rehabilitation and resettlement) in ways that men are not. The trokosi system is perhaps one of the most extreme and visible manifestations of woman-blaming, but it is endemic around the world, whether it is blaming women for provoking men to rape, for prompting domestic violence, or simply for being the mothers of offenders. Again, it is striking that these attitudes persist across cultural, socioeconomic, and political boundaries. Women and girls find themselves incarcerated, controlled, and governed by a range of institutions, both formal and informal, and while the precise nature of the containment and control varies, the common thread is the persistence of the punishment and the exercise of (male) power in relation to women and girls.

---

* Mother-blaming is also common in the psychological research literature in relation to serious violent and sexual offenders.
† For a discussion and analysis of how this contrast operates in U.S. prisons in relation to reproductive rights in particular, see Codd (2012).

One of the most underresearched aspects of this topic is that of the strategies and methods employed by women themselves in order to cope with—and sometimes simply to survive—their own imprisonment or that of members of their families. Women may seek and receive support from within their families and communities, and very often this support comes from other women and girls. In relation to support groups for the partners of male prisoners, it is usually women who organize and run these organizations, and so women find themselves not only supporting their own incarcerated family member(s) but also supporting other women similarly affected. Women do not simply give in and accept everything imposed upon them; many show huge amounts of resourcefulness and courage in order to maintain their family relationships. Often, when governments attempt to improve the experiences of women in prison, or prisoners' family members, the focus tends to be on the physical prison environment, the practicalities of visiting, and on providing programs and schemes for women. If, however, there was more research considering how women cope and support other women, then a more "woman-focused" approach could be adopted, beginning with women's own experiences, attitudes, and views and working up to the design and implementation of services, rather than creating services and programs for the (male) majority, then seeking to fit women in, almost as an afterthought.

The effects of imprisonment on women and girls raise inherent questions of justice and rights that go beyond questions of individual states' responses to prisoner's families and include questions of race, gender, and punishment. Indeed, to focus on these issues as domestic matters linked to individuals states or jurisdictions can serve to conceal injustices; as Benhabib, Morrison, and others have argued "if we are to grasp, and challenge, the major sources of social injustice today, we need to move beyond the state-territorial principle" (Benhabib, 2004; Fraser, 2005; Morrison, 2005; all cited in Aas, 2007). We are faced with a world where, as a consequence of parental imprisonment, numerous children are living without parents, and indeed, as Renny Golden (2005) has pointed out, these children are already living with multiple deprivations. After all, on the whole, it is not the richest or most powerful members of society who find themselves in prison. It is impossible to talk about imprisonment on a global level without talking about globalization and the prison-industrial complex. Prison is an international business that excels at producing its own future customers. Indeed, what prison does best is to produce more prisoners, by rendering its "customers" repeat users and also playing a role in ensuring that their children go on to use the same prison system in the future (rather like fathers and sons following the same cricket or football teams for many generations).

When we talk about imprisonment in "developing" countries, we need to consider the effects of global capitalism not only in terms of the poverty, deprivation, and socioeconomic problems of citizens, but also in terms of how prisons are run and operated. If we consider imprisonment as an international, transnational, and global phenomenon, then we also need to consider prisoners' families. If we can assess the impacts of imprisonment on individual families and communities, then whatever we say about these impacts needs to be assessed in terms of the global scale. We then find ourselves in the position of assessing the costs and benefits of imprisonment on a global level. Imprisonment is not the only way to punish those who do wrong, if punishment is what is socially sanctioned as a response to criminal wrongdoing. It is not inevitable that a state has a high rate of imprisonment. Rose Smith and others, who in their study for the Rowntree Foundation assessed the costs of imprisonment, including health and social care for prisoners' partners and children, through small-scale case studies, found that the costs of imprisonment far exceeded the immediately obvious costs of keeping a prisoner in jail once factors such as substitute child care, health care, and other social costs were factored in (Smith et al., 2007). If this is amplified to a global level, then we are faced with a world where many, many children are living without parents. If we are living in the so-called global village, then we need to consider the costs and benefits of the global village prison. Perhaps the most worrying element for those of us of a critical persuasion is that prison is now a highly profitable global business. This means, therefore, that rather than viewing prison as another demand on taxpayers' money and on state resources, prison becomes a source of profits for shareholders who thus have a vested financial interest in maintaining and expanding the prison population. Thus, in the face of the inexorable expansion of "World Prison Inc.," families suffer "collateral damage" in the pursuit of profit.

Attempts have been made to reform prisons in some countries, as exemplified by the work of Kiran Bedi in India, who famously substantially reformed Tihar prison along therapeutic and community lines, creating an institution that is described in her book as "a virtual ashram" (Bedi, 2007). However, since she left the prison, many of her reforms have been abandoned or, as in the recitation of the morning prayer that she introduced, have been reduced to a matter of ritual and discipline (Gilani, 2011). At first glance, the problem is one of not having reformed the staff and the processes sufficiently, but it also illustrates the persistent power of the prison, the carceral clawback, and the strength of the prison establishment to resist change. In this context, it thus becomes important to consider adopting a far more radical abolitionist perspective and challenge the use and existence of the prison itself (Scott & Codd, 2010).

There is a great deal of work to be done. Criminology is already developing and assessing global and not merely transnational perspectives on a range of phenomena, such as organized crime, transnational policing, the transfer of penal knowledge and policies, and the transborder sex industries. We have already seen the global development of campaigns around domestic and sexual violence, the death penalty, and human rights. Women's and girls' interactions with prison systems raise fundamental questions of social exclusion, marginalization, and justice. Thus, further research is needed that links work on women, girls, prisoners' families, and criminal justice with critical perspectives on punishment and the expansion of the prison-industrial complex, to develop radical, critical, and global feminist perspectives that challenge the power of the prison.

References

Aas, K. F. (2007). Analysing a world in motion: Global flow meets "Criminology of the other." *Theoretical Criminology, 11*, 283–303.

Al Ghairabeh, F. (2008). The effects upon children in Jordan of the imprisonment of their fathers: A social work perspective. *International Social Work, 51*(2), 233–246.

Ameh, R. K. (2004a). Human rights, gender and traditional practices: The trokosi system in West Africa. In A. Kalunta-Crumpton & B. Agozino (eds), *Pan-African Issues in Crime and Justice* (pp. 23–38). Aldershot: Ashgate.

Ameh, R. K. (2004b). Reconciling human rights and traditional practices: The anti-trokosi campaign in Ghana. *Canadian Journal of Law and Society, 19*(2), 51–72.

Amnesty International (2008). *Nigeria: Prisoners' Rights Systematically Flouted.* London: Amnesty International.

Amoah, J. (2007). The world on her shoulders: The rights of the girl-child in the context of culture and identity. *Essex Human Rights Review, 4*(2), 1–23.

Bandele, A. (1999). *The Prisoner's Wife: A Memoir.* New York: Washington Square Press.

Bedi, K. (2007). *It's Always Possible: One Woman's Transformation of India's Prison System.* Honesdale, PA: Himalayan Institute Press.

Benhabib, S. (2004). *The Rights of Others: Aliens, Residents and Citizens.* Cambridge: Cambridge University Press.

Bhana, K., & Hochfeld, T. (2001). *"Now We Have Nothing": Exploring the Impact of Maternal Imprisonment on Children Whose Mothers Killed an Abusive Partner.* Johannesburg: Centre for the Study of Violence and Reconciliation.

Bharucha, R. N. (2007). *Shadows in Cages: Forgotten Women and Children in India's Prisons.* Honesdale, PA: Himalayan Institute Press.

Bilyeu, A.S. (1999). Trokosi–the practice of sexual slavery in Ghana: Religious and cultural freedom vs. human rights. *Indiana International and Comparative Law Review, 9*, 457.

Boaten, A. B. (2001). The trokosi system in Ghana: Discrimination against women and children. A. Rwomire (ed.), *African Women and Children: Crisis and Response* (pp. 91–104). Greenwood Publishing.

Bosworth, M. (1999). *Engendering Resistance: Agency and Power in Women's Prisons.* Aldershot: Ashgate.

Botchway, A. N.-K. (2007–2008). Abolished by law–maintained in practice: The tro-kosi as practiced in parts of the Republic of Ghana. *FIU Law Review*, 3, 369–393.

Braman, D. (2004). *Doing Time on the Outside: Incarceration and Family Life in Urban America*. Ann Arbor, MI: University of Michigan Press.

Braman, D., & Wood, J. (2003). From one generation to the next: How criminal sanctions are reshaping family life in urban America. In J. Travis & M. Waul (eds), *Prisoners Once Removed: The Impact of Incarceration and Reentry on Children, Families and Communities* (pp. 157–188). Washington, DC: The Urban Institute Press.

Breen, J. (2008). The ripple effects of imprisonment on prisoners' families. Jesuit Centre for Faith and Justice, *Working Notes*, 57, 19–24.

Cherukuri, S., Britton, D., & Subramaniam, M. (2009). Between life and death: Women in an Indian state prison. *Feminist Criminology*, 4, 252–274.

Chui, W.H. (2010). "Pains of imprisonment": Narratives of the partner and children of the incarcerated. *Child and Family Social Work*, 15(2), 196–205.

Codd, H. (2000). Age, role changes and gender power in family relationships: The experiences of older female partners of male prisoners. *Women & Criminal Justice*, 12(2/3), 63–93.

Codd, H. (2008). *In the Shadow of Prison: Families, Imprisonment and Criminal Justice*. Cullompton: Willan.

Codd, H. (2012). Baby can I hold you?: Prisoners, reproductive choices and family life. *Contemporary Issues in Law*, 11(4), 227–248.

Condry, R. (2007). *Families Shamed: The Consequences of Crime for Relatives of Serious Offenders*. Cullompton: Willan.

Cook, S., & Davies, S. (eds) (1999). *Harsh Punishment: International Experiences of Women's Imprisonment*. Boston, MA: Northeastern University Press.

Djaba, G. (2008). Personal Communication, June 13, 2008.

Eurochips (2006). *Children of Imprisoned Parents: European Perspectives on Good Practice*. Paris: Eurochips.

Fair, H. (2009). International review of women's prisons. *Prison Service Journal*, 184, 3–8.

Finnegan, F. (2004). *Do Penance or Perish*. Oxford: Oxford University Press.

Fishman, L. T. (1990). *Women at the Wall: A Study of Prisoners' Wives Doing Time on the Outside*. Albany, NY: State University of New York Press.

Fraser, N. (2005). Reframing justice in a globalizing world. *New Left Review*, (November–December), 69–88.

French, H. W. (1997). Ritual slaves of Ghana: Young and female. *The New York Times International*, 7(6), 24.

George, E. (2009). *A Woman Doing Life: Notes from a Prison for Women* (ed. R. Johnson). New York: Oxford University Press.

Gilani, I. (2011). Games the mighty can play in Tihar jail. *Tehelka*, May 24, 2011.

Girshick, L. (1996). *Soledad Women*. Westport, CT: Praeger.

Golden, R. (2005). *War on the Family: Mothers in Prison and the Families they Leave Behind*. New York: Routledge.

Hauser, B. (2003). Born a eunuch? Harmful inheritance practices and human rights. *Law and Inequality*, 1, 1–64.

Henry-Lee, A. (2005). Women in prison: The impact of the incarceration of Jamaican women on themselves and their families. Kingston: The Planning Institute of Jamaica Social Development and Gender Unit.

Hopper, C. (1969). *Sex in Prison: The Mississippi Experiment with Conjugal Visiting*. Baton Rouge, LA: Louisiana State University Press.

Inda, J. X., & Rosaldo, R. (eds) (2002). Introduction: A world in motion. *The Anthropology of Globalization: A Reader* (pp. 1–34). Oxford: Blackwell.

Johnson, E., & Easterling, B. (2012). Understanding unique effects of parental incarceration on children: Challenges, progress and recommendations. *Journal of Marriage and Family, 7*, 342–356.

Johnston, D. (2012). Services for children of incarcerated parents. *Family Court Review, 50*(1), 91–105.

Kaushik, A. (2010). *Human Rights of Women Prisoners in India: A Case Study of Varanasi District Prison*. Koeln: Lambert Academic Publishing.

Kaushik, A., & Sharma, K. (2009). Human rights of women prisoners in India: A case study of Jaipur central prison for women. *Indian Journal of Gender Studies, 16*, 253–271.

Lawston, J. M., & Lucas, A. (2011). *Razor Wire Women*. Albany, NY: SUNY.

Luna, T. (2004). Bolivia's prisons and the impact of law 1008. *Andean Information Network*. http://ain-bolivia.org/index2.php?option=com_content&do_pdf=1&id=64.

Mauer, M., & Chesney-Lind, M. (eds) (2002). *Invisible Punishment: The Collateral Consequences of Mass Imprisonment*. New York: The New Press.

McEvoy, K., O'Mahony, D., Horner, C., & Lyner, O. (1999). The home front: The families of politically motivated prisoners in Northern Ireland. *British Journal of Criminology, 39*(2), 175–197.

Mills, A., & Codd, H. (2007). Prisoners families. In Y. Jewkes (ed.), *Handbook on Prisons* (pp. 671–694). Cullompton: Willan.

Morris, P. (1965). *Prisoners and Their Families*. London: George Allen and Unwin Ltd.

Morrison, W. (2005). Rethinking narratives of penal change in global context. In J. Pratt, D. Brown, M. Brown, S. Hallsworth, & W. Morrison (eds), *The New Punitiveness: Trends, Theories, Perspectives* (pp. 290–307). Cullompton: Willan.

Munro, V. (2002). The emerging rights of imprisoned mothers and their children. *Child and Family Law Quarterly, 14*(3), 303–314.

Murray, J. (2007). The cycle of punishment: Social exclusion of prisoners and their children. *Criminology and Criminal Justice, 7*, 55–81.

Murray, J., Janson, C.-G., & Farrington, D. P. (2007). Crime in adult offspring of prisoners: A cross-national comparison of two longitudinal samples. *Criminal Justice and Behavior, 34*(1), 133–149.

Musengezi, C., & Staunton, I. (eds) (2003). *A Tragedy of Lives: Women in Prison in Zimbabwe*. Harare: Weaver Press.

O'Brien, P. (2001). *Making it in the "Free World."* Albany, NY: SUNY.

Pandey, S. P., & Singh, A. K. R. (2006). *Women Prisoners and Their Dependent Children*. New Delhi: Serial Publications.

Quashigah, E. K. (1999). Legislating religious liberty: The Ghanaian experience. *BYU Law Review, 589*, 602–603.

Quinlan, C. (2010). *Inside: Ireland's Women's Prisons, Past and Present*. Dublin: Irish Academic Press.

Robertson, O. (2007). *The Impact of Parental Imprisonment on Children*. Geneva: Quaker United Nations Office.

Robertson, O. (2008). *Children Imprisoned by Circumstance*. Geneva: Quaker United Nations Office.

Scharff-Smith, P., & Gampell, L. (eds) (2011). Children of Imprisoned Parents. Denmark, Danish Institute for Human Rights, European Network for Children of Imprisoned Parents, University of Ulster and Bambinisenzasbarre.

Scott, D., & Codd, H. (2010). *Controversial Issues in Prisons*. Milton Keynes: OUP/ McGraw Hill.

Smith, B. V. (2006). Analyzing prison sex: Reconciling self-expression with safety. *Columbia Journal of Gender and Law, 15*, 185–234.

Smith, R., Grimshaw, R., Romeo, R., & Knapp, M. (2007). Poverty and Disadvantage among Prisoners' Families. London: Joseph Rowntree Foundation.

Sudbury, J. (ed.) (2005). *Global Lockdown: Race, Gender, and the Prison-Industrial Complex*. New York: Routledge.

Tibatemwa-Ekirikubinza, L. (1999). *Women's Violent Crime in Uganda: More Sinned Against Than Sinning*. Uganda: Fountain Publishers.

Travis, J. (2005). Families and children. *Federal Probation, 69*, 31–42.

Travis, J., & Waul, M. (eds) (2003). *Prisoners Once Removed: The Impact of Incarceration and Re-entry on Children, Families and Communities*. Washington, DC: The Urban Institute Press.

Vetten, L. (2008). The imprisonment of women in Africa. In J. Sarkin (ed.), *Human Rights in African Prisons* (pp. 134–154). Cape Town: HSRC.

Wall Street Journal (2007). Families join convicts in Bolivian prison. 12 April 2007.

Wing, A. K., & Murray Smith, T. (2003). The new African Union and women's rights. *Transnational and Contemporary Problems, 13*, 33–38.

Woods, B. S. (2000–2001). The slave girls of Ghana. *New York Law School Journal of Human Rights XVII*, 875–881.

Criminalization of Beggary
A Critical Look at the Indian Legal Approach

12

A. NAGARATHNA

Contents

Introduction

Beggary is not new to India as it has been in existence since time immemorial. It is a socially and culturally accepted practice in the country. Traditionally, begging has been an accepted way of life in India and giving alms to the needy is inbuilt into the social fabric. In India, it is believed that Lord Shiva once ran his household with the income from scalping, collected by begging among rishis and sadhus (Kamat, V., 1997). Shatrudra (2010) even narrates the tale of Shiva seeking alms. According to certain Hindu texts, the first step in becoming a Hindu monk (*brahmachari*) is to beg for the teacher and for self (Kamat, V., 1997). Ancient Hindu texts refer to it by different names, such as *bhiksham* and *danam*. Giving alms is regarded as a religious duty of everyone, bringing with it blessings and fortune. Thus, for Hindus, giving and sometimes receiving alms are religious duties.

Obligatory almsgiving or zakat is one of the five pillars of Islam and incumbent on all Muslims (Massey et al., 2000). Islam imposes a mandatory annual zakat of 2.5% of one's savings, and it encourages charity. The notion of social justice, according to the Quran, is that "in their (people's) wealth is a 'right' for the beggar and the deprived ... Islam represents the 'right' to social security for the poor and needy." Many Christian societies also regard almsgiving as a form of religious duty.

Current Position in India

According to a survey conducted in 2004, there were about 60,000 beggars in Delhi and over 300,000 in Mumbai, while there were about 75,000 in Kolkata, 56,000 in Bangalore, and 1 in every 354 people in Hyderabad was engaged in begging; there is a possibility of a further phenomenal increase in these numbers.* There are 7.3 lakh beggars across India (Rafiuddin, 2008). About 75%–80% of people are facing starvation and about 500 million people live with hunger and poverty in India (*Combat Law*, 2010).

Factors Responsible for Beggary

A person with a financial crisis or living in poverty may have no option but to beg. A psychological disorder is also a major reason for begging. Associated with this, broken families, addictions to cigarettes, drugs, and alcohol, homelessness, hunger, ill health, and debt are some of the factors responsible for begging. According to a survey of 49 inmates of a beggar home at Vadodara (Gujarat), 39% suffered from psychiatric illnesses, while 74% had a history of addiction, psychiatric illness in the family, and poor family attitude toward them. Table 12.1 shows the psychiatric illnesses present among these inmates (Thakker et al., 2007).

As stated earlier, problems with any type of addiction are a major factor responsible for begging. The aforementioned study by Thakker et al. (2007) also indicates the same, as shown in Table 12.2.

Legal Approach: Then and Now

The imposition of colonial rule in India changed the position and perception of beggars in the country. The Victorians criminalized begging, considering

---

* Data taken from a survey conducted by Action Aid Report 2004, the Beggar Research Institute in 2004, police records, the Council of Human Welfare in 2005, and Delhi School of Social Work in 2008, quoted in Beggary in India, http://www.youthkiawaaz.com/2008/04/beggary-in-india/, retrieved on June 27, 2011.

Table 12.1   Nature of Beggars' Psychiatric Illnesses

Psychiatric Illnesses	No. of Beggars	Sample (%)
Psychosis	11	22.4
Mental retardation	3	6.1
Adjustment disorder	2	4.0
Bipolar I mood disorder	1	2.0
Major depressive disorder	1	2.0
Dementia	1	2.0
Total	19	38.8

Source: Thakker, Y., Gandhi, Z., Sheth, H., Vankar, G. K., and Shroff, S., *The International Journal of Psychosocial Rehabilitation*, 11, 31–36, 2007.

Table 12.2   Nature of Beggars' Addictions

Addiction	Disorder Present	Disorder Absent
Smoking	7 (36.8%)	15 (50%)
Tobacco chewing	7 (36.8%)	14 (46.7%)
Alcohol	3 (15.8%)	6 (20%)
Others	0 (0%)	0 (0%)
DNA	8 (42.1%)	6 (20%)
Total	19	30

Source: Thakker, Y., Gandhi, Z., Sheth, H., Vankar, G. K., and Shroff, S., *The International Journal of Psychosocial Rehabilitation*, 11, 31–36, 2007.

it an embodiment of laziness and moral degeneration (Anonymous, 2011). The criminalization of beggary in India is, in fact, a mala prohibita, carrying with it criminal liability due to the declaration of a law to such effect. Indian beggary laws are based on England's Vagrancy Act of 1824, thus it is essential to understand the reasons behind enforcing this Act.

An analysis of the factors that led to the implementation of vagrancy laws in England shows that the laws on vagrancy in the West and the beggary laws in India are unjustified and not appropriate today, due to the changed socioeconomic conditions. The social and economic conditions prevailing at the time led to the criminalization of vagrants. During the Middle Ages, vagrants were regarded as potential criminals and as a major threat to the community. Earlier legislation in England was aimed at preventing the migration of workers and the crimes associated with such migration. It also reinforced laws regulating the poor by compelling the able-bodied to work for fixed wages (Baker, 2009). In fact, during the Middle Ages, beggary was an accepted practice in Europe and Britain. It was only from the period of Athelstan and Canute to Henry VIII that laws to prohibit vagrancy were enacted. One of the objects of the laws during that period was to provide the feudal lords with a sufficient supply of agricultural labor after the Black Death.* After the decline of the feudal system, the vagrancy laws in England were justified as a means of preventing crime by vagrants who were believed to be a "dangerous class," likely to engage in criminal activity. According to S.J. Alter, these laws were introduced to counter the economic and social threats posed to the social order by the increasing numbers of paupers (Baker, 2009). In the words of Wilson and Kelling (1982), the current stance of England's criminalization of vagrancy is justified with the use of the broken windows theory, which postulates that neighborhood disorder and physical decay, such as public drinking, begging, and vagrancy, will, if left unchecked, send a message to potential malefactors that the area is a defenseless target for criminal activities because no one cares (Baker, 2009). According to Elickson's theory, a regular beggar is like a broken window, a sign of the absence of effective social control mechanisms in that public space (Baker, 2009). The antibeggary laws are justified because the act of begging, unlike many other forms of street nuisance behavior, is likely to signal the erosion of the work ethic (Baker, 2009).

Thus, these laws of yesteryear and the reasons they were enacted are outdated today and go against the established principles of today's laws. Even today, many states, including the United Kingdom, criminalize beggary. In Australia, the state of Queensland is dealing with vagrants, despite huge criticism from civil society.† The Queensland minister for police and corrective services, the Honorable Tony McGrady MP, described the prosecution of the poor under the Vagrancy Act‡ as "unjust" and indicated that criminal sanctions would be removed because they were "incongruent with social programs being developed by the Beattie Government" (Bradfield, 2004). Even the local councils of Brisbane,§ Mount Isa, Townsville, Cairns, Gold Coast, Ipswich, and Toowoomba have criminalized homelessness, thus criminalizing people with insufficient means (Bradfield, 2004). In most Australian

---

* The Statute of Labourers of 1349 was the first enactment to criminalize vagrancy. It aimed at resolving the problem of labor shortage after the Black Death. The Act criminalized traveling and vagrancy (see Baker, 2009, p. 215).
† The Vagrancy, Gaming and Other Offences Act, 1931, defines a vagrant as "any person who has insufficient or no visible lawful means of support, is a habitual drunkard who behaves in a disorderly or riotous manner in a public place loiters or places himself/herself in a public place to beg or gather alms."
‡ Though the Vagrancy Act of Queensland underwent an amendment in 2003, instead of decriminalizing vagrancy, it included an additional offence under the Act, that is, public nuisance, which under the Amendment Act is defined as "a person behaving in a disorderly, offensive, threatening or violent way and also as the behaviour of a person interfering with the peaceful passage through or enjoyment of, a public place by a member of the public."
§ The Brisbane City Council Ordinances prohibit residing or staying overnight in any park; being located in a bus shed and committing any nuisance or interfering with the comfort of any passengers, and stacking or storing any goods.

states and territories, including Victoria, South Australia, Western Australia, Tasmania, and the Northern Territory, the act of begging constitutes a criminal offence with penalties (Walsh, 2004).

Current Indian Legal Approach

Currently in India, 20 states and 2 union territories have antibeggary laws.* The Bombay Prevention of Begging Act of 1959 applies primarily to Bombay and is extended to Delhi. Each state's approach toward the offense and the offender is different, yet all states criminalize begging. The definition of begging under state laws is so wide that a helpless person who survives on alms is made a criminal. It regards a person who appears to be poor or destitute as a beggar. For example, a beggar under section 2(d) of the Bombay Prevention of Begging Act, 1959, is defined as a person "... having no visible means of subsistence and wandering about or remaining in any public place in such condition or manner as makes it likely that the person doing so exists by

---

* The Indian state antibeggary laws are:
  1. The Andra Pradesh Prevention of Beggary Act, 1977, in Andra Pradesh
  2. The Assam Prevention of Beggary Act, 1964, in Assam
  3. The Bihar Prevention of Beggary Act, 1951, in Bihar
  4. Chattisgarh, which has adopted the Madya Pradesh Bikshavirty Nivaran Adhiniyam, 1973
  5. The Goa, Daman & Diu Prevention of Begging Act, 1972, in Goa
  6. Gujarat, which has adopted the Bombay Prevention of Begging Act, 1959
  7. The Haryana Prevention of Begging Act, 1971, in Haryana
  8. The Himachal Pradesh Prevention of Begging Act, 1979, in Himachal Pradesh
  9. The J&K Prevention of Begging Act, 1960, in Jammu and Kashmir
  10. Jharkhand, which has adopted the Bihar Prevention of Begging Act, 1951
  11. Karnataka Prohibition of Beggary Act, 1975, in Karnataka
  12. Kerala, in which the Madras Prevention of Begging Act, 1945, the Trivancore Prevention of Begging Act, 1120, and the Cochin Vagrancy Act, 1120 are in force in different areas of the state
  13. The Madhya Pradesh Bikshavirty Nivaran Adhiniyam, 1973, in the State of Madhya Pradesh
  14. The Bombay Prevention of Begging Act, 1959, in Maharastra
  15. The Punjab Prevention of Begging Act, 1971, in Punjab
  16. The Sikkim Prohibition of Beggary Act, 2004, in Sikkim
  17. The Madras Prevention of Begging Act, 1945, in Tamil Nadu
  18. The Uttar Pradesh Prohibition of Begging Act, 1972, in Uttar Pradesh and also adopted in Uttarakhand
  19. The West Bengal Vagrancy Act, 1943, in West Bengal

The two Union Territories with antibeggary laws are Daman & Diu, which has the Goa, Daman & Diu Prevention of Begging Act, 1972, and Delhi, which has adopted the Bombay Prevention of Begging Act, 1959.

For details, see Press Information Bureau, Ministry of Social Justice & Empowerment, Government of India, based on the information given by Shri D. Napoleon, the minister of state for social justice and empowerment (Napoleon, 2010).

soliciting or receiving alms." Often, a person who is shabbily dressed, including shoe polishers and mechanics, has been wrongfully arrested. The Bombay Act makes begging in public places a crime. Such persons can be arrested by the police with the assistance of officials of the social welfare department. Thus, the power to arrest under the Act is arbitrary, devoid of any guidelines or criteria essential to make a lawful arrest. States have failed to check the unlawful and unfair apprehension of people. They lack the means essential to effectively distinguish beggars from others, such as street performers, mendicants, small vendors, pavement dwellers, and migrants who might solicit alms. In *Manjula S v. State of Maharastra W.P.* [(Civil) No. 1639], a boy who polished shoes was arrested and held liable as a beggar.

The Karnataka Prevention of Beggary Act, 1975, prohibits persons from resorting to begging and provides for the detention, training, and employment of beggars. It also provides for the trial and punishment of beggar offenders and for the relief and rehabilitation of such persons. Section 2 of the Act defines the term "beggar" as

> any person other than a child who (a) solicits or receives alms in a public place whether or not under any pretence such as singing, dancing, fortune telling, performing tricks, or selling articles; (b) enters any private premises for the purposes of soliciting or receiving alms; (c) exposes or exhibits with the object of obtaining or extorting alms, any sore, wound, injury, deformity or disease whether of a human being or of an animal; (d) having no visible means of subsistence, wanders about or remains in any public place in such condition or manner as makes it likely that he exists by soliciting or receiving alms; (e) allows himself to be used as an exhibit for the purpose of soliciting or receiving alms.

This definition itself is so wide that it provides scope for abuse, by criminalizing the public performance of arts and skills for financial benefit.* This provision also adds ambiguity to the law as it excludes from its purview a person who:

(i) is a religious mendicant licensed by the Central Relief Committee to solicit alms in the prescribed manner;
(ii) in the performance of any religious vow or obligation as sanctioned by custom or religion collects alms in a private or public place, without being a nuisance; or

---

* This law prescribes double standards as it wrongfully distinguishes a person who can afford to use big dais, studios, halls, etc., to exhibit his/her talent, art, and skill, from a poor performer, who uses public places such as roads, to showcase his/her talent. For example, Wisdom Gbormegne, a 50-year-old farmer, who lived in the Olta region, was paralyzed and was unable to farm. He moved to the city and now makes money by singing on the streets. If laws like this are implemented, not only will he lose his source of livelihood but he will also be subjected to criminal liability (see http://modernghana.com).

(iii) is permitted in writing by the Central Relief Committed to collect
contributions in cash or kind from the public for any public institution, whether religious or secular or for the furtherance of any object
for the good of the public; or

(iv) is a student collecting alms for the prosecution of his studies.

This provision lacks guidelines clarifying its ambit and is prone to abuse
by alms seekers as well as concerned officers such as the Relief Committees.

Section 11 of the Karnataka Prevention of Beggary Act, 1975, empowers a police officer to arrest a person found begging in public places. The
term "who finds any person other than a child contravening the provisions
of Section 3" is very wide and relieves the arresting officer from the duty
of ensuring the need and necessity of making the arrest and also of ascer-
taining if the person was actually begging. Although section 11 provides
for the removal of the arrested person to the nearest receiving center, which
will, after necessary enquiries, either release the arrested person or forward
him/her to the magistrate, it subjects the arrested person to the unnecessary
inconvenience of arrest and legal procedure for only looking like a (found to
be) "beggar." Thus, instead of adopting a humanistic approach, the antibeggary laws resort to the means of criminalization while addressing the issue.

The beggary laws of Indian states aim to rehabilitate beggars, yet the conditions in such rehabilitation centers are unfit for humans. In fact, media
reports in August 2010 exposed the pathetic conditions of one such center
in Bangalore, where 286 inmates died due to the unhygienic conditions and
food poisoning, while several ran away. "It revealed gross violations, medical
negligence and inhuman attitude of the staff" (Bageshree & Yasmeen, 2010).

Under the current scheme of law, the rehabilitation of a beggar means
criminal liability and detention and thus amounts to nothing more than
imprisonment for being poor. This approach has been hugely criticized by
civil society organizations. In *Ram Lakhan v. State*,* the Delhi High Court
observed this practice as causing "further ignominy and deprivation," leading
to the "dehumanization" of beggars. Unless the assistance provided to beggars
in rehabilitation centers is of good quality, it fails to serve any purpose. In fact,
the Bangalore incident is an indication of gross criminal negligence on the part
of the state and its officials deserve to be prosecuted, not the helpless inmates.

In India, in addition to the antibeggary laws, a few states have shelter
homes/institutions for beggars (Napoleon, 2010a). The central government
provides financial assistance to agencies that take care of children in need of
care and protection, and destitute older persons, under the Integrated Child
Protection Scheme and the Integrated Programme for Older Persons, respectively (Napoleon, 2010b).

---

* 137 (2007) DLT 173/MANU/DE 9811/2006.

Antibeggary Laws of India: Assessment of Their Legality

The antibeggary laws of India, which adopt a punitive approach and impose criminal liability for begging without making essential distinctions, goes against the established principles of the constitution. The antibeggary laws are a sordid tale of disrespect for human life and an abandonment of constitutional norms (Ramanathan, 2011). The right to life guaranteed under Article 21 includes the right to life with dignity and privacy. The antibeggary laws lead to a violation of the rights of a person who lives by seeking alms. They also lead to a curtailment of fundamental freedoms, including that of expression and speech. These laws are also against the human rights recognized by customary international law and the Universal Declaration of Human Rights, the International Covenant on Civil and Political Rights, and the International Covenant on Economic, Social and Cultural Rights (Bradfield, 2004). These laws are also against the notions of natural law, which guarantee basic rights, equity, and justice for all. The antibeggary laws are used in an unjust manner, sometimes even to remove the poor from cities* or to make random arrests. A person "found begging" may be arrested without a warrant, and such arrests are frequent (Ramanathan, 2011).[†]

Criminalization of Beggary vis-à-vis Principles of Criminalization

The current approach of making beggary, which is not mala in se, meaning "wrong by itself," not immoral is, however, declared as a wrong for being

---

* To narrate a few such incidences:
  1. The police and municipal officials of Jaipur decided to remove beggars from major road crossings and tourist destinations, in a bid to woo nonresidential Indians to invest in the state and to portray the city in a good light during the previous Pravasi Bharatiya Diwas in 2011 (see http://daily.bhaskar.com/article/RAJ-JPR-no-city-for-beggars-during-nri-summit-2644260.html).
  2. The Delhi Traffic Police and the Department of Social Welfare removed a number of beggars from the city in order to make the city free of beggars before the Commonwealth Games (see http://www.equitabletourism.org/newsitem.php?AID=926).
† In the words of Usha Ramanathan "Arbitrary arrest of the apparently poor, subjected to a summary enquiry and summary trial, and sentenced to long terms in custody. Can it get worse? It seems it can. There are 'raids' and the 'rounding up' of 'beggars.' There is nothing in the law prescribing "raids" and rounding up, but there is nothing proscribing them either, and it is routine for policemen and "social welfare" officers to exercise them. In 1991, a committee set up by the Bombay High Court accompanied a "police squad" and saw that "the arrest is made of the people who are found on the street in dirty clothes and wandering. They are not actually found begging ... large number of wrong arrests are made which is inhuman and unjust" (see Ramanathan, 2011).

mala prohibita, meaning "acts declared as wrongs by express provisions of law." This approach goes against the established principles of not just criminal law, but also constitutional and human rights jurisprudence.

According to the basic principles of criminalization, the factors that determine the need and necessity of criminalization are the harm caused by an act, the social perception of such an act, and the principles of morality. Further, a conduct must be criminal not just because it is moral or immoral but by considering the possibility of its implementation through the legal machinery.

According to one of the basic principles of criminalization, social perception is one of the most important factors of criminalization. An act, generally regarded as "wrongful" by society at large, deserves to be criminalized. According to some writers, including Farley, a problem will be considered as a social problem if it is widely regarded as undesirable or as a source of difficulties, caused by the actions or inactions of people or of society and affects a large number of people. Beggary, as has been stated, has been in existence in India since time immemorial and also has its roots in the customs and religious texts, which do not regard beggary as "wrongful" in nature. In fact, giving alms to the needy is considered the moral as well as the religious duty of all. According to the "harm-based" approach of criminal law, an act should not be criminalized unless it harms a person. Thus, begging per se, not being harmful in itself but against the principles of morality, is generally considered a crime in India as it fails to fulfill this criterion of criminalization.

According to the principle of proportionality, the sanctions imposed under criminal law must be proportional to the problem that it seeks to deal with, that is the punishment should be proportional to the crime. According to this principle, a state's action must be a rational means to a permissible end, which does not unduly invade protected human rights (Engle, 2009). In fact, the antibegging laws of Indian states go against this principle as they criminalize helpless people seeking alms for a living. The nature of the liability imposed upon a helpless beggar cannot be compared to any injury (of another, unless such offense involves abetment of begging by another) in order to assess its proportionality.

According to the basic principles of criminal law, for an act to be made criminally liable, an element of mens rea (meaning the "state of mind" in form of intention, knowledge, recklessness, negligence, etc.) must accompany it, which is lacking in beggary. Often, a person takes up begging not as a matter of choice, but by chance and under circumstance of necessity, which are justificatory in nature. Most beggars are illiterate and are unaware of the law prohibiting begging. Although ignorance or a mistake of law is not an excuse, the fact that the state has an obligation to make the law "known" to people cannot be ignored. Even if a person "knowingly" begs, it is often under "duress" or under circumstance of "necessity" and hence can be excused.* The pressure of circumstances or acting under threat of another (in cases of organized crime syndicates operating behind beggary), thereby overpowering the free will of the offender, deserves exception from criminal liability.†

As opined by the Canadian Supreme Court in *Perka v. The Queen*:‡

> If the defense of necessity is to form a valid and consistent part of our criminal law it must, as has been universally recognized, be strictly controlled and scrupulously limited to situations that correspond to its underlying rationale.

Thus, as long as the threat under which a person begs is imminent and is proportionate to the wrong committed, the person should not be punished. Similarly, as long as begging is done to save oneself or another from hunger or to fulfill a religious obligation, it does not deserve to be criminalized. Such acts lack the element of "voluntariness" in order to constitute a crime. It would be just and appropriate to consider begging due to threat by another or under necessity as different from crimes committed under circumstances devoid of any degree of directness or immediacy.§

As observed by the Delhi High Court in *Ram Lakhan v. State*:¶

> while in the case of exploitation and compulsion by the ring leaders of a begging racket, the beggar who begs under compulsion of fear for bodily

---

* Even though an act of begging due to poverty or a similar ground of necessity does not come under section 94 of the Indian Penal Code, according to which "Except murder, and offences against the State punishable with death, nothing is an offence which is done by a person who is compelled to do it by threats, which, at the time of doing it, reasonably cause the apprehension that instant death to that person will otherwise be the consequence. Provided the person doing the act did not of his own accord, or from a reasonable apprehension of harm to himself short of instant death, place himself in the situation by which he became subject to such constraint," yet a similar ground of exception from criminal liability for begging is essential. According to the author, if a person begs because they have no other option under threat of starvation, the ground of necessity and acting under economic duress can be justified.

† The author in this regard disagrees with the decision laid down by an English court in *Southwark London Borough Council v. Williams* (1971) 2 AER 175, in which necessity in general and hunger in particular was disallowed as a ground of defense for a crime. In this case, according to Lord Denning, necessity if allowed as a ground of defense will lead to anarchy and disorder in society.

‡ (1984) 2 SCR 232.

§ As rightly pointed out in *R v. Cole* (1994) Crim L R 582, "the peril relied on to support the plea of necessity lacked imminence and the degree of directness and immediacy required of the link between the suggested peril and the offense charged. This defendant robbed two building societies in order to repay debts. The form of defense was 'duress by circumstance' which attempts to extend the coverage of duress by borrowing the idea of an uncontrollable external circumstance forcing a choice by the defendant to break the law."

¶ 137 (2007) DLT 173.

harm from them would have the defense of duress, where the beggar takes
to begging compelled by poverty and hunger, he would be entitled to invoke
the defense of necessity. The common feature of both defenses being the
element of involuntariness or, lack of legitimate choices. It is the absence of
legal alternatives that provides the defense of duress or necessity.

Thus, it is essential that the courts examine if the offender who begs out
of necessity or under duress had any other alternative and if the answer is
negative, the offender should be exempted from liability.

It is unjust to punish a person, such as a disabled orphan or a child, who
receives alms without having any other alternative. Unless the state provides
facilities and opportunities for the livelihood of a person, it must not punish
the person for attempting to get the same by way of begging. Any act done
by an individual for their own and their family's survival without harming
another is a justified act and should not be punished. In such case, the law
must provide an alternative means of livelihood or protection rather than
punishment. In fact, the Ram Lakhan's decision* also takes note of the same
criteria when it states:

> The circumstances that have to be taken into consideration while passing any
> order under the Act are indicated in section 5(6) of the Bombay Prevention
> of Begging Act, 1959 (as extended to the Union Territory of Delhi), such as
> the age and character of the beggar, circumstances and conditions in which
> the beggar was living, reports made by the Probation Officer and such other
> matters as may, in the opinion of the court, require to be taken into consider-
> ation in the interest of the beggar. This is an extremely significant provision.
> It stipulates that in passing any order under the said Act the court shall have
> regard to all considerations mentioned therein ... When the court is required
> to consider the circumstances and conditions in which the beggar was living,
> it necessarily includes the factors such as helplessness, poverty and duress.

Imposing criminal liability on a person who is begging under duress or
necessity fails to achieve the object of the "deterrent" theory of punishment.
A person who begs out of helplessness cannot be deterred by any kind of
punishment, however stringent and harsh it is. A person who is begging out
of necessity is seldom able to make rational choices and hence no punishment
can deter him. The criminalization of beggary is insufficient even to prevent
beggary and it is the above-mentioned factors, such as poverty, that need to
be tackled to prevent beggary. These laws cannot claim to be "preventive" in
approach, as acts of begging out of "necessity" cannot be prevented merely by
criminalizing beggary. Prevention by imprisonment is not a better approach
for tackling beggary in any society. Further, the preventive approach focuses

* 137 (2007) DLT 173.

more on the individual rather than on the entire issue, thus failing to tackle the menace in general.*

Even the theory of retribution fails to explain the criminalization of beggary as there is seldom any victim who would want to take revenge on the wrongdoer in such case.

Even though compensation has never been the primary aim of punishment of any criminal justice system, yet some countries have and are in the course of introducing compensation as an object of criminalization.†

Criminalizing beggary also fails on the principles of "minimization," according to which imposing criminal liability for any act must always be the last option in the absence of another alternative means to curb it. The principle, also known as the proportionality principle, limits the application of criminal law as a last resort to tackle an issue in society. For beggary, there can be other alternative measures such as economic and social rather than punitive. Criminalization is the legislator's ultima ratio and should be used as a last resort, as "uttermost means in uttermost cases" (Jareborg, 2004). According to the theory of utilitarianism, a punishment must be useful and the law imposing such punishment must bring "greatest happiness of greatest number." The antibeggary laws of India go against this theory as it is seldom useful and fails to bring happiness to the larger community.

Even though imprisoning a person in a rehabilitation center may appear to prevent the further commission of an offence, this approach is inhuman considering the nature of the act (of begging) for which it is invoked. Hence, these enactments by way of imprisoning the offender aim to bring in rehabilitation,‡ yet they lack fairness in their approach. Rehabilitation, not "voluntary" in nature, comes in the form of detention. It is often found that a person living on begging continues to do so despite previous convictions

---

* The chapter considers deterrent and preventive theories as different from each other. While the former by inculcating "fear" in the mind aims to deter further commission of the same or a similar offence, the latter by way of incapacitating or such other modes prevents a person from committing an offence.
† For compensation as a form of punishment and an object of criminal law, see Campbell (1984).
‡ According to section 11 of the Karnataka Prohibition of Beggary Act, 1975, a person arrested under the Act must be taken to the receiving center, which, after holding essential enquiries and upon finding that such person was begging, should produce the accused before a magistrate, who shall, after making enquiry, either release the person on bail or detain them in a relief center. According to section 12 of the Act, if such offender is a repeat offender or is unable to comply with required directions, the magistrate can convict the accused and pass a sentence of detention in the nearest relief center for a period of not less than 1 year but extending to 3 years. Expecting one who lives on begging to pay a bail amount is, in fact, indirect denial of bail, thus often leading to detention. Further, according to section 13, a person arrested under this Act, if they are infirm, disabled, decrepit, or suffering from an incurable disease, can be sent to a receiving center. Both the receiving center and the relief center are established by the Central Relief Committee for the reception and temporary retention and relief of beggars.

under the law, as the reasons for the person's begging can be psychological, medical, social, and economic factors, such as, addictions to drugs or alcohol, physical disability, broken family, unemployment, poverty, etc. These factors must be ascertained and appropriately dealt with rather than punishing the beggar and thereby victimizing the one who is already a victim of circumstances. A person begging out of necessity, without any means of a livelihood, will continue to live on alms and their previous convictions will fail to deter them from doing so. The theory of deterrent punishment thus fails to justify the criminal liability imposed by the antibeggary laws of India.

Alternative measures such as tackling poverty, providing employment and vocational training, ensuring the right to food, health, and shelter, must replace the criminalization of beggary. These basic needs, essential for the survival of a human being, are components of the fundamental and human rights guaranteed under the Indian constitution. Hence, the state cannot take the defense of a lack of finances and must at least provide individuals with the means to earn these basic needs themselves. This also requires the political will of the state along with legal measures.

The compensation theory, a form of the punitive damages theories, suggests that punitive damages be considered as a source of compensation (Schmit et al., 1988). However, this theory fails to serve any purpose in the case of the criminalization of beggary as, often, there is no victim to compensate. Rather, providing financial security to the offender is more needed in such cases.

According to the current law,[*] a person arrested must be taken to the receiving center, which after conducting essential enquiries and upon finding that such person was begging should produce the offender before a magistrate, who shall after making enquiries either release him on bail or detain him in a relief center. If the arrested person is a repeat offender or is unable to comply with the required directions,[†] the magistrate can convict the offender and pass a sentence of detention in the nearest relief center for a period of not less than 1 year, which may be extended to 3 years.[‡] In some cases, this detention can be extended to 10 years. Even a person who is infirm, disabled, decrepit, or suffers from an incurable disease will be sent to a receiving center.[§] This entire process of depriving one of their fundamental rights in the name of legal procedure and punishment takes place through a "summary procedure," thereby depriving the accused of a "fair" trial.[¶]

---

[*] For example, section 11 of the Karnataka Prohibition of Beggary Act, 1975.
[†] One such direction can be to furnish bail. Expecting one who lives on begging to pay a bail amount is, in fact, indirect denial of bail, thus often leading to detention.
[‡] For example, section 12 of the Karnataka Prohibition of Beggary Act, 1975.
[§] Both the receiving center and the relief center are established by the Central Relief Committee for the reception and temporary retention and relief of beggars.
[¶] The concept of fair trial generally implies a procedure (of trial) that is "just" in nature with sufficient safeguards for the accused, such as the opportunity to be heard and defended.

Detention and fines are the forms of punishment imposed under all antibeggary laws of India. As has already been discussed, detention fails to serve any purpose. Fines also fail to regulate beggary. It is often for financial aid that a person resorts to begging, and fining such a person is an inapt and useless solution. Imposing a fine is further victimization of a victim of poverty.

Beggary, when scrutinized from the angle of the above-narrated perceptive, fails to fulfill the criteria essential for criminalization and criminal penalty. A criminal law must consider the behavior of a person rather than their economic and helpless condition while committing a crime. The current legal approach of criminalizing beggary with a "punitive" approach is unjustified as it fails to fulfill the objects of punishment, that is, deterrence, prevention, retribution, etc. As already stated, some Indian states criminalize beggary. However, it is true that criminalizing beggary is nothing but criminalizing those who have insufficient means.

These laws are unjust as they criminalize behavior on the basis of housing status rather than their behavior being wrong (Bradfield, 2004). Although India is moving toward adopting a uniform law for the entire nation, through its proposed Abolition of Begging Bill, 2010, it fails to deal with the problem in a humane way. It continues to criminalize beggary instead of regarding beggars as victims of circumstances. The criminalization of beggary can lead to other associated problems, including the flippant treatment of beggars in police stations and in the courts, which is nothing but disrespecting and discriminating beggars for being poor. Even Indian street children are routinely detained illegally, beaten and tortured, and sometimes killed by the police (Human Rights Watch, 1996).

Justified Point of Criminalization

If begging takes the form of a public nuisance or leads to the intimidation and annoyance of another thereby causing "harm," it deserves punitive action. A person taking up begging as a matter of choice for the first time must only be given an admonition, but subsequent acts of begging should be punished.* It is essential to distinguish a person taking up begging because they are unable to find other means of livelihood either because of their health or their age, from a person who voluntarily starts begging despite having the ability and opportunity to earn a living. It is

---

* According to the findings of a study jointly conducted by the Social Welfare Department of Delhi and Delhi University's Department of Social Work, in Delhi many beggars are able-bodied and educated but are forced to beg due to unemployment.

the second category of person who deserves criminal liability.* Indian antibeggary laws only prescribe a period of detention by laying down the minimum and maximum extent of such detention, which is often mandatory in nature, without laying down the grounds to be considered by the deciding authority while determining the extent of the punishment.† Even though a court is supposed to consider grounds such as those previously mentioned, it is not obligatory on its part and is often done in a routine manner.

Abetting Beggary

Although the antibeggary law of India does not punish a person for giving alms, it is possible to do so by interpreting and applying the theory and principle of abetment of crimes. In fact, in Delhi, the Traffic Police Notification makes giving money to beggars a criminal offence for which a fine is imposed. Any motorists giving alms can be held liable under this notification with a fine of Rs. 150 for the first violation and Rs. 300 for the second violation.‡ This practice of imposing criminal liability for giving alms is unjustified, considering the historical and social notions attached to such practice. Hence, giving or soliciting alms per se should not be criminalized as being humane and considerate is not being criminal.

Selling and purchasing children for the purpose of using them for begging warrants an effectual legal measure with a stringent punishment. Persons who kidnap another or maim themselves for the purpose of begging must be considered as aggravated forms of the offence, deserving stringent and deterrent punishment (although the provisions of the Indian Penal Code, including section 363, criminalizes maiming and kidnapping for the purpose of begging, it is seldom used). A person or organized criminal syndicates forcing or luring another to enter into begging must also be subjected to deterrent punishment.

---

* According to a study, of over 5000 beggars surveyed, 4 were postgraduates who used to beg on weekends to supplement their income, 6 were graduates, and 796 had studied up to higher secondary level.
† For example, according to the Anti-Beggary Act of the state of Karnataka, the period of detention is from 1 to 3 years.
‡ This direction of the Delhi Traffic Police (of 2010) provides: "Giving alms to beggars or purchasing articles/wares/goods from roadside vendors at traffic junctions is construed as acts obstructive to the quick discharge and smooth traffic flows at road intersections, and/or hazardous in nature likely to endanger safety of other road users." Violation of this direction is attracted by Rule 22(a) of Rules of the Road Regulations, 1989, framed under section 118 of the Central Motor Vehicles Act, 1988, punishable under section 177 of the Act entailing a fine of Rs. 100 for the first offence and Rs. 300 for the second and subsequent offences (see delhitrafficpolice.nic.in).

Need of Subjective Test with Combined Approach

Often, a person is forced into begging for various reasons, including poverty,* disability, disease, and old age.† It is necessary to find out such reasons and, accordingly, determine the nature of treatment. A person who is forced to beg due to economic reasons needs vocational training and an alternative means of livelihood, while a person who begs because of a physical disability deserves rehabilitation. It is also necessary to distinguish beggars who are mentally ill and provide them with essential medical treatment instead of criminal liability.‡ A person who begs because of their religious objectives and ideological differences also deserves no punishment. On the other hand, beggars who are of the lowest social status or illegal immigrants or those who suffer from ill health require the appropriate measures rather than punishment under law.

As observed by the Delhi High Court in *Ram Lakhan v. State*§

> there are various reasons for which a person begins to solicit alms. Either because he is down-right lazy and doesn't want to work, or because he is an alcoholic or a drug-addict, thus in search of financing his next drink or dose or that he is at the exploitative mercy of a ring leader of a beggary 'gang' or also because he is starving, homeless and helpless. ... It is thus the duty of the court to satisfy them selves that the accused did not have a defense of necessity. Prevention of begging is the object of the said Act. But, one must realize that embedded in this object are the twin goals-Nobody should beg and nobody should have to beg.

Each and every problem associated with beggary, such as poverty, hunger, and lack of shelter, needs to be addressed by the state. It is essential to enact laws in this regard, in order to ensure that the poor can realize their

---

* According to a survey, around 85% of destitute people were earning far below the poverty line before they got into this practice. An Action Aid International study on beggary in India shows that 99% of men and 97% of women got into beggary due to poverty. For details, see the *Hindu* (2011).
† According to a study conducted by Subrata De, in nine cities of four states, out of 85% of the destitute people who entered into begging due to poverty, 25% took to begging because of poverty along with disability, disease, and old age; 15% faced family problems due to poverty; and among women, who constitute less than one-third of the population, family disorganization (21%), disability, disease, and old age (13%) are the reasons for begging.
‡ According to Dr. Yogesh Thakker, in his article in the *International Journal of Psychological Rehabilitation* (quoted by Anonymous, 2011), about 39% of the 49 beggars surveyed in Gujarat's Baroda district by a group of medicos suffer from a psychiatric illness and nearly 74% of them had a history of addiction, psychiatric illness in the family, and poor family attitude toward them. Over 68% admitted to feelings of shame and losing self-esteem, 25% to guilt, 4% to suicidal tendencies, and 8% to antisocial activities.
§ 137 (2007) DLT 173.

basic human rights, including the right to food, shelter, and health. India is already implementing one such law, namely, the National Food Security Act, which is currently awaiting approval from the cabinet. The Act aims to prevent people who fall into the category of "poor," as per certain indicators, from suffering hunger and starvation.

It is essential to address the socioeconomic reasons for beggary rather than indiscriminately criminalizing the act. All forms of faulty, arbitrary, and unfair implementation of laws need effective checks. Magistrates, while exercising their power in determining the need to detain a beggar, must exercise due care and caution and consider all the relevant factors, including the economic, social, and health conditions of the beggar, the possibility of making a living, and the need for sending them to rehabilitation and the period of detention in such rehabilitation centers. The current approach to rehabilitation requires a relook and reframing based on a well-developed custodial jurisprudence, clarifying the nature of the duties and responsibilities of each official in charge of rehabilitating beggars.*

It is essential to adopt a holistic and humanistic approach. It is necessary to deal with all the socioeconomic factors leading to beggary, such as mental illness, domestic violence, failure of maintenance law, drug and alcohol addictions, and unemployment, rather than instantly criminalizing people who seek alms. These problems can be dealt with by an all-inclusive approach, including psychological counseling, rehabilitation, providing employment opportunities, and vocational training. Whenever a person is found seeking alms in public spaces, instead of imprisonment, it is essential to send the person to centers, such as medical centers, rehabilitation homes (without tagging criminal liability with it), and vocational training centers. As of now, there are both political and legal impediments to these approaches, as neither the state nor the provisions of the current laws provide for them. Under the current law, an arrested beggar is sent to a receiving center, which lacks sufficient rehabilitation programs and assistance.

The arrest powers of the police must be limited and restricted only to violent and aggressive behavior of beggars in public places. The police must be sensitized and trained to deal compassionately with an alms seeker. It is essential to formulate certain criteria and guidelines to determine the need to admit a person into a rehabilitation centre in order to avoid indiscriminate subjection to custody. Such an admission must be the choice of the recipient and must not be unnecessarily forced.

* Despite media exposure of the inhuman conditions prevailing in the Bangalore rehabilitation center in August 2010, which clearly showed failure on the part of the state and its officials to discharge their duty with care and caution, no legal action was taken against the wrongdoers who erred in their duty.

It is essential for the state to realize that the problem of beggary is a social and economic concern requiring social and economic measures rather than criminalization. The current legal approach is, in fact, the criminalization not of a menace but of the living conditions of the poor who require the state's assistance instead of its condemnation. It is essential to have a social insight into the issue in order to devise a more practically oriented rehabilitation approach.

Abolition of Begging Bill, 2010: A Look at the Proposed Law

Considering the need for a uniform legal approach for the entire country, the Prevention of Begging Bill, 2010, was presented in the Rajya Sabha on February 25, 2011. An analysis of this bill is essential because if it is passed, it will replace the existing state antibeggary laws.

The bill seeks to prevent beggary by abolishing the act of begging. According to the bill, begging is

> (i) soliciting alms in a public place, including railways, bus-stops, road sides and public transport, by invoking compassion and (ii) entering in any private premises for the purpose of soliciting or receiving alms.

Even though the bill attempts to prevent illegal arrests by requiring that arrests are made only after the arresting officer is satisfied as to the bona fide of the arrested beggar under section 5, it fails to prescribe the criteria to be adopted in arriving at this conclusion. The bill also continues the approach of criminalization by allowing the detention of the arrested person in a receiving center for rehabilitation. Hence, the bill contains certain loopholes and unjust provisions, which exist under current state laws. As mentioned earlier, according to the bill, a person found begging can be arrested by the police, which is a continuation of the "unjust" approach that already exists under the current state laws of India.

However, in comparison to the existing state legislations, the bill seems to be more comprehensive and effective as it seeks to tackle the major issues associated with beggary, such as abetment, use of children, etc. The bill recognizes the fact that there are organized gangs who exploit innocent children and force them into begging, not for the sustenance of such children, but for collecting alms for the gang leaders and organizers. According to section 4 of the bill, a person who forces or encourages any person, including a child in their care, custody, or charge, to beg will be punished with imprisonment for a term that shall not be less than 20 years and if such a person encourages or forces two or more persons to indulge in begging, this person will be punished with imprisonment of not less than 25 years.

The bill obligates the central government to constitute a fund called the "Beggars' Welfare Fund" for the welfare of beggars, which shall be utilized by it, as and when required, for the welfare and rehabilitation of beggars. The bill requires the government to formulate such schemes, work out such plans, including plans for the provision of education, and create suitable infrastructure in every district to enable beggars to take up suitable jobs to earn a livelihood. The bill also requires the appropriate government department to set up destitute homes to provide food, shelter, and protection, to the old, infirm, helpless, and destitute persons to discourage them from indulging in begging. Section 7 of the bill also requires the government to provide employment opportunities to beggars, formulate such schemes, work out such plans, including plans for the provision of education, and create such suitable infrastructure in every district as it considers appropriate. Thus, in this respect, the bill seems to provide "welfare" in the real sense to beggars.

Conclusion

As Mark Tully rightly said, the least that one can do (about the poor in India) is to respect their condition rather than criminalizing it (Kamat, K. L., 1997). The antibeggary laws of India are modeled on the centuries-old vagrancy laws of England, instead of addressing the current socioeconomic issues. These laws, in fact, make people criminally responsible for being poor. This punitive approach does not concur with the principles of criminalization. It fails to effectively fulfill the purpose of punishment, including "deterrence," "retribution," and "compensation." Even though the law aims to introduce rehabilitation, which is currently involuntary, it is in itself not fair or just.

A beggar who is a drug addict or an alcoholic or a physically or mentally disabled person must be provided with appropriate treatment. An aged person or an orphan or a person who voluntarily agrees to undergo rehabilitation can be sent to receiving centers where the emphasis should be on rehabilitation in the true sense. A child found begging must be sent to a juvenile home for rehabilitation. A punitive approach when inevitable, just, and is in accordance with the principles of criminal law, must be allowed. Such an approach is justified in cases of using children for beggary, maiming, and abetting another to beg. People who deliberately and repeatedly resort to beggary deserve a punitive approach. The same can also be extended to beggary associated with other criminal acts such as intimidating and annoying others and not just for "begging per se" without any other option of livelihood. Hence, the punitive approach toward beggary, of punishing parties involved in both giving and receiving alms, has failed to achieve its object.

The fact that, to date, beggary continues to be present and accepted in society is evident of this fact.*

Thus, the antibeggary laws of India are not just against the principles of criminal law but are also unconstitutional in nature. They violate the fundamental rights to life, liberty, dignity, privacy, and freedom and hence go against constitutional morality. Further, these laws are used in an unjust manner, sometimes even to remove the poor from cities. These laws are also against the human rights recognized by customary international law and the Universal Declaration of Human Rights, the International Covenant on Civil and Political Rights, and the International Covenant on Economic, Social and Cultural Rights (Bradfield, 2004). These laws are also against the notions of natural law, which guarantee basic rights, equity, and justice to all.

Beggary is a culturally and socially accepted phenomenon in India, requiring an all-inclusive therapeutic, preventive, reformative, and punitive approach at the minimal level, with a humanistic approach. This combined approach with shades of philanthropy is needed today. Poverty is the worst form of violence,[†] but criminalizing poverty is worse and should be denounced.

References

Anonymous. (2011). Beggary in India. Retrieved on May 11, 2011, from http://www.azadindia.org/social-issues/beggary-in-india.html.

Ashworth, A. (1995). *Principles of Criminal Law*. Oxford: The Clarendon Press.

Bageshree, S., & Yasmeen, A. (2010). Beggars' death probe yet to reach CID, the Hindu, Bangalore, December 28, 2010. Retrieved on December 14, 2010, from http://www.thehindu.com/news/cities/Bangalore/article997138.ece.

Baker, D. J. (2009). A critical evaluation of the historical and contemporary justifications for criminalising beggary. *The Journal of Criminal Law*, 73 JCL 212.

Bernstein, R., & Seltzer, T. (2003). Criminalization of people with mental illnesses: The role of mental health courts in system reform. *The University of the District of Columbia Law Review*, 145.

Bradfield, M. (2004). Nowhere to hide: When the home is not a haven. Retrieved on June 25, 2011, from http://www.qpilch.org.au/_dbase_upl/Nowheretohide.pdf.

Campbell, T. (1984). Compensation as punishment. *UNSW Law Journal*, 7, 338.

Card, R. (2008). *Card, Cross and Jones' Criminal Law*, 18th edn. Oxford: Oxford University Press.

---

* The Safe Streets Act, 1999, of Ontario and Canada criminalizes certain kinds of begging, including aggressive or abusive panhandling. Similarly in British Columbia, the Safe Streets Act of 2004 criminalizes beggary. In the United States, various states, including Illinois, make panhandling legally prohibited, while in the United Kingdom, the Vagrancy Act of 1842 makes vagrancy illegal and even makes it an offence to sleep on the streets or to beg, without considering the reason for doing so.

† Mahatma Gandhi.

Carrodo, M. L. (ed.) (1994). *Justifications and Excuse in the Criminal Law—A Collection of Essays.* London: Garland Publishing Inc.

Child Protection & Child Rights. (2010). Missing children. http://www.childlineindia. org.in/missing-children-india.htm.

Combat Law. (2010). Entitlements of hunger, May–August 2010, p. 26.

Dailybhaskar. (2011). No city for beggars during NRI summit. Retrieved on December 16, 2011, from http://daily.bhaskar.com/article/RAJ-JPR-no-city-for-beggars-during-nri-summit-2644260.html.

Engle, E. (2009). The history of the general principle of proportionality: An overview. *William Journal of International Law and Dispute Resolution,* Forthcoming. Retrieved on June 20, 2011, from SSRN http://ssrn.com/abstract=1431179.

FunOnTheNet. (2012). Beggar mafia. Retrieved on June 14, 2012, from http://www. funonthenet.in/forums/index.php?PHPSESSID=ce0e5e2bdded1aa485c10878f 5671871&topic=234459.msg2944073#msg2944073#ixzz1x1S84Ydg.

Human Rights Watch. (1996). Police abuse and killings of street children in India, Human Rights Watch Children's Rights Project. Retrieved on June 20, 2011, from http://www.hrw.org/legacy/reports/1996/India4.htm.

Jalees, A. (2009). Beggar mafia thrives on lost children—The National. Retrieved on June 20, 2011, from http://www.thenational.ae/news/world/south-asia/ beggar-mafia-thrives-on-lost-children#page2.

Jareborg, N. (2004). Criminalization as last resort (Ultima Ratio). *Ohio State Journal of Criminal Law, 2,* 521.

Kamat, K. L. (1997). The begging profession. Retrieved on October 30, from http:// www.kamat.com/kalranga/bhiksha/begging.htm.

Kamat, V. (1997). Interviews with poverty. Retrieved on November 27, 2010, from http://www.kamat.com/kalranga/bhiksha/index.htm.

Massey, D., Rafique, A., & Janet, S. (2000). Begging in rural India and Bangladesh, Retrieved on July 27, 2011, from http://www.indiaenvironmentportal.org.in/ files/Begging%20in%20and%20Bangladesh.pdf.

Napoleon, D. (2010a). States asked to have anti-beggary law in place in his to Lok Sabha, August 16, 2010. Retrieved on November 26, 2010, from http://news. webindia123.com/news/articles/India/20100817/1567096.html.

Napoleon, D. (2010b). No authentic data on beggars. Press Information Bureau, Ministry of Social Justice & Empowerment, Government of India. Retrieved on April 20, 2011, from http://pib.nic.in/newsite/PrintRelease.aspx?relid=67734.

Neeta, L. (2007). Criminalising beggars instead of rehabilitating them. *InfoChange News & Features,* June. Retrieved on June 1, 2011, from http:www.delhitrafficpolice.nic. in/art.19.htm.

Pereira, M. (2011). Regulation of social functions. Retrieved on June 28, 2011, from http://www.delhitrafficpolice.nic.in/articles/regulation-of-social-functions.htm.

Rafiuddin, M. (2008). Beggars in Hyderabad—A 2 year survey report. Retrieved on June 27, 2011, from http://www.youthkiawaz.com/2008/04/beggary-in-india.

Ramanathan, U. (2011). A constitution amid dire straits. Retrieved on June 14, 2012, from http://www.india-seminar.com/2010/615/615_usha_ramanathan.htm.

Schmit, J. T., Pritchett, S. T., & Fields, L. P. (1988). Punitive damages: Punishment or further compensation? *The Journal of Risk and Insurance,* 55, 453–466.

Shatrudra, S. (2010). Retrieved on June 27, 2011, from http://www.neelkanthdhaam. org/Srspu.html.

Siddique, M. (2008). Rs. 180 Crore—That is the annual earning of beggars in India. Retrieved on May 11, 2011, from http://twocircles.net/2008oct09/rs_180_crore_annual_earning_beggars_india.html.

Storey, T., & Alan, L. (2002). *Criminal Law*. Cullompton: Willan.

Thakker, Y., Gandhi, Z., Sheth, H., Vankar, G. K., & Shroff, S. (2007). Psychiatry morbidity among inmates of the "Beggar Home." *The International Journal of Psychosocial Rehabilitation, 11*(2), 31–36, retrieved on December 20, 2010, from http://www.psychosocial.com/IJPR_11/Illness_in_Beggars_Home_Sheth.html.

The Hindu. (2011). Begging not by choice: Study. Retrieved on July 20, from http://www.hindu.com/2005/07/18/stories/2005071802701300htm.

Walsh, T. (2004). Defending begging offenders 4(1), QUTL JJ. Retrieved on December 25, 2010, from http://www.law.qut.edu.au/ljj/editions/v4n1/pdf/Walsh.pdf.

Wilson, J. Q., & Kelling, G. (1982). Broken windows: The police and neighbourhood safety. *Atlantic Monthly, 29*, 31.

It Is Crime, Not Racism

Victimization of Indian Students in Australia*

13

GAIL MASON

Contents

Introduction

In January 2010, Nitin Garg was stabbed to death on his way to work at a "Hungry Jacks" fast food outlet in the city of Melbourne in Australia (Grace & Miller, 2010). Mr. Garg was 21 years old and was studying accountancy. He was from India. His tragic death came after 6 months of public debate in Australia and India around reports of violence against international students, mainly from India, in Australian cities, particularly Melbourne and Sydney. The responses to Mr. Garg's death from stakeholder groups mirrored, and indeed deepened, the parameters that had shaped the dialogue around the issue of "racial violence against Indian students" since it first attracted public attention in May 2009, when international students staged a public demonstration in Melbourne. It appeared that Mr. Garg was not robbed during the attack and the absence of any apparent motive was sufficient for some commentators to claim that the attack was racially motivated (the absence of a

* Part of this chapter was earlier published as Mason, G. (2010). Violence against Indian students in Australia: A question of dignity. *Current Issues in Criminal Justice, 21*(3), 461–466. Reproduced with permission.

motive is one of the many indicators that can be used to determine whether an incident is a hate crime). On the other hand, the absence of evidence pointing to overt racial overtones on the part of the assailant meant that the Victoria police were not in a position to attribute a racist motive to the crime. None of this is any consolation to Mr. Garg's grieving family. It does, however, signal the polarities of opinion that characterize contemporary debates on racist violence in Australia.

In May 2009, several thousand international students, led by the Federation of Indian Students in Australia (FISA), staged a public protest in the central business district of Melbourne. This protest sought to draw attention to a plethora of long-standing welfare and educational problems faced by international students in Australia (Babacan et al., 2010). The focus or rallying cry of the demonstration was the claim that Indian students living in Melbourne and Sydney were being deliberately targeted for violence and crime that was motivated by racism (Babacan et al., 2010). Although the May 31 demonstration was prompted by high-profile cases, such as the stabbing of Baljinder Singh in the Melbourne suburb of Carnegie on May 25, 2009, protestors also claimed that such incidents formed part of a long history of violent victimization experienced by Indian nationals studying in Australia.

The following week, the Indian prime minister, Manmohan Singh, characterized some of this violence as racist in nature (*Hindustan Times*, 2009). Similarly, the Indian Minister of State of External Affairs, Shashi Tharoor, described the victimization as "a continuing pattern of anti-Indian violence" (Wade, 2009). Throughout the second half of 2009, the issue was given extensive coverage in the Indian media, with some news services strongly condemning the violence as racist; for example: "Australia, Land of Racism" (*Economic Times*, 2009), "Sixth Racist Attack in One Month" (*Times Now*, 2009a), "Race Terror Down Under" (*Times Now*, 2009b), and "Racist Australia?" (NDTV, 2009).

This chapter considers the reactions among Australia's political leaders to this claim of racial victimization. It reports on the results of a study of public documents—including media interviews, press releases, and parliamentary Hansard—on the question of violence against Indian students. In the months following the demonstration, many deep-seated problems in the international education industry were revealed, generating multiple and ongoing reviews of the education, migration, housing, transport, and criminal justice sectors. To the extent that the reviews touched on the wider issues of employment and accommodation, the students' claims of racist violence have been acknowledged by many of these reviews (Graycar, 2010). In the face of severe condemnation of the violence from India and other nations, Australian politicians also sought to respond to the students' claims. I will argue, however, that the nature of this response is concerning. By and large, Australia's political leaders responded with a range of discursive strategies that, ultimately, amounted to a form of denial. This was not simply a denial of the problem of violence itself, but, rather, a denial of the racial character of that violence.

Denial of Racism

Van Dijk (1992) argues that the denial of racism cannot be separated from racism itself: "[o]one of the most crucial properties of contemporary racism is its denial" (p. 87). Australia has its own distinct and volatile history of racism, from the colonization and brutalization of the indigenous population, to the White Australia Policy that operated from the early 1900s into the 1970s, through to contemporary government policy that all too frequently interprets multiculturalism as another word for cultural and moral assimilation (Babacan, 2006; Hage & Couch, 1999; Hollinsworth, 2006). This (albeit shifting) trajectory of racial anxiety has been accompanied by a history of denial that has formulated exclusionary and prejudicial practices and policies as necessary for national security, integration, cultural cohesion, employment, and the like.

The denial of racism is pervasive not just in everyday conversation but also in the "elite discourse" of politicians, media, academia, and corporations (van Dijk, 1992, 1993). Within such public discourse, norms have changed to the point that racism is interpreted as a sign of an uncivilized culture, as evidenced by the emergence of antidiscrimination and equal opportunity laws in most Western countries during the last few decades. Individuals and institutions now seek to employ "impression management" strategies that facilitate "face keeping" or "positive self-presentation" around the issue of racism (van Dijk, 1992, p. 89); for example, through defensive assertions such as "we are not a racist society". Perhaps the most recent Australian example of such denial was evident in the aftermath of the Cronulla riots in Sydney in 2005. The riots involved several thousand, primarily white youths from English-speaking backgrounds, engaging in abuse, intimidation, and violence directed toward people of "Middle Eastern" appearance on and around Cronulla beach (a "revenge" attack was staged the following day by young men identified by police as coming from a Middle Eastern/Muslim background). The overt refusal of Australia's prime minister at the time, John Howard, and a broad body of other "elite" commentators to characterize the violence as racist reflects Australia's long history as a nation in denial (Noble, 2009; Poynting, 2009).

Politicians tend to rely on several interwoven discursive strategies to deny accusations of racism, including: outright denial; avoidance of the word "racism" because of its strong negative connotations; positive self-presentation through the assertion of messages of decency, harmony, and fairness; and the use of euphemisms and deflection onto other problems, such as unemployment, poverty, economic competition, or inner city angst (van Dijk, 1992).

Such "face keeping" is relevant to a nation such as Australia, which is now one of the top 10 receiving countries for the world's mobile tertiary students (*Access Economics*, 2009). India is a leading country of origin for international students in Australia. In 2009, there were approximately 100,000 Indian students studying in Australia, a significant increase from 5 years earlier when there were approximately 30,000 (Hodge & Karvelas, 2009).

In the remainder of this chapter, I argue that most of these discursive manoeuvres are evident in the way Australian parliamentarians, particularly at the federal level, have approached the issue of violence against Indian students. Notable, however, is the scarcity of attempts at outright or literal denial of the kind favored by European and North American politicians (van Dijk, 1992, 1993). Instead, Australian politicians have taken a more circular route to the process of denial by favoring strategies of avoidance, positive self-presentation, and deflection.

The Study

The aim of the current study was to examine how Australian politicians, as the purveyors of "elite" discourse (van Dijk, 1992), responded to the claim of racial victimization against Indian nationals studying in Australia, which, by necessity, required a consideration of the evidence for the claim itself. To do this, the study drew on a database of public documents discussing the violence against Indian students phenomenon compiled in the 12 months following the Melbourne demonstration (June 1, 2009 to May 31, 2010). The purpose of this database was to map the responses to the claim of racial violence among Australian and Indian commentators at both official and informal levels. This database includes: (i) Australian state and federal Hansard; (ii) press releases and interviews from Australian parliamentarians, Indian parliamentarians, the Australian police in Victoria and New South Wales, community groups, and government agencies; (iii) reports of government inquiries, summits, and roundtables; (iv) sentencing hearings for convictions for offenses committed against victims assumed to be of Indian heritage; and (v) media reports in Australia and India, including online blogs attached to Internet media. Excluding repetitious or minor material, a database of approximately 250 key documents was produced.

The study sampled all public statements by federal parliamentarians from this database. It focused on the first 6 months following the May demonstration as this was the period when debates were most acute, Indian students were looking for a response, and there was the opportunity to engage in helpful dialogue around the issue. Using techniques of discourse analysis, the study identified linguistic repertoires employed by Australia's politicians to describe, define, and comment on the victimization of Indian students

(Potter & Wetherell, 1987). This form of discourse analysis is used extensively in scholarship on racism. It aims to identify dominant interpretations by linking the language of leading Australian parliamentarians to wider themes of social and racial inequality.

Results

It is difficult to assess the veracity of the claim that Indian nationals studying in Australia have been the targets of racist violence. Victoria police statistics for 2007–2009 show that 1447 Indian nationals were the victims of crime including robberies and assault, and the police state that Indians living in Melbourne (the capital of the state of Victoria) are disproportionately targeted for robberies (Wilson, 2010). Yet, this does not prove that there is a racial element to this crime. Media reports, however, *do* provide some support for the claim of racial violence. During the 12-month period of the study, more than 20 incidents were reported in the Australian and Indian media of criminal offenses involving a victim identified as a student from India. While there is insufficient evidence in most of these reports to determine whether racism was a factor, some contain victim accounts that point to the presence of racism. For example, in May 2009, Mr. Sourabh Sharma, a 21-year-old student from India, was the victim of an assault and robbery in Werribee, Melbourne, during which the assailants allegedly yelled "Why the f*** did you come here?" (Miller, 2009); in June 2009, Mr. Sunny Bajaj, a 20-year-old student from India, was assaulted in Boronia, Melbourne, by assailants who allegedly called him a "f***ing Indian c***" (*Times of India*, 2009a); and in September 2009, a large group of assailants abused four members of the Singh family, including two students, in a hotel car park in Epping, Melbourne. One of the victims, Mr. Mukhtiar Singh, described the incident as follows:

> They had bottles ... We didn't have a chance to go away, people everywhere around us, everybody was saying, 'go back to India, get out, leave the country', f-word they were using, even the women were screaming like 'go back to your country, go back to India.' (ABC Television, September 16, 2009)

Although the claim of racial violence was eventually acknowledge by Victoria police (ABC Television, 2009), the study found very few instances where an Australian federal politician publicly acknowledged that racism might be a factor in the victimization reported by Indian students during the 6-month period under consideration. However, unlike the parliamentary discourse examined by van Dijk (1992) in Europe and North America, where the extensive use of literal forms of denial was identified, Australian politicians engaged in a more circular, or coded, form of denial. The study identified three major discursive manoeuvres adopted by federal parliamentarians to achieve this denial: avoidance, nationalist rhetoric, and deflection.

Avoiding the "R" Word

Instead of directly or literally denying that racism may be involved in the victimization of Indian students, Australian federal politicians avoided speaking about racism altogether. For example, following her meeting with the Indian prime minister in India in September 2009, the then deputy prime minister Julia Gillard was asked by an ABC journalist: "How do you overcome the perception that Australia's a racist country?." Instead of saying "Australia's not a racist country," Gillard replies:

> I think the important thing is to be here in India and explaining factually to people what has happened and what the Government's response has been. Of course the incidents involving Indian students got a lot of media in India and caused anxiety. That's to be expected. (*ABC 7.30 Report*, 2009)

In other interviews on September 1, 2009, Gillard also sidestepped the question of racist violence by referring to the "treatment of Indian students and offering reassurance that the government was acting on 'welfare and other concerns'" (ABC Radio AM, 2009). In short, she simply refused to utter the "R" word.

Positive Self-Presentation: Nationalist Rhetoric

According to van Dijk (1992, p. 109), parliament is "the prime forum for nationalistic rhetoric" and provides the perfect vehicle for nations to present positive images of themselves, which, in turn, is a common strategy in the overall denial of racism. Such rhetoric has been pronounced among federal politicians in response to the victimization of international students from India. For example, in his address to parliament on June 1, 2009, the day after the student demonstration in Melbourne, the then prime minister Kevin Rudd embedded his condemnation of the violence within positive images of "diversity," "harmony," "tolerance," and "multiculturalism" (rather than the negative image of racism):

> Australia is a country of great diversity, harmony and tolerance. We are a multicultural nation and we respect and embrace diversity – diversity which has enriched our nation, Australia. That is why these recent acts of violence are all the more deplorable. They are equally unacceptable and deserve to be met with the full force of the law. (Commonwealth of Australia, 2009, p. 4905)

While Kevin Rudd alluded to the claim of racism in this parliamentary address, his emphasis on notions of respect and tolerance sidestepped the problem of racism, implying that it is out of the ordinary because it is at odds with "normal" Australian values.

Deflection: Racism versus Crime

Australia's political leaders have not denied the victimization of Indian student's altogether. Rather, they have sought to deflect attention away from racism as a possible cause of this violence by formulating it as a problem of urban violence or crime:

> In fact, there is a much wider problem of urban violence in various parts of some of our largest cities. … These are senseless acts of violence.
> The Australian government is also committed to the safety of all Australians and all those who visit our nation. (Kevin Rudd, Commonwealth of Australia, 2009, pp. 4905–4906)

In asserting their commitment to the safety of "all" visitors and "all" citizens, Australia's federal politicians have sought to neutralize the racial dimension of the victimization by implying that violence is something that could happen to "any" individual, not just people from India or racial minorities (Andersen, 2009; Commonwealth of Australia, 2009).

Discussion

Attempts to downplay the question of racism have come in different guises. The then deputy prime minister and minister for education, Julia Gillard, was careful to condemn the violence but largely avoided directly commenting on whether racism was an element in the offenses: no acknowledgment and no denial. Similarly, the then prime minister, Kevin Rudd, assiduously sought to avoid making any reference to the racism question, choosing instead to praise Australia's commitment to multiculturalism and characterize the victimization of Indian students as part of a larger problem of urban crime and violence.

Together, these discursive strategies—avoidance, nationalist rhetoric, and deflection—amount to a form of denial whereby the victimization reported by Indian students in Australia was formulated, and thereby normalized, as part of a wider crime problem. The obvious concerns about the damage to international trade and Australia's relationship with India are all reasons why the country's political leaders were not, by and large, prepared to speak of, much less acknowledge, racism. Nonetheless, to characterize the victimization as a problem of crime rather than racism is to deny the nature of the harm to the victims and avoid the complexities of causation that lie behind it.

In contrast to Australia's politicians, much has been said about the Indian media's eagerness to characterize the victimization as racist. Some Australian commentators have described it as "hysterical" and "shrill" (it is interesting to remember that feminism has revealed how, historically, the very same language has been used to discredit women). Certainly, sections of the Indian media have responded passionately to the reports they have received of the victimization of Indian nationals while studying in Australia. Any attack on an Indian national in Australia has been quickly described in news reports as racist, irrespective of whether there is accompanying evidence to indicate that racism was a motivating factor.

We can speculate that the eagerness of the Indian media to malign Australia has something to do with cricket or Australia's refusal to sell uranium to India. Nonetheless, beneath this veneer of extravagant reporting, the Indian media have an important point to make. Indian nationals studying in Australia, their families and compatriots back home, have good reason to be angry. Many families have saved hard and sacrificed much to send their children overseas to study in pursuit of what they anticipate will be a better future (both in terms of education and migration). To be confronted with poor educational facilities and substandard teaching programs (Graycar, 2010) would enrage anyone. When coupled with overcrowded living conditions, low-paid employment, and long hours of travel on public transport, it is not surprising that many students feel disgruntled and disillusioned in the face of what must feel like a string of broken promises—and dreams.

India is the world's largest democracy. It is also a nation that has undergone significant change in the last few decades. Buoyed by slogans of "India Shining,"* India's burgeoning middle class is acutely aware of the increasing influence of their nation on the world stage. India's strengthening identity as a nuclear power that can command both fiscal and political forces does much to relegate the humiliation of British colonial rule to a distant memory; but it is still a memory. This tension between an exciting future and a colonized past creates an understandable sensitivity around issues of national pride, respect, and dignity. It only takes a few violent incidents with racist overtones—and certainly, there is evidence that some incidents have been racist—for a deep message of intolerance and cultural disrespect to be conveyed to India. This is how prejudice-related crime works: the negative impact on a targeted community is greater than the sum of its parts. Individual victims experience physical and psychological injury, but, as the Victorian Sentencing Advisory Council recently recognized, several incidents added together quickly send a

---

* "India Shining" was a controversial slogan used by the Bharatiya Janata Party (BJP) in the mid- to early 2000s to signal India's economic success and sense of optimism.

"powerful message of intolerance and discrimination" that can have a "general terrorizing effect" on all members of the target group (Victorian Sentencing Advisory Council, 2009, 8, 1). In assessing the social and political impacts of crimes committed against Indian nationals in Australia, it does not really matter whether the majority of the incidents are motivated by pure racism or not (nor does it matter whether Indians are victimized at a higher rate than other groups or are at greater risk in Australia than they are at home). Some incidents clearly do have racist elements and this is all it takes for a group of people with a common identity to feel under siege: it is the idea that one's community is the target of violent racism that generates the discomfort and consequent anger. As Indian movie star Amitabh Bachchan said in June 2009 when he turned down an honorary doctorate from Queensland University of Technology: "My conscience does not permit me to accept this decoration from a country that perpetrates such indignity to my fellow countrymen" (Doherty, 2009).

The safety and welfare concerns raised by Indian students in Australia have tapped an underlying vein of resentment, at least in some quarters, around the cultural dynamics of the global trade in education. This trade largely involves affluent Western countries selling education, and migration potential, to developing and/or postcolonial nations. Tertiary education in the West is held as the pinnacle of achievement for children of the middle classes in these nations. Some view the normative and assimilationist aspects of this exchange, and the diaspora it encourages, as demeaning and illusory for young Indian men and women, especially when coupled with signs that as international consumers of education, they are not always welcome in countries such as Australia. Some online comments from readers of *Times Now* in late 2009 give a sense of this perspective:

[O]ur Indian counterparts should finally stop craving to live in [foreign] countries because they don't really have anything to give us. (Faizi, Mumbai, September 17 in *Times of India*, 2009b)

Why are Indians demeaning ourselves by wanting to study/immigrate/ live overseas among such white supremacist racist[s]. Such incidents hurt not only the immediate victims but the entire people of India. (Mishra, Mumbai, September 17, in *Times of India*, 2009b)

Could this be the galvanizing moment for us Indians to decide that we shall build our India into our land of dreams rather than going around the world in search of Eldorado? (Nagesh, Bangalore, September 18, in *Times of India*, 2009d)

For others, this is a matter of India's ability to garner respect from other nations:

This incident [referring to an early attack] is horrifying, unpardonable, brutal and pathetic. The world community must raise their voice to stop this

atrocity and heinous crime. ... Now, India will emerge as most developed
country in the world within next 5 to 10 years. India has been progress-
ing fast. ... I believe that you will soon find that the rest of the world will
start paying respect to Indians. (Mrinal Kanti Banarjee, May 30, in *Times
of India*, 2009c)

Violence with prejudicial overtones is the antithesis of cultural,
national, and racial respect for others. The reluctance, and in some cases
complete refusal, of Australia's federal politicians to directly acknowledge
that prejudice is a factor in *some* of the violence that is experienced by
Indian students becomes a sign of further disrespect. It dismisses India's
very real concern that its citizens are good for making curry, driving
taxis, paying fees, serving at petrol stations, or running late night convenience stores, but not good enough—or important enough—to command
us to acknowledge that cultural intolerance and chauvinism do exist in
Australia.

Conclusion

Determining whether it is appropriate to categorize a crime as racist is not
easy. Some of the crimes that have been committed against Indian students
in Australia do have racist features (even if others do not). It is expedient for a
nation's political leaders to deny such racism, blame the victims, or explain it
away as a temporary phenomenon (van Dijk, 1992). Such denial is an attempt
to protect Australia from the "damaging charge of intolerance and racism"
(van Dijk, 1992, p. 97). In the case of violence against Indian students, it has
been possible to achieve denial through circular means that do not require
"elite" commentators, such as politicians, to even engage with the "R" word.
The unfortunate impact of this denial, especially when it comes from those
with the authority of "elite" discourse, is that it diminishes the harm of the
victimization itself. Racial violence is a criminal act of prejudice. The injury
this inflicts cannot be isolated from the prejudicial character of the crime,
which can produce anxiety, resentment, and fear in a whole community of
people. The denial of racism in this context fails to acknowledge this harm
and to address the underlying causes of the problem.

References

ABC 7.30 Report. (2009). Indian visit; International students; Building the
Education Revolution; Award modernisation. Retrieved on 09/09/2009,
from   http://www.deewr.gov.au/Ministers/Gillard/Media/Transcripts/Pages/
Article_090902_.

ABC Radio AM. (2009). Australian politics on education blitz in India. Retrieved on 01/09/2010, from http://www.abc.net.au/am/content/2009/s2672710.htm.

ABC Television (Bourke E). (2009). Indian assault: Victims, police at odds, *ABC News—PM*. Retrieved on 09/09/2010, from http://www.abc.net.au/news/stories/2009/09/16/2688178.htm?section=justin.

Access Economics. (2009). The Australian Education Sector and the Economic Contribution of International Students. Report by Access Economics Pty Ltd for Australian Council for Private Education and Training.

Andersen, B. (2009). India to open door to Australian universities. ABC News. Retrieved on 03/09/2010, from http://www.abc.net.au/news/stories/2009/09/01/2673549.htm.

Babacan, H. (2006). Emerging racisms. Paper presented at the New Racisms, New Anti-Racisms Conference, Research Institute for Humanities and Social Sciences, Human Rights and Equal Opportunity Commission, Department of Anthropology, The University of Sydney, November 3–4.

Babacan, H., Pyke, J., Bhathal, A., et al. (2010). The community safety of international students in Melbourne: A scoping study. Institute for Community, Ethnicity and Policy Alternatives, Victoria University, Melbourne.

Cafagna, J. (2010). Stop and search powers put on show. *The 7.30 Report*, Australian Broadcasting Commission. Retrieved on 03/09/2010, from http://www.abc.net.au/7.30/content/2010/s2787761.htm.

Commonwealth of Australia. (2009). House of Representatives, Debates, vol. HR8. Retrieved on 02/08/2010, from http://www.aph.gov.au/hansard/reps/dailys/dr010609.pdf.

Doherty, B. (2009). Racist attacks force snub by Bollywood great. *The Age*. Retrieved on 03/09/2010, from http://www.theage.com.au/national/racist-attacks-force-snub-by-bollywood-great-20090531-brpm.html.

Economic Times. (2009). Australia, land of racism. Retrieved on 28/09/2010, from http://economictimes.indiatimes.com/News/PoliticsNation/Australia-land-of-racism-/articleshow/4587003.cms.

Grace, R., & Miller, P. (2010). Deadly stabbing: Police return to scene of attack. *The Age*. Retrieved on 03/09/2010, from http://www.theage.com.au/action/printArticle?id=1013677.

Graycar, A. (2010). Racism and the tertiary student experience in Australia. Occasional Paper 5/2010. Canberra: The Academy of Social Sciences in Australia.

Hage, G., & Couch, R. (1999). The future of Australian multiculturalism: Reflections on the twentieth anniversary of Jean Martin's the Migrant Presence. Sydney: Research Institute for Humanities and Social Sciences, University of Sydney.

Hindustan Times. (2009). PM "appalled" at attacks on Indian students in Australia. Retrieved on 18/09/2010, from http://www.hindustantimes.com/indians-abroad/india/PM-appalled-at-attacks-on-Indian-students-in-Australia/420480/Article1-419564.aspx.

Hodge, A., & Karvelas, P. (2009). Hindu extremists burn Rudd effigies. *The Australian*. Retrieved on 18/09/2010, from http://www.theaustralian.com.au/news/hindu-extremists-burn-kevin-rudd-effigies/story-e6frg6n6-1225720021579.

Hollinsworth, D. (2006). *Race and Racism in Australia*. Melbourne: Thompson Social Science Press.

Mason, G. (2011). Naming the "R" word in racial victimization. *International Review of Victimology*, 17(4), 1–18.

Miller, P. (2009). Train gang bashes Indian student. *The Age*, 11/05/2009. Retrieved on 03/09/2010, from http://www.theage.com.au/national/train-gang-bashes-indian-student-20090511-azbq.html.

Noble, G. (2009). "Where the bloody hell are we?" Multicultural manners in a world of hyperdiversity. In: G. Noble (ed.), *Lines in the Sand: The Cronulla Riots, Multiculturalism & National Belonging* (pp. 1–22). Sydney, NSW: Sydney Institute of Criminology Monograph Series.

NDTV. (2009). Racist Australia? NDTV. Retrieved on 28/09/2010, from http://www.ndtv.com/news/specials/overseas_indians.php?page=9.

Potter, J., & Wetherell, M. (1987). *Discourse and Social Psychology: Beyond Attitudes and Behaviour*. London: Sage.

Poynting, S. (2009). Scouring the Shire. In: G. Noble (ed.) *Lines in the Sand: The Cronulla Riots, Multiculturalism & National Belonging* (pp. 44–57). Sydney, NSW: Sydney Institute of Criminology Monograph Series.

Rudd, K. (2009). In: Commonwealth of Australia, Parliamentary Debates, House of Representatives, 1 June, 4905–4906 (Kevin Rudd, Member for Griffith, Prime Minister). http://www.aph.gov.au/hansard/reps/dailys/dr010609.pdf.

Times Now. (2009a). Sixth Racist attack in one month. Retrieved on 05/09/2010, from http://www.timesnow.tv/6th-racist-attack-in-one-month-in-Australia/video-show/4318432.cms.

Times Now. (2009b). Race terror down under. Retrieved on 23/09/2009, from http://www.timesnow.tv/Stop-the-bloodshed-end-violence/videoshow/4327761.cms.

Times of India. (2009a). Thousands rally against racism in Melbourne. Retrieved on 23/09/2009, from http://timesofindia.indiatimes.com/world/indians-abroad/Thousands-rally-against-racism-in-Melbourne/articleshow/4599752.cms.

Times of India. (2009b). What more proof does Australia need? Viewers' opinions. Retrieved on 03/09/2010, from http://www.timesnow.tv/videoopinions/4327479.cms accessed 23/09/2009.

Times of India. (2009c). Stay away from Australia. Viewers' opinions. Retrieved on 03/09/2010, from http://www.timesnow.tv/videoopinions/4318272.cms.

Times of India. (2009d). Debate: Australia finally admits its racism. Viewers' opinions. Retrieved on 03/09/2010, from http://www.timesnow.tv/videoopinions/4327476.cms.

van Dijk, T. (1992). Discourse and the denial of racism. *Discourse and Society*, 3(1), 87–118.

van Dijk, T. (1993). *Elite Discourse and Racism*. Newbury Park, CA: Sage.

Victorian Sentencing Advisory Council. (2009). Sentencing for offences motivated by hatred or prejudice. Victorian Sentencing Advisory Council, Melbourne.

Wade, M. (2009). Indian warning on attacks. *Sydney Morning Herald*. Retrieved on 02/08/2010, from http://www.smh.com.au/world/indian-warning-on-attacks-20090802-e5vz.html.

Wilson, L. (2010). Simon Overland admits Indians are targeted in attacks. Retrieved on 28/09/2010, from http://www.theaustralian.com.au/news/nation/simon-overland-admits-indians-are-targeted-in-attacks. accessed 28/09/2010.

Forced Displacement and Its Implications for Youths' Distress and Posttraumatic Growth

14

AVITAL LAUFER
MALLY SHECHORY-BITTON

Contents

Introduction

Forced displacement from one's home is considered a traumatic event that may be associated with psychological morbidity among children and youth. The negative outcomes may include posttraumatic stress disorder, depression, anxiety, and a host of behavioral problems (Fazel & Stein, 2002, 2003; Heptinstall et al., 2004; Sack et al., 1995; Vernberg et al., 1996). Most of the studies examined internationally forced displacement, refugees, and immigration due to armed conflict. Thus, it is not clear whether displacement is the source of these harmful outcomes, or whether they are the consequences of trauma due to exposure to war and the need to adjust to a new culture (Fazel & Stein, 2002).

Some researchers (e.g., Erol et al., 2005; Greenberg & Keane, 2005) claim that a distinction should be made between forced displacement, which entails transferring to another country, and internal displacement, which entails moving the displaced population from one place to another within a country's borders or cultural regions. As opposed to studies that examine the emotional implications of forced transfer from one country to another among children and youth, research on forced internal migration is very limited.

The Israeli Disengagement Plan gave us the opportunity to examine the effects of government-enforced internal displacement on youth. The current study aims to uniquely contribute to the literature by examining the effects of government-enforced internal displacement on youth who were evacuated from their homes due to a resolution passed by the Israeli government in February 2005, authorizing the evacuation of the Jewish population from their homes to other locations within the borders of Israel. The entire process took 7 days (August 15–22, 2005). Currently, 7 years after the evacuation, most of the evacuees have not yet moved into new permanent housing and they still consider the withdrawal as an act of betrayal by the state (Shechory & Laufer, 2011).

The few studies that were conducted on internal displacement yielded ambiguous results with regard to the implications of transfer for the youths' emotional welfare. Several studies found that forced departure is associated with high levels of emotional distress among the evacuees themselves (Laufer & Shechory, 2008), as well as among those residing in areas adjacent to the evacuated areas (Galili & Lev-Wiesel, 2007; Sagy & Antonovsky, 1987). Other findings showed that forced evacuation had no significant negative implications for the youth (Erol et al., 2005).

An examination of the existing literature on the implications of residential instability also indicates a lack of unanimity. Several studies found that residential instability in childhood was associated with depression and other negative behavioral outcomes (Gilman et al., 2003; Wood et al., 1993; DeWit, 1998). By contrast, other researchers claimed that for some teenagers a new place of residence may constitute an improvement and not lead to the appearance of any negative symptoms (Gilman et al., 2003).

The lack of clarity on the effects of forced evacuation may require a closer examination that would include attention to salutogenic symptoms (positive effects) as well as to pathogenic symptoms (negative effects). Tedeschi and Calhoun (1996, 2004) claimed that traumatic events may result in positive outcomes, which they termed *posttraumatic growth*. Posttraumatic growth is defined as significant changes for the better in self-image, worldview, and relations with others following traumatic events (Tedeschi, 1999). Tedeschi and Calhoun (1996) list five areas of possible improvement or growth after trauma: new opportunities; relating to others; personal strength; spiritual change; and appreciation of life.

To the best of our knowledge, only two studies deal with the association between forced displacement within a country's borders and positive outcomes that may be regarded as posttraumatic growth. The first study examined measures that may indicate signs of growth among adult Israelis who were evacuated following a government decision to transfer Gaza Strip settlements to the Palestinian Authority (Hall et al., 2008). The study found that, alongside the negative implications of the evacuation, there are also visible signs that may point to growth processes. The second study examined Tedeschi and Calhoun's growth measures among youth evacuated involuntarily from their home due to a hurricane and floods (Cryder et al., 2006). In this study, no association was found between the perceived severity of the displacement and growth. In fact, the study found that growth was associated only with personality measures that influence the manner in which the child reacts to trauma.

In light of the above findings, it can be said that the existing knowledge on the connection between forced internal migration within the borders of a country and negative and positive symptoms among youth is limited and needs to be expanded. The current study aims to examine the associations between internal forced displacement and youths' reports on distress and growth. The study also aims to examine whether parent–child relations and gender differences are associated with distress levels and growth resulting from internal displacement.

Due to the importance of the connection with parents during periods of distress and harsh reality (Hair et al., 2008), it is important to examine the extent to which the parent–child relationship is associated with distress levels and growth among the youth who underwent forced displacement following the disengagement plan. Connection to a parent serves as a regulator of children's reactions in a traumatic situation and is the factor that may most influence the reported sense of distress (van der Kolk, 1987; Pynoos et al., 1996). The immediate absence of parents, or chaos in the family resulting from a traumatic event, is liable to exacerbate the effects of trauma and intensify the child's distress. On the other hand, parents may promote adaptation processes in their children by moderating the implications of the traumatic event (Masten et al., 1999; Freud & Burlingham, 1944; Vernberg et al., 1996; Gewirtz et al., 2008). Therefore, continued good relations between parent and child, even in difficult times, constitute a regulator for the youths' sense of tension and serves to reduce distress.

Regarding gender differences, there is a tendency to regard girls as having higher susceptibility compared to boys (Brosky & Lally, 2004; Davis & Siegel, 2000; Groome & Soureti, 2004; Stallard et al., 2004). Girls report more symptoms of fear, anxiety, reexperience, overarousal, and accompanying distress, such as depression and somatization (Durkovic-Belko et al., 2003; Ronen et al., 2003; Vizek-Vidovic et al., 2000), whereas greater distress among boys was manifested by social dysfunction and primarily by a tendency toward dangerous behavior (Shaw, 2003).

The results regarding gender differences in posttraumatic growth have been somewhat inconsistent (for a review, see Linley & Joseph, 2004; Prati & Pietrantoni, 2009), but in studies in which differences have been found, women have reported more growth than men (e.g., Park et al., 1996; Sheikh & Marotta, 2005; Tedeschi & Calhoun, 1996; Weiss, 2002). Therefore, the gender effect in both distress and growth should be considered.

To sum, the current study aims to examine the associations between internal forced displacement and youths' reports on distress and growth. The study also aims to examine whether parent–child relations and gender differences are associated with distress levels and growth resulting from internal displacement.

Method

Sample

The study examined 157 displaced adolescents who were evacuated following the disengagement plan that called for the withdrawal of Jewish settlers and the Israeli defense forces from the Gaza Strip. The sample consisted of 68 (43%) boys and 89 (57%) girls aged 15–19 ($M = 16.47$, SD $= 1.24$). Most of the adolescents were Israeli born (96%) and lived with married parents (91%). The majority of the participants were religious (96%), while others were mainly ultrareligious (2%) or traditional (2%). Almost all the adolescents were present when the evacuation was carried out (87%), and all took an active part in resisting the disengagement plan.

Instruments

Personal background questionnaire: This includes demographic questions (age, gender, family background, etc.). In addition, in order to determine the level of religious observance, the subjects were asked to define themselves by marking the appropriate answer (secular, traditional, religious, or ultrareligious).

Perception of trauma: Single item measuring the effect of the evacuation: "To what extent do you think the evacuation was a traumatic event for you?" Answers on the 4-point scale ranged from "not at all" (1) to "very traumatic" (4) ($M = 3.13$, SD $= 0.90$). The subjects were also asked whether they were present when the evacuation was carried out and whether they were active in resisting the disengagement plan.

Parent–child relationship (attachment to parent): The relationship with the parent measure consists of six questions: "To what extent do your parents understand you?"; "To what extent do you take your parents' opinions into consideration?"; "To what extent is your relationship with your parents a good one?"; "To what extent do you share your thoughts and emotions with your parents?"; "To what extent do your parents know whom you are with when you are not at home?"; "To what extent do you think your parents would help you if you got into trouble." Answers on a 5-point scale ranged from "not at all" (1) to "very much" (5) ($\alpha = 0.80$) ($M = 4.07$, SD $= 0.62$). This measure was used in a previous Israeli study (Shechory & Laufer, 2008).

Psychiatric symptomatology: Psychiatric symptomatology was examined using the Brief Symptom Inventory (BSI) by Derogatis and Spencer (1982). This is a self-report questionnaire that measures general symptoms of psychological distress. It is a short version of the SCL-90 (a psychological self-report symptom scale) consisting of 53 items, each of which is rated on a 5-point Likert scale ranging from 0 ("not at all") to 4 ("extremely").

The responses to the BSI can be analyzed both globally and with symptom specificity. The General Severity Index (GSI) was the global distress index used to calculate the mean score of all 53 items. Ten symptom subscales were also examined: psychoticism, hostility, anxiety, somatization, phobic anxiety, paranoid ideation, depression, obsession-compulsion, interpersonal sensitivity, and additional symptoms. Internal consistencies as measured by Cronbach's alphas were 0.96 for the GSI and as follows for each of the subscales: psychoticism −0.68; hostility −0.77; anxiety −0.82; somatization −0.88; phobia −0.74; paranoia −0.71; depression −0.80; obsession-compulsion −0.80; and interpersonal sensitivity −0.72.

Posttraumatic Growth

To assess posttraumatic growth, we used the Post-Traumatic Growth Inventory (PTGI) (Tedeschi & Calhoun, 1996), adapted by the authors for the current study. The original questionnaire contains 21 items divided into five categories: new opportunities ($\alpha = 0.54$), relating to others ($\alpha = 0.88$), personal strength ($\alpha = 0.82$), spiritual change ($\alpha = 0.80$), and appreciation of life ($\alpha = 0.72$). Pilot interviews with Israeli youth revealed the need to change the PTGI scale to 4 points (1—no change to 4—significant change) rather than the original 6-point scale, as the distinction among the categories was blurred. The questionnaire was used in a previous Israeli study on teenagers and its reliabilities were similar (Laufer & Solomon, 2006). The growth score was calculated as the sum of all the responses (range: 21–84, $M = 47.53$, SD $= 17.46$). The subscales were calculated as the mean of the items. Four levels of growth were defined: no growth (1–21), low growth (22–43), medium growth (44–65), and high growth (66–81) (see also Laufer et al., 2009).

Procedure

As previously mentioned, the sample is a targeted sample whereby research assistants interviewed adolescent girls residing in Judea and Samaria where they gather (youth movement meetings, rallies). The research assistants asked the girls in the relevant age group to participate in the study. As the participants are adolescents, they were given an information page, for them and for their parents, requesting their participation and emphasizing that the questionnaires are for research purposes only.

The questionnaires were distributed some 2 years after the disengagement process. The distribution of the questionnaires began in June 2007 and continued for about 2 months.

Results

Gender Differences in Distress and Growth

Almost half of the youths claimed that displacement was very traumatic ($n = 72$, 45.9%), almost a quarter claimed that it was traumatic ($n = 35$, 22.3%), others that it was somewhat traumatic ($n = 45$, 28.7%), and only 3% ($n = 5$, 3.2%) perceived it as not traumatic. The perceived trauma of the events was found higher among girls ($M = 3.28$, SD $= 0.84$) than boys ($M = 2.91$, SD $= 0.98$) ($Z = 2.36$, $p < .05$), but unrelated to age ($r = 0.15$, ns.). Gender differences were also found regarding the attachment to a parent, with girls reporting a higher attachment to parents ($M = 4.21$, SD $= 0.63$) compared to boys ($M = 3.89$, SD $= 0.65$) ($t(155) = 3.14$, $p < .01$). The attachment to parents was unrelated to age ($r = -0.15$, ns.). Further, age was unrelated to distress symptoms ($r = -0.07$ to 0.15, ns) or to growth ($r = 0.02$ to 0.11, ns).

The gender differences in distress levels were examined with a multivariate analysis of variance and were found to be significant [$F(9, 147) = 6.23$, $p < .001$, $\eta^2 = 0.28$] (see Table 14.1).

Higher levels of distress regarding anxiety, somatization, phobic anxiety, obsessive-compulsive, and interpersonal sensitivity were reported by girls.

Table 14.1 Means, Standard Deviations, and F Values for Distress Symptoms ($n = 157$)

	Boys M (SD)	Girls M (SD)	Total	F (1, 155) (η^2)
GSI	0.74 (0.48)	0.90 (0.68)	0.83 (0.61)	t (155) = 1.58
Psychoticism	0.82 (0.66)	0.84 (0.80)	0.84 (0.74)	0.02 (0.001)
Hostility	1.09 (0.82)	0.88 (0.80)	0.97 (0.81)	2.47 (0.02)
Anxiety	0.71 (0.58)	0.97 (0.85)	0.86 (0.76)	4.49* (0.03)
Somatization	0.27 (0.42)	0.67 (0.79)	0.50 (0.68)	14.73*** (0.09)
Phobic anxiety	0.39 (0.46)	0.78 (0.80)	0.61 (0.70)	13.09*** (0.08)
Paranoid ideation	1.14 (0.75)	1.06 (0.83)	1.10 (0.79)	0.34 (0.002)
Depression	0.84 (0.66)	0.88 (0.78)	0.86 (0.73)	0.11 (0.001)
Obsessive-compulsive	0.92 (0.68)	1.18 (0.94)	1.07 (0.84)	3.86* (0.02)
Interpersonal sensitivity	0.64 (0.55)	0.90 (0.78)	0.79 (0.70)	4.96* (0.04)

*$p < .05$; **$p < .01$; ***$p < .001$.

Table 14.2 Means, Standard Deviations, and *t* Values for Growth—PGI (*n* = 157)

	Boys *M* (SD)	Girls *M* (SD)	Total	F (1, 155) (η^2)
PGI-growth	45.95 (14.72)	48.02 (17.15)	47.14 (16.14)	t (155) = 0.79
Relations with others	2.12 (0.79)	2.19 (0.88)	2.16 (0.84)	0.27 (0.002)
New opportunities	2.09 (0.77)	2.16 (0.87)	2.13 (0.83)	0.24 (0.002)
Spiritual change	2.25 (1.02)	2.61 (1.14)	2.46 (1.10)	4.20* (0.03)
Life evaluation	2.38 (0.91)	2.52 (0.95)	2.46 (0.94)	0.83 (0.005)
Personal strength	2.31 (0.92)	2.40 (0.97)	2.36 (0.95)	0.33 (0.002)

*$p < .05$.

No gender differences were found for the total distress score, or for psychoticism, hostility, paranoid ideation, and depression.

The gender differences in growth levels were examined with another multivariate analysis of variance and were found to be nonsignificant [F (5, 151) = 0.98, ns, η^2 = 0.03] (see Table 14.2). The total growth score did not differ by gender either. As the finding indicates, over half of the adolescents (*n* = 86, 55%) reported high or very high levels of change, while others (*n* = 71, 45%) reported low levels.

Relationships of Distress and Growth with Perception of Trauma and Parent–Child Relationship

Table 14.3 presents zero-order correlations between distress and growth levels and trauma perception and parent–child relationships, for the total sample and by gender. The results indicated several low to moderate correlations.

Two distress symptoms, anxiety and obsessive-compulsive, were positively, although moderately, correlated with trauma perception. The positive correlations hold for the total sample, but are a function of the relationship for boys: the higher the perception of trauma, the greater the reported symptoms. Furthermore, several distress symptoms, the total score, hostility, paranoid ideation, depression, and interpersonal sensitivity were negatively and moderately correlated with the perception of the parent–child relationship. In this case, the negative correlations hold for the total sample, but are a function of the relationship for girls: the higher the perception of the parent–child relationship, the lower the reported symptoms.

Growth levels were positively correlated with both the perception of trauma and the parent–child relationship. New opportunities and personal strength had low positive correlations with trauma perception for the total sample: the higher the perception of trauma, the greater the reported growth. Other dimensions of growth related positively with the perception of trauma only for girls: the higher the perception of trauma, the greater the total score for growth, as well as for relations with others, spiritual change,

Table 14.3   Correlations of Trauma Perception and Parent–Child Relationship with Levels of Distress and Growth, by Gender (n = 157)

	Trauma Perception			Parent–Child Relationships		
	Total	Boys	Girls	Total	Boys	Girls
Distress						
Total GSI	0.14	0.20	−0.18	−0.17*	0.07	−0.23*
Psychoticism	0.10	0.23	−0.16	−0.15	0.01	−0.17
Hostility	0.06	0.21	−0.20	−0.24**	−0.03	−0.22*
Anxiety	0.18*	0.23	−0.18	−0.12	0.12	−0.17
Somatization	0.08	−0.10	−0.05	−0.02	0.08	−0.13
Phobic anxiety	0.11	−0.06	0.04	−0.03	0.12	−0.19
Paranoid ideation	0.05	0.12	−0.13	−0.16*	0.01	−0.17
Depression	0.13	0.24	−0.20	−0.23**	0.05	−0.28**
Obsessive-compulsive	0.23**	0.30*	−0.15	−0.12	0.16	−0.18
Interpersonal sensitivity	−0.03	−0.06	−0.16	−0.19*	−0.07	−0.30**
Growth						
Total PGI	0.15	0.16	0.31*	0.22**	0.12	0.15
Relations with others	0.10	0.09	0.26*	0.19*	0.09	0.13
New opportunities	0.16*	0.19	0.13	0.09	0.13	0.06
Spiritual change	0.11	0.02	0.41***	0.32***	0.14	0.21*
Life evaluation	0.14	0.14	0.37**	0.30***	0.12	0.23*
Personal strength	0.16*	0.23	0.21	0.14	0.10	0.08

$*p < .05; **p < .01; ***p < .001.$

and life evaluation. Furthermore, several dimensions of growth—the total score, relations with others, spiritual change, and life evaluation—correlated positively with the perception of the parent–child relationship. These correlations, although moderate, held for the total sample: the higher the perception of the parent–child relationship, the greater the reported growth. It should be noted, however, that for spiritual change and life evaluation, significant positive correlations were also found separately for girls.

In order to better understand the role of the parent–child relationship in the youths' psychological outcome following trauma, we examined the association between growth and distress, controlled for the parent–child relationship. The association was found to be significant ($r = 0.20$, $p < .05$). To understand how the parent–child relationship affects the association between distress and growth, we used the Baron and Kenny (1986) four-step procedure to explore moderating/mediating effects. This procedure was conducted twice, once with growth as the dependent dimension and once with distress as the dependent dimension. Overall, the procedure permits the decomposition of effects in four steps: (1) distress directly associated with growth; (2) distress directly associated with the parent–child relationship;

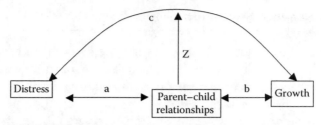

Note: c = mediation, Z = moderation, a and b are direct effects.
All paths in the model except Z are supported.

Figure 14.1 Moderating and mediating relationships.

(3) the parent–child relationship association with growth, controlling for distress; and (4) the association between distress and growth, controlling for the parent–child relationship (paths a, b, and c in Figure 14.1).

The results are presented in Table 14.4. The results suggest that distress and growth are directly and positively associated, as are the parent–child relationship and growth. The parent–child relationship and distress are negatively associated. That is, youth tend to report growth if they are more distressed and if they have good parent–child relationships. The association between distress and growth is also mediated by the parent–child relationship. Youth with good parent–child relationships report a higher level of growth even after controlling for distress; however, youth with bad parent–child relationships report distress events when controlled for growth. The model was tested separately for boys and girls and was not found to be significant; however, the mediation effect was significant in each model.

In addition, we conducted a moderated regression model (path Z in Figure 14.1), which was found to be nonsignificant.

Table 14.4 Coefficients of the Baron and Kenny (1986) Procedure to Examine the Association of Parents–Child Relationships with Distress and Posttraumatic Growth

Dependent	Independent	Controlled	B	SE	t
Growth	Distress		5.70	1.37	4.15***
Relationships	Distress		−0.28	0.05	−5.37***
Growth	Relationships	Distress	3.98	1.32	3.01**
Growth	Distress	Relationships	6.84	1.41	4.87***
Sobel = −1.13, SE = 0.43, Z = −2.59, $p < .01$					
Distress	Growth		0.00	0.00	1.73***
Relationships	Growth		0.01	0.00	3.62***
Distress	Relationships	Growth	−0.22	0.08	−2.76**
Distress	Growth	Relationships	0.00	0.00	2.48*
Sobel = −0.00, SE = 0.00, Z = −2.14, $p < .05$					

*$p < .05$; **$p < .01$; ***$p < .001$.

Discussion and Conclusion

The purpose of this study was to examine the association between internal forced displacement and youths' well-being. More specifically the study investigated the association between parent–child relationships and youths' distress and growth levels following forced displacement. The study findings indicate that the parent–child relations mediated the positive association between distress and growth following internal displacement, thereby indicating that good parent–child relations may lower distress and enhance growth following internal displacement.

According to Tedeschi and Calhoun (1996, 2004), salutogenic and pathogenic aspects are two independent factors that may have a range of connections. Hence, reporting posttraumatic growth is not necessarily followed by a decrease in distress symptoms. Moreover, posttraumatic growth is perceived not as the absence of distress, but rather as a different dimension, which indicates changes for the better in ones cognitive assumptions. The cognitive worldview is now more complex and enables the survivor to find new and positive meaning in the traumatic event (Tedeschi & Calhoun, 1996, 2004). This cognitive change will occur only if the event was traumatic enough to have shattered the existing cognitive worldviews (Janoff-Bulman, 1989). Hence, in order for growth to emerge, some distress is essential.

A positive association between distress and growth was found in this study as well as in previous findings for both adults and youth (e.g., Barakat et al., 2006; Best et al., 2001; Cadell, 2000; Laufer & Solomon, 2006). The positive association between distress and growth indicates that growth tends to exist especially among adolescents who experience distress induced by a traumatic event and may also indicate that growth does not necessarily reduce the negative intensity of the traumatic experience.

Another explanation for the positive association between distress and growth is that it, in fact, indicates that growth is nothing other than a positive illusion on the part of a distressed individual. According to this notion, growth is merely a positive illusion in the service of the self (Westphal & Bonanno, 2007; Davis & McKearney, 2003). Therefore, the presence of growth among those who report distress point to the fact that posttraumatic growth is not a genuine and positive change; had it been a genuine reaction, it would have been negatively associated with distress.

We have no intention of determining which of these two approaches is correct. However, the fact that the parent–child relationship mediated the positive association between distress and growth, supports, in our opinion, Tedeschi and Calhoun's (1996, 2004) assumption that distress and growth are two separate measures that may have a range of associations between them. According to the findings in our study, the association between distress and growth among youth is conditioned by the parent–child relationship.

Positive parent–child relationships promote growth and reduce distress, thereby moderating the association between distress and growth. The role of the parent–child relationship in the growth process indicates that growth is a complex process in which additional factors in general, and parent–child relationships in particular, should be considered.

The ability of positive parent–child relationships to enhance growth may be due to their ability to boost adaptive coping strategies (Holahan et al., 1995). Good parent–child relations also promote disclosure of stressful experiences, which may regulate emotions by changing the focus of attention; either increasing habituation to negative emotions or facilitating positive cognitive reappraisals of threats (Hair et al., 2008; Pedersen & Revenson, 2005). Therefore, adolescents who enjoy good parent–child relations also benefit from better adjustment abilities and decreased distress, which may contribute to their ability to convert the stressful situation into growth.

Former studies indicated that the parent–child interaction is associated with lower levels of adolescent depression (Aseltine et al., 1998) as well as enhanced psychological resilience (e.g., Masten et al., 1999). This indicates the importance of the interaction between the parent and the child even in adolescence. The role of parents in youths' lives and their effect on the development process are notable (e.g., Leung & Leung, 1992; Sweeting & West, 1995; Rosenberg, 1979). The importance of the parents does not diminish in adolescence and neither peers nor school can take their place (Greenberg et al., 1983; Leung & Leung, 1992; Keats et al., 1983). Youth continue to rely on their parents, especially with regard to major decisions and important issues (Frank et al., 1988; Wilks, 1986) and as we found, this is important in stressful situation like force displacement.

The study also found that the youths' perception of trauma regarding the forced evacuation of their homes was only weakly linked to their stress level and was not associated with their reported growth. The result of the study is in line with former studies that found no effect of forced displacement per se (i.e., Erol et al., 2005; Cryder et al., 2006), indicating that the effect of forced evacuation is more the result of the personal and social dimensions of the evacuation, rather than of the actual displacement. However, the period of time from the evacuation to the examination in the current study calls for caution regarding these conclusions.

Gender differences were also examined and reported in the study. Girls reported a higher attachment to parents, a higher trauma perception, and elevated levels of some symptoms of psychological distress. These results are in line with former studies, which indicated that girls tend to perceive stressful events as more traumatic (Brody et al., 1995; Muldoon, 2003), have a higher susceptibility to stress (Durkovic-Belko et al., 2003; Ronen et al., 2003), and are more attached to their parents (Shechory & Laufer, 2011), compared to boys. As for growth, confirming other research (Linley & Joseph,

2004; Prati & Pietrantoni, 2009), no gender differences were reported regarding growth dimensions in the overall mediating model.

Overall, the study findings expand on previous studies that associated a positive parent–child relationship with positive adaptation (e.g., Masten et al., 1999; Aseltine et al., 1998), indicating its ability to enhance growth and lower distress following internal displacement.

Several methodological limitations of this study should be noted. The study is based on a cross-sectional design and its findings are relevant only to a specific point in time. Future researches should employ a longitudinal design in order to shed additional light on the course of emotional distress among youth exposed to internal forced displacement. Another limitation is the use of a specific family dimension—the parent–child relationship—which is a complex dimension that may affect other family dimensions. For example, parent–child relationships were found to positively influence family routines, parental monitoring, and parental supportiveness (Hair et al., 2008; Paschall et al., 2003; Smetana et al., 2002). Thus, good parent–child relations may also enhance youths' well-being through other family dimensions, such as better monitoring and family cohesion, which were found to be associated with lower distress in traumatic times (e.g., Pynoos et al., 1996; Gewirtz et al., 2008). This calls for a more comprehensive examination in future studies on family dimensions that are associated with distress and growth during adolescence.

Caution should also be taken with regard to the use of posttraumatic growth as a variable. The common definition of posttraumatic growth is the individual's positive perception of life following exposure to trauma (Tedeschi & Calhoun, 2004). Some researchers view posttraumatic growth as a coping strategy to reduce stress (Helgeson et al., 2006). The different definitions emphasize the need for further examination of growth in future studies that will include alternative definitions.

Despite the limitations in this study, we believe that it expands on the existing body of knowledge with regard to the psychological effect of youths' forced internal displacement. The study's findings also contribute to our understanding of the growth process and its correlators, including its association with distress and the role of social dimensions such as parent–child relations.

References

Aseltine, R. H., Gore, S., & Colten, M. E. (1998). The co-occurrence of depression and substance use in late adolescence. *Development and Psychopathology, 10,* 549–570.

Barakat, L., Alderfer, M. A., & Kazak, A. E. (2006). Posttraumatic growth in adolescent survivors of cancer and their mothers and fathers. *Journal of Pediatric Psychology, 31,* 413–419.

Baron, R. M., & Kenny, D. A. (1986). The moderator-mediator variable distinction in social psychological research: Conceptual, strategic, and statistical considerations. *Journal of Personality and Social Psychology*, 51, 1173–1182.

Best, M., Streisand, R., Catania, L., & Kazak, A. E. (2001). Parental distress during pediatric leukemia and Post Traumatic Stress Symptoms (PTSS) after treatment ends. *Journal of Pediatric Psychology*, 26, 299–307.

Brody, L. R., Lovas, G. S., & Hay, D. H. (1995). Gender differences in anger and fear as a function of situational context. *Sex Roles*, 32, 47–78.

Brosky, B. A., & Lally, S. J. (2004). Prevalence of trauma, PTSD, and dissociation in court-referred adolescents. *Journal of Interpersonal Violence*, 19, 801–814.

Cadell, S. (2000). The sun always comes out after it rains: Exploring the experience of AIDS caregivers (immune deficiency). Dissertation submitted to the Wilfrid Laurier University, Canada.

Cryder, C. H., Kilmer, R. P., Tedeschi, R. G., & Calhoun, L. G. (2006). An exploratory study of posttraumatic growth in children following a natural disaster. *American Journal of Orthopsychiatry*, 76, 65–69.

Davis, C. G., & McKearney, J. M. (2003). How do people grow from their experience with trauma or loss? *Journal of Social and Clinical Psychology*, 22, 477–492.

Davis, L., & Siegel, L. J. (2000). Posttraumatic stress disorder in children and adolescents: A review and analysis. *Clinical Child and Family Psychology Review*, 3, 135–154.

Derogatis, L. R., & Spencer, M. S. (1982). *The Brief Symptom Inventory (BSI): Administration, Scoring, and Procedures Manual –1.* Baltimore: Johns Hopkins University School of Medicine, Clinical Psychometrics Research Unit.

DeWit, D. J. (1998). Frequent childhood geographic relocation: Its impact on drug use initiation and the development of alcohol and other drug-related problems among adolescents and young adults. *Addictive Behaviors*, 23, 623–634.

Durkovic-Belko, E., Kulenovic, A., & Dapic, R. (2003). Determinants of posttraumatic adjustment in adolescents from Sarajevo who experienced war. *Journal of Clinical Psychology*, 59, 27–40.

Erol, N., Simsek, Z., Oner, O., & Munir, K. (2005). Effects of internal displacement and resettlement on the mental health of Turkish children and adolescents. *European Psychiatry*, 20, 152–157.

Fazel, M., & Stein, A. (2002). The mental health of refugee children. *Archives of Disease in Childhood*, 87, 366–370.

Fazel, M., & Stein, A. (2003). Mental health of refugee children: Comparative study. *British Medical Journal*, 19, 327.

Frank, S. J., Avery. C., & Laman, M. (1988). Young adults' perceptions of their relationships with their parents: Individual differences in connectedness, competence, and emotional autonomy. *Developmental Psychology*, 24, 729–737.

Freud, A., & Burlingham, D. (1944). *War and Children.* New York: International Universities Press.

Galili, R., & Lev-Wiesel, R. (2007). Sense of place among adults who were relocated during adolescence: A retrospective study of Israeli residents of Sinai. *Society & Welfare: Quarterly for Social Work*, 27, 37–53.

Gewirtz, A., Forgatch, M., & Wieling, E. (2008). Parenting practices as potential mechanisms for child adjustment following mass trauma. *Journal of Marital and Family Therapy*, 34, 177–192.

Gilman, S. E., Kawachi, I., Fitzmaurice, G. M., & Buka, S. L. (2003). Socio-economic status, family disruption and residential ability in childhood: Relation to onset recurrence and remission of major depression. *Psychological Medicine, 33,* 1341–1355.

Greenberg, H. S., & Keane, A. (2005). Risk factors for chronic posttraumatic stress symptoms and behavior problems in children and adolescents following a home fire. *Child & Adolescent Social Work Journal, 18,* 205.

Greenberg, M. T., Siegel, J. M., & Leitch, C. J. (1983). The nature and importance of attachment relationships to parents and peers during adolescence. *Journal of Youth and Adolescence, 12,* 373–386.

Groome, D., & Soureti, A. (2004). Post-traumatic stress disorder and anxiety symptoms in children exposed to the 1999 Greek earthquake. *British Journal of Psychology, 95,* 387–397.

Hair, E. C., Moore, K. A., Garrett, S. B., Ling, T., & Cleveland, K. (2008). The continued importance of quality parent–adolescent relationships during late adolescence. *Journal of Research on Adolescence, 18,* 187–200.

Hall, B., Hobfoll, S. E., Palmieri, P. A., Canetti-Nisim, D., Shapira, O., Johnson, R. J., & Galea, S. (2008). The psychological impact of impending forced settler disengagement in Gaza: Trauma and posttraumatic growth. *Journal of Traumatic Stress, 21,* 22–29.

Helgeson, V. S., Reynolds, K. A., & Tomich, P. L. (2006). A meta-analytic review of benefit finding and growth. *Journal of Consulting and Clinical Psychology, 74,* 797–816.

Heptinstall, E., Sethna, V., & Taylor, E. (2004). PTSD and depression in refugee children; Associations with pre-migration trauma and post-migration stress. *European Child & Adolescent Psychiatry, 13,* 373–380.

Holahan, C. J., Valentiner, D. P., & Moos, R. H. (1995). Parental support, coping strategies, and psychological adjustment: An integrative model with late adolescents. *Journal of Youth and Adolescence, 24,* 633–648.

Janoff-Bulman, R. (1989). Assumptive worlds and the stress of traumatic events: Applications of the schema construct. *Social Cognition, 7,* 113–136.

Keats, J. A., Keats, D. M., Biddles, B. J., Bank, B. J., Hauge, R., Wan-Rafaei, B., & Valantin, S. (1983). Parents, friends, siblings, and adults: Unfolding referent other importance data for adolescents. *International Journal of Psychology, 18,* 239–262.

Laufer, A., Hamama-Raz, Y., Levine, S., & Solomon, Z. (2009). Posttraumatic growth in adolescence: The role of religiosity, distress and forgiveness. *Journal of Social and Clinical Psychology, 28*(7), 862–880.

Laufer, A., & Shechory, M. (2008). Alienation and emotional distress among relocated youth following the Gaza disengagement. In N. Ronel, K. Jaishankar, & M. Bensimon (Eds), *Trends and Issues in Victimology* (pp. 222–241). New Castle: Cambridge Scholars Publishing.

Laufer, A., & Solomon, Z. (2006). Posttraumatic symptoms and posttraumatic growth among Israeli youth exposed to terror incidents. *Journal of Social and Clinical Psychology, 25,* 429–447.

Leung, J. P., & Leung. K. (1992). Life satisfaction, self-concept, and relationship with parents in adolescence. *Journal of Youth and Adolescence, 21,* 653–664.

Linley, P. A., & Joseph, S. (2004). Positive change following trauma and adversity: A review. *Journal of Traumatic Stress, 17*(1), 11–21.

Masten, A. S., Hubbard, J. J., Gest, S. D., Tellegen, A., Garmezy, N., & Ramirez, M. (1999). Competence in the context of adversity: Pathways to resilience and maladaptation from childhood to late adolescence. *Development and Psychopathology, 11*, 143–169.

Muldoon, O. T. (2003). Perceptions of stressful life events in Northern Irish school children: A longitudinal study. *Journal of Child Psychology and Psychiatry, 44*, 193–201.

Park, C., Cohen, L. H., & Murch, R. L. (1996). Assessment and prediction of stress-related growth. *Journal of Personality, 64*, 1–35.

Paschall, M. J., Ringwalt, C. L., & Flewelling, R. L. (2003). Effects of parenting, father absence, and affiliation with delinquent peers on delinquent behavior among African-American male adolescents. *Adolescence, 38*, 15–34.

Pedersen, S., & Revenson, T. A. (2005). Parental illness, family functioning, and adolescent well being: A family ecology framework to guide research. *Journal of Family Psychology, 19*, 404–409.

Prati, G., & Pietrantoni, L. (2009). Optimism, social support, and coping strategies as factors contributing to posttraumatic growth: A meta-analysis. *Journal of Loss and Trauma, 14*, 364–388.

Pynoos, R. S., Steinberg, A. M., & Goenjian, A. (1996). Traumatic stress in childhood and adolescence: Recent developments and current controversies. In B. van der Kolk, A. C. McFarlane, & L. Weisaeth (Eds), *Traumatic Stress: The Effects of Overwhelming Experience on Mind, Body, and Society* (pp. 331–358). New York: Guilford.

Ronen, T., Rahav, G., & Rosenbaum, M. (2003). Children's reaction to a war situation as a function of age and sex. *Anxiety, Stress and Coping, 16*, 59–69.

Rosenberg, M. (1979). *Conceiving the Self.* New York: Basic Books.

Sack, W. H., Clarke, G., & Seeley, J. (1995). Posttraumatic stress disorder across two generations of Cambodian refugees. *Journal of American Academy of Child and Adolescence Psychiatry, 34*, 1160–1166.

Sagy, S., & Antonovsky, H. F. (1987). Adolescents' reaction to the evacuation of the Sinai settlements: A longitudinal study. *Journal of Psychology, 120*, 543–556.

Shaw, A. J. (2003). Children exposed to war/terrorism. *Clinical Child and Family Psychology Review, 6*, 237–246.

Shechory, M., & Laufer, A. (2008). Social control theory and the connection with ideological offenders among Israeli youth during the Gaza disengagement period. *International Journal of Offender Therapy and Comparative Criminology, 52*, 454–473.

Shechory, M., & Laufer, A. (2011). Pathways to ideological delinquency: Gender differences among Israeli youth during the withdrawal from the Gaza strip. *International Journal of Offender Therapy and Comparative Criminology, 55*(2), 326–343.

Sheikh, A. I., & Marotta, S. A. (2005). A cross-validation study of the posttraumatic growth inventory. *Measurement and Evaluation in Counseling and Development, 38*, 66–77.

Smetana, J. G., Crean, H. F., & Daddis, C. (2002). Family processes and problem behaviors in middle-class African American adolescents. *Journal of Research on Adolescence, 12*, 275–304.

Stallard, P., Salter, E., & Velleman, R. (2004). Posttraumatic stress disorder follow-ing road traffic accidents: A second prospective study. *European Child and Adolescent Psychiatry, 13*, 172–178.

Sweeting, H., & West, P. (1995). Family life and health in adolescence: A role for cul-ture in the health inequalities debate? *Social Science and Medicine, 40*, 163–175.

Tedeschi, R. G. (1999). Violence transformed: Posttraumatic growth in survivors and their societies. *Aggression and Violent Behavior, 4*, 319–341.

Tedeschi, R. G., & Calhoun, L. G. (1996). The posttraumatic growth inventory: Measuring the positive legacy of Trauma. *Journal of Traumatic Stress, 9*, 455–471.

Tedeschi, R. G., & Calhoun, L. G. (2004). Post-traumatic growth: Conceptual founda-tions and empirical evidence. *Psychological Inquiry, 15*, 1–18.

van der Kolk, B. A. (1987). *Psychological Trauma*. Washington, DC: American Psychiatric Publishing.

Vernberg, E. M., LaGreca, A. M., Silverman, W. K., & Prinstein, M. (1996). Predictors of children's post-disaster functioning following Hurricane Andrew. *Journal of Abnormal Psychology, 105*, 237–248.

Vizek-Vidovic, V., Kutervac-Jagodic, G., & Arambasic, L. (2000). Posttraumatic symp-tomatology in children exposed to war. *Scandinavian Journal of Psychology, 41*, 297–306.

Weiss, T. (2002). Posttraumatic growth in women with breast cancer and their hus-bands: An intersubjective validation study. *Journal of Psychosocial Oncology, 20*, 65–80.

Westphal, M., & Bonanno, G. A. (2007). Posttraumatic growth and resilience to trauma: Different sides of the same coin or different coins? *Applied Psychology: An International Review, 56*, 417–427.

Wilks, J. (1986). The relative importance of parents and friends in adolescent decision making. *Journal of Youth and Adolescence, 15*, 323–334.

Wood, D., Halfon, H., Scarlata, D., Newacheck, P., & Nessim, S. (1993). Impact of family relocation on children's growth, development, school function and behavior. *Journal of the American Medical Association, 270*, 1334–1338.

Theoretical and Practical Models of Criminal Victimization

IV

Forced Marriages, Bride Price, Levirate, and Domestic Violence

15

Victimization of Women and Struggles for Justice and Equity in Selected African Countries

VICTORIA M. TIME

Contents

Introduction

In many countries of Africa, some issues, such as human decency and the welfare of the people, seem to be ignored. What is done is less important than who did it and to whom it was done, as long as a dominant sector of the society is somehow profiting. The victimization of women persists and takes many forms, including domestic violence, forced marriages, bride prices, levirate obligations, and genital mutilations. There has been a plethora of studies on women's victimization in Africa (Bentheim, 2010; Park, 2006; Bunch, 1990; Welch & Sachs, 1987). However, of more relevance to this research are the publications on forced marriages, bride prices, levirate responsibilities, and domestic violence. The extant research on the aforementioned subjects has excluded a careful discussion of the linkage between these acts and criminological theory. For instance, Henry and Milovanovic's constitutive criminology suggests that crime is a "discursive product," that is, acts are only considered crimes when people talk and write about them. The implication is that there would be no crimes if people did not speak about them. They conclude that:

> Our position calls for abandoning of the futile search for causes of crime because that simply elaborates the distinctions that maintain crime as a separate reality while failing to address how it is that crime is constituted as part of society. We are concerned, instead, with the ways in which human agents actively coproduce that which they take to be crime. (Henry & Milovanovic, 1991, p. 307)

Arguably, if their theory was based solely on the premise that crime is the offspring of a discursive product, it could easily be discounted because "not talking about something" does not mean that it does not exist, and while we may discount the causes of a behavior, we cannot ignore their impact. Curiously, this part of their theory mirrors the thinking of those entrenched in a culture where the victimization of women goes unchecked. However, the theory further delves into "ways in which the interrelationships among human agents constitute crime, victims, and control realities" (Akers, 1997, p. 177). This part of the theory also provides a foundation for the subsequent discussion in this chapter.

Additionally, the existing literature reveals that impunity stands in the way of accountability and other modalities of justice, both of which are crucial in curbing these practices and bringing some sort of dignity to the victims. The question of why impunity persists lies in tradition or customs and on judicial systems that either look away or provide lackluster mechanisms of social control. The failure to enforce justice only creates a "breeding ground for impunity" (Anderson, 2011, p. 787).

Some, like Okafo (2009) and Younkins (2002), have written about the merits of tradition and traditional laws, and while tradition or customs are the hallmark of a nation's identity, Time (2012) and Time (2000) have argued that repugnant customary practices should not be preserved, since all they foster is human indignity, dissonance, and strife. This research examines four such customary practices: forced marriages, bride prices, levirate obligations, and domestic violence.

Forced marriage is explained as a union "conducted without the valid consent of one of both parties and is a marriage in which duress—whether physical or emotional is a factor" (FORWARD, 2010; see also Welstead, 2009, p. 51). Adults and children as young as 7 years old can be and have been victims of this repressive practice (see UNFPA, 2005). Park (2006) makes a compelling case for separating child forced marriage from adult forced marriage. He is correct; however, in this study they will be discussed together. A corollary of forced marriage and occasionally independent of it is the bride price. "Bride price is a sum, either in cash or kind, used to purchase a bride for her labour and fertility" (FORWARD, 2010, para. 7). Levirate pertains to a custom whereby "widows are inherited by their late husband's brother or other kin" Kiragu (1996). Abbott et al. (1995, p. 1763) define domestic violence as "assault, threat, or intimidation by a male partner."

Relevance of Study, Procedures, and Setting

The purpose of this chapter is to discuss the realities of forced marriages, bride prices, levirate, and domestic violence and to provide recommendations on how these practices can be curbed, as well as to add to the scarcity of literature on the issues that link criminological theories to the dialogue. Most would agree that forcing a person into a marriage that they do not want to be in, especially a child, and, in essence, selling them to a man for the bride price, borders on slavery. Researchers like Kaye et al. (2005) have linked these practices to domestic violence. Acts like these, including forcing widows to marry their in-laws, persist with impunity in many parts of the world. In these contemporary times, such acts should be a relic of the past. Yet, the fact that numerous scholars still refer to them is indicative of how permissive the acts still are, and why it is necessary that researchers and legislators brainstorm ways to abate them. This study finds relevance by emphasizing the need for immediate and definite action, and by placing the arguments in the context of criminological thinking. Anderson (2011, p. 790) discusses the two-phased question that delegates of the United Nations had to grapple with as they reviewed Nazi wartime issues: (a) "does peace require rectification for the wrongs that started the conflict or (b) is it enough, the United Nations delegates asked, to simply have the absence of war?" The delegates' definitive answer was, "fusing human rights with peace" (Anderson, 2011, p. 790). The antecedent discussion lends support to the fact that while there is the need to stop women's rights violations, there is also the need to fuse the mechanisms of justice to abate impunity.

This chapter represents a qualitative assessment of the realities of these traditional practices across several African countries, some of which have high percentages of girls between the ages of 15 and 19 forced into marriage. Monekosso (2001) provides the following approximations of girls forced into marriage: Mali, 72%; Uganda, 47%; Cameroon, 41%; and Nigeria, 37%. These countries are thus selected for more in-depth scrutiny in this study. Approximations or data quantifying other practices, such as levirate or domestic violence, are not available and do not include women over 19 years old who are also forced into marriage. A content analysis of selected archives enhances the data discussed in this chapter. The archival materials comprise newspaper editorials containing minutia pertinent to this research, journal articles fertile in accounts of the issues, and commentaries further enhance the discussion. Parallels relevant to the study are drawn from other countries as well.

Three research questions form the basis of this research. First, what are the realities of forced marriages, bride prices, levirate, and domestic violence? For instance, what are the health and social issues evident in victims of such practices? Second, how are these patterns relevant to criminological theory? Third, if these behaviors cannot be ethically justified, how can they be minimized?

What are the Realities of Forced Marriages, Bride Prices, Levirate, and Domestic Violence?

Bentheim (2010), IRIN Africa (2007), Kaye et al. (2005), Monekosso (2001), Beswick (2001), Erez and Thompson (1996), Oyebanji (1981), and others have documented the impact of forced marriages, bride prices, levirate, domestic violence, and other crimes against women in Africa. The consequences range from extreme physical violence, health and developmental drawbacks, to psychological and social consequences.

Physical Violence

While each consequence stands apart as atrocious, the egregiousness of axing off the legs of 12-year-old Hauwa Abukar, a recalcitrant minor in Nigeria, by a man she had been forced to marry, highlights the culture of violence and impunity, especially since the man was never charged with a crime (see Black, 2001). In Mali, a 13-year-old who was forced into marriage died the night of her wedding following complications from sexual intercourse with her husband (IRIN Africa, 2007). Bentheim (2010), Mongbo (2007), Park (2006), Beswick (2001), Gender Alert News (2000), and numerous other researchers have reported incidents of violence against women who resist forced marriage. Such violence is manifested through systematic assaults and batteries, rapes, mutilations, and loss of life. These are felonies, which, as a rule, would carry severe penal sanctions, but since the acts are considered culturally induced within the locales where they are perpetrated, the crimes go unpunished and the harms go unredressed. A report to the Human Rights Committee in 2003 states that "domestic violence is an accepted part of daily life in Mali" (OMCT Report, 2003, p. 278), especially since "there are no specific provisions [of the Penal Code] outlawing domestic violence" (OMCT Report, 2003, p. 277).

Health and Developmental Drawbacks

Bentheim (2010), IRIN Africa (2007), Welstead (2009), Black (2001), Monekosso (2001), Erez and Thompson (1996), Bunch (1990), Oyebanji (1981), and others have written about the health issues associated with forced and levirate marriages. Health issues include sexually transmitted diseases such as HIV and AIDS (see Bentheim, 2010; IRIN Africa, 2007), since many of the husbands are not only polygamists, but promiscuous too. Moreover, in order to make the women not desirable to other men, their husbands impregnate them so frequently, even against a doctor's warning, that the women's life may be in jeopardy. Following an interview with a midwife in Uganda, Kaye et al. report that the midwife believed that there was a causal link between the bride price and "reproductive ill-health." The midwife is quoted as saying, "some men think that contraceptives will make women wild, that they may either get more interest in sex, or become more 'carefree' as they know they will not conceive" (Kaye et al., 2005, p. 302). Girls/children forced into sexual relations at such tender ages may be susceptible to early deaths (see IRIN Africa, 2007; Erez & Thompson, 1996) or complications during pregnancies and childbirth (Bentheim, 2010; IRIN Africa, 2007; Kaye et al., 2005), especially when there is limited prenatal care. Without proper care and the correct nourishment, Bentheim (2010) reports that young girls forced into marriage suffer from poorly developed pelvic bones, which may impede healthy and safe childbirth.

Psychological and Social Consequences

Psychological trauma is evident in a forced marriage. The physical and emotional abuses that accompany such marriages scar the women for life. They can never carve out their own identities. Children forced into marriage miss out on childhood as they assume the role of wives and mothers at the dawn of their lives. They are deprived of education, are forever subordinates, and sometimes rendered too timid to ask for basic acts of civility and loyalty from their abusive and promiscuous husbands (see Bentheim, 2010; Immigration and Refugee Board of Canada, 2007). As Chigbu et al. (2010, p. 141) conclude, the leading cause in southeastern Nigeria of husbands' total monopoly in decisions regarding sex, "sex related verbal abuse," as well as "sex related physical violence, and forced sex" are a consequence of "a culture of male dominance." The women and children are given away by their families, and because they are commoditized, it is futile to be recalcitrant. Attempts at escape only exacerbate their plight (see Welstead, 2009; Black, 2001) and, of course, they cannot run back home. Kaye et al. (2005, p. 302), in their ethnographic study in Uganda, quote a non-governmental organization (NGO) employee's observation: "men are dominant in decision-making. The woman has no power for anything. Where the man is suspicious or insecure, domestic violence is common." Another participant in the study states, "Women lack power to make decisions in the home. The culture does not allow them to stand up to the men. The laws also support men" (Kaye et al., 2005, p. 302). In Mali, women who venture to file complaints about domestic violence are pressured into retracting such complaints (see OMCT Report, 2003).

Those women who have the fortitude to ask for a divorce must then fend for themselves and for their children. The children born into these abusive homes grow to know abuse; for those whose parents divorce, they lose the constant presence of their father. Some of these children are exposed to a lifetime of abuse and hardships, and to a culture that they assume is a way of life.

Arguably, Henry and Milovanovic's theory (1991, p. 293), which asserts that crime is only brought about "when others attempt to research, philosophize about, and explain it," does not accord with the realities of the problems documented in different regions of the world, directly associated with forced marriages, levirate, domestic violence, and bride prices. Yet, the theory supports what locales entrenched in the practices think.

Relevance to Criminology and Modalities of Justice

Forced marriages, bride prices, levirate, and domestic violence are not perceived as criminal in the locales where they are carried out, especially since the mothers of the brides were themselves subjected to this process (Benin, 2004). Further, since the existing research on forced marriages, bride prices, levirate, and domestic violence show that impunity has been a hindrance to modalities of justice, one has to further scrutinize the source of impunity. As Time (2013) notes, most of the prominent criminological theories are European and American influenced, and how some of these theories are relevant to other cultures sometimes remains untested. For example, consider Henry and Milovanovic's (1991) constitutive criminology theory. The theory asserts that crime is a "discursive production" brought forth when "agents act out criminal patterns, when others seek to control criminal behavior, and when yet others attempt to research, philosophize about, and explain crime" (p. 293).

As a discursive production, the assumption is that these acts are considered evil only because people talk of them in that light. In essence, the acts are not crimes to the extent that the practices are accepted as a way of life, and no local condemnatory modalities of justice are put in force. There is not much support for this premise. However, Martens (2009, p. 1) sheds light on this issue in his discussion of "race and European attempts to regulate African marriage practices." Martens observes that there is an "innate difference between races," and that there are "environmentalist discourses of 'civilization' and 'savagery' to explain distinctions between themselves [Europeans] and Africans" (2009, p. 1). The drift here is that what Africans see as normal practices are construed and discussed by Europeans as "savagery." Okafo (2009, p. 231) arrives at a similar conclusion, stating that:

> colonization breeds criminalization. This is because a colonizer needs coercive rules and regulations, usually with excessive penalties attached, to obtain compliance with the colonizer's policies, which invariably are out-of-sync and thus unpopular among the colonized.

Neither Marten's nor Okafo's premises are universal, because others, like Bentheim (2010), Clifford (2007), IRIN Africa (2007), Park (2006), Beswick (2001), Erez and Thompson (1996), Kiragu (1996), and Uzodike (1990), see the acts against women as inherently wrong and justify criminal sanctions. Decades before, Brillion (1972, p. 32) explained that:

> There can also be seen a superimposition of two concepts of criminality: one based on modern, codified legislation and the other on customary law. By imposing a criminal code, acts once considered non-criminal were criminalized, such as polygamy, the use of dowry, witchcraft, abortion, infanticide, etc. If there appears to be relatively little crime in Africa, it is apparently because some of the crimes or offenses are absorbed by the old social structures. The people continue to refer to the customary laws or refuse to reveal 'legal' crimes, which they look upon as senseless or harmless. Thus the dark figure of crime could actually be high in Africa.

Acquiescence in an act, silence and inaction, customs or tradition, do not explain away or vitiate the predicate criminality in coercing one human being into a marriage, selling her and calling the sale the bride price, or handing down a woman to an in-law as though she was an undersized garment simply because her husband died; these suggest slavery (see Black, 2001). Williams and Arrigo (2008) explain that our choices and actions ultimately have consequences, even the choice of doing nothing. As they reason, "the 'link' we secure in the chain by choosing a certain action becomes a small, but meaningful, part of a continuing chain of events" (Williams & Arrigo, 2008, p. 34). Not talking about the issue, condones it, and thus perpetuates it; talking about it spreads awareness of it, and legislating against it, provides some deterrent effect. Contributing somehow, even in a minuscule way, to curbing a problem is what Williams and Arrigo refer to as "universal responsibility."

"Constitutive criminology," as Henry and Milovanovic (1991, p. 295) contend, is "concerned with identifying the ways in which the interrelationships among human agents constitute crime, victims, and control as realities." In the context of forced marriages, bride prices, and levirate, such interactions are complicated not only by the financial benefits to the families of the bride, but also by the long-lasting acceptance of the practice under the guise of culture. How can these be crimes in the eyes of the perpetrators when such practices are the staple of long-lasting tradition and families see them as ways to revitalize their economic circumstance? Take Cameroon for example, which is documented as a country where child marriage and forced marriage abound (see Bentheim, 2010; Monekosso, 2001), even though section 61(2) of the 1981 Ordinance and Article 70(1) of the 1981 Civil Status Registration Ordinance speak against the practice of bride price, customary courts disregard the statute. Following customary law, the bride price is an essential condition for a marriage. In essence, impunity does not rest with men who engage in forced marriages and in the practice of bride price; rather, it is fueled by customary courts that solidify such unions. From the researcher's experience, having resided in Cameroon for years, the majority of such marriages are contracted in the villages and small towns where formalized courts are not present, and even when present, tradition, by and large, shapes the thinking and responses to everyday interactions. Additionally, those identified as responsible for enforcing tradition are predominantly men. It goes without saying that the scales of justice from the onset do not tilt in favor of women. This is also the case in Mali. Non-governmental personnel in Mali report that societal pressure, the absence of specific legislations that outlaw oppressive acts, such as those discussed in this study, and a general culture of acceptance that abuse is just a way of life, perpetuate these practices (OMCT Report, 2003).

Henry and Milovanovic (1991) argue that the origins of crime stem from "unequal power relations" that guide a society's view of criminal behavior (Miller et al., 2008). Entrenched in African tradition is the concept of paternalism. Based on this, women are esteemed less, and when the customs are framed to promote male dominance, and the custodians or stakeholders of such customs are male, there is a greater potential for customs to influence not only the behavior of actors, but also the decision-making process. Erez and Thompson (1996, p. 61) conclude that the victimization of women in Africa is "rooted in African culture and are perceived as male normative prerogative." As Time (2012) notes, in Cameroon, domestic violence and other forms of abuse against women have "been accepted as part of the culture"; while Erez and Thompson (1996, p. 61) note that in Sierra Leone, "the status of men and women is clearly defined as dominant and submissive respectively; masculine and feminine traits are traditional and inflexible." In discussing the sexual violation of women in Nigeria, Chigbu et al. (2010, p. 141) blame the prevalence on "a culture of male dominance." In Uganda, Kaye et al. (2005, p. 303) conclude that the bride price "perpetuates the culture of male dominance in prestige, power and decision-making."

Further, even when outsiders condemn repugnant traditional practices, the supposition (since traditional courts seldom, if at all, keep records) is that such condemnations have no deterrent effect. First, traditional courts reinforce the behavior by siding with men. Second, as Time (2012) remarks about Cameroon, it is not uncommon for statutory courts to "apply those customary laws which are outright repugnant." In a Cameroonian case, *Maya Ikome v. Manga Ekemason* CASWP/CC76/85 (unreported) (cited and discussed in Time (2012)), the appellate court failed to recognize a 30-year marriage on the grounds that the bride price was not paid in full. According to the appellate court, a marriage certificate "did not perfect what was already an imperfect union." The "imperfection" was brought about because the bride price had not been fully paid at the inception of the marriage. Erez and Thompson (1996) discuss that customary laws in Sierra Leone endorse child marriages and even though a Prevention of Cruelty to Children Act in the country prohibits sexual intercourse with girls younger than 14 years, it is not uncommon for parents to marry off daughters as young as 9 in order to get the bride price. Additionally, Erez and Thompson note that the same statutory law, which is intended to protect girls younger than 14, also recognizes child marriages. More current research by Park (2006) notes that female slavery, comprising forced marriages and other crimes against girls and women, persists in Sierra Leone because of the entrenched marginalization of women brought about by long-lasting cultural trends and by discriminatory laws and procedures. IRIN Africa (2007) reports that while, theoretically, Malian law has stiff punishments for those who force women into marriages, seldom are such punishments carried out because the families of the women are instrumental in such marriage arrangements.

As a consequence of inaction, piecemeal attempts to tackle the problem, or the absence of legislation, researchers look externally to Western countries and to international conventions and laws when suggesting policies relevant to effective controls. Some, like Bentheim (2010), have noted that the potential of international law to be a deterrent has been stalled by the fact that many men are not charged with these destructive crimes, instead those who are charged at all, are charged with crimes closely associated with, but not directly correlated with forced marriages, such as sexual enslavement, war crimes, or rape (see also Park, 2006).

Drawing from Beccaria (1963), three factors determine the efficacy or deterrent effect of punishment: certainty, celerity, and severity. In the case of those who engage in what outsiders see as repugnant tradition, none of the factors is applicable. It is a way of life. Efforts by international charters and conventions, such as the African Charter on the Rights and Welfare of the Child, the Convention on the Elimination of all Forms of

Discrimination against Women, The Universal Declaration of Human Rights (1948), among others, have not had any deterrent effect. To begin with, such conventions only make it possible for formal courts to prosecute violators, and, as the foregoing discussion suggests, formal courts tend to acquiesce the behavior, thereby promoting impunity. Further, empirical studies of general deterrence reveal that the component of certainty is the most effective factor. Merely issuing condemnatory words without the force of law and the certainty of punishment changes nothing. As Kahan (1996, p. 598) states, "when society deliberately forgoes answering the wrongdoer through punishment, it risks being perceived as endorsing his valuations; hence the complaint that unduly lenient punishment reveals that the victim is worthless in the eyes of the law." Samaha (2011, p. 9) concludes that "if the threat [of punishment] isn't carried out when a crime is committed, condemnation is meaningless, or worse it sends a message that the victim's suffering is worthless." Von Hirsch and Ashworth (2004, p. 21) state that "Punishment conveys censure, but it does not consist solely of it. The censure in punishment is expressed through the imposition of a deprivation ('hard treatment') on the offender." When the certainty of punishment is lax, and if offenders can successfully evade punishment under the canopy of customs, then the practice is likely to persist.

Time (2012), Park (2006), Black (2001), and Bunch (1990) have documented how, despite obvious records of female victimization, society looks away and does nothing or very little. This occurs because women are still voiceless in many societies, and attempts at advancement are thwarted by financial and procedural stalemates. Ultimately, not only are perpetrators immune from retribution, but others are not deterred.

How Can Practices of Forced Marriages, Bride Prices, Levirate, and Domestic Violence Be Minimized?

The author advocates punitive sanctions, victim redress, social welfare programs, and education as strategies to curb these practices. Several African countries have made piecemeal attempts to address some of the problems, but such attempts are insufficient and sometimes contradictory. Take Cameroon for instance, section 344(1) of the penal code speaks against the corruption of youths in any way including debauchery, and stipulates a corresponding punishment of imprisonment from 1 to 5 years, and a fine that may range from 25,000 to 1,000,000 CFA francs, which is approximately U.S.$55 to U.S.$2,200. Subsection 2 of the French version of the code stipulates that such punishment will be doubled if the minor is 16 years old or younger. The English version is silent on this (Cameroon is a bilingual country with English and French as the main languages), and as a consequence, violators escape that punishment. To make the punishment of violators a credible endeavor, laws should be clear and consistent to enable equal justice throughout the country.

In Sierra Leone, the Prevention of Cruelty to Children Act is in force and prohibits sexual acts against children below the age of 14. However, as Erez and Thompson (1996, p. 79) note, the law "approbates and reprobates at the same time: on the one hand, it seeks to protect children under fourteen years; on the other hand, it denies such protection by recognizing child marriages." Park (2006), however, notes that progress has been made in that the Special Court of Sierra Leone now recognizes a forced marriage as a "crime against humanity" and makes it possible for violators to be prosecuted and convicted. This milestone was reached following the recommendations of the Truth and Reconciliation Commission in October 2004, to the government of Sierra Leone. Only time will tell how these theoretical principles translate into actual enforcements. As the commission itself suggests, there must be "accountability" if impunity is to be addressed. A 2008 report (U.S. Department of State) indicates that since the 2003 OMCT Report, Mali now has laws that criminalize spousal abuse; however, law enforcement officers are hesitant to intervene in domestic issues, let alone press charges. Even though, in 2007, the Malian government established a Planning and Statistics Unit with directives to track prosecutions on domestic abuse, the unit is nonfunctional.

Many African countries are signatories to several international treaties, such as the United Nations Convention on the Rights of the Child (1989), The African Charter on the Rights and Welfare of the Child, the Convention against Torture and Inhuman Treatment, The Universal Declaration of Human Rights, and the Convention on the Elimination of all Forms of Discrimination against Women. The point is, the countries where inhumane practices, such as forced marriages, bride prices, levirate, and other forms of cruelty, persist are not unaware of these international prohibitions because they are, in actuality, signatories to these treaties. Yet, in order to tackle the problem seriously, it is vital and imperative that courts faithfully and rigorously enforce these rights and values.

Ironically, customary laws seem to trump statutory law when it comes to enforcement. In Cameroon, for instance, law 69/DF/544 of December 19, 1969, passed in the Francophone Cameroon, and its Anglophone equivalent, law 79(4) enacted on June 29, 1979, give gravitas to customary practices that do not contravene statutory law. One would think that since there is a caveat that customary laws should not run contrary to written laws, such an understanding would be kept intact. This is not the case in Cameroon, and that is true in other African countries because of a male-dominated judicial system and a tradition that feeds impunity. Statutory laws lack enforcement teeth; they require effective legislation as well as effective enforcement. Those who force children and women into marriage, and men who engage in this practice, should be prosecuted. This should not be taken merely as a cultural or private issue; it should be taken as a national issue that needs full judicial attention.

In England, a Forced Marriage Protection Order (FMPO) was enacted in 1996 to protect victims of forced marriages and potential victims, as well as family members and organizations that step in to help victims of forced marriages. This type of legislation is imperative in African countries, especially since, based on tradition, it is rare for an African child to sue a parent. It is, in part, for this reason that Ms. Nafisatu Laushi's lawsuit against her father, who was forcing her to marry a man against her wishes, made headline news (see *BBC News*, September 7, 2002). Girls and women who are recalcitrant should be assured of a safe haven.

Enforcing the rights of victims also means that marriages entered into without consent ought to be nullified. After all, The Universal Declaration of Human Rights, Article 16(2) states that "marriage shall be entered into only with the free and full consent of the intending spouses." Also, the United Nations Convention on the Elimination of All Forms of Discrimination against Women, General Recommendation No. 21, states that: "a woman's right to choose a spouse and enter freely into marriage is central to her life and her dignity as a human being." The problem is that because of limited formal education, many women, particularly those in rural areas, are ignorant of the statutory requirements that promote consent as an integral ingredient for a valid marriage; consequently, some women are lured into customary law marriages that have no legal mandate. Just as they ignorantly and docilely enter into a marriage, that same vulnerability makes them less inclined to leave their abusive husbands.

Determining the absence of consent for minors is easy, because first the law presumes that they cannot give valid consent. Second, where proof is shown that there was parental coercion, or a cultural mandate, lack of consent can be deduced. With regard to young adults, Munby J, an English judge, cautions that courts should be careful to decipher a marriage that was entered into without consent from one where there was valid consent, but from which the woman just wants out. He provides the following guidelines to determine nonconsent:

> Where the influence is that of a parent or other close and dominating relative, and where the arguments and persuasion are based upon personal affection or duty, religious beliefs, powerful social or cultural conventions, or asserted social, familial or domestic obligations, the influence may, as Butler-Sloss LJ put in In re T (Adult: Refusal of Treatment), be subtle, insidious, pervasive and powerful. In such cases, moreover, very little pressure may suffice to bring about the desired result (Re SA Vulnerable Adult with Capacity: Marriage (2006) 1 FLR 867, para. 78).

Further, when a marriage is nullified, the man should make some type of financial restitution to the woman to enable her to resituate. After all, as Bentheim (2010) and Black (2001) indicate, women who are forced into marriage are completely economically dependent on their husbands, and even when they have earned money, it has been exploitative labor. Where there are offspring from the marriage, child support payments should be enforced. A proper collection agency should be in place, otherwise impunity will also manifest itself in this regard. Asset forfeiture and other ways of compelling the man to meet his financial obligation should be put in place. Additionally, trained social workers or counselors should provide extended and intense counseling to the women and children who are victims of such practices.

The United Nations Convention on the Rights of the Child, Article 19 states that:

> State parties shall take all appropriate legislative, administrative, social and educational measures to protect the child from all forms of physical or mental violence, injury or abuse, neglect or negligent treatment, maltreatment or exploitation, including sexual abuse, while in the care of parent(s), legal guardian(s) or any other person who has the care of the child.

Many African countries do not have child protection agencies, and for those that do, such agencies stand only as symbolic institutions with little resources allocated to ensure their efficient operations. These agencies are necessary in every country, especially to help alleviate the plight of children more susceptible to slavery, forced marriages, and other kinds of harmful acts. To make the agencies effective, caseworkers have to be given proper training, monitored carefully, and remunerated reasonably, to deter them from becoming abusive.

Similarly, shelters should be established for women whose dignity is threatened by their families forcing them into nonconsensual marriages or those who are subject to domestic violence or some type of abuse. This is crucial. As Time (2012) notes, in Cameroon, because of the absence of any establishments that provide help for abused women, even the police and hospitals that abused women contact for help, rebuff and turn them away. Law enforcement officers and hospital employees in many African countries need proper training in handling victims of abuse and domestic violence. Further, establishing social support networks is helpful in that women can draw strength from others who have been in similar situations.

Bentheim (2010), Park (2006), Black (2001), and Bunch (1990) have commented on the high proportion of African women who are economically marginalized. Some of the reasons why women fail to acquire upward mobility lie in deep-rooted traditions that allow only sons to acquire an education. According to Women and Literacy (a think-tank group),

in one African country alone the literacy rate among men is 26% while among
women it is 11%. Other statistics further highlight that evidence; of the 1 bil-
lion illiterates in the world, two thirds of them are women! (Sil International,
2010)

This must change if women are to become visible and relevant in matters outside of the home. It is worth noting that in Cameroon and Nigeria,
the literacy rate is high for both genders (CIA, n.d.), but those in rural areas
are still to catch up. While private initiatives to elevate women's and children's literacy in rural areas, such as in the Kom tribe of Cameroon (Sil
International, 2010) and in Nigeria among the Hausas (see Jaulmes, 2007),
have been documented, governments should take the lead in making education mandatory up to a certain minimum level and criminalize parents who
refuse to let their children attend school to gain basic training and education. With access to education, which may include technical or trade skills,
women are more likely to be politically, socially, and economically empowered. Women and Literacy outline the merits of literacy among women. Of
significance, they emphasize how enriching literacy is in enhancing wom-
en's choices on when to get married, the number of children they would
prefer to have, health care issues, and many others (see Sil International,
2010). On the contrary, it is noted that in Liberia, where the illiteracy rate
among women is approximately 58%, forced marriages abound (see Zunia,
2010). Cullen and Agnew (2011, p. 647) surmise that "parent education" as
well as "parent management training programs" are helpful in forestalling
adult offending. Sadat (2011) suggests that crimes against women can be
suppressed if, in addition to other programs in place, women are sufficiently
represented in all disciplines and in international and national institutions
that promote the rights of women.

Even though preventive measures that are introduced to adults may be
helpful, Farrington and Welsh (2007) advocate early prevention programs
since it is clear that programs instituted sooner than later in life more
positively influence the life course of children as they transition to adults.
Targeted programs should not only include individuals, families, and peers,
but should also incorporate community factors as well.

As Cullen and Agnew (2011) explain, enhancement programs in pre-
school are not only effective in curbing delinquency and adult deviance, they
are instrumental in molding other outcomes in life, such as employment and
family stability among others.

Even though formal education is crucial, informal training is also
necessary. Here, community leaders, activists groups, and those personnel affiliated with NGOs should organize frequent town-hall meetings to
inculcate the virtues of human rights to traditional leaders whose beliefs
are still entrenched in the subjugation of women. Of further relevance is

the point that community members should come to the understanding that customs/traditions that are obnoxious and repugnant should be abolished. "Community-based mentoring programs hold promise as efficacious approaches ..." as Cullen and Agnew (2011, p. 647) posit.

Conclusion

Although this study introduces a criminological spin to existing literature, it is not without limitations. The absence of data from the various countries on each of the acts presents problems for readers who are interested in analyzing data. Time (2012), Immigration and Refugee Board of Canada (2007), Ngassa (1999), and Erez and Thompson (1996) have explained that data collection of cases of victimization of women is difficult in many African countries since neither hospitals nor police departments keep records on the women who seek their help. Further, in the villages and rural areas where the majority of such acts occur, there are no police stations, and most of the girls and women have nowhere to file a report. Customary courts typically do not keep marriage registration data; however, more importantly, since the acts are legitimized by customs, they are not considered crimes and thus there is no need to keep records. Even when the BBC and others, such as Bentheim (2010) and Park (2006), make approximations in percentages, those percentages usually relate to forced marriages; hardly any approximations are made on other abusive practices, such as levirate, bride prices, and domestic violence.

This study had three objectives: (1) to highlight the problems associated with forced marriages, levirate, domestic violence, and bride prices; (2) to contribute to the extant literature by providing a nexus between these outdated and traditional practices and criminological theorizing; and (3) to reiterate and expound on proposals pertinent in alleviating or curbing these acts of "slavery," and extending justice to women. Several of the proposals outlined here may require governmental funding. Many African countries are not as destitute as some may think. The problem with some African countries is corruption and mismanagement of public funds (Salih, 2010). The proposals are not overbearing; funds can easily be allocated to sponsor most of them. Other proposals need no funding at all, only a willingness to refine the thought process and to come to the understanding that suppressing and maltreating others, only exposes the weaknesses, insecurities, and deficiencies of the abusers.

Additionally, if these abuses of women have to stop, there must be clear and credible ways of deterring the behavior. If some of these African countries want to catch on with "globalization," they must reformat their policies, customs, and legal systems. Only when credible and objective policies are put in place can impunity be addressed and progress made. Just as a global effort is needed to curb hunger and diseases in Africa, so too is global input necessary and vital to limit female/child abuse and exploitation.

References

Abbott, J., Johnson, R., Koziol-McLain, J., & Lowenstein, S. (1995). Domestic violence against women. *The Journal of American Medical Association*, *273*(22), 1763–1767.

Akers, R. (1997). *Criminological Theories: Introduction and Evaluation*, 2nd edn. Los Angeles, CA: Roxbury.

Anderson, C. (2011). The moral arc of the universe bends long but it bends toward justice: The search for justice in international law. *The Journal of Diplomatic History*, *35*(5), 787–791.

BBC News. (2002). Nigerian girl sues over forced marriage. Retrieved on 10/7/2010, from http://news.bbc.co.uk/2/hiafrica/2242.stm.

Beccaria, C. (1963). *On Crimes and Punishments*. Translated with an Introduction by Henry Paolucci. New York: Macmillan.

Benin. (2004). Saved from forced marriage in Kpessanrou. Retrieved on 10/9/2011, from http://africastories.usaid.gov/search_details.cfm?storyid=312&countryid=2&sectorid=0.

Bentheim, C. (2010). Forced marriage in Africa: Examining the disturbing reality. Consultancy Africa Intelligence. Retrieved on 10/7/2010, from http://www.consultancyafrica.com/index.php?option=com_content&view=article&id+290.

Beswick, S. (2001). "We are bought like clothes": The war over polygamy and levirate marriage in South Sudan. *Northeast African Studies*, *8*(2), 35–61.

Black, M. (2001). Wanted: The right to refuse. *New Internationalist*, August, Issue 337.

Brillion, Y. (1972). Development and crime in West Africa. Paper presented at the *First West African Conference in Comparative Criminology*, Abidjan, Ivory Coast.

Bunch, C. (1990). Women's rights as human rights: Toward a re-vision of human rights. *Human Rights Quarterly*, *12*(4), 486–498.

Chigbu, C., Ekweazi, K., Chigbu, C., & Iwuji, S. (2010). Sexual violation among married women in Southeastern Nigeria. *International Journal of Gynecology and Obstetrics*, *110*(2), 141–144.

CIA. (n.d.). CIA World Fact Book. Retrieved on 10/9/2011, from http://www.ciaworldfactbook.us.

Clifford, C. (2007). Child marriage in Mali continuing to be ignored. Foreign Policy Association. Retrieved on 3/22/2012, from http://foreignpolicyblogs.com/2007/09/06/child-marriage-in-mali-continuing-to-be-ignored.

Cullen, F., & Agnew, R. (2011). *Criminological Theory: Past to Present*, 4th edn. New York, Oxford: Oxford University Press.

Erez, E., & Thompson, R. (1996). Victimization of women in African society. In Fields, C. & Moore, R. (eds), *Comparative Criminal Justice: Traditional and Nontraditional Systems of Law and Control* (pp. 61–82). Prospect Heights, IL: Waveland Press, Inc.

Farrington, D., & Welsh, B. (2007). *Saving Children from a Life of Crime*. New York, Oxford: Oxford University Press.

FORWARD. (2010). Child marriage. Retrieved on 10/9/2011, from http://www. forwarduk.org.uk/key-issues/child-marriage.

Gender Alert News. (2000). Uganda: The facts about the tradition of bride price. *Women's International Network News*, 01457985, Vol. 26, Issue I, 56.

Henry, S., & Milovanovic, D. (1991). Constitutive criminology: The maturation of critical theory. *Criminology, 29*, 293–315.

Immigration and Refugee Board of Canada. (2007). Mali: Prevalence of forced marriages and the consequences of refusing. Retrieved on 3/22/2012, from http://www.unhcr.org/refworld/publisher,IRBC,,MLI,469cd6a0c,0.html.

IRIN Africa. (2007). Mali: Child marriage a neglected problem. IRIN Humanitarian News and Analysis. Nioro du Sahel, 30 August. Retrieved on 3/22/2012, from http://www.irinnews.org/Report/74027/Mali-child-marriage-a-neglected-problem.

Jaulmes, C. (2007). Literacy empowers women and girls in Northern Nigeria. Retrieved on 10/9/2011, from http://www.unicef.org/infobycountry/nigeria_39152.html.

Kahan, D. (1996). What do alternative sanctions mean? *University of Chicago Law Review, 63*, 591.

Kaye, D., Mirembe, F., Ekstrom, A., Kyomuhendo, G., & Johansson, A. (2005). Implications of bride price and domestic violence and reproductive health in Wakiso District, Uganda. *African Health Sciences, 5*(4), 300–303.

Kiragu, J. (1996). Policy overview: HIV prevention and women's rights—Their promotion goes hand in hand. *AIDS Captions*, 8–14. Secondary Source ID: PIP/118343.

Martens, J. (2009). "Civilised domesticity," Race and European attempts to regulate African marriage practices in colonial Natal, 1868–1875. *History of the Family, 14*(4), 340–355.

Miller, J. M., Schreck, C. J., & Tewksbury, R. (2008). *Criminological Theory: A Brief Introduction*, 2nd edn. Boston, MA: Pearson/Allyn & Bacon.

Monekosso, T. (2001). Africa's forced marriages. *BBC News*. Retrieved on 10/9/2011, from http://news.bbc.co.uk/2/hi/africa/1209099.stm.

Mongbo, S. (2007). Women and girls: Victims of the forces of the market and levirate marriage. *Women's Global Network for Reproductive Rights Newsletter*, 88/89, 24–26.

Ngassa, V. (1999). *Gender Approach to Court Action*. Stifung: Saagraph and Friedrich-Ebert.

Okafo, N. (2009). *Reconstructing Law and Justice in a Postcolony*. Surrey: Ashgate.

OMCT Report. (2003). Violence against women in Mali: A report to the Human Rights Committee. Retrieved on 10/9/2011, from http://www.omct.org/files/2004/07/24/eng_2003_07_mali.pdf.

Oyebanji, M. (1981). Proposals for reform of marriage laws in Nigeria. In Aguda, T. A. (ed.), *The Marriage Laws of Nigeria* (p. 151). Lagos: The Nigerian Institute of Advanced Legal Studies.

Park, A. (2006). "Other inhumane acts": Forced marriage, girl soldiers and the special court for Sierra Leone. *Social & Legal Studies, 15*, 315–337.

Sadat, L. (2011). Avoiding the creation of a gender ghetto in international criminal law. *International Criminal Law Review, 11*(3), 655–662.

Salih, M. (2010). Corruption carries high cost, World Bank says. Retrieved on 3/22/2012, from http://ipsnews.net.asp?idnews = 50679.

Samaha, J. (2011). *Criminal Law*, 10th edn. Belmont, CA: Wadsworth/Cengage Learning.

Sil International. (2010). Women and Literacy. Retrieved on 10/9/2011, from http://www.sil.org/literacy/wom_lit.htm.

Time, C. (2012). The Cameroonian woman and the law. In Okafo, C. (ed.), *Grounded Law: Comparative Research on State and Non-state Justice in Multiple Societies* (pp. 493–502). United Kingdom: Wildfire Publishing House.

Time, V. (2000). Legal pluralism and harmonization of law: An examination of the process of reception and adoption of both civil and common law in Cameroon and their coexistence with indigenous laws. *International Journal of Comparative and Applied Criminal Justice*, 24(1), 19–29.

Time, V. M. (2013). Lessons learned about low crime rates in Japan: Field notes from Japanese police officers. In Mackey, D. & Levan, K. (eds) *Crime Prevention* (pp. 397–411). Burlington, MA: Jones & Bartlett.

UNFPA (United Nations Population Fund). (2005). Child marriage factsheet. Retrieved on 10/9/2011, from http://www.unfpa.org/swp/2005/presskit/factsheets/facts_child_marriage.htm.

U.S. Department of State. (2008). Mali: Human Rights Report 2008. Retrieved on 10/9/2011, from http://mali.usembassy.gov/human-rights-report-08-eng.html.

Uzodike, E. (1990). Child abuse and neglect in Nigeria—Socio-legal aspects. *International Journal of Law and the Family*, 4, 83–96.

Von Hirsch, A., & Ashworth, A. (2004). *Proportionate Sentencing*. Oxford: Oxford University Press.

Welch, G., & Sachs, A. (1987). The bride price, revolution, and the liberation of women. *International Journal of the Sociology of Law*, 15(4), 369–393.

Welstead, M. (2009). Forced marriage: Bifurcated values in the UK. *The Denning Law Journal*, 21, 49–65.

Williams, C., & Arrigo, B. (2008). *Ethics, Crime, and Criminal Justice*. Upper Saddle River, NJ: Pearson/Prentice Hall.

Younkins, E. (2002). Customary law as an evolved good shortcut. *Le Quebecois Libre*, 112, 1–9.

Zunia. (2010). Literacy among Sub-Saharan African women. Retrieved on 10/9/2011, from http://www.zunia.org/post/literacy-among-sub-african-women.

Beguiling Eve and Her Innocent Counterpart

Victim-Offender Identities in the Criminal Justice Process

16

COLLEEN MOORE

Contents

Introduction

Victimization is traditionally associated with passivity, helplessness, powerlessness, and vulnerability, and an "ideal victim" necessitates the identification (and prosecution) of an "ideal offender" (Christie, 1986). Further, in contrast to the "fixed" position of the offender (as immoral), the position of the victim can be flexible, depending on their perceived response to the crime that took place. Kearon and Godfrey (2007) present the demise of the victim as having enjoyed a role as the "essential actor" in early modern criminal justice processes, to the "symbolic actor" of the enlightenment, to their current position of "fragmented actor"—to be helped, protected, pitied, or doubted, and even despised. It has been suggested that the idea of "the victim" has become much stronger as they have come to be represented by others in the courtroom, where the "powerful symbolism of vulnerable victims" (Kearon & Godfrey, 2007) was conceived. This image of the "ideal victim" has significantly shaped public, media, and governmental attitudes toward crime and offenders, reinforcing an increasingly complex, fragmented, and paradoxical debate. The victim's role generally remains uncomplicated, providing the victim maintains the "appropriate" veneer of victimhood, but the status of the victim is precarious and can be variously shaped and influenced by cultural forces (Mythen, 2007). The media, as well as jurists, have helped fuel the general public's assessment of the apposite sufferer, as one who has in no way precipitated or contributed to their own victimization—a view that has been promulgated for many years (Kearon & Godfrey, 2007; Weisstub, 1986). The end of the twentieth century saw victim issues begin formally to be addressed by the state and policy makers (Mawby & Gill, 1987) and, through the formalization of measures to address victims' rights, the victim has been (re-)placed (rhetorically, at least) center stage in formal responses to community safety, crime control, and punishment (Mawby & Gill, 1987). The voice of the victim is sought through crime victimization surveys; our policies are shaped to ensure that victims are protected; and victimization is recognized and targeted by the authorities (such as antihate campaigns, domestic violence awareness drives, or safer cities initiatives). Despite such drives to identify "victimization" generally, there are many challenges for those individuals who seek *legal* recourse and recognition if they do not match the prototype. The victim of crime *at court* often remains the "silent and forgotten" actor in the criminal justice system (CJS), which is astonishing, given that most trials would collapse if their cooperation was not forthcoming (Das, 1997).

In this chapter, it is the author's intention to explore the treatment of certain female victimization scenarios in the justice process. The chapter is divided into three sections: first, victims' identities and characteristics will be examined as they present to the justice system as victims of sexual assault, including some of the difficulties that can arise if the victim does not fit the stereotypical prototype of the "rape victim"; secondly, the chapter will examine some recent (misdirected) policy and police initiatives that have sought to aggressively tackle the sexual exploitation of women; finally, the chapter aims to draw attention to the collective benevolence that continues to undermine any serious attempts to address and do away with the endemic exploitation of and hidden violence toward women.

Victims' Roles

It is clear that the victim has several simultaneous roles to fulfil, but when their own behavior is scrutinized and deemed to be deficient, their task is arguably more onerous—especially if they are female (Weisstub, 1986). Some attempts have been made to convincingly portray offenders as victims. Cohen's (1979) observation of the "vacillation between the image of the deviant as mismanaged victim and the deviant as cultural hero" has been explored, as has more recent research that reveals that there is a considerable "victim–offender overlap" (Fattah, 1991). The literature on victim–offender overlap has raised a number of dilemmas in the criminal justice process that remain relatively unexplored in criminology, but what has been identified has, for the most part, examined the link between offending behavior and *previous* victimization. For example, Sampson and Lauritsen (1990) suggest that a deviant lifestyle is largely responsible for the overlap between victimization risk and criminal offending. Self-report studies have primarily sought to understand whether victimization is part of the causal explanation for later offending, and offending for later victimization (Gottfredson, 1984; Sampson & Lauritsen, 1990). What these studies have in common is that they focus overwhelmingly on *male* deviance and the interlinked nature of male offending behavior and victimization. Further, there has been little research to date on the *transformation* that a victim's character can undergo during the investigation or trial of the alleged offender, although victim precipitation has been explored, especially in relation to "domestic" and sexual violence (von Hentig, 1948; Ryan, 1971; Weisstub, 1986). Meloy and Miller (2010) discuss the tenuous and sometimes conflicting legacy that has emerged relating to victim precipitation or victim blaming, which they state was frequently placed on women, serving to protect men's power and privilege, as well as to "offer greater impunity for their infractions." In cases of domestic or sexual violence, victims may seek meaning behind their attack (why me?) and to explain their victimization through their own choices and actions (I had a drink with him). By contrast, victims may believe that they deserved the violence because they are a bad person (Meloy and Miller, 2010). Victim-blaming has been criticized—Ryan's (1971) "wise and plainspoken" analysis of the ideological process that maintains the status quo by (unintentionally) distorting realities in the interests of a specific group is perhaps one of the earliest attempts to understand how it is that we can blame the social problem for our own inconvenience. He suggests that blaming the victim is one of numerous American ideologies that "have rationalized cruelty and injustice." But it is perhaps Weisstub's (1986) seminal work on women's position in the legal arena that throws light on the dilemma that women face in our criminal justice process—regardless of whether they stand as victim or aggressor. If women complain about their treatment by men—*accuse* them, Weisstub argues that they have been characterized "as natural hysterics or masochists who had in their unfemale that is, non-passive, overly sexualized femaleness, *lured men into criminal wrongs*" (my emphasis). The victim has her place, and once she has been declared a victim, she must either be further victimized through "our collective benevolence" (Weisstub, 1986) or exposed as a fraud. Once exposed as a fraud—unreliable and deceitful—it is the job of the legal system to ensure the decimation of her victim status, while maintaining and upholding the status of the "true" unblemished victim—even if it means criminalizing her to achieve such an end. The final section of the chapter will explore some instances where such an outcome seems to have been achieved.

Despite a slight surge of criminological interest in the victim's multifaceted role, to date there has been little research examining how the treatment of the victim during police investigations, as well as cross-examination at trial, can reposition the victim into one of a deviant, even criminal actor, *especially when morals and sexual conduct are scrutinized.* It is the aim of this discussion to highlight some of the processes that can exacerbate such a role transformation, which can have lasting and sometimes punitive results. Using a number of case studies to illustrate some situations in which such transformations can take place, the discussion will critically examine the uncertain and moveable position of the "ideal" victim in relation to the condemnable and immoveable position of the victim *exposed.* If the victim's assertion does not fulfil a set of undefined and ambiguous criteria, it is possible that her allegations can be used to contribute to her own demise.

"False" Allegations

Von Hentig (1948) arguably began the dialogue on victim characteristics when he depicted 12 stereotypical victim types, inter alia "younger women vulnerable to murder and sexual assault" and immigrants. Despite over half a century of consideration of the position and characteristics of the victim, there remains a disproportionate focus on the rights and well-being of the defendant, unless the defendant has already been established as unreliable. However, the character of the victim or witness can be brought to bear on a case—most commonly in allegations of rape and sexual abuse—which can be used to undermine her "reliability." There has been a considerable amount of literature relating to such abuses of trust, which have also been branded as "false allegations." For example, the 1991 case in the United States of Anita Hill, who claimed that Clarence Thomas (her employer) harassed her with "graphic sexual remarks and pornographic films while they worked together at the US Equal Employment Opportunities Commission" (Smith, 1996; *BBC News*, 2010). Hill's case highlighted how a woman making allegations of sexual harassment could be publicly denigrated, while the accused maintained his innocence, even naming Hill as his "most traitorous adversary." Hill has been variously cast as delusional or spurned, seeking revenge, to Brock's (1994) "nutty, and a bit slutty" description that insinuates that Hill was romantically obsessed with Thomas. Brock now describes his book as a character assassination and has since disavowed its premise (Carlson, 2001); he has also apologized to Hill. The allegations made by Hill were not conclusively proven and each maintains their position of "wronged," although the slur did not hinder Thomas, he went on to become a U.S. Supreme Court Justice. In this instance, the maintenance of the status quo (his position) took precedence, arguably at the expense of the accuser's character.

When stories relating to sexual violence make headline news in the United Kingdom, they tend to focus on unusual scenarios. Over 57,000 allegations of sexual assault were reported to the police in 2006, yet Sally Henderson made headlines when she was convicted of perverting the course of justice and jailed for 1 year in 2006 for falsely accusing her husband of raping her (Savill, 2006). Perverting the course of justice rarely makes the news in other contexts, yet in this instance, several national newspapers ran the story, quoting the judge's comments, which branded her a liar. In addition, the prosecutor stated:

> There is nothing more wicked that a woman can do against her husband or partner than to claim rape. But there is very little for a man to do other than say he didn't do it. Hell hath no fury like a woman scorned and her claims were a tissue of lies.

It appears that Sally Henderson did make up these claims against her husband and had done so before to previous partners, and her actions are unquestionably criminal and wrong. However, the number of rape and sexual abuse cases that remain *unprosecuted* far outnumber those in which false allegations are uncovered (Lea et al., 2003). And when rape cases fall apart at, or prior to, trial, rarely do they make the news unless there is another dimension to the story, for example, when the allegations are deemed to be erroneous in some way.

Women who cannot convince the police of an alleged rape may be putting themselves in even further danger by simply reporting them. In 2010, Leyla Ibrahim was found guilty of perverting the course of justice by a Carlisle Crown Court jury (Newstead, 2010) after she failed to identify her attackers, and could not conclusively string the whole story of her attack together. Her assertion that she was attacked in the early hours of January 2009 on a deserted footpath was dismissed. The prosecution claimed she was upset with her boyfriend and lied about the attack "to teach people a lesson." Despite her prosecution, the officer in charge of the investigation, stated, without irony: "The most important thing to me now is to ensure that victims of sex assaults continue to call police immediately. You will be taken seriously." Considering the paucity of successful convictions, and even less publicity relating to them, this advice at the end of a story about the conviction of a woman who claimed to have been raped is astonishing. Leyla Ibrahim is not an isolated case. In 2010, an anonymous woman ("Sarah") was convicted of perverting the course of justice, after retracting allegations of rape made against her husband (Hirsch, 2010). Sarah reported to the police that her controlling husband had subjected her to prolonged domestic abuse, and that he had raped her. She was later persuaded to tell the police that she had made it up "for the sake of the children" (Pidd, 2010) and she withdrew her complaint. Despite the fact that the police were convinced that she was telling the truth, the Crown Prosecution Service (CPS) went ahead with the prosecution and she was sentenced to 8 months in jail. The decision to proceed with charges against her has been defended by prosecutors, who claim that she "actively worked to derail the trial" against her husband, even though their own guidance (CPS, 2009) stipulates that women who withdraw evidence in rape cases are often suffering from pressure or intimidation. (It should be noted, however, that these guidelines were issued after immense pressure from lobbyists and pressure groups.) Although the sentence was later quashed, Sarah's conviction remains, and after serving 18 days, her sentence was replaced with community service and a supervision order for 2 years. Sarah had suffered many years of domestic abuse and sexual assault at the hands of her husband and was intimidated as well as concerned for the welfare of her children when she retracted her complaint (not, she said, because they were false, but because her estranged husband and his sister had "emotionally blackmailed" her into doing so) (Pidd, 2010). If these recent cases were unusual, perhaps they could be put down to a glitch in the criminal justice process, but within a context where, nationally, only 6% of reported rapes result in a successful prosecution, the prosecution of the alleged victim in *any* situation, based on the retraction of a statement or lack of evidence is a travesty. Pidd (2010) suggests that one solicitor she spoke to is aware of 30 more women in similar positions, which, she suggests, "represents a hardening of attitudes against women who report rape." Women who do not appear to present as convincing victims could be interpreted as just one by-product of a CJS in which the police and the CPS treat rape victims with suspicion, because they think many of them are either mistaken about their own experience or outright lying.

The evidence seems to suggest that police responses waiver between benevolent paternalism and outright intolerance of some women's claims. In support of such attitudes, recent U.S. literature on false allegations of rape (Turvey & McGrath, 2011) suggests that they are much more common than previously believed. They state (with little evidence), "given that many false reporters are repeat offenders, a firm zero-tolerance policy and judicious enforcement of the law can save time and money by preventing future false reports from the emboldened." These *emboldened* women, according to the authors, are then further protected by misguided police officers, who mistakenly believe that "exposing, charging, and convicting these individuals will deter *legitimate* (my emphasis) victims from reporting their crimes" (Turvey & McGrath, 2011). Among many spurious claims, the authors invite the readers to consider the scenario of one particular case, in which a woman accused six members of the Duke University Lacrosse Team of raping her during an off-campus party, "Consider the context: The accuser was a stripper with a criminal history, an alleged mental health history, and a history of unfounded claims of being gang-raped...." The authors state that the "accuser told police ten years ago that three men raped her when she was fourteen. None of the men was charged." This in itself does not mean that she made up the allegations, simply that the police did not proceed with the investigation. The characteristics of the alleged victim are presented here as evidence of her unreliability. Unfortunately, such personal judgements are not uncommon and the term *false allegation* seems to be applicable to any case whereby the alleged victim is held somehow accountable for the failure of the case to proceed. The case of Dominique Strauss-Khan, which was played out in the international media, followed a similar pattern. The hotel maid, Nafissatou Diallo, who claimed that Strauss-Khan sexually assaulted her, filed a libel lawsuit against the *New York Post* after the tabloid reported she was a prostitute (Swaine, 2011); prosecutors later dropped criminal charges against Strauss-Khan after losing confidence in Diallo's credibility. An alleged prostitute is not a credible witness, far less a plausible victim of sexual assault, especially if she lied on her immigration papers. In contrast to Diallo's questionable (female) background, Strauss-Khan's (male) reputation is of much greater interest. Allegations of prostitution, racketeering, misogyny, and sexual assault have been explained as "libertine ways" instead of abuses of power. These cases illustrate that a woman's character can very easily be brought to bear against her when she makes an allegation of a sexual assault, and despite calls for such slanderous accusations to be ignored, they continue to seriously impede justice at every stage. The police, media, jurists, prosecutors, and populist pseudoacademics continue to make sweeping and damning generalizations about the acceptable female victim, and the beneficiary frequently appears to be the male position—saved from yet another beguiling Eve, attempting to expose *him* as culpable.

Much of the recent research that has examined attrition in rape cases, is mercifully more robust. Lea et al. (2003) attempt to explain some of the underlying factors that contribute to a crime being NFA-ed (no further action-ed) in England, and suggest that in many cases, the police have followed guidance set out in the Home Office Circular 69/1986, whereby rape allegations could only be no-crimed if the complaint was retracted or the complainant admitted making a false allegation (Lea et al., 2003). However, in some cases, the decision may have been based on other reasons, for example, the complainant was deemed unstable or malicious. When the police record a crime, many factors must be taken into consideration, including the likelihood of a successful prosecution. Lea et al. (2003) found no evidence to suggest that the crime of rape in the southwest of England has a higher rate of false allegations than any other crime, which does not concur with Turvey and McGrath's (2011) findings or interpretation of Lea et al.'s (2003) work. It is worth considering that the term *false allegation* itself is misleading. Turvey and McGrath (2011) do not appear to have understood the concept at all. In their analysis of existing research, they have interpreted NFA-ing as a concrete factor of false allegations—ignoring evidence that suggests that the women may have retracted their complaints for other, well-documented reasons. However, it may be that misinterpreted and misleading allegations as well as deceptive allegations should not be left to the discretion of the police alone to discern and record, which, in turn, can be further confused by uninformed "pseudoresearchers."

It is well established that the prosecution of women as an outcome of their complaint of rape should be avoided, and measures have been implemented in policing that aim to protect the women involved, albeit with slow success. However, there are other, less-documented scenarios in which women's characters and lifestyles have been used not only to damage their chances of a successful prosecution, but also to turn the tables and prosecute them instead. The victimization of certain groups of people remains hidden, and the rights of the victim is still a contentious area of consideration (Mawby & Walklate, 1994), yet victimization that comes about *directly through the criminal procedure* is even less understood, and requires much further research. So far, we have considered the position of women as victims when their background is tenuous and their alleged aggressor is more powerful than they are (from violent husband to the managing director of the International Monetary Fund). The remainder of this chapter will examine cases in which the agenda of the *prevention* of victimization and exploitation of women can be used to further victimize women under the mask of "collective benevolence" (Weisstub, 1986). To begin with, it is necessary to examine the requisites of an "ideal victim."

Ideal Victims' Identities

All victims have something of the uncomfortable "other" about them—a hybrid of outcast and saint (Rock, 2007). Victims, Rock suggests, are "necessarily somewhat disreputable, stigmatised figures, blighted by misfortune, often portrayed as angry and vindictive, perhaps best avoided by lay person and criminologist alike" (Rock, 2007). Women who have a history of sexual promiscuity, "questionable morals," or connections with prostitution are rarely considered reliable witnesses at best, and at worst, their histories or stories can occasionally be the subject of the investigation itself instead of the complaint that brought them to the attention of the police in the first instance. Once it has been established that a woman has a "colorful" past, has had the identity of someone "other," she seems to be unable to shake off her folk-devil mantle. Once she has been "othered" (Levi, 2009), she has a very difficult journey ahead if she hopes to be a credible witness and a legitimate victim. Her identity as a sex worker can take precedence—as Christie (1986) advised us "the creation of 'folk devils' works best when a simple juxtaposition of good victims and evil perpetrators can be made"—and in most visible (media) scenarios, the prostitute is an evil perpetrator unless she has been exploited and forced into slavery.

However, peoples' identities are "robustly plural" (Sen, 2006), and the importance of one identity should not obliterate the importance of the others. As Sen (2006) points out, one or two of our identities may define us in the eyes of the beholder, but a person has to make choices about what relative importance to attach to diverging factors that may compete for precedence. We may appear to be overweight, middle-aged, grumpy, and white, but we may also be a brilliant poker player, a fantastic cook, a loving mother, a wife, a scholar, and a dog owner. Depending upon the situation, it is often the determining factor of the beholder, which defines us. What is known about us depends upon judgments made by others—we are influenced by people with whom we identify (Sen, 2006) and, invariably, we apply what Sen terms a "singular affiliation" to people—the assumption that individuals belong to one collectivity only. For example, women can be defined in the media as "mothers," "rape victims," "sex slaves," or "prostitutes," and this image remains fixed, despite further information that may add alternative dimensions. By contrast, "identity disregard" (Sen, 2006) is also popular, especially in the media—that is, ignoring or neglecting altogether the influence of any sense of identity with others. This could be said to be true of the cases discussed in the first section of this chapter. The reference to a woman's moral character, rather than the identity she has presented with, fits well within these paradigms. Some assumptions about identities can be transformed, but others are fixed and immoveable, especially those that are negative. Latour's (2005) actor-network theory (ANT) is a useful lens to visualize the variety of forces at work in establishing a "social identity." All identities require others to "define who they are, what they should be, what they have been" (Latour, 2005). He suggests that these forces are "constantly at work, justifying the group's existence, invoking rules and precedents, and ... measuring up one definition against all the others" (Latour, 2005). Within ANT, the social is "a type of momentary association which is characterised by the way it gathers together into new shapes" (Latour, 2005)—the sociology of associations— "mothers," "rape victims," "sex slaves," or "prostitutes." It is not incontrovertible that choices are fixed—the ability to doubt and to question is not beyond our reach (Sen, 2006)—but the language and the imagery that is used to illustrate women make it very difficult to shift our swift and certain judgments. Thus, a "rape victim" or a "sex slave" who, it turns out, has voluntarily entered into prostitution is irrefutably corrupt and wholly defined by her negative identity. The current legislation and police activity related to sexual exploitation, for example, can serve to illustrate how such swift and certain judgments are promulgated through the very core of the "justice" process—rendering victimized women as deviant.

The sociology of associations may go some way to explain how, in some instances, a sex worker or a social entrepreneur (what we might call a man who uses his male attributes to survive) may simultaneously be labeled victim, opportunist, or exploiter. Depending upon the situation, a person can assume the qualities of a range of roles or just one, and can be dealt with in accordance to the most defining one. For example, when the police raid a brothel, those initially detained are usually distinct from each other and identified as "victim," "exploiter," "bystander," or "other." "Victims" can be reallocated the role of witnesses, in which case they may be helped, regarded as powerless, or they may be recast as "other" and dismissed. By contrast, "social entrepreneurs" can be perceived as criminal, potentially exploitative, powerful, and punishable. The police, as gatekeepers, along with the CPS—who we may term the *beholders*—are given the power to allocate the appropriate "roles" to those they apprehend, depending upon which slice of identity they embrace at any given time. At some stage throughout this process, initial allocations may move—a victim can become an offender and vice versa.

Targeted Police Activity: Exposing the Exploited

Little attention is focused on the *multiple roles* that people can play in the underbellies of the sex industry in terms of what constitutes the status of a "victim" or an "exploiter," nor the incentives attached to the allocation of a particular "status." This section aims to explore how police activity and targeted crackdowns on brothels have achieved a "multi-edged" result. On the one hand, the country has been alerted to the very serious consequences associated with trafficking and the exploitation of women; however, on the other hand, the threat has been magnified out of proportion—fuelling anxious citizens' fears of "immigrants" and confirming the stereotypical view of the "stolen, trafficked and exploited innocent victim"—all possible, but incomplete identities of the actors involved.

In recent years, the United Kingdom has become a popular destination country for migrant sex workers (Mai, 2010) as well as their "traffickers," and the topic is rarely out of the news. The legislative response to trafficking in England and Wales was introduced at a time when trafficking emerged as a lucrative criminal enterprise (Askola, 2007) and calls were made across the world to address the organized criminal exploitation of human beings. A so-called comprehensive approach has been adopted in England and Wales, which is keen (to be seen) to address the "three Ps" of combating trafficking in human beings (prevention, prosecution, and protection) as well as sexual exploitation in general. A number of police forces across the United Kingdom have dedicated teams and operations in place to combat human trafficking, which have provided researchers inter alia, with some confusing and difficult to disaggregate information (Gilbert & Moore, 2010), especially as most of the police activity has sought to focus on trafficking for *sexual* exploitation (TfSE).

In the United Kingdom, measures have been introduced to address the problems associated with prostitution and "trafficking," based on the criminalization of clients and on the enforcement of more rapid closure orders for establishments suspected of being involved in exploitative dynamics (Mai, 2010). Mai's (2010) findings indicate that the impact of the trafficking legislation is complicated and difficult to interpret, confused and inaccurate (Dasgupta & Murthy, 2009). Trafficking continues to be construed as a wide spectrum of behaviors: from arranging for sex workers to be taxied across London, recruiting and paying for consenting foreign women to travel to England to work as prostitutes (Mai, 2010), to forcing women into conditions of "sexual slavery," which is how the media generally interpret and publicize trafficking cases. In recent years, the scale and *response* to TfSE by the police and the media has far surpassed the degree of successful prevention strategies or convictions. There is also evidence (Davies, 2009) that the focus on TfSE has diverted attention away from some of the more detrimental effects of such intensive policing, such as deportations of women (Mai, 2010), which could be construed as devices that are deliberately intended to hinder the mobility of women, criminalization of victims, and financial rewards through the Proceeds of Crime Act 2002. For example, between November 2004 and June 2009, almost 2 million pounds was recovered through confiscation orders resulting from the prosecutions of people charged with (but not always convicted of) trafficking offenses, and many "rescued" women have been deported. These costly endeavors have arguably reaped relatively small rewards. What is clear is that police raids on brothels have achieved police targets, raised revenue for the police, and heightened the media's interest in and promulgation of the story of the stolen, the enslaved, and the sexually abused trafficked victim—as the ideal victim.

Over the past decade, the police and the government have chosen to focus most of their efforts around trafficking on *sexual* exploitation, rather than trafficking for other exploitative purposes. Askola (2007) suggests that this could be because TfSE invokes complex issues connected to sexuality, freedom, choice, and gender equality, in contrast to trafficking in people for work in private households, sweatshops, construction, illegal drug factories, or agricultural labor, which is more closely related to our precarious economy. A more cynical view would be to explain the concentrated focus on sexual exploitation as justification and promotion of the Police and Crime Act (2009), which further criminalizes behavior associated with sex work. Despite intense and focused police activity, the demand for prostitutes *appears* to have magnified along with its provision, although this in itself is debatable. It is within this confusing spectrum of sex work and exploitation that many women knowingly become sex workers, and they do not fit well within the constructed identities of the victim-actors embroiled within the CJS (sex slave or rape victim).

Prostitutes are often portrayed as victims of circumstance, poverty, predators, or drugs (Markovska & Moore, 2008), arguably because "fallen women" require deeper social and symbolic understanding if they are to be "rescued." The prostitute (similar to the victim of sexual assault) must invoke a particular notion of "victimhood" that positions "victims" of sexual viola-tion as having suffered a "social death" (Phoenix & Oerton, 2005) in order to be deserving. Unsuitable "victimhood" is augmented further when women involved in sex work are called as witnesses in the criminal justice process, where they are still characterized (at least in legal settings) as untrustworthy, disreputable, and suspicious—"victim/offender" actors trapped in the fixed network of immorality and disrepute, which now governs their identities. Through the underground nature of their trade, sex workers are associated with all kinds of illicit behavior, as well as sex, which, in turn, can be used against them should they seek the services of the police—the "beholders." In short, a woman who has not been forced against her will into prostitution does not "deserve" the sympathies of the public or the criminal justice pro-cess, because she has transcended respectable behavior—irrespective of how seriously she has been victimized.

If the authorities are serious about tackling the exploitation of women by men, there are many measures through which they could tackle the more endemic and widespread problem, such as taking women seriously when they report sexual assaults to the police or following up reports of threaten-ing behavior, as was discussed earlier. For, as Phoenix and Oerton (2005) so eloquently surmise, "if rape and sexual assault are a 'fate worse than death,' then it is incumbent upon the government to intervene in the lives of individ-uals so as to prevent the social death of its citizenry." Instead, police activity has focused on low-level, visible sex work—further marginalizing the tar-geted "victim." Although the numbers of recorded solicitations of women by men have fallen by 35% in recent years, soliciting still constitutes a con-siderable bulk of policing activity according to Home Office statistics (see Figure 16.1). By contrast, despite the push played out in the media to address the exploitation of prostitution and TfSE, police activity relating to prostitu-tion appears to be largely concentrated on the street, and directed toward the women themselves and their customers (although the trend does appear to diminishing—see Figure 16.1).

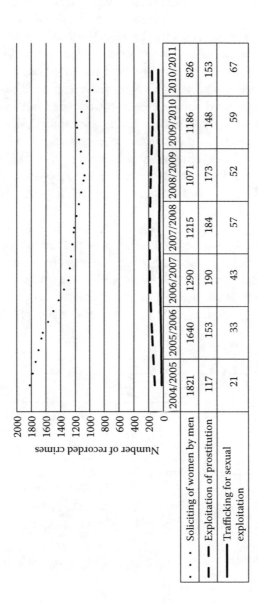

	2004/2005	2005/2006	2006/2007	2007/2008	2008/2009	2009/2010	2010/2011
Soliciting of women by men	1821	1640	1290	1215	1071	1186	826
Exploitation of prostitution	117	153	190	184	173	148	153
Trafficking for sexual exploitation	21	33	43	57	52	59	67

Figure 16.1 Recorded crime statistics 2004–2010. (Data extracted from Home Office, A summary of recorded crime data from 2002-03 to 2011-12, 2012. Retrieved November 5, 2012 from http://www.homeoffice.gov.uk/publications/science-research-statistics/research-statistics/crime-research/historical-crime-data/rec-crime-2003-2012.)

Brothel keeping, by contrast, does not appear to have any available data for initially recorded crime—perhaps the charges are made after further investigation, when TfSE charges are not possible—but the process is not clear. However, in 2009, there were 59 recorded offenses relating to TfSE and 30 went to trial. In the same year, 29 cases of brothel keeping were brought to trial (possibly the remainder of the group were initially arrested under TfSE charges). If this assumption were the case, the results would accord with some of the evidence the author has established while attending trials and piecing together information relating to several specific cases. At various points between arrest and appearance in court, defendants apprehended under serious allegations of trafficking (under sections 57 and 58 of the Sexual Offences Act, 2003) frequently have their charges downgraded, following a guilty plea for a lesser charge, "plea-bargaining," or lack of evidence. While plea-bargaining is not formally acknowledged in the criminal courts of England and Wales, there is much evidence that it does take place (see, e.g., Lea et al., 2003) (Figure 16.2).

The information in Figure 16.2 depicts the progress of three offenses through the CJS in 2009. Despite the unclear routes through which brothel keeping has emerged into the trial process, the rates of conviction in 2009 are similar (82%), when compared to TfSE (80%) and the exploitation of prostitution (92%) from trial to conviction, although it is unclear why three offenders convicted of an offense as serious as TfSE would not be sentenced to custody.

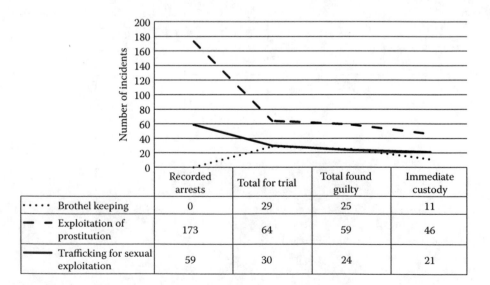

	Recorded arrests	Total for trial	Total found guilty	Immediate custody
····· Brothel keeping	0	29	25	11
− − Exploitation of prostitution	173	64	59	46
——— Trafficking for sexual exploitation	59	30	24	21

Figure 16.2 Progress of brothel keeping, exploitation of prostitution, and trafficking for sexual exploitation through CJS, in 2009. (Data extracted from Ministry of Justice, Table S2.1 (A) Defendants tried and/or sentenced at the Crown Court by offence, sex, and result.)

What is most astonishing, when looking at the aforementioned data, is the comparatively low conviction rate for the exploitation of prostitution. As already discussed, if police are really aiming to protect women from exploitation (which is much more endemic than trafficking), they should arguably concentrate more effort than they currently are, in seeking justice for women in *all* exploitative situations, including sexual assault. The data become more interesting when they are broken down by the sex of the offender, as can be seen in Figure 16.3.

Unlike most other crimes, especially those that fall within the Sexual Offences Act (2003), the conviction rates for men and women are similar for the crimes of brothel keeping (12:13) and the exploitation of prostitution (29:30). These findings are important for a number of reasons: first, it has been established that the position of exploited women is tenuous—their "victimhood" is subjected to scrupulous examination (Meloy & Miller, 2010). In these cases, it is almost impossible to distinguish between male and female exploiters, when we know that women are significantly more likely to be exploited by men; secondly, representing women as equally culpable as exploiters serves to further protect men's power and privilege, by failing to recognize "gender" and victims' experiences of sexual violation and criminal justice (Phoenix & Oerton, 2005) at all; finally, if the law has established that brothel keeping, the exploitation of prostitution, and TfSE are serious crimes that are equally committed by men and women, and that they are equally heinous, it continues to even further obscure the imbalance of sexual, social, and symbolic powers that those very laws aim to address. In other words, the

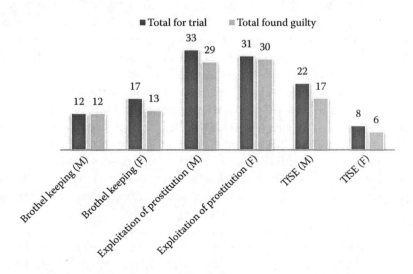

Figure 16.3 Variation between males and females, 2009. (Data extracted from Ministry of Justice, Table S2.1 (A) Defendants tried and/or sentenced at the Crown Court by offence, sex, and result.)

successful police activity, the trial process, and the convictions have served to further exclude and demonize women, rather than highlight the ease with which the endemic, proliferate, and successful exploitation of women by men continues.

Redefining the Stereotypical Victim

The next part of the discussion aims to examine some examples of the type of case that might come to contribute to the statistics presented in the previous section. As discussed, some roles cannot be molded into the fixed identity of offender or victim, and it appears that the prosecution and trial process may exacerbate and further damage opportunities for "justice." If initial allegations as well as their moral character can be used against the "victim" in court, their credibility is nullified. The following cases took place during the previous 5 years. The events are not related and are not generalizable. What connects them is the nature of the *transformation* that took place in regard to the status of the presenting "victim" and the alleged offender.

Case Studies

In a 2008 trial (Cambridge Crown Court), a complainant (Latvian female, aged 26) accused a man called Kalva* of taking her to a house where a group of men raped her. However, despite evidence of a violent and brutal sexual assault, which the complainant claimed he facilitated and encouraged, the charges brought against him were under section 57 (trafficking within the United Kingdom for sexual exploitation) of the Sexual Offences Act, 2003. As part of the defense, the court learned that the complainant had asked Kalva to help her come to England to find work, which he did. He paid for her travel to England and for accommodation in a small English town, and he found her work in a factory. He helped her open a bank account and took her passport, stating that he would keep it for insurance until she had paid off her debt to him. She was thus completely dependent upon him. Although the causes to which these practices have been attributed, such as poverty, lack of sustainable livelihoods, structural inequities in society, and gender discrimination are not necessarily causes in themselves, they do exacerbate the vulnerability of marginalized and disadvantaged groups, thus exposing them to further harm (Sanghera, 2005). However, Kalva was charged with trafficking the complainant *within* the United Kingdom for sexual exploitation. The trial rested on the fact that he *drove her* to the house where she claimed she

---

* Her alleged trafficker—a fellow Latvian who had helped her come to the UK and found her a job.

had been raped (not sexually exploited) and that he waited in another room while the men drugged and raped her. The complainant revealed that she had previously been "sold" as a sex worker in Latvia, but it is unclear what bearing such revelations had on the case in question, except to bring doubt into the minds of the jury as to *her* reliability in this setting. If it is revealed at trial that the victim had previous encounters with the law, or that they have attempted to conceal something that may be relevant to their case (such as having worked as a prostitute), they are exposed as a fraud—unreliable and deceitful; thus, the complainant's character was damaged by reference to her previous work as a prostitute, rendering her account unreliable. A local newspaper printed comments from the prosecution:

> The indication as far as she was concerned was that she was to come here to get work, but the woman was *'no goody two-shoes … [s]he has had a rough life. She comes from a rough place'*. In the past, she has been sold for sex, and it seems Mr Kalva was aware of this background. (*Peterborough News*, 2008)

This "background" defined the victim in the eyes of the jury, the judge, the prosecution, and the media—and the case collapsed.

In a separate trial (2005, Cambridge Crown Court) under section 57, in which the Russian complainant *failed* to acknowledge her past, the presiding judge stated "she dishonestly and persistently stuck to her assertion she had never previously been a prostitute, but there has now been incontrovertible evidence that her assertion is wholly untrue." Directing not guilty verdicts, he said that because the complainant had been proved a liar on that point, it would be difficult to be sure if she was telling the truth on other issues. Her barrister and the police confirmed that the woman had been "manifestly and wholly discredited." Following this ruling, four Albanian defendants were cleared of most charges (of trafficking the Russian woman within the United Kingdom for sexual exploitation, of inciting her into prostitution for gain, rape, sexual assault, making a threat to kill, and theft). These cases illustrate the precarious position that a woman who has a history of sex work can find herself in, should she complain—either about her working conditions or of rape. Added to these problems are the other potential illegalities of the trafficked/exploited person, such as their age, their status within the country, which may be undocumented, their colleagues or peers may be engaging in illegal activities (Sanghera, 2005), as well as the language barriers that can arise in police questioning and the trial itself. All of these additional issues can be barriers to justice, as they can exacerbate a woman's deviance. Furthermore, a considerable gap exists between the demand-driven phenomenon and the intervention strategies proposed (rescue, repatriation, rehabilitation, and prevention, as well as exploring options for legal employment) within England and Wales. When a woman is "freed" or escapes from forced sex work, she is faced with a range of disagreeable prospects, such as testifying against her trafficker and making police statements, which may implicate a wide range of other people, criminal charges herself, and deportation. She is transformed simultaneously into both a victim and a criminal (Sanghera, 2005). Many women are fearful to disclose the truth about their circumstances and opt for immediate deportation, only to return and take up sex work in alternative and possibly safer environments.

By contrast, Keqi Wu (female, 2008, Cambridge Crown Court) was also charged under section 57. As the case came to trial, the trafficking charges were subsequently dropped when Ms. Wu pleaded guilty to the charge of brothel keeping. Such bargaining can frequently happen by offering defendants the opportunity to plead guilty to less serious charges, resulting in no trial (Sanders & Jones, 2007). Despite the media coverage and police claims that when they raided the brothels, they "rescued" victims of TfSE, the case was not one that ended up in the successful conviction data under sections 57 or 58. Indeed, the author witnessed Ms. Wu's barrister describe her client as "so cute," as the defendant awaited her sentence. The media headline that detailed the conviction ran "Masseuse who ran a brothel from a city flat has been jailed for a total of 15 months" (*Cambridge Evening News*, 2008). Roger Harrison, representing Ms. Wu, told the court: "These were free, adult women ... There was no question of exploitation here. These were independent, free adults happy to perform the services they did and the businesses were, partly, developed through the insistence of the clients" (*Cambridge Evening News*, 2008). Wu's case (where it was established that no one was exploited or assaulted) resulted in a conviction (of brothel keeping)—one of the success stories outlined in the previous section. By contrast, the two cases where extensive violence, assault, kidnapping, rape, and exploitation of women *were* an established element of the prosecution—no conviction was achieved. Furthermore, of the three cases, the only defendant successfully convicted was a woman. In addition, Keqi Wu was subsequently forced to hand over £46,000 through a confiscation order. Under the proceeds of crime law, the police are permitted to keep 50% of the assets confiscated during raids and 25% from subsequent prosecutions, with the CPS keeping another 25% and the Inland Revenue the rest—arguably a strong financial incentive to pursue some cases over others.

The following two cases are similar, in that the women involved were both charged with crimes related to brothel keeping. In 2009, Hanna Morris called the police when two armed men entered a flat used by her escort agency, threw petrol around and threatened to set fire to the premises, which were occupied at the time. Although Ms. Morris helped the police with their investigation, and the men responsible were identified, the case against them was dropped, and instead Ms. Morris was charged with managing/keeping a brothel. Despite requests for the prosecution to be dropped, it proceeded to court and Ms. Morris was found guilty, given a 12-month suspended sentence, and ordered to carry out 240 h of unpaid work (Caulfield, 2011). In subsequent discussions, observers have agreed that such prosecutions are detrimental in a number of ways: first, they are "completely contrary to the stated aims of trying to improve the safety of sex workers" (English Collective of Prostitutes [ECP], 2011); they are likely to promote the message of impunity to would-be attackers, thereby increasing the dangers for women working as prostitutes; they could directly discourage the reporting of crimes against potentially vulnerable women; and the threat of serious violent victimization played second fiddle to the pursuance of crimes that are arguably less heinous. Hanna Morris's case is not unique. Similarly, in 2005, Ms. Sheila Farmer (ECP, 2011) was robbed at gunpoint in the flat she shared with other women sex workers. Despite receiving death threats and a petrol bomb attack, she pursued her complaint to the police, and subsequently gave evidence at her attackers' trial, where the judged commended her for her bravery (Farmer, 2012). However, following the trial, the police prosecuted Ms. Farmer for brothel keeping, despite evidence that the women who worked there shared the costs equally, and that she is seriously ill with a malignant brain tumor. Aside from monetary gain from crime proceeds—"legalised pimping" (Farmer, 2012)—the lasting benefits that are achieved by such aggressive policing are perfidious if the police are serious about protecting vulnerable women. Ms. Farmer's case was dismissed from court in 2012, allegedly due to lack of evidence— a full 7 years after her initial complaint to the police, and 18 months after the launch of a campaign to raise awareness of her position, a campaign that arguably had the potential to "open a can of worms" for the authorities (Farmer, 2012).

Farmer's case was dismissed, but prosecutions do not have to end with convictions of women who fail to adhere to acceptable moral identities. In 2010, a jury cleared Claire Finch of running a brothel—a decision described by some sections of the media as throwing Britain's "antiquated" prostitution laws into confusion. Finch admitted offering topless massages with "happy endings" in a small Bedfordshire village. Up to four women worked from her home, offering a range of massage and sexual services. There was no trafficking, coercion, drugs, or underage girls involved, and no public nuisance caused (as with Farmer and Morris). Indeed, two of Finch's neighbors—one a woman of 85—gave evidence on her behalf. Ms. Finch told the court that she wanted to work with other women for the sake of "safety" (as in the case of Sheila Farmer) and "camaraderie." Ms. Finch denied keeping a brothel and was unanimously cleared by the jury (Finch, 2010). This small victory has yet to make a dent in the continued criminal procedures that either actively pursue convictions of marginalized women or neglect their calls for help and protection.

The identity of who is the victim and who is the perpetrator in these types of cases has become even cloudier as a result of the criminal proceedings, and few "victims" appear to have benefitted from the decisions made. As a result of the "justice" process, the victims in these cases have become less obvious, nonexistant in legal terms. Further, "perpetrators" have been recast due to the collapse of their trials. In the aforementioned cases, if the female presents as a victim, either she was recast as a criminal or she "contributed" to the dismissal of her own case due to her sexual aggressiveness—exposed as a fraud—unreliable and deceitful. Obviously, these cases are not generalizable, but they do raise a number of important issues, which deserve further examination.

Recasting the Roles of Victim and Offender

The aforementioned cases have illustrated how victims and offenders can assume conflicting and undeserving identities as they progress through the criminal justice process, as well as the failure of the process itself. Kearon and Godfrey (2007) have alluded to the "confused and contradictory position that victims have offered as both symbolic and real actors in the detection and prosecution of crime and in the public conception of the crime 'problem.'" The victim's circumstances may shift through place and time, but such a transformation of their *standing* occurs in no greater area than as a result of the criminal justice process, through which *justice* is sought. This chapter has demonstrated that alongside the emergence of the *symbolic power* of the victim, we have also seen the (re-)emergence of real, complex, contradictory, and often politically *inconvenient* victims of crime. The inconvenient victim is "emerging as a real actor in critical debates about crime in contemporary society and (increasingly) in the operation of criminal justice...." (Kearon & Godfrey, 2007). The rigidly defined roles of the symbolic victim and the symbolic offender are contributing to the downfall of the credibility of the justice process as it currently stands. In their eagerness to secure a conviction, to be *seen* to be correct, some of the most important issues are being overlooked by our justice gatekeepers, such as justice itself for victims of crime; acknowledgment of wrongdoing; protection from violence; and understanding gendered imbalances of power and exploitation. In short, the enforcement of the law still protects and upholds the position of the righteous male from "beguiling Eve." The idea of an "accurate victimology" is not possible, unless it is taken as an attempt to "get nearer" to the experiences of neglected victims. Although criticism for the continuing false distinction between "victims" and "offenders" and the refusal to acknowledge the overlap between these two groups is not new (Newburn & Stanko, 1994), it still remains a relatively low priority for many. While the justice process is dominated by the aggressive prosecution and punishment of offending behavior instead of attending to the needs of all victims, the victim will remain an idealistic and near-impossible concept.

The moral and judicial response to women who betray signs of "other" or so-called masculine features is not new, and considerable literature is available that examines the concept of the "doubly-deviant, doubly-damned" (Kennedy, 1992; Lloyd, 1995) woman. But from time to time, women's behavior takes a peculiar position in the public's attention, and serves to reinforce political agendas, moral lessons, and family values—whipping up moral panics about unruly, out-of-control women. Goode and Ben-Yehuda (2009) list "five crucial elements or criteria of moral panic: concern; hostility; consensus; disproportionality; and volatility," which have all been applicable to sensational stories about "other," unusual women and the *dangers* that they can present—threatening the ordinary man's blame-free position. Levi (2009) suggests that there are various ways in which "moral entrepreneurs" (e.g., the police, media, and judiciary) can combine to prioritize their preferred panics over other potential contenders, such as "social entrepreneurs"—women actively working in the sex industry. Through the vehicle of moral panic, the media, police, and judiciary have consciously (or "unwittingly") engineered an impenetrable program that encourages the judicial system to focus its attention on the *singular nature* of some women, while requisitioning everything else about them to the legal test— their demands, their victimization, their entrepreneurship, their choices, and their powerlessness. It is also possible to condemn these legal responses as "panicking-for-profit" (Levi, 2009), bearing in mind the funds seized through asset recovery and the proceeds of crime. Yet, as Levi warns, this model neglects the fact that "too much" fear undermines perceptions of the competence of politicians, the police, and the security services, and currently, the media is content to support the hype surrounding raids on brothels and the further criminalization of women who profit from the sale of sex. Cohen's (1972) construction of moral panic involves a public resentment that is whipped up by the media and bureaucratic, cultural/ideological, economic, and personal interests that happen to coincide (see Levi, 2009 for an elaboration, applied to white-collar crime). One of the best approaches to successfully achieving suspicious objectives is to incite publicity through the media, thus enhancing their image and success. The media stories that detail major crackdowns on brothels *reassure* the public and the politicians, regardless of whether the arrests amount to anything. Moreover, stories that expose women who lie about their sexual victimization, comfort the public in the knowledge that if liars are punished, innocents must be safe and justice must be working for truthful, *real* victims. What is clear is that a woman may be gauged by her morals should she find herself in a situation whereby her character is deemed an important part of an investigation. Fortunately, the CPS recently (Booth, 2011) announced that human trafficking victims will not be treated as criminals—a peculiar and anomalous target that belies the attitudes of the CPS toward victims who do not fit the stereotype. A recent headline in a Singapore news outlet, *Asia One* (2011), sums up confused and complicated current attitudes— "Victim turned human trafficker sentenced to 10 years in prison"—no longer a victim, forever a criminal. Our twenty-first-century courtrooms, despite all their emphasis on evidence and due process, do not have the capacity to recognize and acknowledge a victim of exploitation, unless they can be found to be legally blameless. This incapacity to recognize the suffering of others has been described by Weisstub (1986) as a moral lacuna, and likened to psychopathy—the inability to experience what the other side is feeling, "a disengagement of the human self from the objects of their victimizing behaviours". While the justice system continues to define certain groups as lacking in capacity, thus supporting the legal and political "syndrome of the psychopathic lacuna" (Weisstub, 1986), the gates of justice will remain firmly closed to those whose account of suffering is based on the misbehavior of men.

Traditionally, the term *victim* has been "viewed as the 'sufferer' in a simple 'doer-sufferer' model of criminal interaction" (Miers, 1978), but after more than half a century of academic interest and understanding, the treatment of victims is still weak at best, and outright disgraceful in some cases. Women's position in the informal economy is hidden, stigmatized, and difficult to measure (Davies, 2011), but unless we make some attempts to recognize and make sense of the veneers that women have constructed in order to maintain their dignity and social identity, they will continue to be demonized, and the female folk-devil will prevail. As Oscar Wilde (1905) so poignantly recognized, as he served a sentence for "gross indecency between men," "most people are other people." The position of the female victim has been contested and realigned for many years. However, her status as a victim still rests heavily upon her own demeanour. A woman raped may be *a fate worse than death*, but there is nothing more wicked that a woman can do against her husband than *to claim rape*. In a barmy world where sexual abuse and the exploitation of women is endemic, yet almost impossible to prove on an individual level, beguiling "Eve" is presented as more dangerous than her male counterpart—whatever *his* name is.

References

Asia One. (2011). Victim turned human trafficker sentenced to 10 years in prison. July 4.

Askola, H. (2007). *Legal Responses to Trafficking in Women for Sexual Exploitation in the European Union.* Oxford: Hart Publishing.

BBC News. (2010). Wife of Clarence Thomas asks Anita Hill to apologise. Retrieved on October 20, 2010, from http://www.bbc.co.uk/news/world-us-canada-11580897.

Booth, R. (2011). Human trafficking victims will not be treated as criminals, says CPS. *The Guardian*, Sunday July 3.

Brock, D. (1994). *The Real Anita Hill: The Untold Story.* New York: Touchstone Publishing.

Cambridge Evening News. (2008). Woman who ran brothels is jailed for 15 months. July 8, 2008. Retrieved on June 15, 2012, from http://www.cambridge-news.co.uk/Home/Woman-who-ran-brothels-is-jailed-for-15-months.htm.

Carlson, M. (2001). Smearing Anita Hill: A writer confesses. *Time.* Retrieved on June 15, 2012, from http://www.time.com/time/nation/article/0,8599,167355,00.html.

Caulfield, C. (2011). Suspended sentences for brothel trio. *Getsurrey* online. Retrieved on June 15, 2012, from http://www.getsurrey.co.uk/news/s/2090564_suspended_sentences_for_brothel_trio.

Christie, N. (1986). The ideal victim. In Fattah, E. (ed.), *From Crime Policy to Victim Policy: Reorienting the Justice System* (pp. 17–30). Basingstoke, Hampshire: Macmillan Press.

Cohen, S. (1972). *Folk Devils and Moral Panics.* Oxford: Blackwell.

Cohen, S. (1979). Guilt, justice and tolerance. In Downes, D. & Rock, P. (eds), *Deviant Interpretations.* Oxford: Martin Robertson.

CPS. (2009). *CPS Policy for Prosecuting Cases of Rape.* Retrieved from http://www.cps.gov.uk/publications/prosecution/rape.html.

Das, B. B. (1997). *Victims in the Criminal Justice System.* New Delhi: APH Publishing.

Dasgupta, R., & Murthy, L. (2009). Figure it out: Reporting on trafficking in women. Infochange News and Features. Retrieved on June 15, 2012, from http://www.infochangeindia.org/media/related-analysis/figure-it-out-reporting-on-trafficking-in-women.html.

Davies, N. (2009). Inquiry fails to find single trafficker who forced anybody into prostitution. *The Guardian*, October 20. Retrieved on June 15, 2012, from http://www.guardian.co.uk/uk/2009/oct/20/government-trafficking-enquiry-fails.

Davies, P. (2011). *Gender, Crime and Victimization.* London: Sage.

English Collective of Prostitutes (ECP). (2011). Delay to abuse of process case. Retrieved on June 15, 2012, from http://www.prostitutescollective.net/Hanna_Morris_PR.htm.

Farmer, S. (2012). Life is hard enough for prostitutes without our work being criminalised. *The Guardian*, January 6.

Fattah, E. A. (1991). *Understanding Criminal Victimization.* Scarborough, ON: Prentice Hall.

Finch, C. (2010). Experience: I ran a brothel in a country village. *The Guardian*, June 5.

Gilbert, A., & Moore, C. (2010). Human trafficking in the United Kingdom: The journey so far and the road ahead. *The Criminal Lawyer*, 194, 2–4.

Goode, E., & Ben-Yehuda, N. (2009). *Moral Panics: The Social Construction of Deviance*, 2nd edn. Malden, MA: Wiley Blackwell.

Gottfredson, M. R. (1984). Victims of crime: The dimensions of risk. Home Office Research and Planning Unit, UK.

Hirsch, A. (2010). The idea that we are faced with the mutually exclusive objectives of protecting victims of rape and the innocent is false. *The Guardian*, November 26.

Home Office. (1986). Violence against Women Home Office Circular 69/1986. Home Office, London.

Home Office. (2012). A summary of recorded crime data from 2002-03 to 2011-12. Retrieved on November 5, 2012, from http://www.homeoffice.gov.uk/publications/science-research-statistics/research-statistics/crime-research/historical-crime-data/rec-crime-2003-2012.

Kearon, T., & Godfrey, B. S. (2007). Setting the scene: A question of history. In Walklate, S. (ed.), *Handbook on Victims and Victimology* (pp. 17–36). Cullompton: Willan.

Kennedy, H. (1992). *Eve Was Framed: Women and British Justice*. London: Vintage.

Latour, B. (2005). *Reassembling the Social: An Introduction to Actor-Network Theory*. Oxford: Oxford University Press.

Lea, S., Lanvers, U., & Shaw, S. (2003). Attrition in rape cases. *British Journal of Criminology, 43*, 583–599.

Levi, M. (2009). Suite revenge? The shaping of folk devils and moral panics about white-collar crimes. *British Journal of Criminology, 49*, 48–67.

Lloyd, A. (1995). *Doubly Deviant, Doubly Damned: Society's Treatment of Violent Women*. London: Penguin.

Mai, N. (2010). Migrant workers in the UK sex industry. Institute for the Study of European Transformations, London Metropolitan University.

Markovska, A., & Moore, C. (2008). Stilettos and steel toe-caps: Legislation of human trafficking and sexual exploitation, and its enforcement in the UK and Ukraine. In van Duyne, P., Harvey, J., Maljevic, A., von Lampe, K., & Scheinost, M. (eds), *European Crime-Markets at Cross-Roads: Extended and Extending Criminal Europe* (pp. 121–150). Nijmegen: Wolf Legal Publishers.

Mawby, R., & Gill, M. (1987). *Crime Victims: Needs, Services and the Voluntary Sector*. London: Tavistock.

Mawby, R., & Walklate, S. (1994). *Critical Victimology*. London: Sage.

Meloy, M., & Miller, S. (2010). *The Victimization of Women: Law, Policies and Politics*. Oxford: Oxford University Press.

Miers, D. (1978). *Responses to Victimization: A Comparative Study of Compensation for Criminal Violence in Great Britain and Ontario*. Abingdon: Professional Books.

Mythen, G. (2007). Cultural victimology: Are we all victims now? In Walklate, S. (ed.), *Handbook on Victims and Victimology* (pp. 464–483). Cullompton: Willan.

Newburn, T., & Stanko, E. (1994). *Just Boys Doing Business*. Abingdon: Routledge.

Newstead, S. (2010). The family of a Carlisle woman jailed for three years for faking a sex attack have vowed to fight to clear her name "if it takes forever". *Cumberland News*, July 16.

Phoenix, J., & Oerton, S. (2005). *Illicit and Illegal: Sex, Regulation and Social Control*. Cullompton: Willan.

Pidd, H. (2010). I accused my husband of rape. I was locked up—and he was set free. *The Guardian*, November 26.

Rock, P. (2007). Theoretical perspectives on victimization. In Walklate, S. (ed.), *Handbook on Victims and Victimology* (pp. 37–61). Cullompton: Willan.

Ryan, W. (1971). *Blaming the Victim*. New York: Vintage.

Sampson, R. J., & Lauritsen, J. L. (1990). Deviant lifestyles, proximity to crime, and the offender–victim link in personal violence. *Journal of Research in Crime Delinquency, 27*, 110–139.

Sanders, A., & Jones, I. (2007). The victim in court. In Walklate, S. (ed.), *Handbook on Victims and Victimology* (pp. 282–308). Cullompton: Willan.

Sanghera, J. (2005). Unpacking the trafficking discourse. In Kempadoo, K. (ed.), *Trafficking and Prostitution Reconsidered: New Perspectives on Migration, Sex Work, and Human Rights* (pp. 3–24). Boulder, CO: Paradigm Publishers.

Savill, R. (2006). Ex-wife who made false rape claims faces prison. *The Telegraph*, September 30, 2006.

Sen, A. (2006). *Identity and Violence: The Illusion of Destiny*. New York: W. W. Norton.

Smith, J. (1996). *Misogynies*. London: Vintage.

Swaine, J. (2011). Dominique Strauss-Kahn maid files civil suit. *The Telegraph*, August 9. Retrieved on June 15, 2012, from http://www.telegraph.co.uk/finance/dominique-strauss-kahn/8690122/Dominique-Strauss-Kahn-maid-files-civil-suit.html.

Turvey, B., & McGrath, M. (2011). False allegations of sexual assault. In Savino, J. & Turvey, B. (eds), *Rape Investigation Handbook*, 2nd Edition (pp. 269–292). San Diego: Elsevier.

von Hentig, H. (1948). *The Criminal and His Victim*. New York: Schocken Books.

Weisstub, D. (1986). Victims of crime in the criminal justice system. In Fattah, E. (ed.), *From Crime Policy to Victim Policy: Reorienting the Justice System* (pp. 191–209). Basingstoke, Hampshire: Macmillan Press.

Wilde, O. (1905). De Profundis, p. 870, in *The Works of Oscar Wilde* (1990). Leicester: Blitz Editions.

Extending the Logic of Functional Explanations 17
A Theoretical Model to Explain the Victimization Process during an Indian Witch Hunt

SOMA CHAUDHURI

Contents

Introduction

Although the execution of women as witches in Europe and the American colonies, commonly referred to as "the early modern witch craze," ended in the 1700s, some women continue to be labeled and accused as witches in India and other developing nations. According to Federici (2010), a UN report stated that about 25,000 witch killings were recorded in India between 1987 and 2003. It is agreed that the actual figure is much higher, as some incidents (such as those among the workers in the Jalpaiguri tea plantations) rarely appear in the Indian statistics on witch hunts, and that many more women were "tortured, maimed, traumatized for life" (Federici, 2010, p. 13). Over the past few decades, local newspapers in India have reported incidents of witch-hunting at a fluctuating pace. Though the idea of witchcraft accusations seems shocking to most urban, educated Indians, the phenomenon is common among the tribal (*adivasi*) regions in India, such as Bihar, Chhattisgarh, Orissa, Rajasthan, and Jharkhand. While some states have passed anti-witch-hunting legislation, such as Bihar in 1999, Jharkhand in 2001, and Chhattisgarh in 2005, few perpetrators have been brought to justice (Federici, 2010).

In this chapter, I refer to a single case of a witch hunt that took place a few years ago in a tea plantation labor village in the Jalpaiguri district of West Bengal, to develop a theoretical framework that will be useful to understand the witch hunt. I call this village Chandmoni Tea Estate, a fictitious name, given to protect the participants in the study. Further, while narrating the events of the case, I use pseudonyms for the names of people to protect their identities. The inhabitants of this village are *adivasi* tea plantation workers. This migrant *adivasi* population, known as the *Madesia* (people from the middle country), and their descendants currently constitute about 90% of the total workforce in the Dooars tea region. They were brought in from the neighboring state of West Bengal, during the setting up of the first plantations in the region by the colonial owners. Since the local population at the time (*bhumiputras*) resisted working in the plantations as wage laborers, the colonial planters organized the migration of *adivasi* workers from the *Madesia* through *sardars* (middlemen). Family migration was particularly encouraged to ensure a steady supply of labor throughout the years. The planters ruled with the philosophy of isolation and segregation over the *adivasi* workers, a policy that blended well with the global economy of plantation work. However, for the *adivasi* workers, plantation work and their identity as wage earners kept them alienated from the outside plantation population, an identity that continues today and is tied to current plantation politics (Bhowmik, 1981, 2011; Chatterjee, 2001; Dasgupta & Khan, 1983).

The goal of this chapter is not to develop a theoretical model of witchcraft accusations that is applicable across all countries and all communities. Such an attempt would be problematic, particularly given the diversity and the complexity of the communities and time periods where and when the witch hunts are taking place. Instead, the goal of this chapter is to present a theoretical model that works best toward explaining the incident at Chandmoni Tea Estate.

Five Witches and a Jackfruit Tree: Chandmoni Tea Estate 2002

Chandmoni tea garden is located almost 50 miles from the local police station and about 200 miles from the district capital. The plantation is located in the belt of two national parks and is composed of workers from the *Munda*,

Santhal, and *Oraon adivasi* groups. In April 2002, the labor lines were under attack from malaria and diarrhea epidemics, two diseases that are not uncommon in these areas. The Chandmoni plantation has a resident *janguru,* who is both the local priest and the medicine man for the labor lines. The plantation has a government health center that is dysfunctional, and the nearest health center with a doctor is 100 miles away.

Toward the end of July 2002, a driver in the tea estate, 30-year-old Anil, complained of stomach pains. Anil's family, led by his brother (Suresh), consulted the local *janguru* (Hariram) to find a cure for his illness. Hariram prescribed some herbs to calm the stomach pains. When the pains became severe and the *janguru* (male, mid-50s, plantation worker) was unable to cure him, Anil was sent to the hospital. Anil died the next day of an undiagnosed illness. After his death, his family members, headed by his brother, went to the local governing body in the village and expressed concern that Anil could have died from witchcraft. Almost all the villagers in the labor lines (approximately 250 people) attended the meeting. At the meeting, Suresh expressed concern that there was more to Anil's illness than "natural causes." The meeting with the *gram panchayat* was crucial to getting the entire village involved. The village was already under stress caused by the malaria and diarrhea epidemics, and thus it was easy to get the support of the villagers for a witch hunt. Hariram was present at the village meeting.

During the village meeting, it was decided that the local *janguru* would use his powers to uncover what was behind the death of Anil. Suresh decided to pay for the rituals. After a day of rituals that involved animal sacrificing (fowl) and feasting, the *janguru* declared that five women (all between the ages of 40 and 75 years) had used witchcraft and were behind the unusual death of Anil and the increase in the malaria and diarrhea epidemics in the village. The accused women were Atashi, Binshu, Dhanni, Sanchari, and Manshi. The five women identified by the *janguru* as *dains* (witches) were women who were either widows or married, living with husbands, daughters, sons, daughters-in-law, and grandchildren. Thus, they were not destitute women without families. The accused women were employed in the tea plantations as workers or were former employees of the plantation, and all of them lived in the village. They were neighbors, acquaintances, and friends of Anil and his family and were not random strangers who were accused.

The witch hunt of the five women took place in the following week after Anil's death, on a late Friday afternoon, after the tea plantation had closed for the weekend and the managers and supervisors had left for the city. At around ten o'clock in the evening, a group of 30 people, mostly men, went to the houses of the 5 women and dragged them out. The group was led by two men: Lakhan and Buddhiram. Buddhiram had a dispute with one of the accused women's husband. This group was supported by the rest of the village (around 200 people), who prevented the families of the accused women from resisting the attackers. The women were dragged to a small, open courtyard, which had a jackfruit tree right in the middle of it. The children used this area as a playground, and the courtyard was surrounded by huts on all sides. The accused women were tied to the tree one at a time. Their ordeal would continue over the next 2 days. The rest of the villagers kept vigil over the family members of the accused women. When some of the family members of the accused women tried to escape from the village to inform the police, the rest of the villagers prevented them, using threats and physical assault.

Hariram, Suresh, Lakhan, and Buddhiram supervised the witch hunt. Initially, the women were beaten and hit with stones. The first to die was Dhanni (mid-70s, survived by her husband, children, and grandchildren). For the remaining four women, the torture continued until late Sunday evening. The women had nails driven into their forehead to rid the village of the spirits. They were stripped and then beaten with *lathis* and iron rods at regular intervals. Throughout Saturday and Sunday, the *janguru*, who was at the center of the "witch-hunt ritual," held *pujas* in front of the jackfruit tree. At one point, one of the women had a "crucifixion" ceremony to "please" the Christians among the villagers. Throughout the weekend, the villagers kept a tight vigil over the families of the accused women.

On Sunday evening, the murders began. The surviving women had their limbs severed before finally succumbing to their injuries. The bodies of the five women were then hacked into several pieces and thrown into the nearby river. On Monday, the villagers returned to their work at the plantation as if nothing had happened; the families of the murdered women were too scared to report the witch hunt to the plantation management or the police. By Wednesday, the people from the neighboring villages began to find pieces of human limbs and torsos in the river. The police were informed and, by the end of Thursday, over 40 people had been arrested on charges of the murder, physical assault, and torture of the five women. The management of the tea plantation at Chandmoni was unaware of the witch hunt until they were informed by the police.

Critique of Previous Explanations of Witch Hunts and the Need to Revisit Theories of Witch Hunts

Sociological understandings of witch hunts have focused on premodern European and colonial American witch hunts to provide most of the explanations for why witch hunts occur in some societies (Sundar, 2001). Perhaps most popular are the feminist explanations of witch hunts that frame witch hunts as gendered violence, where men target women in power. Power, here, could be manifested in economic wealth, spiritually, or through social positions. For example, Karlsen (1998) argues that New England's system of inheritance (in colonial America) was a major factor in targeting women as witches. Most accused women had no legitimate male heirs in their immediate families and therefore were in a position to inherit or did inherit the property left by their father or husband. These women were thus *aberrations* in a society that had an inheritance system designed to keep property in the hands of men. Similarly, Barstow (1995) attributes witch hunts to competition between men and women during the changing economic and political conditions in premodern Europe. The witch hunts took place at the same time as colonization and the slave trade, and according to Barstow (1995), all three were made possible by the same "ecclesiastical policies and legal changes." Women, slaves, and natives were all objects of exploitation. The witch craze in Europe helped in reinforcing the traditions of misogyny and patriarchal control and demonized the image of the woman (Barstow, 1995, p. 13).

Religious explanations of witch hunts were also popular in explaining the colonial American hunts. Puritans viewed witches as doubly wicked: witches were not only threats to their neighbors' physical and economic well-being, but they were also heretics. Witchcraft was thus viewed as a rebellion against God. The constant fear in New England society was the devil's success in recruiting people to help destroy Puritan churches. The witch in New England was a human with superhuman powers. Foremost among these was her ability to perform "maleficium," that is, to cause harm to others by supernatural means (Karlsen, 1998). Similarly, women healers, who helped during illnesses and childbirth procedures, were common targets during witch hunts. Barstow (1994) writes that a typical witch in Europe was a woman who possessed the power of healing, a power that everyone believed was also the power to kill.

Though gendered explanations of witch hunts were popular (and still are today) among scholars studying the European and colonial American hunts, in the 1960s there arose a need to advocate a global perspective in the study of witchcraft and witch hunts, especially by European historians who acknowledged the importance of research on witch hunts in the developing world. In the last three decades of the twentieth century, most of the research on witch hunts was carried out in the African nations by white Western historians who were driven by a need to understand the newly independent modern states (Hutton, 2002). Hutton goes on to argue that toward the end of the twentieth century, the focus on African communities in witch hunt research was reversed. There arose an abundance of scholarly work by historians on the European and colonial American witch hunts. Although much of this research on colonial and European hunts consists of a close study of a single case or community, Hutton criticizes this research as it rarely studies data outside the Western world. He considers the colonial witch persecutions as "trivial affairs" when the duration and the number of victims are considered, compared to the hunts in the non-Western world (ibid., 2002, pp. 16–17).

Hutton's reflections are perhaps not all accurate. While research on the European and colonial American hunts did increase after the 1960s, research particularly on postcolonial African witch hunts has made a strong theoretical, methodological comeback (Moore & Sanders, 2001). The contrast between the colonial and postcolonial anthropological accounts of African witch hunts lies in the way the phenomena were viewed. Previously, the hunts were studied in isolation: an exotic ritual that was studied in alienation to the sociopolitical events concurrent to the period. For instance, the entire purpose of Evans-Pritchard's (1976) work on witchcraft among the Azande was to demonstrate, through functionalist reasoning, how witchcraft beliefs led to a stabilizing influence on the moral and social system: a form of control system with a negative impact. By comparison, the postcolonial accounts of witchcraft are treated as a reaction of the traditional societies toward a changing moral, economic, and social order, where witchcraft beliefs do not disappear with the advent of modernization, but adapt, change, and reemerge in newer forms.

The divisions of disciplines, geographical areas of research, and different theoretical strands dominate the current field of witch hunts. While each perspective is an important piece of the puzzle on why witch hunts occur, there is a lack of interdisciplinary conversations on the topic. As a result, scholars and researchers of witch hunts are left with a one-sided view of the phenomena, a view that is blurred by the theoretical framework dominant in their disciplines. Despite the criticism, some scholars have been able to transcend disciplinary boundaries through historical perspectives (see, e.g., Comaroff & Comaroff, 1993; Geschiere, 1997; Skaria, 1999) toward an understanding of how witchcraft beliefs are constructed. For instance, Frankfurter (2006), in his book *Evil Incarnate*, traces the construction of evil throughout history, and in different contexts, up to the late twentieth century. His argument was that evil, moral panics, ranging from witch hunts to genocide, are a reaction to getting rid of malevolence and its followers.

In contrast to the popularity of African and Western witchcraft, the study of witchcraft accusations in India is much neglected among global scholars. Of the few studies on contemporary witchcraft accusations in India, the bulk of the research is conducted primarily by social anthropologists (see Bailey, 1992; Bosu, 2000; Carstairs, 1983; Desai, 2008; Kelkar & Nathan, 1991; Nathan et al., 1998; Sundar, 2001), where the focus is on the *adivasi* regions in central India, particularly Madhya Pradesh, Chhattisgarh, Jharkhand, Bastar, and Bihar. However, none of the aforementioned studies focus on the witch hunts among the *adivasi* migrant communities of tea plantation workers in Jalpaiguri.

Scholars studying witch hunts in contemporary India situate gendered conflict, based on myths and folklore, as the dominant reason for witchcraft accusations taking place within *adivasi* communities. This gendered conflict is then placed within property disputes, epidemics, and local politics that erupt into witchcraft accusations against local women. For instance, Barman (2002, p. 1), one of the few anthropologists studying witch hunts in contemporary West Bengal, argues that witch hunts are a form of "persecution" toward widows, who face "a condition of marginality culminating in total exclusion from society." Her analysis, based on the case study of Malda district in West Bengal, India, confirms the findings of previous works on the subject: witch hunts in India are an outcome of property disputes involving widows and husbands' kin (Chaudhuri, 1981; Kelkar & Nathan, 1991; Kelkar & Warrier, 1997; Nathan et al., 1998). The accused women are mostly childless widows, who have a life interest in lands (meaning the right to control the land and its production), which will pass on to their nearest male relative after their death. By accusing them of practicing witchcraft, these men inherit the land immediately. This persecution, according to Barman (2002), is part of a calculated assault on women's traditional rights, which results in the successful establishment of a patriarchal order that forces widows into a subordinate position to the men.

Similarly, Kelkar and Nathan (1991) link witch hunts in the *adivasi* regions of Jharkhand and West Bengal (this does not include the *adivasi* migrant labor community in tea plantations) to the land rights of the widow. The right of a widow to the property of her husband is denied, according to the *adivasi* laws, if her husband's kin are able to prove that she is a witch. Kelkar and Nathan write that *adivasi* women have limited rights over land. In the *adivasi* community of Jharkhand, land is inherited through the male lineage, while women have some, though limited rights over land. Rights over the land for women can be broadly divided into two categories: a life interest in land, which is the right to manage land and its produce; and the right to a share of the produce of the land. This second right (the right to a share of the produce) is further divided into two rights. The first is *kharposh* or a maintenance right. The second is the right to a share of the produce that maybe over the *kharposh*. For example, an unmarried daughter may have a share of the crop that she has helped to harvest. This second right is very important in poor families for their daughters, due to the lack of economic resources (Kelkar and Nathan, 1991). Kelkar and Nathan observe that the "right to a share of the produce of the land" becomes crucial during witchcraft accusations, as the land belongs to the woman and can be transferred to her husband's home. Over the years, this right changed from "rights to a land" to a mere "right to be maintained" for widows, thereby reducing it to the barest minimum possible.

The limited rights over land for *adivasi* women together with the deterioration of their land rights have also given rise to a smaller trend to increase their rights in recent times. For instance, those who do not have sons among the Santhals, Ho, and Munda groups, insist on the transfer of land rights to their daughters, whether living with them or elsewhere (Kelkar and Nathan, 1991). Despite this trend, there is a resistance to women's right to land, from both women and men, who find it difficult to break away from the traditional patrilineal lineage (Kelkar and Nathan, 1991). This struggle over land inheritance has been one of the primary causes for witchcraft accusations against women in the region. The studies by Barman (2002) and Kelkar and Nathan (1991) both point toward the immense pressure on the *adivasi* widows from the male heirs of their husband's family, to give up the land in exchange for maintenance.

However, other literature on witchcraft accusations in India point to factors other than the gendered nature of conflict. For instance, as previously mentioned, Sundar (2001) argues that in Bastar the accused do not fit any pattern of gender, age, dependency, or kinship, and thus attempts to understand these witch hunts should be placed within the context of the contemporary changes that these communities are facing. Sundar's arguments are similar to Federici's (2010) comment that to understand contemporary witch hunts in India, one has to understand how the social crisis caused by economic liberalism has transformed, uprooted, and plundered communities, forcing people to compete for limited resources. Thus, while one should not underestimate the misogyny that these witch hunts reveal, government bodies and international financial institutions are equally responsible for witchcraft accusations in contemporary India (Federici, 2010).

Although the literature on Indian witch hunts primarily identifies gendered conflict related mainly to the struggle over land inheritance and village level conflicts between two parties that escalate into a hunt, as the leading causes for witchcraft accusations, it is difficult to apply the analysis to the witchcraft accusations among the *adivasi* workers in the tea plantations of Jalpaiguri. For one, the *adivasi* worker communities in the tea plantations are migrant laborers, unlike in the other regions of India where the people involved are the original inhabitants of the land. For instance, research on witch hunts in the Jharkhand and Bihar states of India focuses on the agricultural land struggles between the *adivasi* widows and their kin as the leading cause of witch hunts. This analysis does not apply to the plantation workers as the *adivasi* migrant workers do not own any agricultural land in the area. Thus, the struggle over land inheritance between men and women that culminates in witchcraft accusations in Jharkhand, for example, does not make sense in the plantation worker community. All land in the plantations that the tea plantation workers live and work in belong to the plantation owners.

Second, the geographical location of the plantations, the economic conditions of the tea plantation community and the place of the *adivasi* migrant workers within it, makes them a distinctive case, different from other *adivasi* communities in India. The migrant labor community in the plantations is a unique community, with social, political, economic, and historical conditions that differ from those of the *adivasis* in the rest of India. To further elaborate on this point, while witchcraft accusations in the places of origin of these groups have found gender and economic conflicts to be significant indicators for witch hunts, the migration to the tea plantations and the adjustment of life from agricultural laborers to wage workers had a considerable impact on the daily lives of the *adivasi* migrant workers. Thus, while the practice of witchcraft accusations and the witch hunts that followed have continued throughout the years, the practice has changed in form.

Thus, while I am not suggesting that previous studies on witch hunts in India are of little use, I argue that, given the unique position of the *adivasi* migrant worker communities in the tea plantations, it is difficult to analyze the phenomenon from previous studies on India. The context is different here as these accusations are taking place within a migrant community, compared to witchcraft accusations in Bastar, Jharkhand, or Chhattisgarh, where the community is indigenous. Thus, a theoretical perspective that focuses on the witchcraft accusations in the tea plantations promises to contribute toward a rigorous understanding of witch hunts in that region. Here, I respond to Federici's (2010) call to take a deeper look at the institutional reasons for the continuation of witchcraft accusations among plantation workers. The following text is devoted to discussing why there will be a need to revisit previous theories and extend the logic of the theoretical explanations of witch hunts in order to analyze the Chandmoni case.

Perhaps pertinent to the need to revisit prior theories are the special characteristics of the Chandmoni case. While all the victims in the Chandmoni case were female, the case lacked the criteria of *persecution*, a term that is widely popular among feminist scholars and Western scholars on witch hunts. The term *persecution* is understood to mean harassing to afflict or injure because of a group's beliefs or characteristics. Acts committed against a religious group may be deemed persecution by observers or by believers, while people committing those acts may see them as necessary to preserve social order and safety. Thus, the concept of persecution refers to strategic attempts encouraged by the dominant powerful groups in a society, directed at groups that threaten them (Jensen, 2007). The targets of ritual violence in persecution are symbolic of real targets, that is, the targets are symbolic of a group or category that constitutes a real threat to the persecutors. In others words, where witch hunts are categorized under persecution, the accused witches are symbolic of the female threat to patriarchy (Jensen, 2007). The planned and calculated attack on the threat group is also another defining characteristic of persecution that does not end with a single attack. Rather, in persecution, the strategic attacks culminate in a mass wave of attacks toward the threat group.

In other words, Western feminists and some Indian scholars (Barman, 2002) framed the witchcraft accusations as persecutions. However, the witch hunt in Chandmoni did not seem to be a structured group activity.* Rather, it seemed to be motivated by individual interests, where the hunt for witches died out as soon as the interest was satisfied. For instance, of the five women who were accused as witches in the Chandmoni Tea Estate, four of them had prior conflicts with some of the villagers. These conflicts had nothing to do with Anil's illness, but were related to unpaid debts. Ramlal, a plantation worker, explained how the witches were selected:

> It seemed very random...the selection of the women...but you know that nothing is random. The names [of witches] that Hariram called out were all pre decided. Suresh's friend Lakhan, had paid an additional five hundred rupees to the *janguru* to call out Sanchari's name. Lakhan and Sanchari's husband had a dispute over money. Sanchari's husband accused Lakhan of stealing money from him. So Sanchari's accusation was not random. Same with Atashi, Binshu and Dhanshi...their accusations were related to disputes that they had. Manshi's accusation however was random. She was an old woman...maybe that is why she was selected.

Ramlal's explanations on the motivations behind the accusations of the four women are tied to the calculated category of witch hunts, while the attack against Manshi fall's under the surprise category of hunts. In the first instance, the targeted women are aware of the accusations against them. There are usually some prior conflicts, such as a property dispute, between the accuser and the accused, where the local beliefs in *dains* are manipulated to launch a witch hunt against the accused woman. In the surprise category of witch hunts, the accused women have no warning beforehand of the witchcraft accusations against them. The immediate cause that instigated the hunt was, in most cases, an ailment in the household of the accuser, as we see in Manshi's case, where Anil's death triggered such a response (for a detailed discussion on the two categories of hunts, see Chaudhuri, 2012).

Second, the inheritance theories explaining witch hunts do not seem to fit in with the Chandmoni incident. None of the five accused women had property or land issues that would benefit the accuser's family or friends through their (the women's) successful accusations. Instead, what is unique to cases in contemporary India, and that includes the Chandmoni incident,

---

* One can argue that there is some structure to the Indian hunt. However, two characteristics of the Indian hunt work against its categorization under persecution. One, Indian hunts are "individually" motivated to achieve personal interests for the accuser. In the process, the accuser gathers support from the group. Second, and related to the first, because these hunts are individually motivated, and not a structured group activity against another group, they do not result in panic waves. Thus, a single case of a witch hunt does not lead to a series of hunts, in the Indian cases.

is the dual construction of deviants: *dains* become deviants from the perspective of their fellow villagers and accusers, while the accusers themselves are viewed as deviants from the perspective of the police and legal codes. In the cases where there has been police intervention, the accusers have been prosecuted under sections of the Indian Penal Code that deal with murder. For instance, when the police finally intervened in the Chandmoni incident, the accusers were arrested, and the community was traumatized by the police onslaught. Such a situation requires a new term in the study of witch hunts—*dual deviance*—a term that looks at the process of witchcraft accusations from the perspective of the moral entrepreneurs. Dual deviance occurs when both the "accusers of witchcraft" and the individuals who are labeled as "witches" are categorized as deviants. In the following section, I will discuss the proposed theoretical framework needed to explain the logic behind the Chandmoni witch-hunt incident.

Extending Witch-Hunt Theory: Dual Deviance, Scapegoat, and Stinchcombe's Analysis of the Logic of Functional Explanation

The concept of dual deviance involves deviance at two levels. Level one consists of two groups: the deviant group and the moral entrepreneur group (the labeling group). The deviant group is the group whose actions (regardless if these actions are factual or assumed) are considered to be a threat to the moral order of the community that this deviant group and the moral entrepreneurs belong to. The moral entrepreneur group is the group that seeks to maintain the moral boundaries of the community, and is also assigned the task of labeling the deviant group as deviant. Becker coined the term *moral entrepreneur* in *Outsiders* (1963); it consists of rule creators and rule enforcers. Rule creators can be seen as moral crusaders, who are chiefly concerned with the successful persuasion of others based on what they think is moral (and therefore defining deviance), but are not concerned with the means by which this persuasion is achieved. Moral crusaders must have power and public support, generate public awareness of the issue, and be able to propose an acceptable solution to the problem that is enforced by rule enforcers (Becker, 1963).

Applying this logic to the Chandmoni incident, at level one of the model of dual deviance, the accused *dains* are the deviants in the community, who are responsible for the harm and misfortune in the lives of the *adivasi* villagers. Here, the accusers, the *janguru*, and the village headman acted as the moral entrepreneurs who saw the witches as a threat to the stability of the community—a moral panic—responsible for causing Anil's illness. The moral entrepreneurs (which included the core group of accusers, the *janguru*, and *panchayat* members) were instrumental in justifying the need to look for supernatural spiritual causes behind the ailments and deaths within the community. *Dains* were identified as the culprits, who were blamed for all the miseries in the plantation worker communities and for making the powers of the *janguru* to cure Anil, ineffective. Here, the *adivasi* workers, who were constantly under pressure due to the nature of the plantation economy, connected the micro village-level strain of ailments to witchcraft, rather than blaming the deaths on the lack of proper medical aid for the workers. For them, the ailments became the necessary proof that witchcraft was at work, and joining forces with the accusers became a natural choice; a choice that was necessary not just to get rid of the witchcraft but to seek justice against the *dains*. As one *adivasi* worker explained,

> there is so much pressure and struggle in our daily lives...one has to do something...kill something...so that we feel that momentarily we have some power over our lives. It perhaps gives the community some respite. Momentarily of course, till the harassment by the police and outsiders start. Hospitals, medicines, doctors are something we do not have here. So at work we have the troubles over wages and treatment. And at home it is the old story of ailments and deaths.

The *dain* becomes the symbol of all oppression and misery and thus the witchcraft is no longer a personal matter. The witchcraft is now a concern of the community, a label that the moral entrepreneurs have been successful in implementing.

At the next level in the model of dual deviance, the moral entrepreneurs (the accusers, the *janguru*, and *panchayat* members) are transformed to the category of deviants by a third group of people, typically outside the community of the deviant group and the labeling group at the first level. Even though this third group is outside the community, they are a part of the larger community that the groups in the first level belong to. This third group then acts as the moral entrepreneurs in the second level, while the labeling group in level one is transformed as the deviant group and the original deviant group is transformed as victims. In the Chandmoni case, this group of new moral entrepreneurs are the police, the state, and other institutions, whose members are typically non-*adivasis*, and who view the accusers as the new deviants. At this level, witch hunts are seen as a phenomenon that is harmful toward the *adivasi* community, and the victims are the accused witches who are innocent (see Figure 17.1a and b).

While this model of dual deviance can help in understanding the incident of the witch hunt at Chandmoni Tea Estate from the perspective of the moral entrepreneurs, it is important to understand the role of the accused women in the bigger rhetoric of tea plantation politics. Sociologists studying the phenomenon of witch hunts have used a variety of theories from the

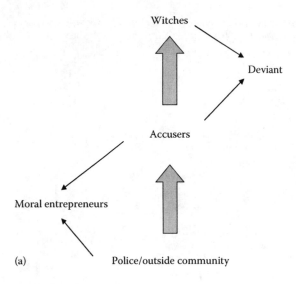

Figure 17.1 (a, b) Model of dual deviance.

deviant behavior literature to study witch hunts (Erickson, 1962; Jensen, 2007; Ben-Yehuda, 1980). The most popular among them are the functional theory and the scapegoat theory. While the functional standpoint (Erickson, 1962) refers to deviance as the "normal" response to "abnormal" social conditions, scapegoating refers to the punitive or negative treatment of people or groups who are held accountable for crises or problems they did not cause. In scapegoating, the target takes the blame for the crisis that is threatening the group, either "as an intentional diversionary tactic or as a cathartic displacement of anger and frustration" (Jensen, 2007, p. 53).

In the Chandmoni Tea Estate incident, the five accused women were used as scapegoats in the moral struggle of the community because of the failure to cure Anil. They were selected not because they were *dains*, but because their accusations were important to distract the focus of the *adivasi* community from the real causes behind Anil's death: lack of health care in the region, constant stress of epidemics, and the tremulous relationship between the workers and the plantation owners over living and wage conditions (see Talwar et al., 2005). The *adivasi* workers were stuck in a plantation economy for generations, where the careful strategy of isolation and alienation of the workers by the planters (Bhowmik, 2011) has resulted in the creation of a marginalized and oppressed working class. The threat of witchcraft brings out feelings among the *adivasi* workers that they need to exert control over their lives.

For some, the fear of *dains* along with the need to take control over their lives, leads the *adivasi* migrant workers to join the witch hunt. For others, witch hunts are a good opportunity to settle scores. In the following narrative,

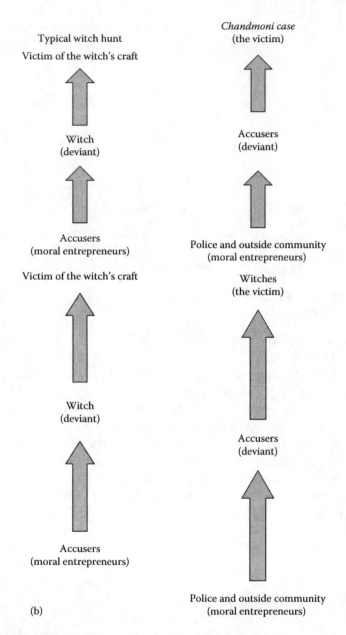

Figure 17.1 (Continued)

Sunil, a villager, who was at the meeting when the causes behind Anil's death were revealed to the villagers in the Chandmoni Tea Estate incident, mentions the event leading to the creation of the scapegoats:

> They [Anil's brother and family] were very upset…came to the meeting drunk…Started telling the village that there was witchcraft involvement in

the issue. And then what, other people in the village joined in ... some of them were just looking for an opportunity to create trouble in the village. They started supporting Suresh ... there was a lot of people ... they all looked like they wanted to do some harm.

Frustration over the continuing epidemics, anger, and encouraged by alcohol and miscreants are some of the reasons behind the support for the hunts. The accusations against the woman in the Chandmoni Tea Estate witch hunt were made to provide evidence that there was no conspiracy in the witchcraft accusations: the five women were selected because they were guilty of witchcraft. The ailment argument leading to the witchcraft accusations became crucial in convincing the community to join the hunt.

For the *adivasi* migrant workers, the *dain* represents all that is wrong in their lives. A logic that might work to explain the witch hunts in Jalpaiguri is to view witchcraft accusations as functional responses when social order is threatened, and the accused women become credible scapegoats for alienation by workers. The functional explanation of witch hunts from a sociological theoretical perspective can be best explained by Jensen (2007), who applies Stinchcombe's logic of functional explanations (1968).* Jensen explains:

> Some type of threat either to society or to some members of a society or to some members of a society (e.g., plague), leads to a decline in security. The minus sign between the threat and the homeostatic variable means as the threat increases, security decreases. People do not like such a state and begin to search for a response (e.g., scapegoating). The minus sign between security and the response means that as security declines, the search for response increases. Finally for the response to function as expected, it has to reestablish security (the homeostatic condition)—hence, the positive sign between the response and the homeostatic variable. In the example, scapegoating increases and security increases (i.e., a positive relationship). A variety of different threats, homeostatic variables, and responses can be found in the witch hunt literature. (2007, p. 40)

Applying Stinchcombe's model and Jensen's adaptation to the hunts among the *adivasi* migrant workers, one can explain why the hunts continue to occur. Among the *adivasi* workers, a threat to society or some of

---

* Functionalism came under harsh criticism from the 1970s. Stinchcombe's model seems to answer most of the criticisms leveled at functionalism. "Nothing is assumed about the nature of homeostatic variables—except, of course, that they must be of certain practical value to a group of people ... Change, while provoked by extraneous factors, is inherent to the system ... Moreover the model is not alien to a notion of revolution. And since the environment of a system can never be controlled, there is also no need to assume an end-state involving total equilibrium" (Arditi, 1988). Arditi extends Stinchcombe's model to show how equilibrium structures, structural conditions, and social conflicts are variations of the extended functional model.

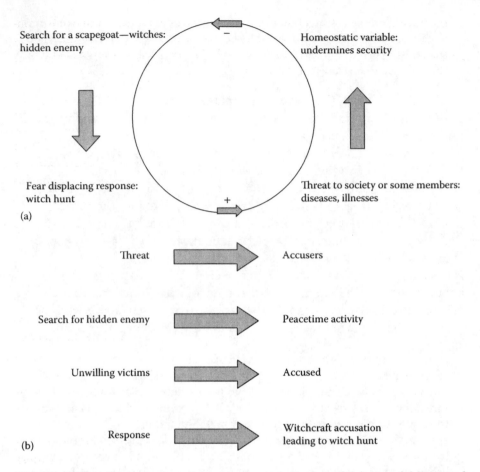

Figure 17.2 (a, b) Scapegoat theory and witch hunts: The logic of functional explanations. (Adapted from Jensen, G. F., *The Path of the Devil: Early Modern Witch Hunts*, Rowman and Littlefield, New York, 2007; Stinchcombe, A. L., *Constructing Social Theories*, Harcourt, Brace and World, New York, 1968.)

its members can occur in the form of diseases or illnesses. This threat is entrenched in insecurities about wages, employment, and politics in the plantations. This undermines security in the society and elicits a response in the form of the hunt for a scapegoat that would take the blame for undermining the stability in the community. The scapegoat takes the form of witches, and the fear-displacing response takes the form of witch hunts (see Figure 17.2).

Conclusion: Explaining the Chandmoni Incident with the Logic of Functional Explanations

At the very outset, Chandmoni had all the characteristics of a community in stress: a series of epidemics, the failure of the state-sponsored health system, and an unresponsive management. Anil's death created the homeostatic condition of the community to be unstable, partly because Anil's family was relatively better off than others in the village (Anil earned more than the workers in the plantation as he was a driver for a private party) and partly because of the failure of the *janguru's* medications to cure Anil.

To ensure that his position remained intact and unchallenged, the *janguru* did what other moral entrepreneurs would do: necessitated the need to hunt for a scapegoat who would be blamed for the "real" causes behind the epidemics. The scapegoats would all have to be *dispensable* and *valid* or credible threats. The search for the *dain* was thus justified, as *dains* are the hidden enemy: meaning that they could be their neighbors, friends, or acquaintances, who have a secret identity. The five accused women were randomly selected and were in no position of power to retaliate against the hunts. If anything, they were in positions that made them socially vulnerable: old women, women with weak economic backgrounds, and women with families that were in conflict with powerful families in the village.

For the moral entrepreneurs (the *janguru*, *panchayat* members, and supporters of Anil's brother), the women represented the evil force that needed to be discarded. The extensive hunt, and the torture that went on for days, were a crucial display of triumph over evil. The hunt was so important in the psyche of the villagers that they kept vigil so that there would be no outside interference during the torture and the murders. It was the perfect response of a community under threat.

But does violence over *dains* restore order in the plantation *adivasi* community? Violence is often used as a means to disrupt order (riots, genocides), and it is often the beginning of anomie. However, in the context of witch hunts, the violence against the accused woman is symbolic: getting rid of the plague that is responsible for the misery. Violence can thus be both disruptive (from the point of the police, the state, and the non *adivasi* community) and restitutive (justice for the wronged, in this case the *adivasi* community). Thus, the *adivasi* workers look toward the *dain* as the image of misery, an image that can be destroyed and shamed through the witch hunt, and the *adivasi* man can restore his honor.

References

Arditi, G. (1988). Equilibrium, structural contradictions, and social conflicts: Revisiting Stinchcombe. *Sociological Forum, 3,* 282–292.

Bailey, F. G. (1992). *The Witch Hunt or the Triumph of Morality.* Ithaca, NY: Cornell University Press.

Barman, M. (2002). *Persecution of Women: Widows and Witches.* Calcutta, India: Indian Anthropological Society.

Barstow, A. L. (1995). *Witchcraze: A New History of the European Witch Hunts.* London: Harper Collins.

Becker, H. S. (1963). *Outsiders: Studies in the Sociology of Deviance.* New York: Free Press.

Ben-Yehuda, N. (1980). The European witch craze of the 14th to 17th centuries: A sociologist's perspective. *American Journal of Sociology, 86,* 1–31.

Bhowmik, S. (1981). *Class Formation in the Plantation System.* New Delhi, India: People's Publishing House.

Bhowmik, S. (2011). Ethnicity and isolation: Marginalization of tea plantation workers. *Race/Ethnicity, 4,* 235–253.

Bosu, M. S. (2000). Gender relations and witches among the indigenous communities of Jharkhand, India. *Gender Technology and Development, 4,* 333–358.

Carstairs, G. M. (1983). *The Death of a Witch: A Village in North India 1950–1981.* London: Hutchinson.

Chatterjee, P. (2001). *A Time for Tea: Women, Labor, and Post/Colonial Politics on an Indian Plantation.* Durham, NC: Duke University Press.

Chaudhuri, A. B. (1981). *Witch Killings Amongst Santals.* New Delhi, India: Ashish Publishing House.

Chaudhuri, S. (2012). Women as easy scapegoats: Witchcraft accusations and women as targets in tea plantations of India. *Violence Against Women, 18,* 1213–1234.

Comaroff, J., & Comaroff, J. (1993). *Modernity and Its Malcontents: Ritual and Power in Postcolonial Africa.* Chicago, IL: University of Chicago Press.

Dasgupta, P. K., & Khan, I. A. (1983). *Impact of Tea Plantation Industry on the Life of Tribal Laborers.* Calcutta, India: Anthropological Survey of India.

Desai, A. (2008). Subaltern vegetarianism: Witchcraft, embodiment, and sociality in central India. *South Asia: Journal of South Asian Studies, 31,* 96–117.

Erickson, K. T. (1962). Notes on the sociology of deviance. *Social Problems, 9,* 307–314.

Evans-Pritchard, E. E. (1976). *Witchcraft, Oracles and Magic Among the Azande.* Oxford: Oxford University Press.

Federici, S. (2010). Women, witch hunting and enclosures in Africa today. *Sozial Geschichte Online, 3,* 10–27.

Frankfurter, D. (2006). *Evil Incarnate. Rumors of Demonic Conspiracy and Satanic Abuse in History.* Princeton, NJ: Princeton University Press.

Geschiere, P. (1997). *The Modernity of Witchcraft: Politics and the Occult in Postcolonial Africa.* Charlottesville, VA: University Press of Virginia.

Hutton, R. (2002). The global context of the Scottish witch hunt. In Goodare, J. (ed.), *The Scottish Witch Hunt in Context* (pp. 16–32). Manchester: Manchester University Press.

Jensen, G. F. (2007). *The Path of the Devil: Early Modern Witch Hunts.* New York: Rowman and Littlefield.

Karlsen, C. F. (1998). *The Devil in the Shape of a Woman: Witchcraft in Colonial New England.* New York: W. W. Norton.

Kelkar, G., & Nathan, D. (1991). Women, witches and land rights. In Kelkar, G. & Nathan, D. (eds), *Gender and Tribe: Women, Land and Forest* (pp. 88–109). New Delhi, India: Kali for Women.

Kelkar, G., & Warrier, M. (1997). Indigenous Asia: Knowledge, technology and gender relations. *Gender Technology and Development, 3,* 313–319.

Moore, H., & Sanders, T. (eds) (2001). *Magical Interpretations, Material Realities: Modernity, Witchcraft and the Occult in Postcolonial Africa.* London: Routledge.

Nathan, D., Kelkar, G., & Xiaogang, Y. (1998). Women as witches and keepers of demons: Cross-cultural analysis of struggles to change gender relations. *Economic and Political Weekly, 33,* 58–69.

Skaria, A. (1999). *Hybrid Histories: Forests, Frontiers and Wildness in Western India.* New Delhi, India: Oxford University Press.

Stinchcombe, A. L. (1968). *Constructing Social Theories.* New York: Harcourt, Brace and World.

Sundar, N. (2001). Divining evil: The state and witchcraft in Bastar. *Gender, Technology and Development, 5,* 425–448.

Talwar, A., Chakraborty, D., & Biswas, S. (2005). Study on closed and re-opened tea gardens in North Bengal. *Paschim Banga Khet Majoor Samity* and International Union of Food, Agriculture, Hotel, Restaurant, Catering, Tobacco, Plantation and Allied Workers' Association (IUF).

From Criminal Spin to Positive Criminology

18

NATTI RONEL

Contents

> Ben Azai said: Run to do even easy mitzvah (*good deed; commandment*) and run away from any sins, for doing mitzvah leads to more mitzvah and sinning leads to further sinning.
>
> **—Ethics of Our Fathers 4:2**

Introduction

More often than not, the study of crime, violence, and related behaviors emphasizes the negative aspects in people's lives that are associated with or lead to deviance and criminality. A common but partial understanding is that human relationships are affected more by destructive encounters than by constructive or positive ones—"the bad" is often considered to be stronger than "the good" (Baumeister et al., 2001). Prominent criminological theories tend to exemplify the dominant role of the bad in criminology: neglect; social rejection and alienation; association with strong criminal influences; reaction to social strain; lack of self-control; past trauma and conditions of risk; and criminal careers (Hagan, 1988; Shoham et al., 2004). Consequently, an expected and reasonable response to crime, violence, and deviance is a stronger force that attempts to solve the problem of criminality and its effects by removing offenders from society, by punishing them, and by retaliating—all largely negative experiences. But does this really solve the problem effectively—can it stop people from engaging in violent or criminal behaviors? Can it really bring relief to the pain and suffering of victims of crime? Can it improve the quality of life of societies? Unfortunately, the power of "the negative" in solving crime and its outcomes is partial and temporary. It is a solution aimed at a change of "the same order," following the known distinction of Watzlawick et al. (1974). Therefore, another step is necessary, generating a transformation of a different order. And that is where positive (different from positivistic) criminology plays a role in changing the picture. In the following, I will introduce this innovative perspective in criminology. But before that, I will briefly introduce a recent phenomenological theory of criminology that describes and interprets one aspect of criminal behavior, namely, the criminal spin (for a more detailed description of this theory see Ronel, 2009, 2011). The spin model describes the problem; positive criminology offers an approach to its solution.

Phenomenology of the Criminal Spin

Various authors, representing different perspectives, have undertaken the task of explaining crime and deviance. Most have attempted to provide causal explanations for criminal and deviant behaviors. Since its inception, criminology has offered a wide selection of such explanations, which often lead to corresponding responses (e.g., Goode, 2002; Hagan, 1988; Shoham et al., 2004). Careful scrutiny of the causal explanations of crime reveals that although most of them make good sense and are founded on evidence, in many cases they also contradict each other (e.g., Blumstein et al., 1988; DeLisi & Vaughn, 2008; Maruna, 2004). The reason for this confusion is that causal explanations are usually dependent on time, space, and content, describing and explaining certain behaviors by certain people within a certain context (Klein, 1998; Muftić, 2009). Nevertheless, concentration on the phenomenology of criminality itself, as a human experience within human consciousness (Katz, 2002), may reveal a common essence of those behaviors considered to be criminal, regardless of their particular causes, context, and content. Consequently, I suggest that we can discern a common process in the phenomena of most criminal behaviors, notwithstanding their varying features. The phenomenology of different criminal behaviors in different settings reveals a typical flywheel-like process of a criminal spin, which gives these behaviors their unique character and leads to undesired yet unavoidable results.

A criminal spin is an event or a set of events that represent a process of escalation in criminal behavior, accompanied by a cycle of criminal thinking or corresponding emotions. A criminal spin occurs when there is a sudden, rapid, or gradual acceleration of behavior that is considered criminal. The process arises as an almost inevitable chain of events, linked to one another in the generation of ever-intensifying criminal behavior. The overall process is one of a spinning flywheel; once set in motion, it preserves its own continuity. All components work coherently to increase the movement and create an integrated process that is stronger than the sum of the parts and factors that comprise it (Collins, 2001). Usually, if nothing interferes with the natural order of events, this process leads to a crisis that halts its movement, or reaches a peak and then subsides.

As a criminal spin progresses, there is a noticeable weakening of self-control, although the person involved may deny this and may perceive himself or herself as "being in control." Sometimes, the individual consciously attempts to gain or regain control over the situation; however, this might even increase the spin, as happens during domestic battering (Ronel & Tim, 2003). For some individuals, the loss of control in such situations reflects a generally low level of self-control (Hay & Forrest, 2006; Hirschi & Gottfredson, 1994). However, contrary to the claim of the general theory of deviance, there are individuals that give up their sense of self-control only during a particular process, while demonstrating a strong desire for control and displaying such control in other aspects of their life and at different times (Piquero et al., 2010). As the spin theory is phenomenological, it does not look for the causes of the present lack of control, whether they are internal, external, both, or none. The focus is on the various phenomena related to the spin process itself.

Similar to any human phenomenon, a criminal spin involves behaviors, emotions, and cognition that interact together in the spin process. Any of these may ignite the spin process: behavior may stimulate cognition and emotions, emotion may lead to behavior and cognition, or cognition might precede a criminal behavior, with or without a corresponding emotion.

A criminal spin may be presented in acute or chronic phases. During the acute phase, the individual exhibits a one-time only event that denotes a criminal spin, or may exhibit separate, unrelated such events. However, the spin might enter into a chronic phase, where the individual is trapped in related or recurring episodes of an acute criminal spin, or a sequential development of criminal, deviant, or violent activity. Apparently, a chronic spin is manifested in the development of a criminal lifestyle or career (Farrington, 1995). In that sense, there is no difference between a career criminal and a criminal career (Blumstein et al., 1988; DeLisi, 2005; DeLisi & Vaughn, 2008), as they both represent the chronic criminal spin.

Parallel to the individual level, a criminal spin may be detected in groups as well: a group may exhibit behavior patterns that represent an acute or a chronic criminal spin. When this happens, the group operates as a whole that is larger than its parts, with the potential for generating further criminality among its members (Akers & Jensen, 2006; Battin et al., 1998; Battin-Pearson et al., 1998; Porter & Alison, 2006; Winfree et al., 1994). Furthermore, one may detect a criminal or deviant spin in even larger entities, such as a neighborhood (Schuerman & Kobrin, 1986), certain geographical areas (Weisburd et al., 2010), across cultures and social classes (Fagan et al., 2007), or even at a national level, as for example in the case of Nazi Germany.

Certain characteristics are common to the phenomenology of all cases of individual or group criminal spins. These features may be weak and temporary in the acute phase, but stronger and persistent in the chronic phase. First, the spin involves an intensification of behaviors, thoughts, and feelings that are increasingly and narrowly directed to the spin route. Second, the process assumes a "life" of its own and preserves its continuity. This leads to the third feature, a gradual or sudden loss of self-control and less ability to behave out of free choice. Fourth, the individual is increasingly self-centered and occupied by his or her own wishes, desires, fears, or distress, while the ability to consider others or to empathize with them diminishes (Ronel, 2000). In addition, the individual is concerned more with the immediate than the future consequences. A growing self-centeredness leads to a greater separation of that person—from others, from himself or herself, and from spirituality (this is further elaborated on in the following text). Fifth, two motives operate within the consciousness in spin: the first is an "I must" motive, which appears when the consciousness initially enters, or is in the course of the spin process, filled with the perception of an existential threat or a need. This creates a sense that any action that can remove this threat and regain one's safety should be taken. The self-centered consciousness typically becomes limited by the spin and directs itself toward surviving the threat. The second is an "I can" motive, that is, a perception of the individual's personal legitimacy and ability to perform the criminal act. This motive represents the cognitive and emotional states that, at least temporarily, accept, support, and allow the chain of behaviors based on a sense of personal capacity and legitimacy to continue to the desired end, while minimizing the possibility of other consequences.

Based on this description, it is possible to detect a criminal spin and even to predict its direction when it has just started, at the individual, group, community, or societal level. When confronted with a criminal process, experienced individuals may evaluate the level, nature, and degree of the spin process. Such an evaluation, at any level, may guide the appropriate intervention. The existence of a criminal spin indicates the intensity and level of the desirable intervention. Usually, an external intervention that is noticeable and stronger than the spin is required, since the spin is a self-perpetuating process. While law enforcement might provide such an external intervention, it usually targets only some of the characteristics of the criminal spin. For example, punishment and deterrent measures might at times reduce or even end the "I can" motive, sometimes providing the only way to break a chronic spin, but if the "I must" motive (and self-centeredness, as well) are not addressed, the individual may be drawn back into an active criminal spin. The high recidivism rate of chronic offenders verifies this claim. Therefore, it is also necessary to generate a complementary transformation that has the ability to reduce both the "I can" and "I must" motives, to restore self-control and reduce self-centeredness. Positive criminology is a perspective that encompasses various models aimed at these objectives.

Foundations of Positive Criminology

Hatred is overcome only by non-hatred.
—**The Buddha** (*Dammapada*)

Love is the only remedy for hate. It blossoms only in the heart of a fearless man ... Goodness must be joined with knowledge.
—**Gandhi** (in Settel, 1995)

Positive criminology is a new concept that explicitly focuses on various experiences of the good that may assist individuals, groups, and communities in turning away from criminality and its consequent harm and suffering (Ronel & Elisha, 2011). It seeks the knowledge of goodness in a criminological context, following Gandhi's maxim cited above. Parallel but contrary to the spin model, which indicates a progression of criminal activity with a decrease in the ability of individuals and groups to desist from it, positive criminology indicates the growing ability of individuals and communities to refrain from criminal, violent, or deviant behavior. Positive criminology is oriented to human strengths, resilience, and positive encounters that can assist individuals in abstaining from crime and deviant behaviors. It promotes social inclusion and unifying and integrating forces in individual, group, social, and spiritual dimensions.

An individual in a criminal spin usually exhibits an increased degree of self-centeredness, as noted. The development of self-centeredness entails a process of separation from others, who are increasingly perceived to be object-like (potentially threatening or rewarding), to the point of social, existential, and spiritual alienation. Being together with a peer group of like individuals—a gang or a criminal subculture, for instance—does not reduce the sense of existential separation from humanity at large, as it usually indicates the separation of that group from noncriminal society (Braithwaite, 2000).To reverse that process, an authentic unification, which is usually positively experienced, is needed. Therefore, the possibilities of inclusion, integration, and unity are central to positive criminology and, in fact, represent its positive direction. For that reason, the separation–unification vector is basic to understanding the progress of a criminal spin and recovery from it, where unification denotes the positive route. Accordingly, the term *positive criminology* takes on another meaning, that is, the criminology of integration, inclusion, and unification.

In the social dimension, the promotion of social inclusion represents the positive vector, sometimes as the first source of transformation. It marks an initial reduction in self-centeredness and alienation. Similarly, existential integration of the self within humanity, where others are perceived as less object-like (Shoham & Addad, 2004), and the construction of an integrative consciousness center of pro-social norms (Timor, 2001) constitute another dimension of positive unification, indicating reduced self-centeredness and an increasing ability to resist immediate gratification. Finally, the direction toward unification with a spiritual power greater than the self represents the positive vector in the spiritual dimension, constructing a meaning that also supports the reduction of self-centeredness and indicates increasing self-control with the aid of the spirit (Ronel, 2000).

The perspective of positive criminology refers to uniting influences that share two common features: first, they are largely considered as good and are experienced by targeted individuals as positive, and second, they may assist these individuals in developing the ability to refrain from criminal or deviant behavior. The first feature is based on and shared with positive psychology (Gable & Haidt, 2005; Seligman & Csikszentmihalyi, 2000). An essential notion of positive psychology is that the study of positive experiences is complementary and should not be secondary to that of negative processes. Investigations of how positive emotions help build enduring personal resources (Fredrickson, 2001), for example, may be adapted to the study of the target population of criminology (Ronel, 2006).

Positive criminology takes this further by means of its second quality, that is, the determining of crime prevention and desistance as the desired outcomes of positive experiences. Accordingly, the positive experiences are meaningful because of their ability to enhance a transformation that can prevent or stop criminal spins at any phase and level. Positive criminology acknowledges the ability of offenders and ex-convicts to reform and rehabilitate under certain circumstances, and highlights the importance of positive conditions and human encounters in any effective rehabilitation process.

Positive criminology is a field distinct from positive psychology, notwithstanding the shared emphasis on the impact of "the positive." First, as said, it is specifically aimed at crime prevention and desistance, a specification not necessarily held by positive psychology. Second, although some of the resources and means to attain this goal are psychological in character, as various scholars of psychology indicate (e.g., Martin & Stermac, 2010), others represent other-than-psychological spheres and issues. These include, for example, law-enforcement issues, such as restorative justice (e.g., Shachaf-Friedman & Timor, 2008), and sociological processes, such as the sociology of acceptance (Bogdan & Taylor, 1987). Third, positive criminology spotlights individuals and groups that are engaged in, at risk for, or victims of deviant or criminal activities. This focus is naturally absent in positive psychology; it indicates a specific knowledge. For example, target individuals of positive criminology might be at any stage or phase of a criminal spin, at times requiring a combined response of positive influences with those that can forcibly and immediately halt a spin if the positive ones are insufficient (Wilson & Kelling, 1982).

The target population of positive criminology often reports an experience of challenging and adverse backgrounds. These developmental factors include exposure to a wide range of negative experiences. Positive criminology represents a perspective that takes into account the complexity of the offending individuals in terms of their personal, environmental, and cultural characteristics, including their strengths and potential for personal, social, and spiritual growth. Consequently, risk factors are also perceived in terms of their potential for growth and development, rather than simply as indicators of vulnerability and destruction (Antonovsky, 1979; Ronel & Haimoff-Ayali, 2009). Studies that can be associated with a positive criminological perspective have revealed several personal strengths among different types of rehabilitated offenders, such as taking personal responsibility, finding new meaning in their lives, and maturation (e.g., Biernacki, 1986; Maruna, 2004; Ronel, 1998b), in addition to variables such as obtaining external assistance (e.g., family, treatment, voluntary support groups such as Alcoholics Anonymous [AA] and Narcotics Anonymous [NA], and religious organizations). These and other studies emphasize the importance of cultivating positive human strengths following risk and crisis events, in order to achieve higher levels of well-being and positive growth (Bogenschneider, 1996; Fraser, 1997; Ronel & Levy-Cahana, 2010).

Positive Criminology in Theory and Practice

Positive criminology is founded on a perspective that is shared by different theories and approaches in criminology. I will briefly describe some of the most prominent of these. It should be noted that other theories and approaches may also be included under this term, if they encompass the same elements of unification, positive experience, and abstinence from criminality.

Reintegrative Shaming

Braithwaite's (1989) reintegrative shaming is a major theory in criminology that represents the positive perspective well. A central component of this theory is a distinction between a person's identity and behavior, which allows for self-correction and social rehabilitation (Braithwaite et al., 2006). Such a distinction can be found in religious traditions such as Judaism, Christianity, and Zen Buddhism (Brazier, 1995; Miller & Delaney, 2005); in modern spiritual approaches, such as the 12-step program (Ronel, 2000); and in humanistic and positive psychology. Reintegrative shaming is based on the idea that rehabilitative interventions may be most effective when they include condemnation of the wrong criminal behavior (shaming), along with the acceptance and reintegration of the individual by the community (Braithwaite, 2000). This perception is parallel to the one presented here, which stresses the importance of social inclusion in ending a criminal spin. Disintegrative shaming occurs when the offender is functionally excluded from society and negatively labeled by normative members of society. According to the labeling theory (Becker, 1963; Robbers, 2009), such social rejection can reinforce criminal behavior. The spin model would predict the same (Ronel, 2011), based on the progress toward growing separation and exclusion. Here, social rejection and exclusion mark the negative route, and reintegration indicates the positive one, as both reintegrative shaming and positive criminology claim.

Restorative Justice

Restorative justice represents a school of thinking and an intervention approach in criminal justice that is also consistent with the perspective of positive criminology. It holds that intervention should focus on the relationships harmed as a result of an offense and the people involved in the conflict (Braithwaite, 2000; Shachaf-Friedman & Timor, 2008; Timor, 2008; Zehr, 1995). In the language of positive criminology, the offending behavior is perceived as increasing the separation within society: separation between the wrongdoer, the victim, and the community. Therefore, restorative justice is aimed at reintegration within society of the perpetrator, the victim, and the community. The purpose of restorative justice is to right wrongs—to help heal and better the physical and nonphysical damage that arises from the offense committed. Righting the wrongs mainly takes the form of responding to the emotional, social, and material needs of the victim of the offense, paving the way for the reintegration of the perpetrators after they take responsibility for their actions. All the restorative justice programs that have been developed on this basis in recent years encourage reintegration with society and its members by methods such as mediation, conflict settlement, rehabilitation, and the inclusion of offenders and victims in the community. According to the positive criminology perspective, such practices have the potential to help individuals reintegrate themselves as well.

Rehabilitation

As emphasized earlier, positive criminology is associated with abstaining from crime. Crime desistance, correction, and rehabilitation are long-standing concepts in criminology, although their ability to fulfill their objectives has been seriously questioned (e.g., Anstiss, n.d.; Ward & Maruna, 2007). According to Robinson (2008), rehabilitation is currently enjoying renewed legitimacy following its evolution and transformation, and the inclusion of a moral dimension. Correspondingly, public opinion has indicated some optimism about the effectiveness of rehabilitation (Piquero et al., 2010). Moreover, current research in criminology has clearly proved the effectiveness of rehabilitative practices that take into account the actual needs of the offending individuals and especially their motivation for positive future outcomes (Maguire & Raynor, 2006; Ross & Hilborn, 2008; Ward et al., 2007). Although positive criminology and rehabilitation practices are concerned with crime desistance, positive criminology includes only those practices of rehabilitation that are experienced as positive by target individuals. They are usually aimed at achieving change by exploring the individuals' strengths rather than controlling their faults (Van Wormer & Davis, 2003; Ward & Maruna, 2007); they are future-oriented (desistance-oriented) rather than past-oriented (problem-oriented); and they enable a transformation of the self-narrative into a positive, or at least normative one (Maruna, 2004). To demonstrate, Ward and Maruna (2007) and Ward et al. (2007) presented two effective rehabilitation practices, the first aimed at reducing the risk of undesirable behavior, and the second based on the "good life model," which is more inclusive and is consistent with positive criminology.

Recovery

The discussion of recovery is closely related to that of rehabilitation. The literature on recovery in the field of addiction can be applied to any domain in criminology (Best et al., 2010; Heaps et al., 2009; White et al., 2006). From the perspective of positive criminology, the process of recovery from criminality entails not only abstinence from criminal conduct (which is an initial condition of the recovery process), but also promoting physical, mental, and social well-being by means of a spiritual evolution (White & Kurtz, 2005). Therefore, positive criminology suggests a shift from the "problem-and-treatment" paradigm to a recovery paradigm, where recovery is a process in which behavioral problems are gradually resolved by developing physical, emotional, spiritual, relational, and occupational health (Best et al., 2010; McNeill, 2006). A recovery system of care refers to a whole network of informal relationships and human services that integrate professionals with indigenous paraprofessionals to support the long-term recovery of individuals and families (White et al., 2006). Similar to other positive criminology approaches, recovery involves an achievable vision that includes the integration of individuals, families, and communities. Enduring support in the community is essential for the continuation of the recovery journey; it often includes mutual aid and other peer support of the type that self-help groups provide.

Self-Help Groups and the 12-Step Program

One of the most popular approaches in the Western world for self-change in the field of addiction is that of 12-step self-help groups. Self-help groups, in general, and particularly 12-step groups, which emphasize spiritual and moral change, represent another aspect of positive criminology. The groups serve as a place for learning and practicing new behavior and values, alongside spiritual development. Research conducted among addicts who participated in the 12-step program at Alcoholics Anonymous (AA) and Narcotics Anonymous (NA) self-help and mutual-help groups has identified several therapeutic elements that help addicted individuals in their recovery process (McCrady & Miller, 1993). These include, to name a few, enjoying the benefits of "helper therapy" (Riessman, 1965), spiritual awakening through faith in a higher power that helps them abstain from psychoactive substances (Ronel & Humphreys, 1999–2000), transformation of anger and resentment into forgiveness (Hart & Shapiro, 2002), being part of a "grace community" that represents the highest morality far above the morality of its members (Ronel, 1998a), and sponsoring another person in the recovery process (Crape et al., 2002). Research indicates that self-help organizations such as NA constitute a bridge to recovery, connecting the drug subculture to the general dominant culture (Ronel, 1998b).

The 12-step program originated in AA and was then adopted by other self-help organizations that target a variety of problems, such as drug addiction (NA), eating disorders (Overeaters Anonymous [OA]), and emotional disturbance (Emotions Anonymous [EA]) (Room, 1993). From its inception, the 12-step program caught the attention of professionals as a possible expert approach to therapy, first limited to addiction (White, 1998), and later extended into other fields, such as domestic violence (Ronel & Tim, 2003) and victim assistance (Brende, 1993; Ronel, 2008). It might therefore be perceived as a general professional treatment method and program for recovery, also known as grace therapy (Ronel, 2000). In a professional setting, the 12 steps may be adapted to the changing needs of the participants (Brende, 1995). The program emphasizes the spiritual nature of change and recovery as a continuous process and a unifying way of life, where the recovering individuals gain growing recognition of a higher power and practice integration within their communities—that of their peers and the wider community.

Research on Positive Criminology

Positive criminology is a new term. It was developed on the foundation of the results of several studies by my research group, and also served as the basis for other studies, a few of which will be described here.

The Impact of Volunteers on Those They Help

A series of studies examined the impact of a personal encounter with perceived goodness on individuals in problem situations. Human goodness was represented by volunteers who were perceived as truly altruistic by their target beneficiaries, hence the term *perceived altruism*. The studies focused on the encounter between lay volunteers and (a) at-risk street youth in a mobile outreach service (Ronel, 2006); (b) at-risk youth in drop-in centers for youth at risk in Israel (Ronel et al., 2009); (c) at-risk youth and graduates at a boarding village for adolescents who are removed from their homes (Lavie, 2008); and (d) prisoners recovering from addiction who participated in a Vipassana course in a rehabilitation prison (Frid, 2008). The results of all the studies were dramatically consistent and showed that (a) the beneficiaries knew that volunteers were servicing them and this was highly significant to them; (b) they perceived these volunteers as true altruists; (c) they were so satisfied that they preferred the volunteer services over those of the paid workers; and (d) they were positively affected by the encounter with voluntarism. Meeting the volunteers raised their awareness of giving without expecting a reward, which sharply contradicted their former view of the world as a battlefield. In some cases, the example set by the volunteers inspired the beneficiaries to consider volunteering themselves. Finally, they were sometimes able to generalize the altruistic image to the entire service and overcome their initial objections to a service run by the establishment. The volunteers provided a living example of the possibility of human goodness through personal encounters and demonstrated the existence of a responsive society with mutual, unconditional caring. The proposed explanation refers to the contrast between the example of the volunteers and the marked self-centeredness of individuals in problem situations, which shifted slightly as a result. These results suggest practical implications for innovative interventions with individuals in problem situations and illustrate the significance of the science of goodness and positive criminology practice.

Volunteering for Others

Positive criminology focuses on the impact of goodness on individuals in problem situations, both as beneficiaries and as givers. Several studies have demonstrated that allowing individuals in problem situations to volunteer for the benefit of others can promote rehabilitation and transformation (Burnett & Maruna, 2006; Ross & Hilborn, 2008). In our research group, Uzan (2009) focused on the experience of young offenders in Israel who participated in a community volunteer activity of helping people with needs. Uzan found that the youngsters perceived this activity as a highly significant experience that led them to a process of introspection and a decision to change their way of life. The conclusion, which is consistent with other studies (see Ross & Hilborn, 2008, for a full description), was that participation in initial altruistic activities can develop and strengthen internal virtues (e.g., responsibility, caring for others, and goodness) that motivate individuals from the criminal subculture to adopt pro-social attitudes, norms, and behaviors.

Social Acceptance and Life Transformation in Rehabilitation of Imprisoned Sex Offenders

Ward and colleagues (e.g., Ward, 2002; Ward & Gannon, 2006) have provided extensive research on the impact of a positive perspective represented by the "good life model" on the rehabilitation process of sex offenders. Our research team conducted the first study of imprisoned sex offenders based explicitly on the perspective of positive criminology (Elisha, 2010). The purpose of this qualitative study was to identify the internal and external factors that assist imprisoned sex offenders in their recovery and change process.

Most participants reported personal and social changes during their current imprisonment (the research period) that they deemed significant to their recovery. They attributed the changes to the support they received from various sources, both inside and outside the prison, particularly spouses, parents, therapists, and religious figures. The participants interpreted the support as social acceptance of them; however, this was not construed as unconditional acceptance, but as one that required them to take responsibility and make a significant change. It might also be referred to as love with boundaries, containing components similar to those included in the reintegrative shaming mechanism (Braithwaite, 1989, 2000). The research findings also suggest that positive changes can be achieved even under such harsh conditions as imprisonment, but only if these conditions are accompanied by those of positive criminology.

Conclusion

A person in a criminal spin is expected to continue in the spin until it reaches a peak with unpleasant results, or until it is met by an external force greater than that of the spin. Since a criminal spin, and especially a chronic one, usually results in increasing harm to others and to the perpetrator, there is a need for a social response that might end the spin and minimize its harm. This is a duty of society toward the victims of the criminal spin, toward itself as a whole, and even toward the spinning individuals, who usually have no control over the process. Unfortunately, the prevailing social response is "more of the same." Sometimes, this is necessary in order to bring about change. However, the effectiveness of such a solution in ending a spin process is questionable, and something different is also needed. Positive criminology offers "more" that is not "of the same." It does not compete with traditional law enforcement, but attempts to complement it. In many if not most cases, this complementary process can produce better results than those claimed by conservative law enforcement. Furthermore, its results can have long-lasting effects; if correctly practiced, the positive has stronger recovery potential than the negative, and unification, inclusion, and integration are more durable than separation practices in promoting criminological health and welfare.

References

Akers, R. L., & Jensen, G. F. (2006). The empirical status of social learning theory of crime and deviance: The past, present, and future. In F. Cullen, J. P. Wright, & K. R. Blevins (eds), *Taking Stock: The Status of Criminological Theory* (pp. 37–76). Piscataway, NJ: Transaction Publishers.

Anstiss, B. (n.d.). The effectiveness of correctional treatment. Retrieved October 6, 2009, from http://www.corrections.govt.nz/research/the-effectiveness-of-correctional-treatment.html.

Antonovsky, A. (1979). *Health, Stress and Coping*. San Francisco, CA: Jossey-Bass.

Battin, S. R., Hill, K. G., Abbott, R. D., Catalano, R. F., & Hawkins, D. J. (1998). The contribution of gang membership to delinquency beyond delinquent friends. *Criminology, 36*(1), 93–115.

Battin-Pearson, S. R., Thornberry, T. P., Hawkins, D. J., & Krohn, M. D. (1998). Gang membership, delinquent peers, and delinquent behavior. *Juvenile Justice Bulletin*. U.S. Department of Justice: Office of Justice Programs.

Baumeister, R. F., Bratslavsky, E., Finkenauer, C., & Vohs, K. D. (2001). Bad is stronger than good. *Review of General Psychology, 5*(4), 323–370.

Becker, H. (1963). *Outsiders: Studies in the Sociology of Deviance.* New York: The Free Press.

Best, D., Rome, A., Hanning, K. A., White, W. L., Gossop, M., Taylor, A., & Perkins, A. (2010). Research for recovery: A review of the drugs evidence base. Edinburgh: Scottish Government Social Research.

Biernacki, P. (1986). *Pathways from Heroin Addiction: Recovery without Treatment.* Philadelphia, PA: Temple University Press.

Blumstein, A., Cohen, J., & Farrington, D. P. (1988). Criminal career research: Its value for criminology. *Criminology, 26*(1), 1–35.

Bogdan, R., & Taylor, S. (1987). Toward a sociology of acceptance: The other side of the study of deviance. *Social Policy, 18*(2), 34–39.

Bogenschneider, K. (1996). An ecological risk/protective theory for building prevention programs, policies, and community capacity to support youth. *Family Relations, 45*(2), 127–138.

Braithwaite, J. (1989). *Crime, Shame and Reintegration.* Cambridge, MA: Cambridge University Press.

Braithwaite, J. (2000). Shame and criminal justice. *Canadian Journal of Criminology, 42*(3), 281–298.

Braithwaite, J., Ahmed, E., & Braithwaite, V. (2006). Shame, restorative justice and crime. In F. Cullen, J. Wright, & K. Belvins (eds), *Taking Stock: The Status of Criminological Theory* (pp. 397–417). Piscataway, NJ: Transaction Publishers.

Brazier, D. (1995). *Zen Therapy.* New York: Wiley.

Brende, J. O. (1993). A 12-step recovery program for victims of traumatic events. In J. P. Wilson & B. Raphael (eds), *International Handbook of Traumatic Stress Syndromes* (pp. 867–877). New York: Plenum.

Brende, J. O. (1995). Twelve themes and spiritual steps. In G. S. Everly Jr. & J. M. Lating (Eds), *Psychotraumatology* (pp. 211–229). New York: Plenum.

Burnett, R., & Maruna, S. (2006). The kindness of prisoners: Strengths-based resettlement in theory and in action. *Criminology & Criminal Justice, 6*(1), 83–106.

Collins, J. (2001). *Good to Great.* New York: HarperCollins.

Crape, B. L., Latkin, C. A., Laris, A. S., & Knowlton, A. R. (2002). The effects of sponsorship in 12-step treatment of injection drug users. *Drug and Alcohol Dependence, 65*(3), 291–301.

DeLisi, M. (2005). *Career Criminals in Society.* Thousand Oaks, CA: Sage.

DeLisi, M., & Vaughn, M. G. (2008). The Gottfredson-Hirschi critiques revisited: Reconciling self-control theory, criminal careers, and career criminals. *International Journal of Offender Therapy and Comparative Criminology, 52*(5), 520–537.

Elisha, E. (2010). Positive characteristics among prisoners who are sexual offenders and their impact on the perception of incarceration as an opportunity for change and correction of life. Unpublished doctoral dissertation, Bar-Ilan University (in Hebrew, English abstract).

Fagan, J., Wilkinson, D. L., & Davies, G. (2007). Social contagion of violence. In D. Flannery, A. Vazsonyi, & I. Waldman (eds), *The Cambridge Handbook of Violent Behavior and Aggression* (pp. 688–723). Cambridge: Cambridge University Press.

Farrington, D. P. (1995). The development of offending and antisocial behavior from childhood: Key findings from the Cambridge study in delinquent development. *Journal of Child Psychology and Psychiatry*, 36, 929–964.

Fraser, M. W. (ed.) (1997). *Risk and Resilience in Childhood*. Washington, DC: NASW.

Fredrickson, B. L. (2001). The role of positive emotions in positive psychology: The broaden-and-build theory of positive emotions. *American Psychologist*, 56(3), 218–226.

Frid, N. (2008). Vipassana workshops in jail. Unpublished master's thesis, Bar-Ilan University (in Hebrew).

Gable, S. L., & Haidt, J. (2005). What (and why) is positive psychology? *Review of General Psychology*, 9(2), 103–110.

Goode, E. (2002). *Deviant Behavior*. Tel Aviv: Open University of Israel (Hebrew edition).

Hagan, J. (1988). *Modern Criminology*. Singapore: McGraw-Hill.

Hart, K. E., & Shapiro, D. A. (2002). Secular and spiritual forgiveness interventions for recovering alcoholics harboring grudges. Paper presented at the Convention of the American Psychological Association, Chicago, IL.

Hay, C., & Forrest, W. (2006). The development of self-control: Examining self-control theory's stability thesis. *Criminology*, 44(4), 739–774.

Heaps, M. M., Lurigio, A. J., Rodriguez, P., Lyons, T., & Brookes, L. (2009). Recovery-oriented care for drug-abusing offenders. *Addiction Science & Clinical Practice*, 5(1), 31–36.

Hirschi, T., & Gottfredson, M. A. (1994). The generality of deviance. In T. Hirschi & M. A. Gottfredson (eds), *The Generality of Deviance* (pp. 1–22). New Brunswick, NJ: Transaction Publishers.

Katz, J. (2002). Start here: Social ontology and research strategy. *Theoretical Criminology*, 6(3), 255–278.

Klein, M. W. (1998). Street gangs. In M. Tonry (ed.), *Crime and Punishment* (pp. 111–132). Oxford: Oxford University Press.

Lavie, M. (2008). The influence of volunteering on the beneficiaries. Unpublished master's thesis, Bar-Ilan University (in Hebrew).

Maguire, M., & Raynor, P. (2006). How the resettlement of prisoners promotes desistance from crime: Or does it? *Criminology & Criminal Justice*, 6(1), 19–38.

Martin, K., & Stermac, L. (2010). Measuring hope: Is hope related to criminal behaviour in offenders? *International Journal of Offender Therapy and Comparative Criminology*, 54(5), 693–705.

Maruna, S. (2004). Desistance from crime and explanatory style: A new direction in the psychology of reform. *Journal of Contemporary Criminal Justice*, 20(2), 184–200.

McCrady, B. S., & Miller, W. R. (eds) (1993). *Research on Alcoholics Anonymous*. New Brunswick, NJ: Rutgers Center for Alcohol Studies.

McNeill, F. (2006). A desistance paradigm for offender management. *Criminology & Criminal Justice*, 6(1), 39–62.

Miller, W. R., & Delaney, H. D. (2005). Psychology as the science of human nature: Reflections and research directions. In W. R. Miller & H. D. Delaney (eds), *Judeo-Christian Perspectives on Psychology* (pp. 291–308). Washington, DC: APA.

Muftić, L. R. (2009). Macro-micro theoretical integration: An unexplored theoretical frontier. *Journal of Theoretical and Philosophical Criminology*, *1*(2), 33–71.

Piquero, N. L., Schoepfer, A., & Langton, L. (2010). Completely out of control or the desire to be in complete control? How low self-control and the desire for control relate to corporate offending. *Crime & Delinquency*, *56*(4), 627–647.

Piquero, A. R., Cullen, F. T., Unnever, J. D., Piquero, N. L., & Gordon, J. A. (2010). Never too late: Public optimism about juvenile rehabilitation. *Punishment & Society*, *12*, 187–207.

Porter, L. E., & Alison, L. J. (2006). Examining group rape: A descriptive analysis of offender and victim behaviour. *European Journal of Criminology*, *3*(3), 357–381.

Riessman, F. (1965). The "helper therapy" principle. *Social Work*, *10*, 27–32.

Robbers, M. L. P. (2009). Lifers on the outside: Sex offenders and disintegrative shaming. *International Journal of Offender Therapy and Comparative Criminology*, *53*(1), 5–28.

Robinson, G. (2008). Late-modern rehabilitation: The evolution of a penal strategy. *Punishment & Society*, *10*(4), 429–445.

Ronel, N. (1998a). Self-help groups as a spontaneous Grace Community. *Social Development Issues*, *20*(3), 53–72.

Ronel, N. (1998b). Narcotics Anonymous: Understanding a bridge of recovery. *Journal of Offender Rehabilitation*, *27*(1/2), 179–197.

Ronel, N. (2000). From self-help to professional care: An enhanced application of the 12-step program. *Journal of Applied Behavioral Science*, *36*(1), 108–122.

Ronel, N. (2006). When good overcomes bad: The impact of volunteers on those they help. *Human Relations*, *59*(8), 1133–1153.

Ronel, N. (2008). Grace therapy for recovering victims: A restorative 12-step based therapy. In M. S. Sundaram, K. Jaishankar, & S. Ramdoss (eds), *Crime Victims and Justice: An Introduction to Restorative Principles* (pp. 399–408). New Delhi: Serial Publications.

Ronel, N. (2009). The criminal spin. In K. Jaishankar (ed.), *International Perspectives on Crime and Justice* (pp. 126–145). Newcastle upon Tyne: Cambridge Scholars Publishing.

Ronel, N. (2011). Criminal behavior, criminal mind: Being caught in a criminal spin. *International Journal of Offender Therapy and Comparative Criminology*, *55*(8), 1208–1233.

Ronel, N., & Elisha, E. (2011). A different perspective: Introducing positive criminology. *International Journal of Offender Therapy and Comparative Criminology*, *55*(2), 305–325.

Ronel, N., & Haimoff-Ayali, R. (2009). Risk and resilience: The family experience of adolescents with an addicted parent. *International Journal of Offender Therapy and Comparative Criminology*, *54*(3), 448–472.

Ronel, N., & Humphreys, K. (1999–2000). World-views transformations of Narcotics Anonymous members in Israel. *International Journal of Self-Help and Self-Care*, *1*(1), 101–127.

Ronel, N., & Levy-Cahana, M. (2010). Growing-up with a substance-dependent parent: Development of subjective risk and protective factors. *Substance Use & Misuse*, *46*(5), 608–619. doi:10.3109/10826084.2010.527417.

Ronel, N., & Tim, R. (2003). Grace therapy: Meeting the challenge of group therapy for male batterers. *Clinical Social Work Journal*, *31*(1), 63–80.

Ronel, N., Haski-Leventhal, D., Ben-David, B. M., & York, A. S. (2009). Perceived altruism: A neglected factor in initial intervention. *International Journal of Offender Therapy and Comparative Criminology, 53*(2), 191–210.

Room, R. (1993). Alcoholics Anonymous as a social movement. In B. S. McCrady & W. R. Miller (eds), *Research on Alcoholics Anonymous* (pp. 167–188). New Brunswick, NJ: Rutgers Center for Alcohol Studies.

Ross, R. R., & Hilborn, J. (2008). *Rehabilitating Rehabilitation: Neurocriminology for the Treatment of Antisocial Behavior.* Ottawa, Canada: Cognitive Centre of Canada.

Schuerman, L., & Kobrin, S. (1986). Community careers in crime. *Crime and Justice, 8* (Communities and Crime), 67–100.

Seligman, M. E. P., & Csikszentmihalyi, M. (2000). Positive psychology: An introduction. *American Psychologist, 55*(1), 5–14.

Settel, T. S. (1995). *The Book of Gandhi Wisdom.* New York: Carol Publishing.

Shachaf-Friedman, E., & Timor, U. (2008). Family-group conferencing in Israel: The voices of victims following restorative justice proceedings. In N. Ronel, K. Jaishankar, & M. Bensimon (eds), *Trends and Issues in Victimology* (pp. 57–87). Newcastle upon Tyne: Cambridge Scholars Publishing.

Shoham, S. G., & Addad, M. (2004). *The Insatiable Gorge.* Tel Aviv: Babel (in Hebrew).

Shoham, S. G., Adad, M., & Rahav, G. (2004). *Criminology.* Tel Aviv: Schocken (in Hebrew).

Timor, U. (2001). Balagan: Delinquency as a result of the lack of a center of norms and consciousness. *International Journal of Offender Therapy and Comparative Criminology, 45*(6), 730–748.

Timor, U. (2008). An informal approach to delinquents and their victims: An alternative to standard punishment. In N. Ronel, K. Jaishankar, & M. Bensimon (eds), *Trends and Issues in Victimology* (pp. 32–56). Newcastle upon Tyne: Cambridge Scholars Publishing.

Uzan, T. (2009). The descent into crime and the experience of volunteering as reflected in life stories of youth at risk. Unpublished master's thesis, Bar-Ilan University (in Hebrew).

Van Wormer, K., & Davis, R. D. (2003). *Addiction Treatment: A Strengths Perspective.* Pacific Grove, CA: Brooks/Cole-Thomson.

Ward, T. (2002). Good lives and the rehabilitation of sexual offenders: Promises and problems. *Aggression and Violent Behavior, 7,* 513–528.

Ward, T., & Gannon, T. A. (2006). Rehabilitation, etiology, and self-regulation: The comprehensive good lives model of treatment for sexual offenders. *Aggression and Violent Behavior, 11,* 77–94.

Ward, T., Mann, R. E., & Gannon, T. A. (2007). The good lives model of offender rehabilitation: Clinical implications. *Aggression and Violent Behavior, 12,* 87–107.

Ward, T., & Maruna, S. (2007). *Rehabilitation.* London: Routledge.

Watzlawick, P., Weakland, J., & Fisch, R. (1974). *Change: Principles of Problem Formation and Resolution.* New York: W. W. Norton and Co.

Weisburd, D., Telep, C. W., & Braga, A. A. (2010). *The Importance of Place in Policing: Empirical Evidence and Policy Recommendations.* Stockholm: Swedish National Council for Crime Prevention.

White, W. L. (1998). *Slaying the Dragon: The History of Addiction Treatment and Recovery in America.* Bloomington, IL: Chestnut Health Systems/Lighthouse Institute.

White, W. L., & Kurtz, E. (2005). The varieties of recovery experience: A primer for addiction treatment professionals and recovery advocates. Chicago, IL: Great Lakes Addiction Technology Transfer Center.

White, W. L., Kurtz, E., & Sanders, M. (2006). *Recovery Management*. Chicago, IL: Great Lakes Addiction Technology Transfer Center.

Wilson, J. Q., & Kelling, G. L. (1982). Broken windows: The police and neighborhood safety. *The Atlantic Monthly, 249*(3), 29–38.

Winfree, L. T., Mays, G. L., & Vigil-Backstrom, T. (1994). Youth gangs and incarcerated delinquents: Exploring the ties between gang membership, delinquency, and social learning theory. *Justice Quarterly, 11*(2), 229–256.

Zehr, H. (1995). Justice paradigm shift? Values and visions in the reform process. *Mediation Quarterly, 12*(3), 207–216.

Intimate Partner Violence Victimization

Perspectives from Spouses of Alcohol Dependents

19

K. JEEVITHA

L. N. SUMAN

Contents

Introduction

Intimate partner violence (IPV) has been recognized as a prevalent and serious problem for more than 20 years. Violence by adult intimate partners has been defined as aggressive or controlling behavior that ranges from mild to severe, spanning physical, sexual, and emotional abuse. In acknowledging that domestic violence can include husband-to-wife and wife-to-husband aggression, it is generally accepted that women are the targets of spousal violence, particularly of a severe and physically injurious nature (Stets & Straus, 1990). The National Family Health Survey-III (NFHS-III) of India, carried out between 2005 and 2006, found that a significant proportion of married women had been physically or sexually abused by their husbands. The survey indicated that, nationwide, 37.2% of women experienced violence after marriage (NFHS-III, 2006).

The evidence regarding alcohol and marital violence has been extensively reviewed. Briefly, case-control studies of violent men, alcoholic men, and abused women, and epidemiological studies of the general population and of women in health-care settings have consistently found an association between the indices of heavy drinking and the occurrence of domestic violence. For example, 20%–93% of battered women consider their partners to be problem drinkers or alcoholics (Leonard, 1993). O'Farrell and Murphy (1995) found that significantly more wives of alcoholics, in comparison to a matched, community sample, experienced husband-perpetrated violence, particularly of a severe nature. Carroll et al. (2002) reported that alcohol abuse leads to a reduction in caring, a diminution of emotional attachment, and a lessening of the desire for emotional intimacy from one's partner. This harms the marital relationship and leads to marital estrangement, which, in turn, enhances the risk for marital dissolution.

Benegal et al. (2005) carried out a survey of alcohol use in Karnataka, Southern India, as part of a collaborative multinational study on "Gender, Alcohol and Culture." They found that in a sample of 502 male alcohol users, 50% reported that they became more aggressive toward other people after drinking. The study also found that alcohol-using males were three times more likely to have been physically aggressive toward their spouses as compared to male abstainers. More recently, Flake and Forste (2008) examined the relationship between familial characteristics and the likelihood of experiencing domestic violence in five Latin American countries: Columbia, Dominican Republic, Haiti, Nicaragua, and Peru. Data from the demographic and health surveys of more than 30,000 women in the age range of 15–49 years and living with a partner were analyzed. The results revealed that partner alcohol use was positively associated with domestic violence across all data sets. Alcohol use by the male partner had the strongest and most consistent effect on the likelihood of experiencing domestic violence, followed by cohabitation and female-dominant decision making.

Murphy et al. (2001) found that partners of-violent alcoholic patients had more antisocial personality characteristics, greater alcohol problem severity, higher relationship distress, and a stronger belief in the links between alcohol consumption and relationship problems. These lead to the victimization of the spouse, which, in turn, adversely affects the spouse's health. The literature has consistently reported that domestic violence has a severe impact on the health of the victim. Studies have revealed that women exposed to domestic violence suffer from mental health problems (Moracco et al., 2004; Kumar et al., 2005), chronic malnutrition (Ackerson & Subramanian, 2008), gynecological problems, temporary or permanent disabilities, depression, and suicide (Kaur & Garg, 2010).

In a prospective study of partner aggression (Fals-Stewart, 2003), two clinical samples of men (domestic violence treatment and alcoholism treatment) recorded their daily drinking using a diary format while their female partners recorded incidents of aggression by the men toward them, also using a diary format. This study found that the odds of partner aggression by men increased on days when the men consumed alcohol, especially the days when drinking was heavy, and that this relationship was stronger for severe aggression than for less severe aggression. Thus, the association between alcohol use and aggression or violence is fairly well established.

O'Farrell et al. (2004) examined partner violence before and after behavioral couples therapy (BCT) for 303 married or cohabiting male alcoholic patients, using a demographically matched nonalcoholic comparison sample. In the year before BCT, 60% of alcoholic patients had been violent toward their female partner, five times the comparison sample rate of 12%. In the first and second years after BCT, the violence decreased significantly from the year before BCT, and clinically significant violence reductions occurred for patients whose alcoholism remitted after BCT. Structural equation modeling indicated that greater treatment involvement (attending BCT sessions and using BCT-targeted behaviors) was related to lower violence after BCT and that this association was mediated by reduced problem drinking and enhanced relationship functioning. In another study, Roozen et al. (2009) reported that Community Reinforcement and Family Training (CRAFT) was a useful approach to manage IPV among alcohol abusers. They noted that CRAFT helped the partner to (i) recognize and safely respond to potential violence, (ii) improve communication with the alcohol abuser, (iii) decrease stress, (iv) improve self-efficacy, and (v) assist in encouraging the unwilling alcohol abuser to enter treatment.

According to Klostermann (2006), the link between alcohol use and IPV has implications for treatment irrespective of whether alcohol use directly leads to aggression or indirectly mediates the violent behavior. In a review of the treatment options available, he noted that there is a lack of agreement about the best approach for IPV among patients entering substance abuse treatment. He pointed out that treatment providers should develop strategies to reduce IPV and these strategies would have to be incorporated and integrated with the regular treatment of substance use problems. However, few studies in India have examined the nature of the domestic violence against spouses by men diagnosed as having alcohol dependence. The current study attempts to overcome this lacuna.

Methodology

The aim of this study was to examine the nature of the domestic violence experienced by spouses of alcohol dependents (SADs).

Operational definition of domestic violence: In the current study, domestic violence has been defined in accordance with the Domestic Violence Act enacted by the Government of India in 2005. According to the Act, any act or omission or commission or conduct of the respondent shall constitute domestic violence in case it:

(a) Harms or injures or endangers the health, safety, life, limb or wellbe-
    ing, whether mental or physical, of the aggrieved person or tends to
    do so and includes causing physical abuse, sexual abuse, verbal and
    emotional abuse and economic abuse; or
(b) Harasses, harms, injures or endangers the aggrieved person with
    a view to coerce her or any other person related to her to meet any
    unlawful demand for any dowry or other property or valuable
    security; or
(c) Has the effect of threatening the aggrieved person or any person
    related to her by any conduct mentioned in clause (a) or clause (b); or
(d) Otherwise injures or causes harm, whether physical or mental, to the
    aggrieved person.

Sample

The study had two groups of subjects. Group I was composed of 30 SADs and Group II was composed of 30 spouses of nonalcohol/nondrug dependents. Subjects who were living with their husbands and who had a working knowledge of English and Kannada were included in the study. The mean age of the subjects in Group I was 35 years. Their mean education was 12 years. The mean duration of marriage was 13 years and the mean duration of alcohol consumption of their partners was 12 years. In Group II, the mean age of the subjects was 37 years. Their mean education was 12 years and the mean duration of marriage was 18 years. The majority of the sample were Hindus (85%), from a middle socioeconomic status (80%), belonging to nuclear families (68%), and most of them were homemakers (90%) in both the groups. A family history of alcohol dependence (family of origin) was found to be greater in Group I than in Group II, with a significant difference between the two groups ($\chi^2 = 19.26$; $p'.01$). Marital details suggested that there were significantly more consanguineous marriages in Group I when compared to Group II ($\chi^2 = 15$; $p'.01$).

Inclusion criteria for Group I:

- A primary diagnosis of alcohol dependence syndrome in the husband (ICD-10 criteria).

Inclusion criteria for Group II:

- Female subjects whose husbands do not have psychoactive substance
  abuse/dependence.

Exclusion criteria for Group I:

- Women whose husbands have poly substance abuse/dependence or other psychiatric disorders.

Common exclusion criteria for Group I and II:

1. Subjects with ongoing psychotic illness
2. Subjects with cognitive deficits
3. Subjects dependent on psychoactive substances
4. Subjects with major physical illnesses

Description of Tools

(1) *Sociodemographic Data Sheet (SDS)*: This was prepared for collecting information about the subject's name, age, education, consanguinity of marriage, duration of marriage, number of children, occupation (if any), income, details of other family members, and family income. Information was also obtained about the duration of drinking of the alcohol dependents and any history of alcohol abuse/dependence in the families of origin of the spouses.

(2) *Semistructured Interview Schedule*: This was prepared by the investigators to assess domestic violence. The interview schedule involved asking the spouses questions on various areas of domestic violence, such as physical abuse, verbal abuse, emotional abuse, and sexual abuse, in accordance with the Protection of Women from Domestic Violence Act (2005) of India. According to this Act:

- (i) "physical abuse" refers to any act or conduct which is of such a nature as to cause bodily pain, harm or danger to life, limb, or health or impair the health or development of the aggrieved person and includes assault, criminal intimidation and criminal force;
- (ii) "sexual abuse" includes any conduct of a sexual nature that abuses, humiliates, degrades or otherwise violates the dignity of woman;
- (iii) "verbal and emotional abuse" includes-
  - (a) insults, ridicule, humiliation, name calling and insults or ridicule specially with regard to not having a child or a male child; and
  - (b) Repeated threats to cause physical pain to any person in whom the aggrieved person is interested.
- (iv) "economic abuse" includes-
  - (a) deprivation of all or any economic or financial resources to which the aggrieved person is entitled under any law or custom whether payable under an order of a court or otherwise or which the aggrieved person requires out of necessity including, but not limited to, household necessities for the aggrieved person

and her children, if any, *stridhan*, property, jointly or separately owned by the aggrieved person, payment of rental related to the shared household and maintenance;

(b) disposal of household effects, any alienation of assets whether movable or immovable, valuables, shares, securities, bonds and the like or other property in which the aggrieved person has an interest or is entitled to use by virtue of the domestic relationship or which may be reasonably required by the aggrieved person or her children or her *stridhan* or any other property jointly or separately held by the aggrieved person;

(c) prohibition or restriction to continued access to resources or facilities which the aggrieved person is entitled to use or enjoy by virtue of the domestic relationship including access to the shared household.

The interview schedule has a total of 34 questions exploring the above-mentioned areas. Each area is rated on a 10 cm Visual Analogue Scale to assess the severity of violence. The two ends refer to "no abuse" and "worst possible abuse." SADs were asked to rate their experience of domestic violence when their husbands were sober and when they were intoxicated in order to determine the influence of alcohol consumption on aggression.

Procedure

SADs who met the inclusion and exclusion criteria for the current study were requested to give consent to participate in the study. Written informed consent was obtained from all the subjects. The interviews were carried out individually in the hospital setting. The subjects of Group II were recruited from the community after interviewing them about their husbands' alcohol use. Written informed consent was obtained from all the subjects. The interviews were carried out in individual sessions in the participants' homes. The interviews took about 1 hour for the subjects in Group I to complete as most of them were overcome with emotion and frequently broke down while giving details of their traumatic experiences. The duration of the interviews with subjects in Group II took approximately 30 minutes.

Analysis of Data

The data obtained from the interviews were qualitatively analyzed. Descriptive statistics, that is, percentages were used to calculate the number of subjects experiencing violence in the different domains. Ratings on the Visual Analogue Scale were analyzed using a t-test to examine the significance of difference between the two groups.

Ethical Considerations

1. The study was cleared by the institute's ethics committee.
2. Written informed consent was obtained from all the subjects.
3. The confidentiality of the results obtained was assured and maintained.
4. Psychological help was offered to those who sought it or they were referred to an appropriate professional.
5. Subjects were informed that they were free to leave the study at any time.

Results

Among Group I, seven (23.30%) subjects reported severe forms of physical abuse from their partners, such as being physically attacked (Table 19.1). Many of them stated that their partners, while in an intoxicated state, had also attempted to strangle them. However, they did not report the injuries for which they had to be hospitalized or receive treatment. Two (6.60%) subjects reported mild to moderate forms of abuse, such as being stopped from going to work or meeting their family and friends. Their partners had also tried to harass them at their workplace while in an intoxicated state. Further, they also reported that in a sober state, their partners would deny any such happenings and instead accuse them of lying about such events. Twenty-one (70%) subjects reported no physical abuse.

Two (6.60%) subjects reported severe forms of sexual abuse, such as attempts to have sexual intercourse when they did not want to or their partner threatened to use some degree of force but intercourse did not occur. They had also experienced marital rape. One (3.5%) subject reported mild to moderate forms of abuse where the partner had engaged the spouse in sexual play (fondling, petting, etc., but not intercourse) even when she did not want to, while 27 (90%) reported no sexual abuse.

Twenty-seven (90%) subjects reported severe forms of emotional/verbal abuse, such as name calling by their husbands and using foul language. They had been humiliated or insulted by being called names, criticized, or received

Table 19.1 Percentage of SADs Reporting Different Types of Domestic Violence

Type of Abuse	High (%)	Mild–Moderate (%)	No Abuse (%)
Physical abuse	23	7	70
Sexual abuse	7	3	90
Emotional abuse	90	10	—
Economic abuse	10	23	67

sexual comments in front of others. They were also threatened with the physical harm or death of their close associates, friends, or family members. They had also been threatened with divorce or the ending of the relationship even if they did not want to. Three (10%) subjects reported mild to moderate forms of abuse where their partners acted very cold or distant when angry and would refuse to discuss any problems. Their husbands would become angry/upset when household chores, such as meals or the laundry, were not ready when they wanted it or they were not done to their satisfaction. No spouse reported the absence of emotional/verbal abuse.

Three (10%) subjects reported severe forms of economic abuse, such as being deprived of economic or financial resources to which they are entitled under law, such as property, valuables, money, and the like. Their partners, without prior notice or permission, had disposed of household assets, valuables, shares, securities, bonds, and other valuables that the subjects and their children had an interest in or were entitled to use or enjoy under the law, for the purpose of warding off the debts they incurred when buying alcohol or for gambling purposes. Seven (23.30%) subjects reported mild to moderate forms of abuse where their partners had forced them to hand over their earnings or money or to get money from their parents. Twenty (66.60%) subjects reported no economic abuse.

Of the 30 subjects who reported domestic violence in Group I, 17 (56.60%) subjects reported severe forms of domestic violence, while 13 (43.30%) subjects reported mild to moderate forms of domestic violence, and no spouse reported the absence of violence. Of the 30 subjects who reported domestic violence in Group II, 23 (76.60%) subjects reported mild domestic violence in the form of emotional/verbal abuse, where partners acted cold or distant when they were angry and refused to discuss any problems. Seven (23.30%) subjects reported the absence of domestic violence.

Table 19.2 shows that there is a very high significant difference between the two groups on domestic violence. The findings also reveal that SADs have

Table 19.2 Mean, SD, and *t*-Value on Visual Analogue Scale for the Two Groups

Sl. No.	Variables	Group I ($n = 30$)		Group II ($n = 30$)		
		Mean	SD	Mean	SD	*t*
1	Physical abuse	2.10	3.67	0	0	3.13*
2	Sexual abuse	0.80	2.53	0	0	17.26**
3	Emotional/verbal abuse	7.70	1.32	1.13	0.77	23.26**
4	Economic abuse	1.67	2.80	0	0	3.25**
5	Overall domestic violence	7.47	1.63	1.64	0.76	19.17**

Note: df = 58.
*$p < .05$; **$p < .01$.

Table 19.3 Mean, SD, and *t*-Value on Visual Analogue Scale in Sober and Intoxicated States for Group I

Sl. No.	Variables	Intoxicated		Sober		
		Mean	SD	Mean	SD	*t*
1	Physical abuse	2.10	3.67	0.67	1.58	1.96*
2	Sexual abuse	0.80	2.53	0.43	1.61	0.66
3	Emotional/verbal abuse	7.70	1.31	3.80	1.99	6.95**
4	Economic abuse	1.67	2.80	1.07	1.89	0.97

Note: df = 58.
*p < .05; **p < .01.

reported very high rates of physical abuse, sexual abuse, emotional/verbal abuse, and economic abuse meted out to them by their partners when compared to non-SADs, who have not reported any abuse in these areas except emotional/verbal abuse. Further, they have also reported emotional/verbal abuse as being the highest form of abuse when compared to the other forms of abuse. Domestic violence had a significant negative impact on SADs, leading to high levels of psychological distress.

Table 19.3 shows that physical abuse and emotional/verbal abuse are significantly higher when the partner is in an intoxicated state than when sober. These findings indicate that alcohol use is a significant instigator of violence.

Discussion and Conclusion

The SADs in the current study reported poorer marital satisfaction and lack of support and care from their spouses. They had also contemplated ending their marriage because of the constant domestic violence. However, due to the social stigma faced by divorced women and the lack of viable options, they were forced to stay in their marriage. Chengappa (1986, p. 73) had similarly observed that "if more families have not broken up, it is because most Indian wives fear the stigma attached to divorce." Thus, the situation in India has not changed much even after 25 years. Suman and Nagalakshmi (1995) reported consistent findings, where alcoholic families were characterized by poor communication patterns, lack of mutual warmth and support, spousal abuse, and poor role functioning. The spouses of alcoholics expressed greater dissatisfaction in all areas of family functioning, than the alcoholics.

The interviews revealed that most of the SADs were very distressed and had symptoms suggestive of depression. They had poor sleep and appetite, a sustained low mood, and ideas of hopelessness and helplessness. These findings are in sync with those reported by Rajendran and Cherian (1992), who reported that the majority of the wives of alcohol abusers reported financial problems, daily quarrels, and physical assaults. Many of the wives suffered from various physical and mental health problems and manifested high levels of stress and stress-related symptoms. In a recent study, Dawson et al. (2007) also found that women whose partners had alcohol problems were more likely to experience victimization, injury, and mood disorders. They were also likely to have poorer health and a lower psychological quality of life when compared to women whose partners did not have alcohol use problems.

The current study also observed that physical abuse and emotional/verbal abuse are significantly higher in an intoxicated state than when sober. These findings reveal alcohol as the instigator of violence. These results are in keeping with those reported by Coker et al. (2000), who estimated the frequency and correlates of IPV by type (physical, sexual, battering, or emotional abuse) among women aged 18–65 years. They found that alcohol and/or drug abuse by the male partner was the strongest correlate of violence. In a sample of 772 women surveyed at a health clinic, their male partner's alcohol use was significantly associated with the commission of IPV after the effects of age, employment, race, the battered woman's substance abuse, violence in the family of origin, and access to guns were removed. Most of the alcoholic husbands neglected their family responsibilities and a majority of the wives of alcohol abusers reported financial problems, daily quarrels, and physical assaults.

The results of the current study indicate that early screening of spouses for the presence of psychological distress and disturbed marital relations is required. Once screened, prevention can be carried out at various levels. Primary prevention involves focusing on spouses who have not been exposed but are at a greater risk, such as spouses whose partners have started drinking as social drinkers or abuse alcohol although they are not dependent. Thus, the goal is to build a strong social support system and provide alcohol dependency education. Secondary prevention can be targeted at spouses who are already experiencing the negative aftermaths of alcohol dependents. These programs can include information and skill building. Finally, tertiary prevention, which involves sociocultural programs in communities or through self-help groups, such as Al-Anon, can be implemented.

References

Ackerson, L. K., & Subramanian, S. V. (2008). Domestic violence and chronic malnutrition among women and children in India. *American Journal of Epidemiology*, *167*, 1188–1196.

Benegal, V., Nayak, M., Murthy, P., Chandra, P., & Gururaj, G. (2005). Women and alcohol in India. In Obot, I. S., & Room, R. (eds), *Alcohol, Gender and Drinking Problems: Perspectives from Low and Middle Income Countries* (pp. 89–124). Geneva: World Health Organization.

Carroll, J. J., Robinson, B. E., & Flowers, C. (2002). Marital estrangement, positive feelings toward partners, and locus of control: Female counselors married to alcohol-abusing and non-alcohol-abusing spouses. *Journal of Addictions and Offender Counseling, 23,* 30–40.

Chengappa, R. (1986). Alcoholism, the growing malaise. *India Today,* April 30, 72–80.

Coker, A. L., Smith, P. H., McKeown, R. E., & King, M. J. (2000). Frequency and correlates of intimate partner violence by type: Physical, sexual, and psychological battering. *American Journal of Public Health, 90,* 553–559.

Dawson, D. D., Grant, B. F., Chou, S. P., & Stinson, F. S. (2007). The impact of partner alcohol problems on women's physical and mental health. *Journal of Studies on Alcohol and Drugs, 68,* 66–75.

Fals-Stewart, W. (2003). The occurrence of intimate partner violence on days of alcohol consumption: A longitudinal diary study. *Journal of Consulting and Clinical Psychology, 71,* 41–52.

Flake, D. F., & Forste, R. (2008). Fighting families: Family characteristics associated with domestic violence in five Latin American countries. *Journal of Family Violence, 21,* 19–29.

Kaur, R., & Garg, S. (2010). Addressing domestic violence against women: An unfinished agenda. *Indian Journal of Community Medicine, 33,* 73–76.

Klostermann, K. C. (2006). Substance abuse and intimate partner violence: Treatment considerations. *Substance Abuse Treatment, Prevention and Policy, 22,* 1–24.

Kumar, S., Jeyaseelan, L., Suresh, S., & Ahuja, R. C. (2005). Domestic violence and its mental health correlates in Indian women. *British Journal of Psychiatry, 187,* 62–67.

Leonard, K. E. (1993). Drinking patterns and intoxication in marital violence: Review, critique, and future directions for research. In Martin, S. E. (ed.), *Alcohol and Interpersonal Violence: Fostering Multidisciplinary Perspectives* (pp. 253–281) (Research Monograph No. 24). Rockville, MD: NIH.

Moracco, K. E., Brown, C. L., Martin, S. L., Chang, J. C., Dulli, L., Loucks-Sorrell, M. B., Turner, T., Bou-Saada, I. G., & Starsoneck, L. (2004). Mental health issues among female clients of domestic violence programs in North Carolina. *Psychiatric Services, 55,* 1036–1040.

Murphy, C. M., O'Farrell, T. J., Fals-Stewart, W., & Feehan, M. (2001). Correlates of intimate partner violence among male alcoholic patients. *Journal of Consulting and Clinical Psychology, 69,* 528–540.

National Family Health Survey-III (NFHS-III). (2006). Fact sheet. Ministry of Health and Family Welfare, Government of India, New Delhi.

O'Farrell, T. J., Fals-Stewart, W., Murphy, M. & Murphy, C. M. (2004). Partner violence before and after individually based alcoholism treatment for male alcoholic patients. *Journal of Consulting and Clinical Psychology, 71,* 92–102.

O'Farrell, T. J., & Murphy, C. M. (1995). Marital violence before and alcoholism treatment. *Journal of Consulting and Clinical Psychology, 63,* 256–262.

Rajendran, R., & Cherian, R. R. (1992). Levels of stress in wives of alcoholics. Madras: Addiction Research Centre, unpublished report.

Roozen, H. G., Blaauw, E., & Meyers, R. J. (2009). Advances in management of alcohol use disorders and intimate partner violence: Community reinforcement and family training. *Psychiatry, Psychology and Law, 16*(Supplement), S74–S80.

Stets, J. E., & Straus, M. A. (1990). Gender differences in reporting marital violence and its medical and psychological consequences. In Straus, M. A. & Gelles, R. J. (eds), *Physical Violence in American Families* (pp. 151–165). Brunswick, NJ: Transaction Publishers.

Suman, L. N., & Nagalakshmi, S. V. (1995). Family interaction patterns in alcoholic families. *NIMHANS Journal*, *13*(1), 47–52.

The Protection of Women from Domestic Violence Act. (2005). Ministry of Law and Justice, Government of India, New Delhi.

Conclusion

NATTI RONEL
K. JAISHANKAR

Crime is a burden—to individuals, groups, and states. Although there are individuals, groups, and even states that may temporarily profit from crime, the pain and suffering that it causes are much more universal and it might backfire on those who have gained a temporary profit from it. Global crime is no different. Naturally, our aim is to reduce global crime, thereby minimizing the harm it causes. During the last decades, desistance from crime has become a mature topic of interest for criminologists (e.g., Maguire & Raynor, 2006; Maruna & LeBel, 2010; McNeill, 2006), at least on the individual level. Desistance is defined as the process of abstaining from crime among those who have previously engaged in a sustained pattern of offending (Maruna, 2001). It is understood that individuals usually do not just "quit crime" by making a decision and walking away, in the same way they might change their job. For various reasons, including the stigma of having a criminal record, the cycle of crime and punishment can become a repetitive loop that is difficult to escape from—a chronic spin (Ronel, Chapter 18, this volume). A better metaphor for desisting from crime is recovering from an addictive behavior such as gambling or substance use. Desistance from crime will probably involve some false stops and starts, sometimes called "relapses."

The desistance literature has also inspired an applied school of thought, sometimes known as the "desistance paradigm" or "desistance-focused practice." Farrall (2004) distinguishes "desistance-focused" perspectives from "offending-related" approaches on the basis that, whereas the latter concentrates on targeting or correcting offender deficits, the former seeks to promote those things thought to be associated with desistance (such as strong social bonds, prosocial involvements, and social capital). Others have argued for a shift from "deficit-based" interventions (focusing on risk factors and "needs" as defined by the experts) to "strengths-based" approaches that seek to promote "good lives" as defined by the person themselves (e.g., Ross & Hilborn, 2008; Ward et al., 2007; Ward & Maruna, 2007).

The desistance literature offers several suggestions for intervention with *individual* desisters that might increase the chances for prolonged desistance. The following suggestions represent the positive criminology perspective (Ronel, Chapter 18, this volume): focus on strong and meaningful relationships; give strong optimistic messages and avoid labeling; focus on strengths and not just on risks; recognize and mark achievements toward desistance; make practical assistance the priority; work with parents and partners; and work with support communities. All of these are on the individual and local level; however, can such a perspective become valid on a global level? What would global crime desistance look like, what might it teach, and can a positive criminology perspective be applied to global criminology as well, to meet the challenges of global criminology? Since global criminology is still a young field, these questions remain open for new explorations, conceptualizations, and learning by trial. A possible direction might be revealed by the knowledge of victimology.

Victimology signifies a shift in the focus of study and intervention from the criminals to the victims and from criminality to victimization (Lindgren & Nikolić-Ristanović, 2011), in a similar way to the change of direction and the suggestion of a complementary perspective by positive criminology and the desistance literature. Not surprisingly, the growth of victimology and its global acceptance are almost simultaneous to the emergence of the desistance paradigm. Both call for a shift from being overly focused on crime and its characteristics, to a different perspective: that of victims and their supporters and that of desistance. In addition to the time relation, can these two separate approaches be related in the case of global criminology? Can we suggest a stance that represents global victimology and global crime desistance? Since knowledge of crime desistance is mostly on the individual level and victimology is more developed in the global perspective, we may assume that the development of global crime desistance practice might follow that of global victimology. For example, victims' rights is a recognized topic with a growing global interest, as we observe in declarations and conventions of victims' rights—as individuals and as groups—and some assimilations of these rights into various legal systems worldwide (Parmentier, 2009; Shapland, 2010). Another example is human trafficking, where victimology-based interventions direct social responses on a global level (Lindgren & Nikolić-Ristanović, 2011). Of course, there is much yet to do in order to minimize the suffering caused by global crime and to increase global crime desistance enterprises; however, the globalization of related knowledge is a possibility and we believe that global criminology, as a field of study, will provide it.

In the global village, crime and deviance unfortunately play a powerful and detrimental role. Hence a better—and global—response is called for. Any such effort should stand on the solid ground of well-founded intercultural ethics, manifest in projects of international and local cooperation and, of course, share scholarly knowledge from around the world. The First International Conference of the South Asian Society of Criminology and Victimology (SASCV), held at Jaipur, India, 15–17 January 2011, provided such ground, where high-standard professional and multicultural ethics met with a broad range of accumulated knowledge in an international and regional undertaking. We further hope that the high-quality chapters selected from the conference that are presented in this book will open new vistas of understanding of crime and victimization.

References

Farrall, S. (2004). *Rethinking What Works with Offenders: Probation, Social Context and Desistance from Crime*. Cullompton: Willan.

Lindgren, M., & Nikolić-Ristanović, V. (2011). *Crime Victims: International and Serbian Perspective*. Belgrade: Organization for Security and Cooperation in Europe, Mission to Serbia, Law Enforcement Department.

Maguire, M., & Raynor, P. (2006). How the resettlement of prisoners promotes desistance from crime: Or does it? *Criminology & Criminal Justice*, 6(1), 19–38.

Maruna, S. (2001). *Making Good: How Ex-Convicts Reform and Rebuild their Lives*. Washington, DC: American Psychological Association.

Maruna, S., & LeBel, T. (2010). The desistance paradigm in correctional practice: From programs to lives. In F. McNeill, P. Raynor & C. Trotter (eds), *Offender Supervision: New Directions in Theory, Research and Practice* (pp. 65–89). Cullompton: Willan.

McNeill, F. (2006). A desistance paradigm for offender management. *Criminology & Criminal Justice*, 6(1), 39–62.

Parmentier, S. (2009). To be or not to be a victim: On the developing notion of victimhood under the European convention. In O. Hagemann, P. Schäfer & S. Schmidt (eds), *Victimology, Victim Assistance and Criminal Justice* (pp. 43–60). Mönchengladbach: Niederrhein University of Applied Sciences.

Ross, R. R., & Hilborn, J. (2008). *Rehabilitating Rehabilitation: Neurocriminology for Treatment of Antisocial Behavior*. Ottawa, Canada: Cognitive Center of Canada.

Shapland, J. (2010). Victims and criminal justice in Europe. In S. G. Shoham, P. Knepper & M. Kett (eds), *International Handbook of Victimology* (pp. 347–372). Boca Raton, FL: CRC.

Ward, T., Mann, R. E., & Gannon, T. A. (2007). The good lives model of offender rehabilitation: Clinical implications. *Aggression and Violent Behavior*, 12, 87–107.

Ward, T., & Maruna, S. (2007). *Rehabilitation*. London: Routledge.

Index